WHAT WORKS IN CORRECTIONS

In *What Works in Corrections,* Doris Layton MacKenzie examines the effects of correctional interventions, management policies, and treatment and rehabilitation programs on the recidivism of offenders and delinquents. She reviews different strategies for reducing recidivism and describes how the evidence for effectiveness is assessed. MacKenzie examined thousands of studies to identify those with sufficient scientific rigor to enable her to draw conclusions about the effects of various interventions, policies, and programs on recidivism. Systematic reviews and meta-analyses were performed to further examine these results. In this book, she assesses the relative effectiveness of rehabilitation programs (e.g., education, life skills, employment, and cognitive behavioral), treatment for different types of offenders (e.g., sex offenders, batterers, and juveniles), management and treatment options for drug-involved offenders (e.g., drug courts, therapeutic communities, and outpatient drug treatment), and punishment, control, and surveillance interventions (e.g., boot camps, intensive supervision, and electronic monitoring). Through her extensive research, MacKenzie illustrates which of these programs are most effective and why.

Doris Layton MacKenzie, Ph.D., is professor in the Department of Criminology and Criminal Justice at the University of Maryland. She earned her masters and doctorate degrees in psychology from the Pennsylvania State University and was awarded a visiting scientist position at the National Institute of Justice, U.S. Department of Justice. In this capacity, she provided expertise to federal, state, and local jurisdictions on correctional boot camps, correctional policy, intermediate sanctions, research methodology, experimental design, statistical analyses, and evaluation techniques. As an expert in criminal justice, MacKenzie has testified before U.S. Senate and House committees. She has recently co-edited a book with Gaylene Styve Armstrong about correctional boot camps titled *Correctional Boot Camps: Military Basic Training or a Model for Corrections?* Currently, she is co-director of the International Prison Project and has been invited to present her work at the United Nations.

CAMBRIDGE STUDIES IN CRIMINOLOGY

Other books in the series:

Life in the Gang: Family, Friends, and Violence, by Scott Decker and Barrik Van Winkle

Delinquency and Crime: Current Theories, edited by J. David Hawkins

Recriminalizing Delinquency: Violent Juvenile Crime and Juvenile Justice Reform, by Simon I. Singer

Mean Streets: Youth Crime and Homelessness, by John Hagan and Bill McCarthy

The Framework of Judicial Sentencing: A Study in Legal Decision Making, by Austin Lovegrove

The Criminal Recidivism Process, by Edward Zamble and Vernon L. Quinsey

Violence and Childhood in the Inner City, by Joan McCord

Judicial Policy Making and the Modern State: How the Courts Reformed America's Prisons, by Malcolm M. Freeley and Edward L. Rubin

Schools and Delinquency, by Denise C. Gottfredson

Delinquent-Prone Communities, by Don Weatherburn and Bronwyn Lind

White Collar Crime and Criminal Careers, by David Weisburd and Elin Waring, with Ellen F. Chayet

Sex Differences in Antisocial Behavior: Conduct Disorder, Delinquency, and Violence in the Dunedin Longitudinal Study, by Terrie Moffitt, Avshalom Caspi, Michael Rutter, and Phil A. Silva

Delinquent Networks: Youth Co-Offending in Stockholm, by Jerzy Sarnecki

Criminality and Violence among the Mentally Disordered, by Sheilagh Hodgins and Carl-Gunnar Janson

Situational Prison Control: Crime Prevention in Correctional Institutions, by Richard Wortley

Corporate Crime, Law, and Social Control, by Sally S. Simpson

Series list continues following the Index.

What Works in Corrections

Reducing the Criminal Activities of Offenders and Delinquents

Doris Layton MacKenzie

University of Maryland

CAMBRIDGE UNIVERSITY PRESS
Cambridge, New York, Melbourne, Madrid, Cape Town, Singapore, São Paulo

Cambridge University Press
40 West 20th Street, New York, NY 10011-4211, USA

www.cambridge.org
Information on this title: www.cambridge.org/9780521806459

First published 2006

Printed in the United States of America

A catalog record for this publication is available from the British Library.

Library of Congress Cataloging in Publication Data

MacKenzie, Doris L.
What works in corrections : reducing the criminal activities of offenders
and delinquents / Doris Layton MacKenzie.
p. cm. – (Cambridge studies in criminology)
Includes bibliographical references and index.
ISBN-13: 978-0-521-80645-9 (hardback)
ISBN-10: 0-521-80645-3 (hardback)
ISBN-13: 978-0-521-00120-5 (pbk.)
ISBN-10: 0-521-00120-X (pbk.)
1. Criminals – Rehabilitation – United States. 2. Criminals – Rehabilitation – United States – Evaluation. 3. Corrections – United States. 4. Recidivism – United States – Prevention. I. Title. II. Series: Cambridge studies in criminology (Cambridge University Press)
HV9304.M24 2006
364.3 – dc22 2006000775

ISBN-13 978-0-521-80645-9 hardback
ISBN-10 0-521-80645-3 hardback

ISBN-13 978-0-521-00120-5 paperback
ISBN-10 0-521-00120-X paperback

To

David Robert MacKenzie

Contents

Acknowledgments

A large number of people helped me with this book. I especially recognize Larry Sherman and Jerry Lee. They have provided inspiration and financial support, and I truly appreciate this. Larry was responsible for first starting me on this line of research, and I owe him a great debt. Fawn Ngo helped throughout the process of writing this book with editorial assistance and encouragement. Without her help I would not have been able to complete it. David Wilson was invaluable in teaching me the technique of meta-analysis. A large number of graduate students assisted in all phases of this work; to them I extend my thanks.

PART ONE

STRATEGIES FOR REDUCING CRIME

CHAPTER ONE

Strategies for Reducing Recidivism

Which correctional strategies, programs, policies, and interventions effectively reduce crime? That is the question addressed in this book. Obviously, other issues such as costs and justice are important in public policy decisions. However, the degree to which crime is reduced is always important, and, in the eyes of many, it is the primary reason for or goal of corrections. In this book, therefore, I focus solely on the effectiveness of these policies in *reducing crime*. The decision whether a particular strategy is effective is made on the basis of scientific evidence.

Although crime reduction is one of the major, if not the major, goal of correctional policy, the goals of sentencing are somewhat different. Traditionally, four major goals are attributed to sentencing: retribution, rehabilitation, deterrence, and incapacitation. Retribution refers to just desserts: the idea that people who engage in criminal behavior deserve to be punished. This is an important purpose of most sentences. The three other goals of sentencing are similar to those of corrections. These goals are utilitarian in purpose, emphasizing methods to protect the public and reduce crime. The three goals differ, however, in the mechanism expected to provide public safety. The first, deterrence, emphasizes the onerousness of punishment; offenders will be deterred from committing crimes as a result of a rational calculation that the costs of punishment are too great. From this perspective, the punishment is so repugnant that neither the punished offender (specific deterrence) nor others (general deterrence) will commit the crimes. The second, incapacitation, deprives offenders of the capacity to commit crimes because they are physically detained in prison; when offenders are in prison they cannot continue to commit crimes in the community. The third sentencing goal, rehabilitation, is directed toward changing offenders so they will not continue to commit crimes.

Within corrections, debate continues about the most viable strategies for reducing crime. Some argue for incapacitating large numbers of offenders so they will not continue committing crimes in the community. Others believe that offenders make rational choices to commit crimes and that they will be deterred from these activities if the punishment is sufficiently onerous. A third group focuses on the ability of correctional programs to change offenders so that they will not continue to commit crimes. Many who take this perspective believe crime will be prevented through rehabilitation or treatment directed toward changing the offender. Finally, some believe correctional programs will reduce crime by increasing control over offenders while they are in the community or by involving them in some type of physically and/or mentally stressful experience(s). These latter programs attempt to combine aspects of incapacitation, deterrence, and/or rehabilitation.

There are a wide range of strategies, programs, policies, and interventions currently in use in corrections. One heuristic approach classifies these various strategies into the following categories: (1) incapacitation; (2) deterrence; (3) rehabilitation; (4) community control; (5) structure, discipline, and challenge programs; and (6) other combinations of rehabilitation and control (MacKenzie, 2002). Obviously, these categories are not mutually exclusive. They represent different strategies for controlling crime in the community. Most strategies, programs, and interventions have some theoretical rationale for expecting a reduction in crime; they differ enormously in the mechanism anticipated to produce the reduction.

Incapacitation deprives the offender of the capacity to commit crimes, usually through detention in prison or jail or through capital punishment. There are numerous strategies that fall under the five other types of interventions categorized previously. Deterrence is punishment designed to be so repugnant that neither the offender nor others will commit the crime in the future. A heavy fine for criminal activities is an example of the use of deterrence to attempt to reduce crime. Rehabilitation-oriented programs such as cognitive skills, education, employment services, and life skills are directed toward changing the offender to prevent future criminal behavior of the treated individual. Community control or the surveillance and supervision of offenders in the community is an attempt to reduce the delinquent or offender's capacity and/or opportunity for criminal activities. Intensive supervision, electronic monitoring, and home confinement are examples of increased community control. Structure, discipline, and challenge programs use physically and/or mentally stressful experiences designed to change offenders in positive ways (rehabilitation) or deter them from later crime. Examples are wilderness programs, outward bound, and the recently popular correctional boot camps. Finally, other programs attempt to combine rehabilitation and control or structure by increasing the surveillance and control, or the structure and discipline, while at the same time providing rehabilitation services. Two recent examples of these programs are drug courts and correctional boot camps that incorporate drug treatment or other rehabilitation programs.

CHANGES IN THE PHILOSOPHY AND PRACTICE OF CORRECTIONS

The philosophy and practice of sentencing and corrections have changed dramatically in the past thirty years. For the first seven decades of the twentieth century, sentencing and corrections strongly emphasized rehabilitation. This changed during the 1970s when this emphasis gave way to a focus on fairness and justice. In this model, sentences were expected to reflect just desserts and not some utilitarian motive. Subsequently, sentencing practices moved to a crime control model, emphasizing the use of incapacitation to reduce crime. During the 1980s and 1990s, the crime control model became increasingly popular. These changes in the goals of corrections have been associated with an enormous increase in the number of people in the United States who are under some form of correctional supervision. Changes in the philosophy and practice of sentencing and corrections have clearly had a major effect on these rates. However, there is no consensus about what specifically has caused the changes, the effect of the changes, and their intended and unintended consequences.

The Age of Indeterminate Sentencing and Rehabilitation

In the 1960s, all U.S. states, the federal government, and the District of Columbia had indeterminate sentencing systems. The emphasis of sentencing and corrections was on rehabilitation. Theoretically, both the juvenile and adult correctional systems focused on treating individuals adjudicated for delinquent or criminal offenses. During this time, prisons were referred to as "correctional institutions" and prison guards became "correctional officers."

Under the indeterminate model of sentencing, legislatures set maximum authorized sentences; judges sentenced offenders to imprisonment, probation, and fines and set maximum durations; correctional officials had power over granting good time, earned time, and furloughs; and parole boards set release dates. In some states the indeterminacy of the sentences permitted sufficient leeway to permit courts to sentence offenders to prison for time periods from one day to life. Professionals, typically the parole board, were assigned the task of determining when the offender had made sufficient progress to be awarded supervised release in the community.

After the sentence was imposed, decision making was almost totally the prerogative of correctional authorities or parole boards. Parole boards, in various forms, had the responsibility to set conditions of release for offenders under conditional or supervised release, the authority to return an offender to prison for violating the conditions of parole or supervised release, and the power to grant parole for medical reasons. Reductions in the length of prison sentences could be given for satisfactory prison behavior (good time) or for participation in work or educational programs (earned time).

The idea behind indeterminate sentencing was individualization of sentences. Judges gave sentences with a wide range between the minimum and maximum length of time (e.g., zero to twenty years) the offender had to serve in prison. Offenders were supposed to be released when they were rehabilitated. Decisions about release were the responsibility of prison authorities and the parole board. Officials were given broad authority to tailor new sentences, to promote the correction and rehabilitation of the offenders, and to safeguard offenders against excessive, disproportionate, or arbitrary punishment.

Theoretically, two underlying beliefs appear to explain the philosophy behind indeterminate sentences – one environmental and the other psychological (Rothman, 1980). Environmental explanations focused on the wretchedness of the inner city slum environments and questioned how an individual growing up in these environments could be held responsible for later criminal behavior. Fairness dictated that offenders be treated as individuals; anything else was vengeful. The psychological perspective considered offenders ill and, therefore, in need of treatment as a cure for the illness. In either case, the criminal justice system was responsible for changing lawbreakers into law abiders.

The recommendations made by a panel of experts in the 1960s is evidence of the strong focus on rehabilitation. This panel was formed in response to President Lyndon Johnson's 1965 address to the U.S. Congress, in which he called for the establishment of a blue ribbon panel to examine the problems of crime in our Nation. Prominent among the panel's recommendations was an emphasis on probation and parole. According to the panel, caseloads should be reduced to an average ratio of thirty-five offenders per probation or parole officer; all releasees from institutions should receive adequate supervision; all jurisdictions should provide services for "felons, juveniles and adult misdemeanants who need or can profit from community treatment; and, probation and parole officials should develop new methods and skills to aid in reintegrating offenders through active intervention on their behalf with community institutions" (President's Commission on Law Enforcement and Administration of Justice, 1967:166).

Similarly, the panel's recommendations for institutions reflected the emphasis on rehabilitation, services and reintegration: "Model, small-unit correctional institutions for flexible, community-oriented treatment" should be established (page 173); educational and vocation training programs should be upgraded and "extended to all inmates who could profit from them" (page 175); "modern correctional industries aimed at the rehabilitation of offenders" should be instituted (page 176); and "graduated release and furlough programs should be expanded" (page 177) and coordinated with community treatment services (page 177). Prosecutors were urged to make discriminating discharge decisions by "assuring that offenders who merit criminal sanctions are not released and that other offenders are either released or diverted to non-criminal methods of treatment" such as diversion to community treatment (page 134). Out of these recommendations grew the Omnibus Crime Control and Safe Streets Act of 1968.

These recommendations, as well as the indeterminate sentencing structure, clearly demonstrate that the emphasis at the time was on rehabilitation with a focus on community treatment, diversion, reintegration, and education and employment programs. However, it should be noted that despite the philosophical emphasis on rehabilitation, in actual practice, these programs were often poorly implemented and funded.

A Time of Change: 1970–2000

The decade of the 1960s had begun with great optimism about the promises that a new frontier would be created and a more equitable order achieved. By the end of the decade, belief in "the great society" had given way to a despairing distrust of the state. The fallout from this thinking for correctional policy was immense because inherent in the rehabilitative ideal was a trust in criminal justice officials to reform offenders. Some people questioned the unbridled discretion available to criminal justice decision makers who gave preferential sentences to the advantaged and coerced inmates into conformity. Others wished to return to earlier times when "law and order" reigned in our country, and they called for a "war on crime" to preserve the social order. The times were ripe for major changes in the criminal justice system. A virtual revolution occurred in sentencing and corrections policies and practices in the seventies and thereafter.

One of the most visible influences on this change was Martinson's 1974 summary of a more elaborate report by Lipton, Martinson, and Wilks (1975). Martinson described the results of the research team's assessment of 231 evaluations of treatment programs conducted between 1945 and 1967. From this research, he concluded that "[w]ith few and isolated exceptions the rehabilitative efforts that have been reported so far have had no appreciable effect on recidivism" (Martinson, 1974:25). This report was widely interpreted as demonstrating that "nothing works" in the rehabilitation of offenders. Subsequently, a National Academy of Science panel reviewed the results and agreed with Martinson (Sechrest, White, & Brown, 1979).

Not everyone agreed with Martinson's conclusions. Critics argued the work was flawed for two major reasons (Palmer, 1983; 1992). First, the methodology that had been used in most of the research was so inadequate that only a few studies warranted any unequivocal interpretations, and second, the majority of studies examined programs that were so poorly implemented they could hardly be expected to have an effect on future criminal activities. Despite the concern that the research did not support such a conclusion, the phrase "nothing works" became an instant cliché and exerted a powerful influence on both popular and professional thinking.

Several factors may explain why at that point in time Martinson's conclusion became so widely accepted. Cullen and Gendreau (2000) argue that the historical times were ripe for a full-scale attack on rehabilitation and the indeterminate sentencing model. From this perspective, the decade of social turbulence preceding the publication of Martinson's article profoundly affected many Americans. Inequities based on gender, race, and class had been exposed and challenged. Protests, riots, and bombings about issues such as civil rights and the war in Vietnam were common occurrences. Within the criminal justice system, the 1971 riot and slaughter of inmates and guards at Attica prison demonstrated the extent to which government officials would go to suppress offender protests over prison conditions. The public began to question the past faith in the ability of social institutions to solve social problems. In regard to corrections, the question was: Could judges and correctional officials be trusted to exercise the extreme discretion permitted by the rehabilitative ideal?

For many, the answer to this question was no; the officials should not be given such wide discretion. However, liberals and conservatives differed in why they wanted to limit discretion. Conservatives argued that the judges and parole boards were too lenient; they used their discretion to release predatory criminals who continued to victimize innocent citizens. Liberals argued that the discretion given to officials was coercive and ineffective. Because officials could not really tell when offenders were rehabilitated, why should they have the power to decide when the individual should be released? If the professionals who were responsible for rehabilitation could not demonstrate that they could effectively change offenders (as the Martinson report indicated), then their authority and autonomy in establishing the length of sentences should be severely restricted so that they would have less control over people's lives. Furthermore, they argued, the wide discretion often results in disparity and unfair sentences that are not remedied through the parole release system. As a result of the wide discretion allotted to officials in the criminal justice system, offenders with similar past histories convicted of similar crimes often served widely disparate sentences whereas those with disparate histories and crimes served similar sentences. Critics of the indeterminate sentencing system argued that poor and minority offenders were discriminated against, imprisoned offenders were coerced into programs, and offenders who challenged prison conditions were denied parole.

The Justice Model of Sentencing and Corrections

The proposed solution to the problems of sentencing and corrections was to return to a justice model of sentencing and corrections (American Friends Service Committee, 1971). From this perspective, sentences should be decided on the basis of fair and just sentencing policies. The model is based on retributive notions of deserved punishment, or the idea that the sentence should fit the crime. Offenders would receive their just desserts – the deserved punishment – nothing more, nothing less. Advocates argued that prisons should not be used to achieve any public end. In their opinion, it is not morally justified to use people in particular ways to achieve public goals. Punishment should be proportionate to the crime but not be designed to achieve some utilitarian motive such as rehabilitation or crime control. The only relevant factors to consider in sentencing are the crime(s) of conviction and the offender's past history of criminal activity. Under this model, individualized treatment and discretion would be eliminated; thus, all offenders would be treated similarly by the criminal justice system.

The justice model carried with it direct implications for public policy. Offenders should be given substantial procedural protections throughout all stages of criminal justice system processing. Thus, legal rights of inmates became very important to the courts and corrections.

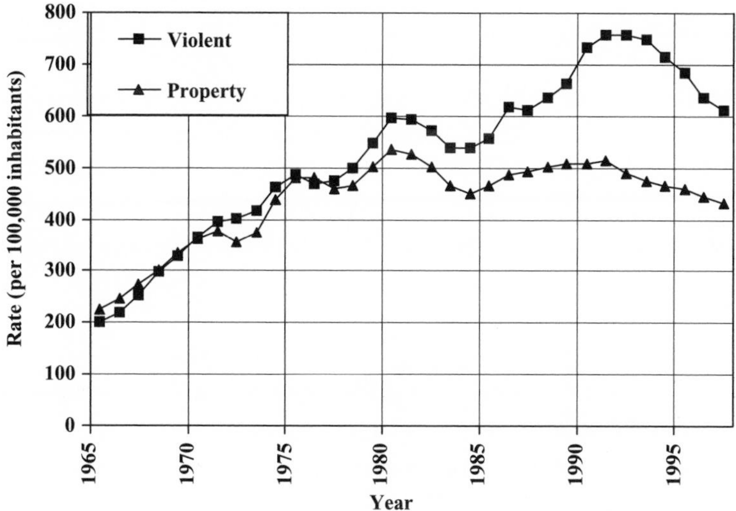

Figure 1.1. U.S. crime rate (offenses known to the police), 1965–1997.

Rehabilitation, if used, should be voluntary and not coerced. The largest policy effect was the need to change from an indeterminate sentencing model to determinate or *flat* sentencing. Under this sentencing method, a specific crime would carry a clearly identified sentence length, not a broad minimum and maximum; parole release would be eliminated; and sentence lengths would be determined by guidelines that considered only the past history of criminal activity and the current crime of conviction.

Crime Control: Incapacitation and Deterrence

Although proponents of the justice model were arguing in favor of this change away from a rehabilitation model, others began to argue for changes that would increase the crime control aspects of sentencing and corrections through incapacitation and deterrence. Crime rates escalated during the period from 1965 to 1975 (and continued through the early 1990s; see Figure 1.1), and this may have led to the increased emphasis on the need to control crime. "Law and order" advocates attacked rehabilitation as coddling criminals. They wanted to implement policies that would limit the ability of judges and correctional officials to mitigate the harshness of criminal sanctions. They advocated "get tough" proposals for mandatory minimum sentences and lengthy determinate sentences as methods for reducing criminal activities through incapacitation and deterrence.

The concept of incapacitation is simple – for as long as offenders are incarcerated they clearly cannot commit crimes outside of prison. That is, crime is reduced because the incarcerated offenders, while in prison, are prevented from committing crimes in the community. During the mid-1970s, interest in incapacitation as a crime prevention strategy grew, in part because of concerns about the efficacy of rehabilitation raised by the Martinson report, rising crime rates, and public fear of crime. The inherent logical utility of keeping offenders behind bars so that they could not engage in criminal activity drew support for incapacitation strategies.

Most people accept the notion that crime prevention through incapacitation is one primary justification of imprisonment (Zimring & Hawkins, 1995). Generally accepted, also, is the fact that some individuals should be incarcerated for long periods of time as retribution for the seriousness of their offenses and because they pose a threat if released. However, questions arise about how broadly the incapacitation strategy should be used and whether it is a cost-efficient and cost-effective crime prevention strategy. Some ask that prison space be reserved for only a small, carefully selected group of dangerous repeat offenders. Others advocate a general incapacitation strategy that would incarcerate a substantial number of felons. The success of incapacitation in reducing crime in the community remains a controversial subject (see Chapter 3, Incapacitation).

Increases in prison populations shifted societal attention toward a more selective strategy of incapacitating a small group of offenders. Encouragement for selective incapacitation as a crime control strategy also benefited from research that revealed a small number of very active offenders (6 percent of the cohort) accounted for a disproportionately large number of the arrests (52 percent) in a Philadelphia birth cohort (Wolfgang, Figlio, & Sellin, 1972). Incapacitation advocates argued that crime could be reduced if these "career criminals" were identified and incapacitated.[1] This selective incapacitation

[1] See Chapter 3, this volume, for a discussion of the difficulties in identifying career criminals.

strategy would identify offenders who were most likely to commit serious crimes at a higher frequency so that they could be incarcerated for longer periods of time. Further support for the benefits of incapacitation as a correctional strategy came from the proposal that, although there were enormous costs to incarcerating large numbers of felons, there were also substantial costs if they were released and continued to commit crimes, such as costs of criminal processing, loss to victims, and so forth (Zedlewski, 1987). Some of the practices that can be attributed to these incapacitation strategies are habitual offender laws,[2] abolishment of parole, mandatory sentences, and the more recent three-strikes laws.

War on Drugs. The "war on drugs" was another major factor that affected sentencing and corrections. The expansion of criminal sanctions for drug crimes began in the 1970s but picked up speed in the 1980s with the declaration of a war on drugs and the passage of the Anti–Drug Abuse Acts of 1986 and 1988. From a crime control perspective, it was thought that increasing arrests and punishment for drug offenses would be effective in reducing illegal drug use and sales. As described subsequently, this war had and continues to have a profound effect on correctional populations and minorities (Tonry, 1995).

Intermediate Sanctions. As a result of disillusionment with the effectiveness of rehabilitation and the focus on justice and incapacitation, intermediate sanctions were proposed as an ideal way to provide a range of sanctions between probation and parole (Morris & Tonry, 1990). Theoretically, these sanctions could be scaled in severity to be proportionate to the seriousness of the crimes committed. Furthermore, the additional control and threat of sanctions were expected to either deter offenders from future criminal acts or restrict them (in a sense incapacitate them) so they would not have the opportunity to reoffend.

Most jurisdictions in the United States have some type of intermediate sanctions programs. These programs have been variously called

[2] Although habitual offender laws had been enacted by many states in the 1960s, they became popular again during this time.

correctional alternatives, intermediate sanctions, community corrections, or, more recently, correctional options. Intensive supervised probation or parole (ISP), house arrest, boot camp prisons, and day reporting centers are some of the more common intermediate sanctions. Frequently, they are used in conjunction with other tools of supervision such as urine testing or electronic monitoring. The sanctions are used as either front-end options for probationers or as back-end options for those released on parole or community supervision.

Prior to the 1970s, intermediate sanctions were referred to as community corrections; at that time the focus was on providing services and rehabilitation. In contrast, the intermediate sanctions of the 1980s and 1990s involved increased control over offenders. Typical requirements for offenders in ISP programs were more frequent meetings with correctional agents, periodic urine tests, substance abuse treatment, and verification of employment. The focus was on increasing control over offenders and making community supervision more onerous so that the punishment was retributive. In part, this was in response to the attitude that probation was nothing more than a slap on the wrist and, therefore, did not provide either a deserved punishment or a method to reduce the criminal activities of offenders while they were supervised in the community.

Truth in Sentencing. The amount of time offenders serve in prison is almost always shorter than the time they are sentenced to serve by the court. For example, Ditton and Wilson (1999) found that prisoners released in 1996 served an average of thirty months in prison and jail, or 44 percent of their average eighty-five-month sentences. Under indeterminate sentencing, decisions are made by professionals in low-visibility settings with high discretion and are unlikely to be influenced by public sentiment and passion. In the past three decades, sentencing requirements and release policies became more restrictive; pressure for longer sentences and uniform punishment led to mandatory minimums and sentencing guidelines. However, prison crowding, good time reductions, and earned time incentives continued to result in early release of prisoners. In response, many states increased the severity of sentencing laws by enacting restrictions on the possibility of early release; these laws became known as "truth in sentencing." The

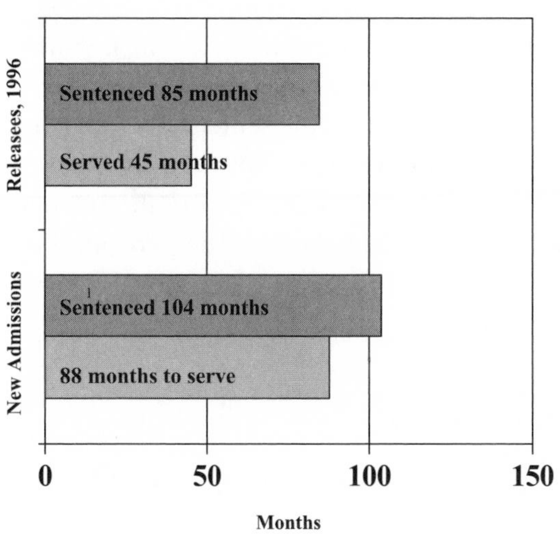

- Violent offenders released from state prison in 1996 were sentenced to an average of 85 months; they served about 50% or an average of 45 months
- Under truth-in-sentencing laws, violent offenders would serve 85% of sentence; new admissions to prison were sentenced to an average of 104 months so they would be expected to serve an average of 88 months (e.g., 85%)

Figure 1.2. Discrepancy between sentence and time served, comparing state prisoners released from prison in 1996 to the expected time served for new admissions.

truth-in-sentencing laws require offenders to serve a substantial portion of the prison sentence imposed by the court before being eligible for release. The laws are premised on the notion that juries, victims, and the public are entitled to know what punishments offenders will suffer at the time judges order it.

This philosophy gained momentum in the 1990s. To provide incentives to states to pass truth-in-sentencing laws, the U.S. Congress authorized grants to build or expand correctional facilities through the Violent Offender Incarceration and Truth-in-Sentencing Incentive Grants Program in the 1994 Crime Act. To qualify for the grants, states had to require people convicted of violent crimes to serve not less than 85 percent of their prison sentences.

Two-thirds of the states established truth-in-sentencing laws using the 85 percent test. In part to satisfy the 85 percent test and thereby qualify for federal funds for prison construction, states limited the powers of parole boards to set release dates, or of prison managers to award good time or earned time, or both. The laws reduced the discrepancy between the sentence imposed and actual time served in prison (as shown in Figure 1.2).

Most states target violent offenders under truth-in-sentencing laws; however, the definition of truth in sentencing varies among the states. For example, states such as Florida, Mississippi, and Ohio require *all* offenders to serve a substantial portion of the sentence before being eligible for release (Ditton & Wilson, 1999). Furthermore, there is variation in the percent of the sentence states require the offender to serve as well as the crimes covered by the law. The percent of the sentence required to be served in most states varies from 50 to 100 percent of a minimum sentence.

CONTROVERSY OVER COSTS

A great deal of controversy continues to exist about the use of incapacitation to control crime in the community. Cost is an important factor in almost all the debates. In the 1980s, as incarceration rates continued to climb, people began to complain about the rising costs of corrections. They questioned whether the high costs were worth the benefits gained by continually incarcerating such a large number of people. In response, Zedlewski (1987) pointed out that there were social costs to releasing offenders and these costs must be calculated and weighed against the costs of incarceration. If an offender is released and continues to commit crimes, there are additional costs to the criminal justice system such as the costs of arrests, revocation hearings, and court proceedings; there are also costs for the victims such as loss or additional private security.

Zedlewski's argument that there are social costs to releasing offenders had direct policy implications. Policy makers could justify additional expenditures on prison construction as a means to keep offenders in prison and, thereby, save the social costs of release. That is, constructing and operating prisons were worth the expense to save the social costs that would be incurred from releasing these offenders into the community. This argument was used to support additional prison construction.

The idea that there are social costs to releasing offenders from prison ignited a controversy that still rages. Some researchers have attempted to calculate the costs of crime, but there exists a controversy over which numbers to use in calculations. These researchers have varied opinions as to what costs are legitimately included and how the elements should be calculated. For example, should the calculations include criminal justice system costs, monetary costs to victims, private security costs, health care expenses, and the pain and suffering of victims and/or risk of death? Should the costs include tangible and intangible costs to victims, cost to others (victims' families, insurance companies, businesses, and society), and/or costs of preventing crime (theft insurance, guard dogs)?

Once decisions are made about what social costs to include, the actual number of crimes prevented by incarceration must be estimated. If each crime carries some social costs, the problem is determining how many crimes offenders would commit if they were in the community and not in prison. All evidence suggests that official statistics do not provide adequate information for these estimates, and so researchers have used self-report data for this purpose. Estimates vary across studies and recent findings suggest that the estimates of criminal activity will differ greatly if offenders are given a sentence to community supervision (MacKenzie, Browning, Skroban, & Smith, 1999). Furthermore, these estimates become more difficult because offenders have criminal careers that span a certain number of years. They are more active at some points in their careers, and their criminal activity usually declines as they get older (Blumstein, Cohen, Roth, & Visher, 1986); therefore, estimates of the number of crimes offenders would commit if they were in the community must take career length into consideration.

Once the estimates of the cost of crime to society and the average number of crimes committed are calculated, the yearly social costs of not imprisoning an offender can be determined. This figure is weighted against estimates of what it costs to keep an offender in prison. The result represents the benefit of imprisonment.

Instead of arguing about the specific calculations of the costs and benefits of incarceration, others reject the social costs calculations completely. They argue that the imputed costs of victim "pain and suffering" takes no account whatsoever of suffering by imprisoned offenders or by offenders' partners, children, and communities. From their perspective, the cost-benefit assessments require weighing inherently incommensurable values, and the attempts to do so have reached a dead end. They argue that it may be more productive to compare the cost and benefits of alternative crime prevention policies and not attempt to calculate the social costs of crime. Both groups in this debate include knowledgeable scientists who are aware of the complexity of the problems. At this time, there is no clear answer to the debate.

CONCLUSION

In this book, I focus on correctional strategies designed to reduce crime. I use the term *strategies* broadly to include various programs (e.g., vocational education), policies (e.g., incapacitation), and interventions (e.g., urine testing). Most of these strategies have some theoretical rationale for expecting a reduction in crime; however, they differ greatly in the proposed mechanism for crime reduction. Some interventions rely on the philosophies of incapacitation or deterrence to reduce the criminal activities of offenders, whereas others focus on rehabilitation. Still others attempt to control behavior, provide structure and discipline or challenge, or combine rehabilitation with control. The major question addressed in this book is, Which of these strategies are effective in reducing crime? It goes without saying that there are many different and important aspects to any decision about correctional strategies. Decision makers are interested in many different issues when they make a decision about correctional interventions. For example, cost-effectiveness and public acceptance are two important considerations.

Reducing crime is one of the major goals of the majority of correctional strategies. Furthermore, once we understand whether a program has an effect on crime, decisions on other considerations are easier and clearer. For instance, if we know that correctional boot camps are ineffective in reducing the later criminal behavior of offenders, we could then move to decisions about whether the programs had any other benefits such as cost reduction or good public relations. Too often discussions of effectiveness are confused because the criterion for establishing whether different strategies are effective is not clearly articulated. This confusion is greatly diminished if the measure of effectiveness is unambiguously defined as I have done in this book – effectiveness here refers to a reduction of criminal activity.

Furthermore, discussion of all factors that might be important in considering a correctional strategy would triple the size of each chapter, making the book prohibitively long.

As discussed in this chapter, the types of correctional interventions used in the United States have changed in the past thirty years, in part as a result of changes in correctional philosophy. Prior to the 1970s, most programs emphasized rehabilitation. The justice model led to programs that varied the amount of retribution. From this perspective, intermediate sanctions could be used to vary the retributive nature of the sentence. However, the largest change occurred with the crime control model of corrections. Interventions were designed to reduce crime through incapacitation and deterrence.

In this book, I examine various correctional strategies and draw conclusions about the effectiveness of the different strategies. The outcome of interest is crime reduction. In the next chapter, I argue for the importance of using scientific evidence and present the type of evidence that will be used to determine effectiveness. In the following chapters, I examine the evidence of effectiveness or ineffectiveness for the various strategies. In the final chapters of the book, I summarize these findings.

CHAPTER TWO

Evidence-Based Corrections

SCIENTIFIC EVIDENCE FOR WHAT WORKS

Strategies for reducing crime should be based on scientific evidence. By the term "evidence-based corrections," I refer to the need to use scientific evidence to make informed decisions about correctional policy (MacKenzie, 2002; MacKenzie, 2001; MacKenzie, 2000; MacKenzie 2005). That is the subject of this book.

In this book, I use four different approaches to evaluate the research and assess the effectiveness of crime reduction strategies: (1) reviews of the research literature, (2) meta-analyses used to examine groups of studies, (3) simulation studies, and (4) a scientific methods scoring system that uses the direction and significance of studies. There are several reasons for using different methodologies to review and assess the research and to draw conclusions about effectiveness in crime prevention. First, some strategies of crime prevention do not lend themselves to program evaluation that can be easily categorized using the scientific methods score designed to assess the quality of the science. Second, by using different methods to assess effectiveness, it is possible to discern agreement among the different methods.

LITERATURE REVIEWS

Reviews of the research literature have traditionally been used to determine whether there is evidence that some particular program, strategy, or intervention is effective in producing the intended outcome (e.g., reduce recidivism). The reviewer, usually someone who is knowledgeable about the topic area, examines the studies and draws conclusions about the findings based on the direction and significance of the results. This method of drawing conclusions about a program area is highly subjective, and it is difficult for someone else to determine exactly how conclusions were drawn. Many reviews are unsystematic and lack explicit and transparent methods, preventing others from understanding why studies were excluded, how they were critically appraised, and how conclusions were made about effectiveness.

Replication is an important part of science, and it is difficult to replicate literature reviews. For example, Martinson and his colleagues conducted a review of the literature and concluded that, with few exceptions, nothing was effective in rehabilitating offenders (Lipton, Martinson, & Wilks, 1975). Yet, later researchers who examined a similar body of research concluded that there was sufficient evidence to conclude that some programs work for some offenders (Andrews, Zinger, Hoge, Bonta, Gendreau, & Cullen, 1990; Palmer, 1975).

In this book, I use literature reviews as one approach to judge the effectiveness of several programs. These are used primarily when current reviews of the literature are available and little additional research has been completed in the past five or six years that would change the conclusions from these previous reviews. Frequently, several different researchers have reviewed the literature and have drawn similar conclusions about the effectiveness or ineffectiveness of the programs.

META-ANALYSES

A second method I use to draw conclusions about effectiveness is meta-analysis. Broad assessments of the literature have benefited from the rise of this new statistical technique (MacKenzie, Wilson, & Kider, 2001; Farrington & Petrosino, 2001). Meta-analysis enables researchers to aggregate the continuously growing body of empirical studies to examine and compare the effect of some intervention. Meta-analysis is a method of summarizing, integrating, and interpreting selected sets of scholarly research (i.e., empirical studies that produce quantitative findings; Lipsey & Wilson, 2001).

Meta-analysis is a method of encoding and analyzing the statistics that summarize research findings from research reports. The procedure begins with a clear definition of which studies will be eligible for inclusion in the analysis. Once the eligibility criteria are defined, an intensive search is made for all studies, published and unpublished, that might fit the criteria. This usually results in a large number of studies in the area of interest. These studies are carefully examined, and those that are potentially eligible are located and examined in more depth. Usually only some proportion of these studies are deemed eligible. Each independent sample in the eligible studies is the *unit of analysis* for the systematic review. For each independent sample, an effect size statistic is calculated and used as the outcome measure in the meta-analysis. The effect size is a standardized measure of the difference between the treatment and comparison group. Where possible, characteristics of the samples, the treatment, and the methodology of the study are coded and used as variables in the statistical analysis.

The meta-analysis of correctional boot camps (see Chapter 14) that my colleagues and I completed can be used as an illustration of the technique. First, we identified the characteristics of studies that would be eligible for the analysis. Eligible studies for the meta-analysis included quasi-experimental and experimental evaluations of a correctional residential program with a militaristic environment and compared the recidivism of participants to a comparison group who received another correctional sanction. After defining the eligibility criteria, we searched for eligible studies. The intensive search identified 771 unique documents, of which 144 were deemed potentially relevant. These studies were located and evaluated for eligibility. In the meta-analyses in this book, studies were eligible if they were in the English language, had a comparison group, and were completed after 1970 or 1980. The date selected depended upon our evaluation of the similarity of the programs to currently operating programs. We wanted to generalize the results to programs that were being implemented in corrections today.

For the boot camp meta-analysis, 29 studies in 37 documents (i.e., more than one document was located for the same study) were judged eligible for inclusion in the systematic review. The 29 studies resulted in 44 distinct samples that provided the primary unit of analysis for the systematic review. We coded information on the samples (e.g., age group, race), the programs (e.g., therapeutic programming in daily schedule, aftercare), and the study methods (e.g., random selection, attrition). This information was used to examine whether these attributes made any difference on the impact of the programs. For example, if we had information about the characteristics of the samples, we could enter this data into the models to ask whether the results of the meta-analysis differed by gender, race, or age. Using program information, we could ask whether the results of the analysis differed depending upon the length of the program or if the amount of individual counseling had an impact on outcomes. Equally important were the variables related to the method of the study. With this information we could ask where the results differed as a function of whether the study used an experimental design with random assignment to treatments or whether subject attrition made a difference. It was disappointing to find that many of the studies did not describe the characteristics of the samples and the programs with much detail, so we were unable to include much data on these in the meta-analysis.

Meta-analysis solves some of the problems inherent in literature reviews. Like reviews of the literature, meta-analysis is a method of drawing conclusions based on a group of research studies. The difference is that meta-analysis uses a particular statistical methodology for combining the results of quantitative research studies. The meta-analysis statistical technique uses data from a group of studies, all examining a similar program, to draw conclusions about the effectiveness of the program. One of the major benefits of meta-analyses is that the analyses can be replicated by other researchers. In some areas, such as the rehabilitation literature, there is a body of research using meta-analysis to examine the effectiveness of programs (see, e.g., Andrews et al., 1990). Wherever possible in this book, I use information from meta-analyses when I draw conclusions about the effectiveness of different types of correctional interventions.

In many chapters, I include a forest plot of the effect sizes from the studies examined. These plots illustrate the effect size comparisons between the experimental and control groups and whether these differences are significant. These plots are useful graphic displays of results using meta-analytical techniques.

The Campbell Collaboration: Systematic Reviews and Meta-analysis

The Campbell Collaboration is an exciting new development in social science research (www.campbellcollaboration.org/). The Collaboration is designed to facilitate the preparation, maintenance, and accessibility of systematic reviews of research on the effects of social science interventions. One section of the Collaboration, the Justice Group, focuses on crime and justice topics.

Researchers have long grappled with the problem of understanding how to interpret the results of separate but similar studies. Meta-analysis provides a more precise way of determining the "success" of interventions. However, not all meta-analyses use explicit methods and not every rigorous review uses quantitative methods. For these reasons, the term *systematic review* has become popular to describe scientific syntheses using explicit methods.

There is growing consensus that systematic reviews can be important in evidence-based decision making. However, there are several obstacles that have limited their usefulness. First, many systematic reviews are one-time efforts that are completed and published. Such reviews are not updated with new studies, and, thus, the information eventually becomes outdated. Second, a systematic review may not include all relevant studies; in particular, unpublished studies and reports are often excluded. This limits its utility because reliance solely on published studies produces a biased sample and is therefore inadequate (Lipsey & Wilson, 1993). Finally, there is the problem of dissemination and lack of uniformity. Reviews are often published in academic journals that are not reader friendly for most policy makers and practitioners. The Campbell Collaboration was designed to address some of the problems with current systematic reviews and meta-analyses.

The Cochrane Collaboration in health care is the precedent for the Campbell Collaboration (see www.Cochrane.org; Petrosino, Boruch, Farrington, Sherman, & Weisburd, 2003). The Cochrane Collaboration was organized to address the concerns of Archie Cochrane, who criticized health care professionals for ignoring scientific evidence. The organization conducts systematic reviews on health care. The reviews are prepared electronically, structured with the same exact detail, and updated periodically as new evidence becomes available.

The Campbell Collaboration will build on the Cochrane precedent but will focus on what works in social policy. The Justice Group of the Collaboration will coordinate the preparation, maintenance, and accessibility of reviews relevant to crime and justice. During the first year, the Justice Group solicited reviews in twenty-five areas of intervention. Currently, the Campbell Collaboration has solicited reviews on such topics as interventions for offenders with co-occurring disorders, Scared Straight, community-based programs for juveniles, outpatient treatment for drug-involved offenders, and treatment for sex offenders. When this work is completed and available, it will greatly assist decision makers, researchers, and the general public by offering the best evidence on the effectiveness of crime and justice interventions.

SIMULATIONS

Another technique that is used to determine the effectiveness of some programs is simulation research. Simulations are complex statistical techniques used to predict the future by "simulating" future conditions based on various estimates. For example, incapacitation research uses statistical models to estimate the crimes prevented by various policy decisions. Such studies do not easily lend themselves to the effect size calculations used in meta-analyses or the scoring methodology used for evaluating specific programs. For this reason, I review the literature on incapacitation and, on the basis of the simulation research as well as the literature reviews, I draw conclusions about the effectiveness of incapacitation strategies.

ASSESSING THE SCIENTIFIC METHOD AND SIGNIFICANCE OF STUDIES

The fourth method I use to draw conclusions about the effectiveness of various correctional strategies and programs is a technique developed by University of Maryland researchers to assess the effectiveness of various types of crime prevention programs (Sherman, Welsh, Farrington, & MacKenzie, 2002; Sherman, Gottfredson, MacKenzie, Eck, Reuter, & Bushway, 1997).

Determining What Works in Correctional Programming

An innovative technique for determining what works in crime prevention was developed by University of Maryland researchers in response to a request by the U.S. Congress. The U.S. Congress requested a comprehensive evaluation of the effectiveness of state and local criminal justice and community efforts to prevent crime. The evaluation was to be independent and employ rigorous and scientifically recognized standards and methodologies. The culmination of this effort was the publication of a report to the U.S. Congress of more than six hundred pages, "Preventing Crime: What Works, What Doesn't, What's Promising" (hereafter the "Maryland Report"; Sherman et al., 1997; Sherman et al., 2002). The Maryland Report reviewed the research in seven different settings: family, school, police, community, place, the labor market, and in the criminal justice system. Within this context, the report evaluated the quality of the research methods of more than five hundred studies of various crime prevention programs. This assessment, along with the direction and significance of the research results, was used to draw conclusions about what works in preventing crime.

Traditional crime prevention efforts are directed toward people who are not yet involved in crime. In contrast, the University of Maryland researchers employed a broader perspective on crime prevention that included any setting capable of reducing crime in the community. From this perspective, strategies and programs in criminal justice settings (i.e., in the courts and corrections) that focus on reducing the criminal activities of known offenders were included in the definition of crime prevention. That is, because past criminal behavior is the best predictor of future criminal behavior (Andrews & Bonta, 2003; Sampson & Laub, 1990), it is reasonable to expect that crime can be prevented by preventing the criminal behavior of known offenders. Because the majority of offenders serve time in the community on probation, parole, or some other type of supervised release and because those who are incarcerated will eventually be released into the community, it is beneficial to focus attention on the future criminal activities of these individuals.

Chapter 9 in the Maryland Report addressed crime prevention in the criminal justice system, focusing on research funded by the

U.S. Department of Justice (MacKenzie, 1997). The chapter centered on options for dealing with actual offenders once they are identified so that crime in the community can be reduced. Many of these strategies and interventions reflected the crime control perspective of correctional interventions (e.g., correctional boot camps, intermediate punishments). Subsequently, the state of Washington Joint Legislative Audit and Review Committee asked me to extend this research to include additional correctional programs (MacKenzie & Hickman, 1998), including many of the programs the state of Washington operated in their correctional system (e.g., education, vocation, prison industries, cognitive behavior therapy). These programs are commonly used in other correctional systems as well and are more rehabilitation-oriented than the programs assessed in the Maryland Report. This book extends the findings from these earlier reports. The following sections describe the scientific merit scoring procedure in more detail.

The Scientific Method Scoring Procedure

The University of Maryland researchers developed a two-step procedure for drawing conclusions about what works in crime prevention. The first step was to locate and assess each individual study for the quality of the research design and methodology. This was based on the scientific rigor of the study and the internal validity of the research methodology. The second step was to examine each topic area for research quality and the direction and significance of the results. That is, within each topic area, the results of the evaluations were summarized to draw conclusions about what works, what does not, what is promising, and what we do not know. For instance, all boot camp evaluations were located, and each study was assessed for scientific rigor (MacKenzie, 2001; Chapter 13 this volume). In the case of juvenile boot camps, four evaluations were located. Each evaluation was judged to be of high quality because they each used an experimental design and there appeared to be no major problems with assignment and attrition.

Following this assessment of the quality of the research, the direction and significance of the results were examined. Again, using juvenile boot camps as an example, the four identified studies were examined;

three of the studies found no significant differences between the boot camp youths and the control groups in recidivism. In the fourth study, the boot camp youth did worse than the controls. Therefore, the conclusion was that there was no evidence juvenile boot camps were effective in reducing criminal activity; in other words, at this point in time given the research evidence, juvenile boot camps "do not work." Of course, conclusions about most of the topic areas were not as easy because, in general, the quality of the research was much lower.

Some of the authors of the chapters in the Maryland Report assessed the impact of programs on criminal or delinquent activity as well as risk variables (e.g., drug use by juveniles, poor school performance, unemployment, etc.). In contrast, the review of studies in the criminal justice setting (which included courts and corrections) focused solely on whether the programs reduced criminal activities. Of course, it is important to note that each program or crime prevention strategy has effects other than crime reduction. For example, the analysis of the costs and benefits of a program is critically important in any examination of relevant issues (Welsh & Farrington, 2000a; Welsh & Farrington, 2000b). A high quality, intensive treatment program for offenders can be relatively costly; the advantages of the program must be weighed against the costs. Such issues, among others, are important in policy decisions. The problem is that many times other issues make the effectiveness difficult to discern and/or the crime reduction effect of the program is assumed but not articulated. For these reasons, I focused my attention on the effectiveness of correctional programs and strategies in reducing criminal activities while acknowledging that crime reduction is only one factor among many that are important to consider.

Step One: Determining scientific rigor. The first step in the process of assessing studies for scientific rigor was to locate as many studies as possible within each topic area (e.g., intensive supervised probation, drug treatment, boot camps, etc.). In most cases, studies conducted within the past ten years were used because older work is less relevant to the present social conditions and correctional programming. Both published and unpublished research reports were included. To be included in the assessment, the study had to include information on criminal activities or recidivism. The scientific rigor of each study was assessed using a coding form to document research design, selection problems, attrition, statistical analysis, statistical controls, and sample size (see Sherman et al., 1997 for copy of the form). The results of the assessment were used to give each study a scientific rigor score. Scores ranged from one to five, with five indicating the highest level of scientific rigor. Studies assigned a particular methods score share the following features:

Level 1 Studies. This level indicates some correlation between the program and measure(s) of recidivism. Usually there was no comparison group. Studies in this category were judged to be so low in scientific rigor that they were not used to assess the effectiveness of the correctional programs.

Level 2 Studies. These studies indicated some association between the program and recidivism but were severely limited because many alternative explanations could not be ruled out, given the research design. Frequently in the correctional evaluations, these studies used dropouts or nonvolunteers as the comparison group, and no variables were included in the statistical analysis to control for initial differences between groups.

Level 3 Studies. These studies contained a comparison between two or more groups, one receiving the program and one without the program. The design of the study and the statistical analysis assured reasonable similarity between the treated group and the comparison(s).

Level 4 Studies. This level indicates a comparison between a program group and one or more control groups with controls for other factors or a nonequivalent comparison group that is only slightly different from the program group.

Level 5 Studies. This level is considered the "gold standard" because studies employ random assignment and analysis of comparable program and comparison groups, including controls for attrition.

Step Two: Drawing conclusions about what works. Clear conclusions about programs that work, do not work, or are promising require a high level of confidence in the research findings. Emerging results continually add new pieces to the puzzle. Old research results must be reconsidered in light of new findings, and these may lead to different conclusions. The best one can claim to know about effectiveness is based only on the quality and quantity of the available evidence at one point in time. Thus, I am not asserting that my conclusions in this book will hold for the future. Rather, this is a summary of where we are at this point in time – what we know about the effectiveness of correctional interventions, strategies, and programs.

Because there are many consequences of claims about "what works," it is important to use a reasonably high threshold for the strength of scientific evidence; however, the current state of evaluation research creates a dilemma. If we use only studies that score at level five (the gold standard) on the scientific merit scale, there would be few evaluations to use in assessing programs. For example, a high threshold for making decisions about what works would require at least two level-five studies showing that a program is effective (or ineffective), with the preponderance of the evidence in favor of the same conclusions. Yet employing such a conservative approach to determine what works would leave us with very little research from which to draw conclusions.

Obviously, there is a trade-off between the level of certainty in the conclusions that can be drawn and the level of useful information that can be gleaned from the available research. Excluding findings from studies that score moderately on scientific merit would waste a great deal of useful information. Thus, to make use of the available research, the University of Maryland researchers adopted a middle road between reaching few conclusions with great certainty and many conclusions with little certainty. This meant they eliminated studies of very weak methodology. Studies had to reach the bar of scientific rigor with a minimum score of three.

Descriptive or process evaluations and those scoring a one on the scale were eliminated from consideration because they could not reasonably be used to determine whether the program was effective in reducing recidivism. Studies scoring a two were very common; however, because many alternative explanations for the results could not be ruled out (e.g., the scientific merit of the studies was so low), we decided to use these only to provide additional information about an area of study (e.g., preponderance of evidence) but not to draw conclusions. Although studies that scored at level two lacked strong scientific rigor and cannot provide the sole basis for conclusions about effectiveness, they do provide some worthwhile information. This is particularly true in program areas that include very scant evaluation research. These admittedly weak studies may be the only information available. In program areas that are more researched, level two studies become part of the preponderance of evidence but do not serve as the primary sources of evidence. Here, the findings are given reduced weight relative to those of more scientifically rigorous evaluations.

In the University of Maryland crime prevention work, we developed decision rules using scientific strength and substantive findings from the available evaluations and classified each program area into one of four categories: what works, what does not, what is promising, and what is unknown. The decision rules were as follows:

What Works: We were reasonably certain these programs reduce recidivism in the kinds of contexts (and with the types of participants) in which they have been evaluated, and for which the findings should generalize to similar settings in other places and times. Programs defined as "working" must have at least two level-three evaluations with statistical significance tests showing effectiveness and the preponderance of all available evidence supporting the same conclusion.

What Does Not Work: We were reasonably certain these programs fail to reduce recidivism in the kinds of contexts (and with the types of participants) in which they have been evaluated and for which the findings should generalize to similar settings in other places and times. Programs classified as "not working" must have at least two level-three evaluations with statistical tests showing ineffectiveness and the preponderance of all available evidence supporting the same conclusion.

What Is Promising: These are programs for which the level of certainty from available evidence is too low to support generalizable conclusions but for which there is some evidence predicting that further research could support such conclusions. Programs are defined as "promising" if they have at least one level-three evaluation with significance tests showing their effectiveness in reducing recidivism and the preponderance of all available evidence supports the same conclusions.

What Is Unknown: Any program not included in one of the previous three categories is defined as having unknown effects. There is simply not enough research employing adequate scientific rigor upon which to draw even tentative conclusions. Program areas with unknown effects should not be interpreted as ineffective. Succinctly put, the jury is still out.

An advantage of this scoring system with clearly specified decision rules about what works, what does not, what is promising, and what is unknown is that other scientists can replicate our findings. Obviously, the scoring is based more on the internal validity of the research than the external validity.

DETERMINING WHAT WORKS

The following chapters in this book examine different correctional and court interventions. I refer to these variously as interventions, strategies, programs, or treatments because many people use the term "intervention" to refer specifically to therapeutic or rehabilitative efforts. In this book, I examine the crime reduction effectiveness of not only therapeutic programs (e.g., drug treatment, cognitive skills programs) but also of more punishment-oriented interventions such as intermediate sanctions and of correctional strategies such as incapacitation. Various methods of assessing effectiveness, including literature reviews, meta-analyses, simulations, and the methods score are used to determine whether an intervention reduces crime. Where possible, I use the University of Maryland scoring system, systematic reviews, and meta-analyses to draw conclusions about what is effective in reducing crime. The following chapters examine these different interventions and assess the effectiveness of the interventions.

CHAPTER THREE

Incapacitation

GROWTH IN CORRECTIONAL POPULATIONS

A dramatic increase in the offender population accompanied the changes in sentencing and correctional philosophy that began in the 1970s. The increase in incarceration rates was unprecedented (see Figure 3.1). From 1930 until 1975 the average incarceration rate had been relatively stable at 106 inmates for every 100,000 individuals in the population. The rate fluctuated only slightly, from a low of 93 inmates per 100,000 to a maximum rate of 137 (Blumstein & Beck, 1999; Sourcebook, 2000). That time period was the age of indeterminate sentencing and rehabilitation.

As shown in Figure 3.1, after 1975 incarceration rates grew tremendously. By 1985 the incarceration rate for state or federal prisons was 202 per 100,000 adults in the population, and this continued to climb to 411 in 1995 and 478 in 2000. Prisons are operated by state or federal agencies and hold longer term, sentenced prisoners. Jails are operated by local counties or cities and hold those who are awaiting trial or sentencing or who have been sentenced to short sentences (one or two years at most). When jail populations are added, the total incarceration rate in year 2000 was 699 individuals per 100,000 adults. More than 1.3 million prisoners were under U.S. federal or state jurisdiction by the end of 2000; more than 2 million were incarcerated either in a local jail or a state or federal prison (Sourcebook, 2000). Additionally, incarceration rates rose faster for women than for men (a 364 percent increase in the number of female prisoners per 100,000 residents compared to a 195 percent increase for males) and for minorities

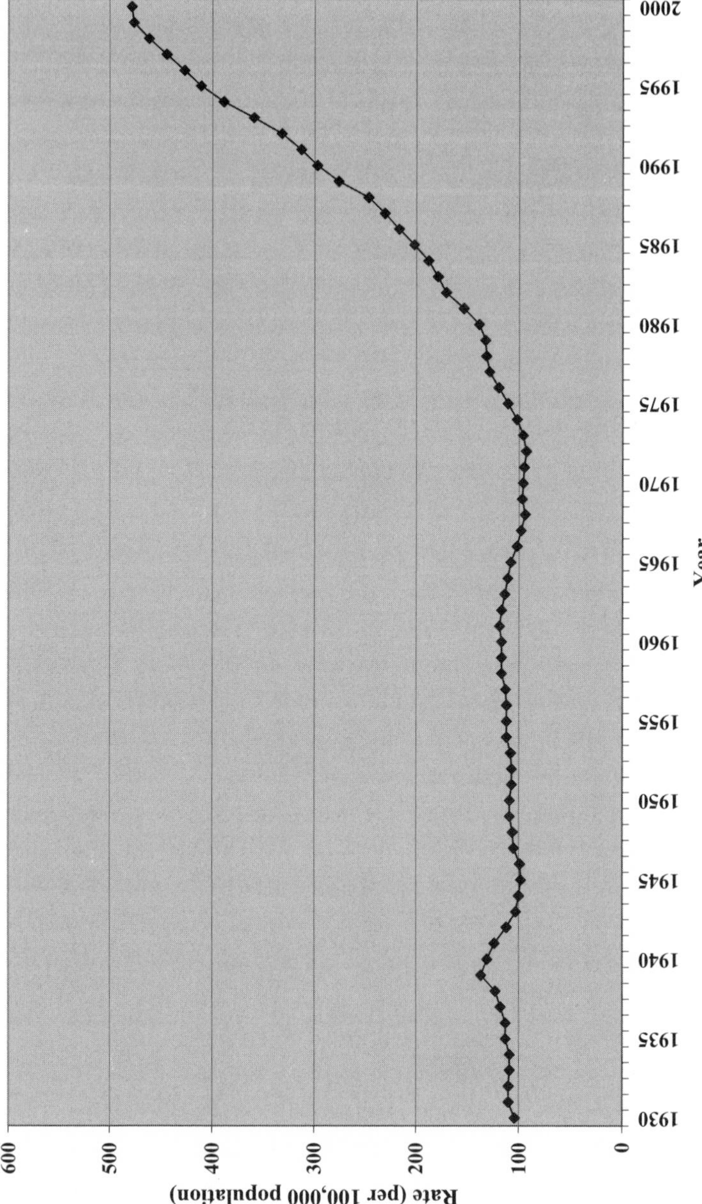

Figure 3.1. U.S. incarceration rate in state and federal institutions (1930–2000).

(increases of 184 percent and 235 percent for African Americans and Hispanics, respectively) compared to whites (a 154 percent increase) (Blumstein & Beck, 1999).

During the 1930 to 1975 time period there were only two deviations from the relatively stable incarceration rate: a rise at the end of the Great Depression and a decline during World War II. This strikingly consistent rate led Blumstein and Cohen (1973) to propose a "theory of the stability of punishment." They argued that societies maintain a stable incarceration rate by balancing the tolerance of marginal crimes against the costs (financial and political) associated with raising the incarceration rate. However, shortly after they made this proposal, incarceration rates in the United States began a rapid increase, and the stability of punishment theory was dismissed. In its place Blumstein, Cohen, and Miller (1980) proposed the demographic shift hypothesis to explain the growth. From this perspective, the growth in the prison population was the result of a shift in the number of people in the prison-eligible population as a result of the large demographic bulge in the U.S. population caused by the post–World War II baby boom generation. That is, the largest cohort of the baby boomers were in the peak ages of incarceration, and therefore the increase in the imprisonment rates was caused by a larger number of individuals in the population who were most at risk for incarceration.

Subsequently, it became obvious that the increases in rates were well beyond that which would be expected by demographic shifts alone (MacKenzie, Tracy, & Williams, 1988). Recent research examining the changes that have taken place in the past twenty-five years has attributed the increase in the prison population to changing prison policies such as sentencing guidelines, mandatory minimum prison terms, and restrictions on parole release (Reitz, 1998; Tonry, 1996b) In comparison to the past, a higher proportion of those who are arrested in the United States are sentenced to prison and those who are committed to prison stay there for longer periods of time (Cohen & Canela-Cacho, 1994). Furthermore, the growth in incarceration rates has not been uniform across all the types of crime. The dominant factor in the growth in incarceration rates is the increase in the number of arrests for drug crimes (Blumstein & Beck, 1999; see also Tonry, 1995). The growth in incarceration for nondrug offenses is accounted for by increases in the number of prison commitments per arrest and increases in time served.

Increases in the U.S. correctional population were not limited to prison and jail inmates alone. The number of individuals on probation and parole also grew substantially. Probationers include adult offenders whom courts place in community supervision instead of incarceration, whereas parolees include those adults conditionally released to community supervision whether by a decision of the parole board or by mandatory conditional release after serving a prison term. Nearly 4.6 million adult men and women were on probation or parole at the end of 2000, up from 1.3 million in 1980 (Bureau of Justice Statistics, 2001). For 2000 this represents a rate of 1,836 probationers and 347 parolees for every 100,000 adults in the population. From 1980 until 2000, the number of people on probation grew 243 percent and the number on parole grew 229 percent (Bureau of Justice Statistics, 2001).

Overall, the total U.S. adult population under the jurisdiction of federal, state, and local correctional authorities reached an all-time high of almost 6.5 million in 2000, up from 1.8 million in 1980 (Bureau of Justice Statistics, 2001). One in every 32 adults, or 3.1 percent of the country's adult population, were either incarcerated in prison or jail, or on probation or parole at the end of the year 2000. The majority of these adults (71 percent) were on probation or parole.

CHANGES IN CRIME RATES

One of the first questions many people ask after seeing the rising incarceration rate is, What impact has this had on public safety? The question centers on whether the changed focus on crime control through incapacitation and deterrence has been effective in reducing crime in the community, preventing crime, and/or increasing public safety. In other words, has the dramatic increase in correctional populations been associated with a corresponding decrease in the crime rate? The answer is not clear. There are other factors that may produce changes in either the crime rate or the incarceration rate, or both simultaneously; furthermore, there is no simple association between the two.

Index crimes are the crimes used by the U.S. Federal Bureau of Investigation (FBI) in the Uniform Crime Reports (UCR) as indices for recording changes in crime rates over time; they consist of violent crime index offenses (i.e., murder, forcible rape, robbery, aggravated assault) and serious property crime index offenses (i.e., burglary, larceny/theft, motor vehicle theft, arson) known to the police. Figure 3.2 shows the rates of property and violent index crimes known to the police and the rate of incarceration for state and federal prisons from 1965 until 2000 (Sourcebook, 2000). As shown, the relationship between crime and incarceration rates is not simple and varies greatly by the period examined. For example, the incarceration rate was stable from 1965 until approximately 1972, after which it moved steadily upward. In contrast, crime rates fluctuated during the same period. Violent crime rose from 1971 until 1981, fell through 1985, rose again until 1991, and has been declining ever since. Property crime rates experienced similar fluctuations.

Another way of measuring crime is through victim surveys. Unlike the UCR, these surveys do not depend on victims reporting crime to the police. The National Crime Victimization Survey (NCVS), conducted by the U.S. Bureau of the Census for the U.S. Bureau of Justice Statistics, obtains data from interviews with individuals in households selected as representative of the U.S. population. On one hand, changes in violent crime victimization rates during the past twenty-five years are very similar to the changes in official rates obtained through the UCR. Similar to the trends shown in the UCR, violent crime victimization rates fluctuated between 1973 and 1994 and then began a steady decline through 2000 (Rennison, 2001). Property crime victim rates, on the other hand, have fallen since 1974.

A difficulty in trying to determine the effect of the incarceration rate on crime rates is that one or both may be caused by some other factors at play during the time studied. Changes in demographics, labor markets, or other economic, social, cultural, or normative factors may influence the rates. Any apparent relationship may be spurious. Researchers have attempted to study the relationships with complex statistical models. Although almost everyone acknowledges that the increased incarceration rates have had some effect on decreasing crime rates, a great deal of controversy exists about

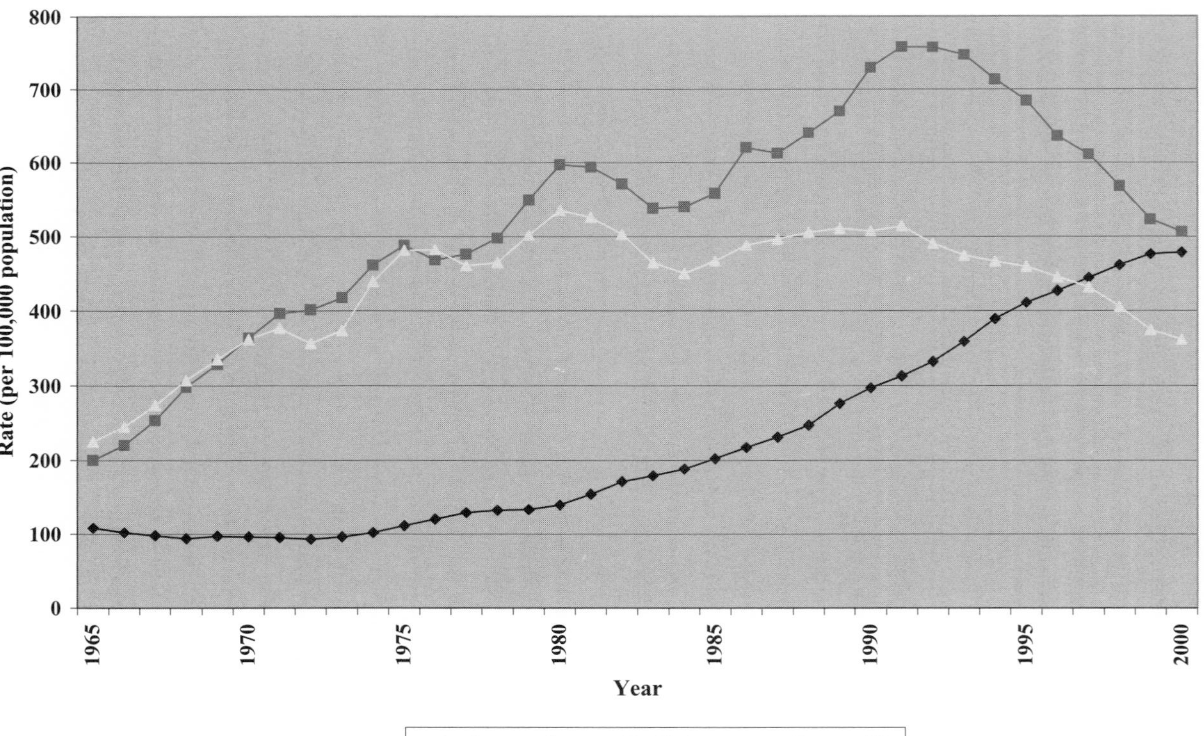

Figure 3.2. U.S. incarceration rate and violent and property crime rates (1965–2000).

the size of the impact (Donohue, 1998; Rosenfeld, 2000; Spelman, 2000).

INCAPACITATION STRATEGIES

The crime control strategy is based on the belief that incapacitation will be successful in reducing crime because offenders in prison cannot continue to commit crimes in the community. A secondary benefit of incarceration is thought to be the indirect effect of deterring (or inhibiting) others from committing crimes because of the threat of incarceration (general deterrence effect). Furthermore, individuals who spend time in prison may be deterred from continuing their criminal activities when they are released (a specific deterrent effect). During the mid-1970s, interest in incapacitation as a crime prevention strategy grew, in part because of concerns about the efficacy of rehabilitation, rising crime rates, and public fear of crime. Additional support for the benefits of incapacitation as a correctional strategy came from the proposal that although there were enormous costs to incarcerating large numbers of felons, there were also substantial costs if they were released and continued to commit crimes (in terms of such factors as criminal processing, loss to victims, etc.; Zedlewski, 1987). Some of the practices that can be attributed to these incapacitation strategies are habitual offender laws, mandatory minimum sentences, and the more recent three-strikes laws.

Originally, incapacitation strategies were supported because of what seemed to be the logical utility of keeping offenders in prison so they could not commit crimes. In some jurisdictions the increases in incarceration rates were accompanied by decreases in crime rates, leading some people to conclude that incapacitation strategies were successful in reducing crime. However, careful scientific examination requires more than an association between two variables because both could easily be caused by some third factor.

The more rigorous research examining the effectiveness of incapacitation strategies uses simulation or mathematical models to estimate the impact of incarceration on offending in the community (Spelman, 1994; Zimring & Hawkins, 1995). The estimation of crime prevention benefits obtained through incarceration is a complicated process. It should be noted that this research makes use of complex statistical models with reasonable estimates of the relevant factors completed by a respected group of researchers. Although there is still debate about the estimates used in the statistical models, it is important to distinguish the predictions in this research from unscientific estimates given in some policy debates. For example, Zimring and Hawkins (1995) describe one unscientific estimate that predicted a $300 billion savings in the cost of crimes prevented, which, as noted by Zimring and Hawkins, was greater than the federal deficit or the national defense budget at the time.

The majority of the studies examining the effect of incapacitation demonstrate a small but positive effect in reducing crime. There is some controversy over what is considered a "small" effect. Frequently, the crime prevention effect of incarceration is associated with significant increases in prison populations. Debates continue about whether the reduction in crime is worth the additional costs for building and maintaining prisons and jails and whether there are other more cost-effective methods of crime reduction.

Time Series Models

Studies of the impact of incapacitation policies make use of two different statistical techniques: (1) time series and (2) individual-level modeling. The time series models examine the relationships between crimes and prison populations. Researchers have studied this association both at the national and state level. Frequently, homicide data are used as the dependent variable in these time series regressions because data are available for more years and suffer less from underreporting (Marvell & Moody, 1998). Studies using U.S. national-level data generally report a 15 percent decline in homicides with each 10 percent increase in the prison population (Devine, Sheley, & Smith, 1988; Marvell & Moody, 1998). These studies use statistical controls such as age structure, economic factors, military activity, and executions; that is, factors that may be related to changes in either the incarceration rate, the crime rate, or both.

Studies have also examined the impact of incapacitation policies and the association of these policies with changes in crime and incarceration rates within states (Levitt, 1996; Marvell & Moody, 1994; 1998). In general, they find increases in prison population are associated with crime reduction but the association is smaller than the estimates from national-level data. For example, Levitt estimates that each additional prisoner eliminates 0.004 murders, 0.05 rapes, 1.2 assaults, 1.1 robberies, 2.6 burglaries, and 9.2 larcenies annually.

Using econometric modeling, Levitt (1996) attempted to examine the impact of the prison population growth rates on crime by identifying states with court orders to reduce prison overcrowding. He used panel data from a group of twelve states for the years 1971 to 1993. For some part of this period the entire prison systems of these states were under court order to reduce overcrowding. In the analysis he examined the period before the litigation and compared this to the litigation period. His assumption was that overcrowding litigation has an effect on the prison population rate but has no impact on the crime rate; thus, changes in the crime rate during the period of litigation demonstrates the impact of prison population on the crime rate. Replications in the twelve states control for potential historical effects or some spurious effects occuring during the time of the study that affect both rates. As a result of this work, Levitt estimated that incarceration of each additional prisoner averted about fifteen index offenses each year, mostly property crimes.

Estimating Crime Rates and Criminal Careers

The second method of examining the impact of crime control through incarceration makes use of mathematical models based on estimates of individual-level offending. To estimate the effect of incarceration on individual-level offending, researchers have to be able to estimate individual-level offense rates. The question is, How many crimes would offenders commit if they were in the community?

Early research on incapacitation used official records of arrests or convictions to estimate the individual-level offense rates (Blumstein & Cohen, 1979; Clarke, 1974; Greenberg, 1975; Petersilia & Greenwood, 1978; Van Dine, Conrad, & Dinitz, 1977). However, official rates reflect only those crimes that come to the attention of the police; offenders are not arrested for the vast majority of crimes they commit (Blumstein & Cohen, 1979; Greenwood & Abrahamse, 1982; MacKenzie, Browning, Skroban, & Smith, 1999). This presented a major problem for the researchers because estimates based on official arrests or convictions greatly underestimated the number of crimes one individual actually commits.

The length of time offenders continue to commit crimes, or the "criminal career," presented another estimation difficulty. Early researchers had no way of estimating how long individual offenders would continue to commit crimes during their lifetime. That is, researchers needed to know the length of offenders' "careers" of crime. When did they begin their criminal activity? When was their rate of criminal activity highest? When did they desist from committing crimes? If an offender incarcerated at age forty was near the end of his career then locking him up for twenty years would not prevent many crimes in the community because he would have desisted anyway. Thus, the available official data did not provide sufficient information to enable researchers to effectively estimate either individual offense rates or criminal careers.

Self-report surveys of prisoners conducted during the late 1970s and early 1980s were designed to answer the questions about the individual crime rates and criminal careers of offenders (Chaiken & Chaiken, 1982; Greenwood & Abrahamse, 1982; Peterson & Braiker, 1980; Peterson, Braiker, & Polich, 1981; Peterson, Chaiken, Ebener, & Honig, 1982). These surveys asked offenders who were entering prison to report how many crimes they committed per month during a recent period when they were in the community. From these self-reports, estimates of the number of crimes offenders commit per year could be calculated. These yearly estimates, called *lambda*, are used in simulation models to estimate how many crimes were averted each year for the offenders who were kept in prison. Additionally, questions about offending patterns at different ages gave researchers information on the stages of criminal careers (e.g., initiation, length, high rate periods, desistance). Using these estimates in simulation or mathematical models, researchers examine the number of crimes prevented by actual and hypothetical criminal justice practices and sanctioning policies. The size of the incapacitative effects depends on estimates of lambda, assumptions about the length of the career, and the type of sanctioning policy used in the analysis.

Estimating lambda is no easy task; estimates vary substantially by crime type. For example, recent studies of prison inmates (English,

1993; Horney & Marshall, 1991) and probationers (MacKenzie et al., 1999) have found lambdas of 13.7–24.9 for robbery, 43–117.2 for theft, and 32–37.4 for drug dealing. Furthermore, the fact that there are a large number of offenders who commit few crimes (low lambda) and a small proportion who commit a large percentage of crimes (large lambdas) results in the mean being skewed toward larger numbers (Visher, 1987). In her examination of the differences in reported robberies for a group of prison inmates, Visher found the average number of robberies per year was 43.4. In contrast, because of the skew, the median number of robberies was 3.75 per year. All of these issues in estimating lambda present problems for researchers when they attempt to use lambda in mathematical models to estimate the number of crimes averted.

Another problem in estimating the number of crimes an offender would commit in the community arises when arrests, probation, or alternative sanctions are considered. Recent research by my colleagues and myself suggests that criminal activity may substantially decline after arrest and during probation (MacKenzie et al., 1999). Of twenty offenders who committed thefts in the year before arrest, we found only two continued to steal during probation. Furthermore, prior to probation, active thieves committed 43 thefts per year, whereas active thieves on probation reported committing only 10.5 thefts a year. The results were similar for all crimes investigated (burglary, forgery, robbery, assault, and drug dealing); both the number of active offenders and the number of crimes committed per year declined when the offenders were on probation. On the basis of these findings, we would expect prisoners who are given alternative sentences in lieu of prison to have lower lambdas because they were arrested and sentenced to community sanctions. Thus, estimates of lambda based on the prearrest period as used in many studies may greatly overestimate the crime savings because these offenders would be offending at a much lower rate if they had been sentenced to community sanctions.

Collective versus Selective Incapacitation

It is important to distinguish between two types of incapacitation strategies: collective and selective (Greenberg, 1975). Collective strategies refer to crime reduction accomplished through traditional offense-based sentencing and imprisonment policies and changes in these policies such as mandatory minimum sentences. Sentences are usually based on the seriousness of the conviction and the offender's prior record under a "just desserts" philosophy of sentencing. Under a collective strategy, offenders convicted of a similar offense with a similar past history receive similar sentences. In contrast, selective strategies attempt to improve the efficiency of imprisonment as a crime control strategy by tailoring sentences to individual offenders. Selective strategies attempt to identify offenders who will commit serious crimes at high rates in the future in order to sentence them to longer periods of imprisonment. Thus, selective incarceration attempts to decrease crime by keeping high-rate, serious offenders in prison for longer periods of time.

Continuing increases in prison populations and research findings of large differences in the crime rates of individual offenders moved attention toward a more selective strategy of incapacitating a small group of offenders. Initially, interest in selective incapacitation as a crime control strategy came from research that revealed a small number of very active offenders (6 percent of the cohort) accounted for a disproportionately large number of the arrests (52 percent) in a Philadelphia birth cohort (Wolfgang, Figlio, & Sellin, 1972). Similarly, self-report surveys of prison inmates found the majority of offenders reported committing offenses at a fairly low rate; however, a small fraction of the prisoners reported committing crimes at a substantially higher rate (Chaiken & Chaiken, 1982; Marquis, 1981; Peterson et al., 1982). In other words, a relatively small number of offenders were responsible for a large amount of crime. Incapacitation advocates argued that crime could be reduced if these "career criminals" were identified and incapacitated. The goal of selective incapacitation is to identify the offenders who are predicted to commit serious crimes at high rates in the future so they can be incarcerated for long periods of time.

In the face of constraints on available prison resources, the issue for criminal justice policy was how to allocate a limited number of cells among competing offenders. In support of the selective incapacitation sentencing policy, Greenwood and Abrahamse (1982) argued that increasing the length of time served by the predicted high-rate offenders, while at the same time reducing the time served by those who were predicted to be low-rate offenders, could reduce crime rates without a corresponding increase in prison populations. Ideally, the worst (those who commit the most numerous and/or the most serious crimes), active (not yet at the end of their career of crime) criminals would be identified and put in prison.

EFFECTIVENESS OF INCAPACITATION STRATEGIES

In general, reviews of the collective incapacitation strategies demonstrate a modest reduction in crime combined with substantial increases in prison populations (Visher, 1987). Visher provides a review of three different types of incapacitation studies: (1) collective strategies that attempt to ascertain how much crime was prevented by the sanctioning and imprisonment policies, (2) collective strategies that estimate the potential crime reduction under different hypothetical policies, and (3) selective strategies. Estimates of the crimes prevented by imprisonment policies vary greatly depending upon what estimates of lambda are used (e.g., UCR, NCVS, self-report from different samples) and the time period investigated. According to Visher the sentencing practices and policies that doubled prison populations during the 1970s and early 1980s resulted in an estimated crime reduction of 10 to 30 percent. Furthermore, the large increase in prison populations prevented only an additional 6 to 9 percent of all robberies and burglaries.

Similarly, investigations of the impact of alternative imprisonment policies demonstrate a relatively small impact on crime reduction associated with a large increase in prison populations. Most of these studies relied on histories of the arrests and convictions of a sample of offenders and investigated the impact of imposing a five-year prison term for anyone convicted of a previous felony conviction. Cohen (1983) concluded that a general policy of five-year terms of imprisonment for any serious offense would produce decreases in crime of approximately 15 percent. Similarly, in her review of these studies, Visher

(1987) concluded that the five-year mandatory prison terms would have averted approximately 10 to 20 percent of all index offenses in the jurisdictions studied.

Early support for a selective incapacitation strategy came from research by Greenwood and Abrahamse (1982) examining whether such policies could reduce the robbery rate in California. According to their results, the use of a selective incapacitation strategy could reduce the robbery rate by about 15 percent, and the number of incarcerated robbers would be reduced by about 5 percent. They cautioned that their analysis had several limitations, and they suggested that the work should be replicated in other jurisdictions.

Other researchers reviewed Greenwood and Abrahamse's results and concluded that the original analysis greatly overstated the effects of the proposed selective incapacitation strategy (Cohen, 1983; Spelman, 1994; Visher 1987; von Hirsch & Gottfredson, 1984). In 1983, the National Academy of Sciences panel on criminal careers commissioned a reanalysis of the original survey data (Blumstein et al., 1986). The estimates resulting from this study indicated substantially smaller incapacitative effects than those found by Greenwood and Abrahamse; furthermore, substantial increases in the prison population were predicted. In her review of studies of selective incapacitation, Visher concludes that this strategy may achieve a 5 percent reduction in robbery with a 5 to 10 percent increase in prison populations.

To be successful, selective incapacitation depends upon predictive accuracy. Offenders who will commit the most crimes in the future must be identified and incarcerated for longer periods of time; yet, research demonstrates that the prediction of offenders' behavior is difficult. For example, Greenwood and Turner (1987) used retrospective data (e.g., self reports of criminal behavior prior to incarceration) to predict future arrests and found the data had poor predictive accuracy (i.e., their scale was only about 50 percent accurate in predicting future arrests). Additionally, the small differences in arrest rates between the groups classified as high and low risk did not justify the large differences in sentence lengths that would be required for these offenders if significant selective incapacitation effects were to be achieved. In another study, Gottfredson and Gottfredson tried to improve prediction by using components of the "criminal career" such as the rate of offending and the nature and potential patterning of offending. The results demonstrated little improvement in prediction accuracy. They conclude that "the utility of incapacitation as a crime control strategy seems constrained by the limits imposed by predictive validity and perhaps by the nature of the criminal career" (Gottfredson & Gottfredson, 1986:441).

Criminal justice processes may play a part in determining the effectiveness of incapacitation policies. It appears that high-rate offenders are overrepresented among inmates and low-rate offenders are found among offenders who remain free. During periods of high incarceration, inmates entering prison have lower median offense rates in comparison to those entering when incarceration rates are low (English & Mande, 1992; Miranne & Geerken, 1991). Therefore, the relative crime savings through incapacitation differs depending upon the incarceration rate. On one hand, when incarceration rates are high, additional prisoners reduce the number of crimes in the community much less because the additional offenders being imprisoned are actually low-rate offenders. On the other hand, when incarceration rates are low, additional offenders who are incarcerated have a greater impact on reducing criminal activity in the community because they are high-rate offenders.

Cohen and Canela-Cacho (1994) studied the relationship between incarceration and levels of violent crime using both national data and corrections data from six states. The study focused on the crime control effects of incarceration, especially whether incarceration was an effective strategy for controlling violent crimes and the merits of pursuing alternative incarceration policies. They used sophisticated estimating techniques that took into consideration the fact that high-rate offenders are overrepresented among inmates while low-rate offenders are disproportionately found among the offenders who remain in the community and the fact that termination of criminal careers reduces the crime prevention effects derived from increases in incarceration. They estimate that the incapacitation effects during periods of low incarceration rates are probably much greater than previously estimated, and that the increasing numbers of offenders being incarcerated today bring only marginal returns for incapacitation effects (the law of diminishing returns). This occurs because the expanding prison populations are likely to include an increasing number of offenders who would be low-rate offenders.

The focus on tougher sentencing laws has led to increasingly rigid sentencing statutes, and these have particularly impacted repeat offenders. By 1994 thirty states had introduced three-strikes legislation, and ten had passed tougher sentencing for repeat offenders (Benekos & Merlo, 1995). The "three strikes and you're out" baseball metaphor is used throughout the country in reference to criminal sanctions that become increasingly severe for each conviction an offender receives until they are considered to be "out": in prison for life. Greenwood and colleagues (1996) estimated the crime prevention impact of the California three-strikes law, one of the most sweeping of the laws. Although the first two strikes accrue for serious felonies, the third strike that triggers the life sentence can be for any felony. According to their estimates, the new law would reduce serious felonies committed by adults in California between 22 and 34 percent below what would have occurred had the previous law remained in effect. One-third of these prevented felonies would be violent crimes such as murder, rape, and assault. The remaining two-thirds of the prevented crimes would be less violent felonies, such as less injurious assaults, and most robberies and burglaries of residences. This crime reduction effect would come at a price of $4.5–6.5 billion annually because of the rise in prison population. The authors tested several alternative models to see if other less costly options would be as effective as the three-strikes laws. Although these options were predicted to drop the costs, they also decreased the effectiveness.

The researchers caution that although their results appear encouraging for crime prevention, they would come at great financial cost because of the large estimated increase in prison population. For example, the California three-strikes law, if applied in all eligible cases, would reduce the number of serious felonies in a year by about 28 percent or 329,000 crimes. However, this would cost an additional $5.5 billion a year in additional criminal justice funding for the additional costs of the construction and operation of prisons. This can be translated as a cost of $16,000 per serious felony prevented. Clearly, issues related to the costs of incapacitation policies are closely linked to decisions about effectiveness.

UNINTENDED AND INTENDED CONSEQUENCES OF INCAPACITATION

There is growing concern that the increased incarceration rates, especially the unprecedented rates in the United States today, may affect other institutions such as families, communities, and schools in a manner that increases crime and social disruption or that at minimum offsets any crime reduction effect of increased incarceration (Lynch & Sabol, 2000; Rose & Clear, 1998). The argument goes this way: Social institutions such as families, neighborhoods, communities, education, and labor markets provide and enforce norms of behavior that keep most people from engaging in criminal activity. When the ties or bonds to these institutions are weakened or lost, individuals become more marginalized, and such individuals have higher levels of violence and crime (Sampson, Raudenbush, & Earls, 1997). Historical changes have occurred that have particularly impacted young African American inner city males (Wilson, 1996). In the past twenty years labor force participation among African Americans in inner cities declined dramatically and the percent of female-headed households increased (Sampson & Wilson, 1995). At the same time, participation in the drug trade increased (Blumstein, 1995). The violence attendant to the drug trade further weakened ties to the social institutions.

The high rate of incarceration is hypothesized to have exacerbated the problems in the inner cities. In the past, when incarceration rates were low, members of some families were imprisoned, but this was sufficiently unlikely that it did not have a strong effect on communities. However, when the incarceration rates are so high that 10 percent of the adult males in a community are imprisoned at any time and the majority of males have been in correctional institutions at some point in their lives, incarceration may adversely affect the community in ways that it did not in the past. For example, incarceration weakens families by removing men from families. The remaining family members may be less effective in supervising and controlling children, especially teenagers. Furthermore, incarceration reduces the supply of marriageable men, leaving more single mothers to support and raise the children. Moreover, there is evidence that imprisonment reduces an inmate's connection to the labor force (Bushway, 1998), which further promotes family disruption and violence (Sampson, 1987). The very communities hit hardest by incarceration are those already negatively impacted by recent historical changes. These low-functioning neighborhoods are depleted and every available resource is needed.

From one perspective, the removal of criminal males may benefit a community because they are no longer committing crimes. From another perspective, this assumes that the offenders are solely a drain on the community. This may be a faulty assumption. Offenders, even while involved in criminal activities, may provide important sources of support for the community or its individual members (Hagan & Dinovitzer, 1999). Some ethnographic research demonstrates offenders represent both assets and liabilities to their communities. The point is not that they are model citizens but that they contribute to the support of the family and community stability. If they are incarcerated, these resources are withdrawn, and they might not be restored even after the offender is released because ties are loosened or broken beyond repair. Children may be so negatively impacted that crime in the more distant future may increase. In any case, the importance of this discussion is the possibility that incarceration policies may have had negative effects on inner city, underclass communities that exacerbate already existing problems. Thus, as a direct consequence of incapacitation policies, these communities may experience more, not less, disorganization and crime (Rose & Clear, 1998).

The control philosophy represents an increased reliance on imprisonment, surveillance, and custody. Feeley and Simon (1992) refer to this as a "new penology." In their view, the new penology represents a shift of interest away from the traditional criminology concerns about individuals to an interest in actuarial consideration of aggregates. Instead of a concern with punishing individuals, attention is directed toward managing aggregates of dangerous groups. This has led to new discourses revolving around probability and risk assessment instead of clinical diagnosis and need assessment. Rehabilitation and reintegration are no longer valued. The fear is that the United States has moved to a new understanding of poverty that characterizes a segment of society as the underclass, whose members are permanently excluded from social mobility and economic integration.

According to Feeley and Simon the underclass is understood as a permanently "marginal population, without literacy, without skills, and without hope; a self-perpetuating and pathological segment of society that is not integratable into the larger whole" (467). Underclasses made up largely of minority populations may be separated physically and institutionally from mainstream social and economic life in the United States. The new penology may reflect this new vision of poverty.

CONCLUSIONS

Research examining the effectiveness of incapacitation policies clearly reveals that

- incapacitation policies prevent crime in the community and
- a small number of offenders commit a disproportionate share of crime. If these offenders could be incapacitated, a large number of crimes would be prevented.

However, there are many unresolved questions that make the effectiveness of this strategy questionable. Most important are the following issues:

- Debates continue about the amount of crime prevented through incapacitation and about how much should be considered a large reduction in crime.
- Research has not been successful in predicting which offenders will be the high-frequency offenders in the future; therefore, targeting them for longer prison sentences is impracticable.
- Increased use of incapacitation as a crime prevention strategy must address the expected increases in imprisonment rates and the associated financial costs that accompany such strategies.
- Large increases in the use of incapacitation may have limited returns because the additional offenders not now incarcerated are lower frequency offenders who would not be committing many crimes in the community; thus, incarcerating them would reduce the return on investment for every new dollar expended.
- Large increases in the use of incapacitation may also have limited returns because offenders who are incarcerated for lengthy periods

of time may be at the end of their criminal career and therefore would not be committing crimes in the community anyway.
- True estimates of the crimes prevented are difficult to obtain because both the frequency of criminal participation and the duration of careers must be estimated.

Furthermore, recent studies have revealed that increases in imprisonment rates that have occurred in the past twenty-five years have had a major detrimental impact on minority populations in urban environments (Tonry, 1995; Feeley & Simon, 1992). Finally, collateral consequences of the increased use of imprisonment have been identified, namely, the negative effects on human and social capital of those incarcerated, their families, and their communities (Rose & Clear, 1998) that need to be considered when addressing effectiveness.

CHAPTER FOUR

Perspectives on Rehabilitation

INTRODUCTION

For years after Martinson and his colleagues published their treatise on treatment in corrections, a common mantra regarding rehabilitation was "nothing works" (Martinson, 1979; Lipton, Martinson, & Wilkes, 1975); obviously, this is not true. Research demonstrates that some programs are effective (as discussed in this book). Furthermore, researchers have identified some principles that appear to be important for effective programs. In this chapter, I review some of the issues of concern to those interested in rehabilitation.

ACADEMIC DISCIPLINES AND TERMINOLOGY

Before discussing the principles of rehabilitation and the evidence supporting these principles, I want to clarify differences in the use of several terms. The meanings of the terms *rehabilitation, treatment,* and *research* differ depending upon the academic discipline of the person using the term. In the following sections, I discuss these differences.

Human Service Delivery

Criminologists use the terms *rehabilitation* and *treatment* differently depending on their academic discipline. Most psychologists working in the field of criminology define rehabilitation and treatment as some type of human service delivery. Others use the terms more generically. The latter group refers to probation and parole as treatments or rehabilitation. In meta-analyses or assessments of program effectiveness, researchers use rehabilitation to refer to a wide range of management strategies. They would include probation or intensive supervision with increased control as treatment even if these programs did not include any human service delivery. For example, in their review of the rehabilitation literature, Lipton, Martinson, and Wilkes (1975; Martinson, 1976) refer to probation, imprisonment (sentence length), and parole as "treatments." In contrast, psychologists would not consider programs to be rehabilitative if they did not have human service components. I try to separate these terms by using rehabilitation to refer to programs with human service components. I refer to other programs as management strategies or interventions.

In part, the confusion in terms is due to the common use of the term *treatment* to mean the experimental condition in a research study. Both groups refer to the experimental condition in research as the treatment. From this perspective, anything that is being studied is a treatment.

Law and Science: Different Perspectives

Early in my boot camp research, I was asked by a lawyer to "find how boot camps work." I was offended. As a scientist, I do not go into a research project trying to find what I might want to find. I enter the research with a question: "Do boot camps work?" I operationalize the terms by defining boot camps (e.g., short-term programs with military basic-training atmospheres) and work (e.g., reduce recidivism, reduce costs). Then, I proceed to do the research and try to stay as objective as I can about the answer so I will not influence the outcome. I want the empirical research to help me answer the questions. Although I use my experience, opinions of authorities, and past research to help me formulate the questions, I do not use these to answer the questions. This is very different from what a lawyer means by research. The law profession looks to past precedence and authorities for guidance to answer the question, not empirical research. Legal research entails a search for past precedence and authorities in order to support one perspective. In law, one takes a position and then tries to find support for this position.

The lawyer's research perspective is dramatically different from the scientist's. Scientists attempt to protect themselves from letting their subjective opinions influence the research results. In this book, I attempt to draw conclusions on the basis of empirical research. This is the basis of the argument for evidence-based corrections.

TREATMENT INTEGRITY AND PROGRAM IMPLEMENTATION

In part, Martinson's work was a critique of the way correctional programs were designed and operated. It is important to reiterate that later reviews of Martinson's work clearly demonstrated that he was not concluding in his treatise that no correctional program could work. His major point was that at the time of his study, there was little evidence to tell us what works. Two factors led him to this conclusion. First, it was impossible to tell if programs were effective because most of the studies did not examine interventions that had *program integrity*. Implementation of effective programs in corrections is a function of the ability of policy makers, program administrators, and service deliverers to translate knowledge and theory into practice with integrity (Leschied, Bernfeld, & Farrington, 2001). A program has integrity if it incorporates such things as a clearly identified rationale consistent with the human service theoretical literature, qualified and trained staff to deliver the program, treatment methods shown to be effective, and a consistent protocol. Thus, one of the principles of effective programming is that programs must have integrity.

Program integrity is also concerned with *dosage* issues. Programs with dosage integrity are of sufficient length to have an expected impact on participants. Although we have not yet gotten to the point where we know exactly what dose is needed for particular offenders with specific problems, it is clear that there is some optimal or sufficient level of treatment that is required to change offenders. For example, a program with poorly trained staff delivered once a week for one hour for ten weeks to high risk offenders probably does not have treatment integrity.

The importance of program integrity may seem self-evident. Yet at present, as occurred with the programs Martinson studied, many programs provided to correctional clientele do not have integrity. Departments of corrections operate under severe financial constraints. At times, programs for offenders are provided by poorly trained, ill-paid staff or the amount of time spent in the programs is extremely limited.

Many people today argue in support of more detailed descriptive or process evaluations of programs being studied so that researchers know specifically what is being delivered to whom (Leschied et al., 2001). This information would permit others to judge the integrity of the service delivery. Details about implementation issues would be invaluable for meta-analysts because the variables could be used within the analyses to assist in identifying important components of programs. That is, meta-analysts could examine whether factors such as time in program or the type and level of staff training had an impact on the outcome of particular programs.

POOR RESEARCH DESIGNS

The research designs of the studies were the second problem with the literature reviewed by Martinson. Many of the studies were so poorly conducted from a research design point of view that it was impossible to tell what the outcomes meant. In other words, the studies had little internal validity. No conclusions about the effect of the programs could be made because the research designs were so poor. For example, reviewers of the research could not tell if the treatment and comparison groups differed prior to the treatment because the groups were not randomly assigned to conditions or not matched in any way. If the groups differed prior to treatment, one cannot conclude that the treatment had an effect because differences between groups following treatment could be due to the prior differences that existed. Thus, Martinson's conclusion that nothing works was really a critique of the poorly designed studies of inadequately implemented programs.

The Maryland methods scoring system is a method for making this issue more transparent so that researchers, policy makers, and the public can easily see the quality of the research. If the quality is high (e.g., high score on the methods scale), one can be more certain that the results are believable based on the research design. A low score indicates that the research design permits many alternative explanations for the results and one cannot be sure that any effects were attributable to the treatment.

Researchers' involvement in an intervention may contribute to improved study design (Cullen & Gendreau, 2000). Lipsy (1992) completed a meta-analysis examining 397 studies of juvenile delinquency interventions. His initial analysis examined the effect of these interventions on delinquency behavior. He and his colleagues coded more than 154 items for methods variables (e.g., study design, attrition), study context (date published), nature of treatment (type, duration, intensity), and characteristics of subjects (race, sex, age, prior delinquency). One of the things the research demonstrated was the effect of the researchers' involvement in interventions. In situations in which the researcher provided the treatment or was influential in the treatment, there were larger effect sizes than when researchers only evaluated the interventions. Possibly, when researchers are involved in program implementation they may ensure the program integrity remains higher. This may explain the larger effect sizes in these studies.

DISCRETION AND DISPARITY

One reason Martinson's work had such a major impact on the philosophy of corrections was the historical context of the times. In the beginning of the 1960s, many in the United States had great hope about our ability to solve social problems. It was a time of optimism. We believed we could walk on the moon, solve our social problems, and show other countries how to become democracies. President Johnson's "great society" slogan expressed the great optimism of the times. However, as the sixties came to an end, attitudes in the United States had changed. The society was in turmoil. Citizens pushed for equality. People questioned the "great society." The civil rights movement and the women's movement fought for equal rights for their respective groups. Research demonstrated that minorities were not treated the same as others by the criminal justice system. Riots in prison made the public aware of the problems of inmates. Protests against the Vietnam War divided the country. As a result of these social disruptions, many citizens began to distrust U.S. social institutions. For the criminal justice system, this distrust of social institutions led to questions about the amount of discretion in the system. From this perspective, if judges could not be trusted to make fair and just decisions, then their power should be limited.

For corrections, this distrust combined with the Martinson report led people to question the system of indeterminate sentencing that had become the norm in the U.S. correctional system. Rehabilitation had been the philosophy of corrections since the turn of the century during the progressive movement. According to this philosophy, the major goal of corrections was to rehabilitate offenders. Offenders received sentences with wide differences between the minimum they must serve and the maximum they could be required to serve. Once offenders were determined to be rehabilitated, they were released. Parole boards and correctional personnel determined when offenders were considered to be rehabilitated.

There were several obvious problems with the system. First, if there were no effective programs, as many mistakenly concluded from Martinson's report, then corrections was not rehabilitating offenders. Second, researchers demonstrated that the system resulted in discriminatory treatment, particularly for minority offenders. Offenders with similar past histories and crimes of conviction often received widely disparate sentences. Conversely, offenders convicted of vastly different crimes with very different past histories of offending were given similar sentences. This seemed basically unfair and often appeared to reflect prejudice toward minorities.

Despite the fact that the philosophical model of corrections changed away from rehabilitation to just desserts and crime control, many researchers and practitioners continued to support and study rehabilitation. They argued against the "nothing works" philosophy and suggested that a careful reading of the outcome literature would provide "bibliotherapy for cynics" (Gendreau & Ross, 1979; Palmer, 1996). In particular, a group of Canadian psychologists continued to study the effectiveness of rehabilitation programs in the Canadian correctional system. I refer to Canadian researchers such as Gendreau, Andrews, Bonta, and Ross as the Canadian School. They have been extremely important in keeping the rehabilitation/human service research moving forward. As a result of this continuing research, some general principles of correctional treatment have been identified (Andrews & Bonta, 2003). As previously discussed, one of the principles is the need for treatment integrity. A second is the importance of targeting "dynamic criminogenic needs."

THE NEED PRINCIPLE

One question that arises when discussing rehabilitation is, What factors should be the target or targets of the human service components of rehabilitation programs? The answer forms another principle of effective correctional programming – interventions should target known predictors of crime and recidivism that can be changed. These are called dynamic criminogenic needs. They are human deficits directly related to the propensity to commit crime that can be changed in rehabilitation programs. Research has shown that criminogenic needs include such characteristics as procriminal attitudes, procriminal associates, impulsivity, weak socialization, below average verbal intelligence, risk taking, weak problem solving and self-control skills, early onset of antisocial behavior, poor parental practices, and deficits in educational, vocational, and employment skills. Research also demonstrates that these factors are directly related to criminal activities. In contrast, some factors that are targeted in rehabilitation programs are not necessarily criminogenic.

One good example of a characteristic not necessarily related to criminal activity is self-concept or self-esteem. Self-esteem is unrelated or only weakly related to recidivism (Cullen & Gendreau, 2000). Offenders and juvenile delinquents can and often do have high self-esteem. They may be good at their criminal behavior. Targeting their self-esteem in treatment will not necessarily change their criminal behavior. Thus, self-esteem is not necessarily a criminogenic need.

Criminogenic needs can be static or dynamic. Characteristics such as age, race, and gender are considered static because they cannot be changed with rehabilitation programs. Although these characteristics may be correlates of criminal activity (hence criminogenic), they cannot be changed in rehabilitation, and therefore these are not targets of treatment. For example, more males are convicted of crimes than females, so "maleness" is a correlate of crime and hence criminogenic. However, treatment cannot change one's sex, so it is a static factor. Dynamic factors such as procriminal attitudes, criminal associates, impulsivity, and self-control are the targets of treatment programs. These dynamic needs can be changed through rehabilitation.

In sum, dynamic criminogenic needs are factors directly related to criminal behavior (criminogenic) that can be changed in treatment (dynamic). The dynamic criminogenic needs should be the targets of treatment.

Identifying Criminogenic Needs

An important issue is how to identify criminogenic factors so they can be the target of treatment. Research has identified factors that are associated with criminal behavior. Ideally, correctional rehabilitation programs would target the dynamic factors that correlate most strongly with criminogenic activity.

For example, in a meta-analysis of 372 studies of correlates of criminal behavior, Gendreau and his colleagues found the strongest correlates to criminal behavior (highest correlations) were antisocial attitudes, antisocial associates, antisocial temperament, antisocial personality, behavioral history, and parental/family factors. Personal education and vocational achievement were less strongly correlated. The lowest correlates with criminal behavior were lower class origins and personal distress/psychopathology (e.g., anxiety, depression, self-esteem, alienation, anomie) (Gendreau, Andrews, Goggin, & Chanteloupe, 1992). Thus, factors that are most highly correlated with criminal behavior may be the most logical targets of correctional rehabilitation programs. On the basis of this research, Andrews and Bonta (2003) refer to antisocial attitudes, antisocial associates, a history of antisocial behavior, and antisocial personality as the "big four" risk factors. If these can be changed with rehabilitation then theoretically future criminal behavior should decline.

In another research study, Andrews, Dowden, and Gendreau (1999) examined 374 tests of the effectiveness of programs on reducing recidivism. They examined the impact of programs that focused on specific targets of intermediate change. They classified each study according to the target of the program that was studied (e.g., antisocial cognitions, fear of punishment). If the program was successful in changing this intermediate target then recidivism should theoretically be reduced. They found programs that focused on personal targets were most successful in reducing recidivism. These were antisocial cognitions, skill deficits, antisocial associates, and family processes aimed at enhancing quality of relationships, as well as improved supervision, academic and vocational education, and substance abuse targets.

Surveys of other research support these studies. After reviewing the literature on correlates of risk for criminal behavior, Andrews and Bonta (2003) propose a group of eight characteristics as the "big eight" risk factors: antisocial attitudes, antisocial associates, a history of antisocial behavior, antisocial personality pattern, problematic circumstances at home (family/marital), problematic circumstances at school or work, problematic leisure circumstances, and substance abuse. The first four make up the "big four." Note that other than the history of antisocial behavior, all of the big eight are dynamic criminogenic needs that could be targeted in rehabilitation programs. Furthermore, although past history of antisocial behavior cannot be a target, current and future antisocial behavior could be. Targets that focus on fear of official punishment, personal distress, mental health, physical activity, conventional ambition, and family matters (other than problematic circumstances at home) were not effective in reducing criminal activities in the studies reviewed by Andrews and Bonta.

TREATMENT MODALITY

Almost consistently, reviews of the literature, systematic reviews, and meta-analyses demonstrate that correctional programs that are skill oriented, based on a behavioral or cognitive-behavior theoretical model, and multimodal are more effective than other modes of treatment (Andrews et al., 1990; Palmer, 1996; Lipsey, 1992; Redondo, Sanchez-Meca, & Garredo, 1999). Cognitive-behavioral and behavioral treatment programs are based on social learning principles. These techniques employ modeling, graduated practice, role playing, reinforcement, extinction, resource provision, concrete verbal suggestions, and cognitive restructuring. Multimodal programs treat all of the deficits simultaneously. Skill-based programs teach offenders skills they need to resist antisocial behavior. Approaches such as casework, individual counseling, and group counseling do not appear to be effective. These interventions are self-reflective, verbally interactive, insight oriented, and less structured. Punishment approaches do not target criminogenic needs.

Lipsey's meta-analysis (1992; 1995) and Losel's review of meta-analyses (1995) are good examples of the findings regarding treatment modalities. For example, Lipsey meta-analyzed 397 studies of juvenile delinquency interventions. He and his colleagues rated every study on 154 dimensions (e.g., characteristics of methods, treatment, and delinquents). Treatment modality had the largest effect. Treatment that was behavioral, skill oriented, or multimodal was associated with larger effect sizes than interventions based on deterrence, family counseling, group counseling, or individual counseling. Lipsey compared the effect of skill-oriented, behavioral, and multimodal treatments to other interventions. If the other interventions resulted in 50 percent recidivism, the skill, behavioral, and multimodal treatments reduced recidivism by 20 to 40 percent, resulting in recidivism rates as low as 30 percent. These results were similar to Andrew and colleague's findings (1990) for "clinically relevant" treatment for adult offenders.

Losel (1995) reviewed 13 meta-analyses of correction treatment and found results supportive of Lipsey and Andrew et al.'s findings. However, the meta-analyses that Losel reviewed differed in size; the smallest included 8 studies and the largest included 443 studies. Also, most focused on juvenile interventions and few examined adult interventions (n = 4) (Andrews et al., 1990; Antonowicz & Ross, 1994; Losel & Koferl, 1989; Redondo et al., 1999). Across all the meta-analyses, the highest effect sizes were found when the mode of treatment was behavioral, skill oriented, and multimodal.

THE RISK PRINCIPLE

The Canadian School of researchers also proposes a risk principle. From their perspective, treatment should be delivered to offenders at the highest risk for recidivism. One reason for this proposal is that low risk offenders may not continue to commit crimes in the future even without treatment. Thus, treatment is best reserved for those who are at the highest risk for recidivism.

Research support for the risk principle has been mixed. Andrews and Bonta (2003) review four studies examining risk level and intensity of treatment. In support of the principle, high risk offenders had lower recidivism when they were given more intense treatment. When low risk offenders were given intense services, the treatment had either a minimal or a negative effect on recidivism. In contrast to this support for the risk principle, Antonowicz and Ross (1994) found no support for the principle in their meta-analysis, and Lipsey (1995) found only weak support.

Risk Classification

In many stages of criminal justice processing, decisions must be made about the risk offenders present to the community. For example, decision makers must decide who to release pretrial, who to intensively supervise in the community, and who to release from prison on parole or supervised release. Risk classification is how risk is determined in order to make these decisions (Van Voorhis, 1997; 1993). Such decisions are made with either clinical assessment or actuarial approaches. In clinical assessment, a knowledgeable person uses informal, nonobservable criteria for deciding on the risk an individual presents to the community. In comparison, the actuarial approach differs from clinical decision making because explicit criteria for decisions are validated by research. Comparison between clinical assessments and actuarial classification clearly demonstrates the superiority of the actuarial approaches.

Actuarial risk classification techniques are developed in one of two ways: empirically or theoretically (MacKenzie, 1989). The empirical systems are developed using empirical data to select the items that are most strongly related to recidivism. These items are used for a summated risk classification scale.

Theoretical schemes select variables that are theoretically related to recidivism. These variables are empirically tested, and those that are most strongly correlated with recidivism are used in a summated risk classification scale. The theoretically developed scales are more apt to use dynamic criminogenic items in the scales and, therefore, are more beneficial for use in combination with rehabilitation programs.

RESPONSIVITY PRINCIPLE

Responsivity has also been proposed as an important principle of rehabilitation. This concept refers to rehabilitation program delivery in a style and mode consistent with the learning styles and abilities of the offenders. For example, programs requiring a high level of verbalization and cognitive maturity may not be appropriate for many offenders. Although this proposal has face validity, there is little research demonstrating the effectiveness of programs designed for different types of offenders.

Andrews et al. (1990) reviewed four programs that addressed these issues. Offenders judged to be more or less amenable to treatment, mature, empathetic, or conceptual participated in programs that varied in psychodynamic focus, level of structure, and supervision by volunteers, respectively. In all of the studies, the appropriate treatment led to greater success as measured by recidivism or success rates. For instance, offenders with low conceptual levels had lower recidivism if they received a program with a higher level of structure. Similarly, offenders with low maturity did better in highly structured programs, whereas those with more maturity did better with low structure. Thus, there is some evidence supporting the responsivity principle.

However, there is a continuing debate about how to design effective rehabilitation programs responsive to the issues of women, ethnic minorities, psychopaths, and mentally disordered offenders. In particular, as we discuss in the rest of this book, there are a limited number of studies examining the effectiveness of programs for female offenders.

SUMMARY

Five principles of rehabilitation have been proposed:

- program integrity
- criminogenic needs;
- skill-oriented, behavioral/cognitive theoretical models
- risk
- responsivity.

Although all of these principles appear logical and have a certain amount of face validity, research support for several is limited (e.g., risk, responsivity). One of the difficulties of the meta-analyses of the programs and interventions is that they are generally highly theoretical. The meta-analysts combine many different types of programs into the analyses. This makes it very difficult for practitioners and policy makers to use the results for decision making. For this reason, in this book, I have focused on clearly defined programs that are operated in the courts and correctional systems. Thus, the meta-analyses and method score assessments that my colleagues and I have completed, reported in the following chapters, are designed to investigate effectiveness at the program level.

PART TWO

THE EFFECTIVENESS OF REHABILITATION PROGRAMS

CHAPTER FIVE

Academic Education and Life Skills Programs

INTRODUCTION

Educational programming in prisons originally focused on religious instruction. Such instruction was expected to help offenders achieve spiritual enlightenment (Gerber & Fritsch, 1995; Teeters, 1955). Consistent with the beliefs of those responsible for the early penitentiary movement, offenders were thought to need time to reflect on their crimes and repent. Religious instruction was expected to help in this process of penitence. However, during the reformatory era, the focus of education programs changed from religious instruction to basic literacy and communication skills.

The reformatory age began in 1876 when Zebulon R. Brockway first proposed his theory of rehabilitation at the first conference of the American Prison Association (the forerunner of the current American Correctional Association). Since that time academic education has been a cornerstone of correctional programming. As superintendent of the first reformatory at Elmira, New York, Brockway brought his revolutionary ideas into practice. The goal was to reform youth. The reformatory was designed to provide a physically and mentally healthy environment where youth would have access to academic education and extensive vocational training. Brockway believed that law-abiding behavior was attainable through legitimate industry and education (Reagan & Stoughton, 1976). Elmira was used as a model for both adult prisons and juvenile reformatories throughout the United States.

During the age of rehabilitation, from the turn of the century until the mid-1970s, educational programs were considered a mainstay of correctional rehabilitation. By 1930, academic and vocational educational programs were operating in most prisons, where they were considered to play a primary role in the process of rehabilitation. From the original basic literacy programs, the type and variety of educational programs grew to include opportunities for a high school or general equivalency diploma (GED), vocational education (see Chapter 6 on vocational education and employment programs), life skills programs, postsecondary or college education, and educational release.

EDUCATIONAL PROGRAMS TODAY

Despite the "tough on crime" rhetoric of many politicians and decision makers, there appears to be a general belief that education has benefits in its own right (Applegate, Cullen, & Fisher, 1997; Cullen, Skovron, & Scott, 1990). Although the focus of corrections in the United States turned away from rehabilitation to just desserts and crime control models during the 1980s and 1990s, prisons continued to offer academic education. For juveniles and youthful adults, academic education was legally mandated. However, correctional administrators did not limit the programs to only those for whom education was legally required. A survey of all state and federal adult correctional facilities conducted in 1995 by the Bureau of Justice Statistics found that 87 percent had educational programs (Stephan, 1997). More than 75 percent of the facilities offered basic adult education and secondary education programs. Almost a quarter of the inmates participated in some type of education. A third of the facilities provided access to college course work.

One reason for the continuing emphasis on educational programs is the strong correlation between educational level and criminal activity. Prison inmates are, on average, less educated and have fewer marketable job skills than the general population (Andrews & Bonta, 2003). Incarcerated adults also have high rates of illiteracy. Ryan (1990) estimates that half of America's inmates are illiterate if sixth grade achievement is used as a cutoff. According to several researchers, the average reading level of incarcerated offenders may be below the fifth grade level. More than one-half of all prison inmates have not completed high school, and those who have are often two to three grade levels behind in actual skills (Tewksbury & Vito, 1996).

Adult Basic, Secondary, and Literacy Programs

Administrators responsible for developing educational programs in prison are faced by the need to design programs that span primary, secondary, and postsecondary levels. This is particularly difficult in adult correctional systems where the academic grade levels of the prison population frequently range from primary grades through postgraduate. There seems to be a consensus that prison education programs should begin with literacy.

Literacy has been defined in many ways but is usually characterized by grade level. The first mandatory literacy requirement established in the federal prison system in 1981 used an ability to function academically at a sixth grade level as the definition of basic literacy. This initial mandatory literacy level was increased to an eighth grade level in 1985 and to a high school diploma or GED in 1991. The federal mandatory literacy program has served as a model for state prison systems. In a survey of state prison systems, Di Vito (1991) found that 26 percent of the systems had mandatory educational programs. Support for the importance of literacy and mandatory programs came from many directions. For example, in the 1970s, the Fourth United Nations Congress on Prevention of Crime and Treatment of Offenders endorsed the compulsory literacy education of prisoners. In 1992, the American Bar Association officially endorsed literacy programs and adopted a model state prison mandatory literacy bill.

Even states that do not have mandatory literacy requirements use incentives to encourage school enrollment. Incentives for participation vary from a reduction of sentence to daily stipends, extra institutional privileges, and promotion to a higher paid or better class of job. Inmates who do not attend the mandatory programs are sanctioned through the regular disciplinary process for misconducts, or they lose the daily stipend or good time.

Life Skills Programs

Recently, *life skills* components have been added to many academic curriculums. Many academic education programs do not address a number of other important skill deficits that may hinder offenders in their attempts to function successfully in everyday life in the community (Finn, 1998). The life skills programs are designed to address such deficits. For example, the curriculum of a life skills program might include instruction on how to search for a job, balance a checkbook, budget, control anger, make decisions, and set goals. The actual curriculums of the life skills programs vary greatly.

Postsecondary Programs

The consensus about the desirability of literacy programs in prisons does not appear to extend to postsecondary education (PSE). Although college programs have a long history in U.S. prisons, their acceptability has ebbed and flowed. College programs in prisons began shortly after World War II, in part because of veterans' education benefits that extended to prisoners. Nothing in the law prohibited veterans who were prisoners from receiving funds for college education. By the late 1960s, Adams (1968) found that 75 percent of the forty-six prison systems he surveyed had some college-level program.

Most classes originally took place in prisons where instructors from nearby colleges provided accredited courses. Later, some prison systems began study-release programs where prisoners could participate in regular classes on college campuses; however, these programs were flooded with problems. Often student-inmates took a long time to return to the prison and stopped off for unauthorized activities. Furthermore, parents of free-world students complained that they did not want their children exposed to the criminal inmates.

Another boost to the prison college programs came from Pell grants designed to help low- and middle-income families with college expenses, for which many prison inmates qualified. However, critics of the prison college programs complained that such grants should not be made available to prisoners. During the 1990s, laws were passed prohibiting Pell grants for those convicted of drug possession or facing the death penalty or life in prison without the possibility of parole. The 1994 Crime Bill prohibited inmate-students from receiving federal Pell grants (Batiuk, Moke, & Rountree, 1997).

THEORETICAL RATIONALE FOR ASSOCIATION BETWEEN EDUCATION AND RECIDIVISM

Conspicuously absent from the research literature in the area of education is a discussion of a theoretical explanation for the connection between education and postrelease offending. Few correctional educators articulate the precise mechanism by which they expect the intervention to impact future offender behavior. There are many possible ways education may bring about changes that will reduce the future criminal activities of offenders.

One mechanism by which education will theoretically affect recidivism is through improvement of inmate cognitive skills. The way individuals think influences whether they violate the law. Deficiencies in social cognition (understanding other people and social interactions), problem solving abilities, and the sense of self-efficacy are all cognitive deficits (or "criminogenic needs"; Andrews et al., 1990) found to be associated with criminal activity (Foglia, 2000). Educational programs that increase offenders' social cognitions, ability to solve problems, and belief in their ability to control events in their lives may reduce their future offending.

Other research demonstrates a connection between executive cognitive functioning (ECF) and antisocial behavior. ECF is defined as the cognitive functioning required in planning, initiation, and regulation of goal-directed behavior (Giancola, 2000). It would include such abilities as attention control, strategic goal planning, abstract reasoning, cognitive flexibility, hypothesis generation, temporal response sequencing, and the ability to use information in working memory. From this perspective, education may be important in reducing crime because it improves the ability to use and process information.

Some researchers and educators argue that the importance of education may be in its ability to increase individuals' maturity or moral development (Batiuk et al., 1997; Duguid, 1981; Gordon & Arbuthnot, 1987). For example, academic instruction can help instill ideas about right and wrong, and these ideas may be associated with changes in attitudes and behaviors. Education may also mitigate the harsh conditions of confinement or "pains of imprisonment" and reduce prisonization, the negative attitudes that are sometimes associated with incarceration. In this way, education may provide a basis for reconstruction of law-abiding lifestyles upon release from prison (Harer, 1995a).

In contrast to the perspective that educational programs will increase general problem solving, perspective taking, executive cognitive functioning, or stage of development, economic theories of crime hypothesize that the programs are important in reducing offending more directly via increased skills and employability. Employability may increase for several reasons. One, the offenders may obtain necessary credentials, such as a high school diploma or GED, that make them eligible for jobs for which they previously would not have been considered. Second, the educational programs may provide them the skills needed for specific jobs. From this perspective, education would increase an offender's chances of getting and keeping legitimate employment after release, thereby eliminating the need to commit crimes for financial gain. There is some evidence that education in prison is associated with an increase in employment. In a review of the research, Gerber and Fritsch (1995) examined the impact of educational program participation on postrelease employment and concluded that inmates who participated in or completed prison education programs were more likely to be employed after release.

Obviously, the academic curriculum will differ depending upon the theoretical rationale for the relationship between education and offending. Although a general liberal arts curriculum might be crucial for increasing cognitive functioning, changing ones' antisocial beliefs, or increasing moral development, it might be less apt to provide specific job skills. If gainful employment is the theoretical link to reducing crime, then education programs would focus more directly on teaching the specific job skills offenders will need to find work in the community. Indeed, Duguid, Hawkey, and Pawson (1996) argue that evaluations should examine these theoretical differences in programs and intermediate outcomes to determine "what works for whom, when, why and in what circumstances" (74).

EFFECTIVENESS OF EDUCATION AND LIFE SKILLS PROGRAMS

Despite the fact that education programs are one of the cornerstones of corrections intervention, the quantity and quality of the research examining the effectiveness of such programs in reducing recidivism is severely limited. In part, this seems to be due to the belief that educational opportunities should be offered to all inmates. Thus, an experimental design where inmates are randomly assigned to either education or some alternative does not seem to be acceptable to many administrators and educational staff. From one perspective, this speaks to how important educators and correctional staff and administrators consider the opportunity for education. From another perspective, it has severely limited our ability to determine how effective these programs are in reducing recidivism.

In his well-known study of rehabilitation, Martinson (1974) reviewed studies of education and vocational training for both juveniles and adults. Similar to his conclusions in other areas, Martinson concluded that overall "it can safely be said that they provide us with no clear evidence that education or skill development programs have been successful" (27) in reducing recidivism. He cautioned that these results could easily be due to flaws in the research design. In addition, interpretation of the results is difficult because of the disparity in the programs, the populations affected, and the institutional settings. Similarly, Linden and Perry (1983) reviewed the literature and concluded that although there was evidence that educational programs successfully increased academic achievement, they had not demonstrated their effectiveness in reducing postrelease offending.

More recent reviews of the research assessing educational program effectiveness in reducing criminal offending have been more positive. Gerber and Fritsch (1995) disagreed with Martinson's (1974) conclusion in their review of research on prison education programs. They reconsidered six of the evaluations contained in the original Martinson report and found that although three of the evaluations Martinson reviewed failed to produce statistically significant results, two others found a positive and significant relationship between adult education programming and recidivism (the one remaining study was too poorly designed to enable any conclusions). On the basis of their findings, Gerber and Fritsch concluded that there was evidence that adult education programs can successfully reduce recidivism. Similarly, Taylor (1994) concluded that PSE programs were effective in reducing recidivism.

Subsequently, my colleagues and I at the University of Maryland reviewed the research and assessed each study's methodology. We identified twelve adult basic education (ABE)/GED programs and five life skills evaluations examining the impact of education on later recidivism of offenders that were scored two or greater on the research methods scale (Cecil, Drapkin, MacKenzie, & Hickman, 2000; MacKenzie & Hickman, 1998). However, in our analysis, we limited our review to studies completed after 1980 and that met or exceeded a research methods score of three (the minimum standard for methodological rigor) to draw conclusions about effectiveness. Of the twelve basic education studies, only five were scored at three or greater and were used for determining the effectiveness of the programs in reducing the later recidivism of the offenders (Anderson, 1995a; Harer, 1995a; 1995b; Jeffords & McNitt, 1993; Walsh, 1985).

Of the five studies that we reviewed, many failed to use significance tests and those that did employ statistical tests failed to produce significant findings in favor of program participation. In most cases, the effect sizes were moderate or small. Our examination of the studies and the comparison groups led us to conclude that the critical variable did not appear to be merely program participation but the extent of involvement in the educational curriculum and/or program completion. Using the Maryland criteria for decisions about what works, we concluded ABE programs show *promise* as a means of reducing offender recidivism. Our decision was based on the study by Walsh (1985) that showed significantly lower recidivism for GED participants in comparison to nonparticipants, in addition to the preponderance of evidence from the other studies. The results were not strong enough to conclude that the programs work. It should also be noted that the Walsh study examined the effectiveness of a GED program for probationers, and this was one of the few studies to examine a program offered to offenders in the community.

In our review of life skills evaluations, we scored four of the studies three or greater (Melton & Pennell, 1998; Miller, 1995; 1997; Ross, Fabiano, & Ewles, 1988). In general, the life skills participants had lower recidivism rates; however, similar to the basic education/GED programs, few of the studies used statistical tests to determine significant differences, and overall the effect sizes were moderate or small. The magnitude of program effectiveness varied based on the comparison group. When life skills participants were compared with offenders who received no programming (e.g., a probation-only comparison group), life skills participation was associated with a reduction in recidivism. Conversely, when the life skills participants were compared to a group participating in a cognitive skills program, the effectiveness of life skills training was not as clear. Of the four studies of life skills programs, only two employed statistical tests (Melton & Pennell, 1998; Miller, 1997), and neither reported significant differences in recidivism between participants and control groups. In the remaining studies where nonstatistical comparisons were made, there was inconsistency with respect to the direction of the effects. These results led us to conclude that there was insufficient evidence to draw any conclusions regarding the effectiveness of life skills programs in reducing recidivism.

To further examine the effectiveness of correction-based education, my colleagues and I conducted a meta-analysis of evaluations of correctional educational programs (Wilson, Gallagher, Coggeshall, & MacKenzie, 1999; Wilson, Gallagher, & MacKenzie, 2000). We began this research with an intensive search for evaluations of educational programs (life skills programs were not included in this meta-analysis because these were often provided by staff who were not educators) and located several additional studies not included in the prior review (Cecil et al., 2000). In total, we identified twenty-seven program-comparison contrasts: six of ABE, three of GED, five of combined ABE and GED, and thirteen of PSE.

According to the results of the meta-analysis, those participating in the ABE, GED, and combined ABE or GED recidivated at a lower rate than comparison groups. However, the results were not significant for the ABE and GED programs alone. When all of the participant groups were combined (i.e., ABE, GED, and ABE/GED combined) and compared to the control groups, there was a significant difference between the participants and the comparisons. We estimated that program participants recidivated at a rate of 41 percent relative to a base recidivism rate of 50 percent for the comparison group. PSE programs also demonstrated a significant reduction in recidivism for the participants. Compared to a base recidivism rate of 50 percent for the comparison, we estimated the participants would recidivate at a rate of 37 percent.

What is important to recognize is that the significant results of the meta-analysis cannot be interpreted as showing that educational program activities caused the decrease in reoffending. The vast majority of the studies included in the meta-analysis scored a two or three on the methods score. The typical study used a simple quasi-experimental comparison group design that contrasted naturally occurring groups of participants with nonparticipants. Although approximately half of the studies performed some form of post hoc matching or statistical control, such controls were generally restricted to adjustments for age and race distributions. Thus, the generally positive findings may result from differential characteristics of the offenders that existed prior to the program and not as a positive effect of program participation itself. That is, these groups could differ prior to the program on important characteristics such as motivation to change, self-control, or social bonds.

Little research has examined in particular what works for whom, when, and why. None of the studies included in the meta-analysis was based solely on a sample of women. Overall, nineteen studies included females but only fifteen provided sufficient information to calculate their percentage in the sample; in this subset of fifteen studies, women represented 21 percent of the study sample, and thus the results cannot be generalized to programs serving women. Furthermore, it is important to recognize that none of the programs were designed to be culturally relevant for racial or ethnic minorities or to address the specific needs of women. Coffey and Gemignani (1994) also point out that many juvenile facilities are separated from mainstream academic communities; therefore, correctional education is apt to be unaware of many of the reform movements and research on effective practices in education.

Given some of the limitations noted for previous reviews, for present purposes, I conducted an additional assessment to examine the impact of educational and life skills programming on recidivism, this time restricting the studies under examination to those scoring a three or higher on the methods score. Tables 5.1 and 5.2 list all of the studies included in previous reviews along with the methods score, corresponding recidivism rates, and follow-up time; the accompanying Appendices 5.1 and 5.2 provide a description of each study.

Academic Education Programs

Citation	Effect
Linden et al., 1984 (MP)	3.29
O'Neil, 1990	3.26
Langenbach et al., 1990	3.20
Burke & Vivian, 2001	2.49
Walsh, 1985	2.49
Batiuk et al., 1997	2.37
Blackburn, 1981	2.37
Linden et al., 1984 (BCP)	1.93
Jeffords & McNitt (TYC), 1993	1.64
Steurer et al., 2001	1.44
Harer, 1995b	1.34
Anderson, 1995 (GED)	1.26
Anderson, 1995 (College)	1.17
Adams et al., 1994	1.06
Anderson, 1995 (ABE)	.93
Harer, 1995a	.44
Mean Odds-Ratio (16)	**1.16**

Figure 5.1. Forest plot showing odds ratio and 95 percent confidence interval for studies of academic education programs.

Figure 5.1 represents the results of a meta-analysis of sixteen independent samples from thirteen educational treatment programs [note: the studies by Linden, Perry, Ayers, & Parlett (1984) and Anderson (1995a) include multiple distinct samples]. The primary recidivism measures used to calculate effect sizes were rearrest (n = 6) or return to prison (n = 10). For the Linden et al. study, the return to prison rate for major offenses was employed in calculating the effect size. The effect sizes listed for the Harer (1995a) and Adams et al. (1994) studies were calculated by combining both control groups and taking the weighted mean of the groups' recidivism measures, producing a singular comparison measure. The most recent recidivism measures for each study were used, representing the longest follow-up period. Twelve studies included in Table 5.1 were excluded because of low methods scores. As shown, the majority of effect sizes favored the treatment group, although many of these were non-significant differences. Nevertheless, nine of the studies significantly favored the treatment group, and the overall effect size indicated the treatment group had significantly lower recidivism rates than the control group. Given these results, there is sufficient evidence to

TABLE 5.1. *Studies of educational treatment programs showing recidivism rates and length of follow-up*

Study (methods score)	Measure of recidivism	Recidivism: Experimental (%)	N	Control (%) #1/#2/#3	N	Follow-up period (in months)
Linden et al., 1984 (5)	Return to Prison		30		26	96
	(Minor Offense or Tech. Violation)					
	BCP	5.9		14.3		
	MP	7.7		0.0		
	(Major Offense)					
	BCP	58.3		64.3		
	MP	61.5		75.0		
Harer, 1995b (4)	Rearrest/Parole Revocation[1]	35.5	534	44.1	671	36
Harer, 1995a (4)	Rearrest/Parole Revocation[1]	30.1	183	39.0/41.5	182/254	36
Adams et al., 1994 (3)	Return to Prison	23.0	5,051	21.6/23.7	1,359/8,001	44–36
Anderson, 1995a (3)	Return to Prison[1]					24
	ABE	32.3	1,060	30.6	3,765	
	GED	27.4	1,303	32.3	4,629	
	College	26.5	976	29.8	3,467	
Batiuk et al., 1997 (3)	Return to Prison[2]	19.9	95	37.0*	223	120
Blackburn, 1981 (3)	Rearrest/Return to Prison	37.0	189	58.0*	189	N/A
Burke & Vivian, 2001 (3)	Reincarcerated[1]	46.8	32	68.7	32	60
Jeffords & McNitt, 1993 (3)	Rearrest	41.3	475	53.5*	1,242	12
Langenbach et al., 1990 (3)	Return to Prison	40.0	360	68.0*	360	60

Steurer, Smith, & Tracy, 2001 (3)	Rearrest	48.0	1373	57.0*	1797	36
O'Neil, 1990 (3)	Return to Prison	3.9	129	11.5*	129	24
Walsh, 1985 (3)	Rearrest	24.0	50	44.0	50	43.2
Boudouris, 1985 (2)	Rearrest/Parole Revocation	38.0	245	59.0	305	48–96
Clark, 1991 (2)	Return to Prison	26.4	356	44.6*	630	12–42
Gaither, 1976 (2)	Return to Prison	14.0	4,444	24.0*	1,850	120
Holloway & Moke, 1986 (2)	Rearrest[1]	25.3	95	38.5/48.0	116/106	12
Hull, Forrester, Brown, Jobe, & McCullen, 2000 (2)	Return to Prison[1]	19.1	451	38.2/49.1	469/1,307	180
Lockwood, 1991 (2)	Rearrest	27.0	92	40.0	92	24
McGee, 1997 (2)	Return to Prison[1]	13.1	754	37.5	771	79.2
Piehl, 1995 (2)	Return to Prison[3]	33.5	212	43.3	450	36
Porporino & Robinson, 1992 (2)	Readmission to Prison	30.1	899	35.7*/41.6*	462/375	13.2
Ramsey, 1988 (2)	Rearrest[1]	32.0	100	32.0/38.0	100/100	60–72
Schumacker, Anderson, & Anderson, 1990 (2)	Rearrest, Technical Violation, or Conviction[1]	27.0	248	32.0	287	12
Siegel & Basta, 1997 (2)	Felony Rearrest		81/56		51	60
	GED	24.0				
	PALS	35.0		46.0		
	Conviction					
	GED	21.0		22.0		
	PALS	20.0				

[1] No significance tests reported.

[2] Calculated recidivism rate for treatment group from reported odds ratio assuming mean recidivism rate for comparison group.

[3] Calculated recidivism rate for nonparticipants from data in Table 3 of original study.

* Significantly different from experimental group $p < 0.05$.

TABLE 5.2. *Studies of life skills programs showing recidivism rates, length of follow-up, and sample characteristics*

Study (methods score)	Measure of recidivism	Recidivism				Follow-up period (in months)
		Experimental (%)	N	Control (%) #1/#2/#3	N	
Melton & Pennell, 1998 (4)	Rearrest (M)	0.34	147	0.37	188	12
	Conviction (M)	0.84		0.79		
Ross, Fabiano, & Ewles, 1988 (4)	Conviction[1]	48	17	18/70	22/232	18
	Imprisonment[1]	11		0/30		
Miller, 1995 (3)	Rearrest[1]	8	61	17	18	6
Miller, 1997 (3)	Conviction/Pending Charge[1,2]	29	55	27	48	12
	Return to Prison[1]	31		38		
Austin, 1997 (2)	Return to Prison Of	44	256	49	144	36
	Recommitted, Due to New Offense[1]	25	113	37	70	

[1] No significance tests reported.

[2] Rates recalculated from original results to exclude two noncontrol group treatment samples; when all four treatment samples are combined, conviction rate equals 19 percent and return to prison rate equals 22 percent for treatment group.

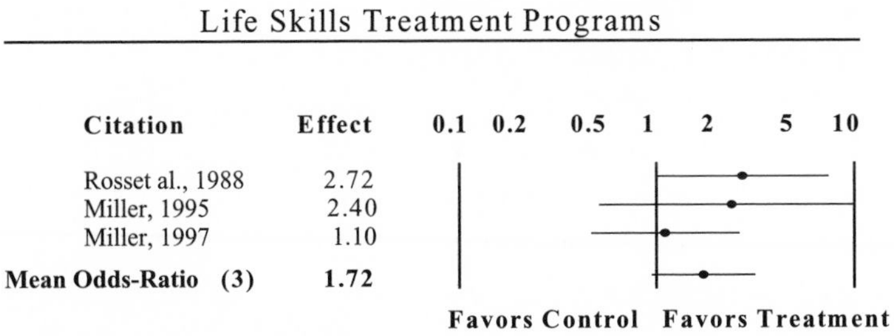

Life Skills Treatment Programs

Citation	Effect
Rosset al., 1988	2.72
Miller, 1995	2.40
Miller, 1997	1.10
Mean Odds-Ratio (3)	**1.72**

0.1 0.2 0.5 1 2 5 10

Favors Control **Favors Treatment**

Figure 5.2. Forest plot showing odds ratio and 95 percent confidence interval for studies of life skills treatment programs.

conclude that academic education programs are effective in reducing recidivism.

Figure 5.2 presents the results of three studies examining the effect of life skills education on recidivism [note: the study by Melton and Pennell (1998) was excluded from the plot because the authors did not report the standard deviation for the measure of recidivism]. The measures of recidivism utilized in calculating the effect sizes are rearrest (n = 1), conviction (n = 1), and conviction and/or pending charges (n = 1). The most recent recidivism measures for each study were also used, representing the longest follow-up period. One study from Table 5.2 was excluded because of low methods scores. Although the results indicate a positive treatment effect, the difference was nonsignificant.

CONCLUSIONS

What Works?

Do correctional education programs reduce the recidivism of offenders? According to our decision-making rules, there is sufficient evidence to say that the results from the ABE, GED, and PSE educational programs effectively reduce future offending. Overall, the meta-analysis demonstrated that participants in educational programs had lower recidivism. Furthermore, several ABE/GED studies (Jeffords & McNitt, 1993; Langenbach, North, Aagaard, & Chown, 1990; Walsh, 1985) that scored three or more on the research methods scale demonstrated significant differences in recidivism between participants and nonparticipants.

PSE is also effective in reducing recidivism. Significant differences between participants in college programs and controls were found in studies by Batiuk et al. (1997), Blackburn (1981), and O'Neil (1990). In addition, although several of the studies did not provide tests of significance (see Table 5.1), for most of these studies, the treatment group had lower rates of recidivism. Overall, in the majority of the studies of both ABE/GED and PSE, the participants had lower recidivism; thus, the preponderance of evidence supports the conclusion that corrections-based educational programs are effective in reducing recidivism.

In spite of this, given the abundance of educational programs for offenders in prison or in the community, the dearth of methodologically rigorous studies is surprising. As seen in Table 5.1, the median methods score was two, slightly fewer studies were scored three, and quasi-experimental or true experimental studies were rare. Moreover, most of the evaluations suffered from selection problems. That is, those who volunteered for educational programs were compared to either a group who chose not to participate or those who dropped out of the programs. In both of these situations, we can assume that the voluntary participants differed in some important way from the other group members prior to the educational program; therefore, any differences in recidivism may be due to these initial differences and not anything that happens in the program. Notwithstanding these methodological flaws in the extant research, there is sufficient evidence from our assessments of the research quality, significance tests, and meta-analysis to conclude that correctional education programs work to reduce recidivism.

What We Do Not Know

Currently, there is insufficient evidence to draw conclusions about the effectiveness of life skills training programs. Evaluations routinely neglected to report statistical tests, and those that did so reported nonsignificant differences between the participants and the comparison groups. Furthermore, the results from the studies were inconsistent with regard to the direction of the effects.

APPENDIX 5.1. STUDY REFERENCE, DESCRIPTION, AND METHODS SCORES (IN PARENTHESES) OF ACADEMIC EDUCATION TREATMENT FOR OFFENDERS

Adams et al., 1994 **(3)**

Texas prison inmates admitted and released between March 1991 and December 1992 participating in academic program compared only to (1) participants in both academic and vocational education and (2) nonparticipants.

Anderson, 1995a **(3)**

Inmates released from Ohio prisons FY 1992 who participated in ABE, GED, or prison-based college program compared to three separate groups of nonparticipants; constructed based on reading score, highest grade completed, and prior educational programming.

Batiuk et al., 1997 **(3)**

Inmates in Ohio released between 1982 and 1983 who graduated from the Wilmington College Associates Degree Program compared to inmates who did not receive education.

Blackburn, 1981 **(3)**

Inmates at the Maryland Correctional Training Center released between 1970 and 1978 who participated in an associate of arts degree program through the College Program offered by Hagerstown Junior College compared to a matched group of nonparticipants.

Boudouris, 1985 **(2)**

Inmates released from Iowa State Penitentiary participating in education programs compared to substance abusers, treated and untreated.

Burke and Vivian, 2001 **(3)**

Inmates released from the Hampden County Correctional Center in Ludlow, Massachusettes, between January 1993 and October 1993 who completed at least one three-credit college course compared to a demographically matched control group of inmates who did not take college courses.

Clark, 1991 **(2)**

Males participating in the New York Department of Corrections Inmate College Program during the 1986–87 academic year who successfully completed the program, compared to program noncompleters who either withdrew or were removed.

Gaither, 1976 **(2)**

Inmates who had been discharged or paroled between August 1965 and December 1974 participating in the TX Department of Corrections Junior College Program compared to inmates who were eligible for the college program but did not participate.

Harer, 1995b **(4)**

Federal Bureau of Prison inmates participating in education programs (ABE, GED, ACE, PSE) compared to nonparticipants.

Harer, 1995a **(4)**

Federal prison inmates released between January 1987 and June 1987 who had served at least one year and completed at least one education program (ABE, GED, ACE, PSE) compared to those (1) completing at least half of the courses and (2) completing no courses.

Holloway and Moke, 1986 **(2)**

Inmates released between January 1982 and October 1983 who graduated from the Lebanon Correctional Institution associate degree program compared to (1) inmates with a high school diploma or GED who attended no more than two quarters of the program and (2) inmates without a GED or high school diploma and no participation in the associate program.

Hull et al., 2000 **(2)**

Virginia Department of Correctional Education records of inmates in the Virginia Department of Correcions released between 1979 and 1994 examined; academic program completers compared to noncompleters and nonparticipants.

Jeffords and McNitt, 1993 **(3)**

Youth in the Texas Youth Commission released on parole or independent living or discharged between July 1990 and June 1992 who received a GED compared to those who did not receive a GED before release.

Langenbach et al., 1990 **(3)**

Oklahoma prison inmates participating in the Oklahoma Televised Instructional System PSE program compared to a matched group of nonparticipants.

Linden et al., 1984 **(5)**

Inmates at British Columbia and Matsqui Penitentiaries in 1972 who volunteered to participate were randomly assigned to a university-level education program or to a comparison group receiving normal prison activities.

Lockwood, 1991 **(2)**

Inmates released between 1981 and 1987 from three New York prisons who participated in a prison college program and completed more than sixty credits compared to a demographically matched control group of inmates who completed thirty or fewer credits.

McGee, 1997 **(2)**

Adult inmates in Illinois who completed requirements for an associate degree or postsecondary vocational certificate between July 1992 and June 1993 compared to inmates released between July 1991 and June 1995 who had not completed either of the programs.

O'Neil, 1990 **(3)**

Alabama prison inmates released in 1983 who participated in the PSE program are compared to randomly selected group of eligible nonparticipants.

Piehl, 1995 **(2)**

Male inmates released from WI Department of Corrections between October 1988 and August 1992 who completed an educational program compared to inmates who were eligible but did not participate.

Porporino and Robinson, 1992 **(2)**

Inmates in the Correctional Service of Canada who participated in ABE in 1988 and who successfully completed ABE grade-eight level compared to (1) ABE participants released before completion and (2) ABE participants who withdrew from the program.

Ramsey, 1988 **(2)**

South Carolina prison inmates released between fiscal year 1982–1983 and 1984–1985 participating in the Palmetto Unified School District ABE program who received a GED compared to (1) program participants who did not achieve a GED and (2) nonparticipants.

Schumacker et al., 1990 **(2)**

Adult releasees from nineteen correctional institutions in a midwestern state who received academic training compared to only releases who did not enroll in any coursework.

Siegel and Basta, 1997 (**2**)
Felony probationers in Pima County, Arizona, between March 1988 and June 1992 graduating from the GED or Principle of the Alphabet Literacy System (PALS component of the adult education program LEARN compared to candidates who were eligible but did not participate in either program.

Steurer et al., 2001 (**3**)
Cohort of inmates released from incarceration between 1997 and 1998 in Maryland, Ohio, and Minnesota participating in correctional education programs compared to nonparticipants.

Walsh, 1985 (**3**)
Male probationers under supervision of the Lucas County Adult Probation Department, Toledo, Ohio between 1979 and 1981 participating in a GED program matched to control group of nonparticipants.

APPENDIX 5.2. STUDY REFERENCE, DESCRIPTION, AND METHODS SCORES (IN PARENTHESES) OF LIFE SKILLS EDUCATION TREATMENT FOR OFFENDERS

Austin, 1997 (**2**)
Inmates between March 1994 and November 1996 were recruited for the thirteen-week Life-Attitude-Skills-Education-Retraining program located in Dauphin County Prison; graduates were compared to a group of inmates who did not participate.

Melton and Pennell, 1998 (**4**)
Inmates who volunteered and met the screening criteria were randomly assigned to the Staying Out Successfully life skills program or to the control group of inmates who received regular programming.

Miller, 1995 (**3**)
Eligible inmates from four Delaware prisons participating in the first cycle of the Delaware Life Skills Program compared to a control group of eligible applicants who did not receive life skills but who may have participated in other correctional programs.

Miller, 1997 **(3)**
Same as Miller (1995) with longer follow-up period.

Ross et al., 1988 **(4)**
High-risk male probationers in Ontario assigned to Life Skills Training group compared to (1) cognitive skills participants and (2) regular probation.

CHAPTER SIX

Vocational Education and Work Programs

INTRODUCTION

Work has been an important part of the daily activities of inmates from almost the inception of penitentiaries. Originally, the Pennsylvania penitentiary system called for solitary confinement without work. The rationale for this was to give offenders time to reflect on their crimes and repent; however, the terrible psychological and physical effects of such isolation soon became apparent. To maintain their health, inmates were provided with moral and religious instruction and work. They were expected to work from eight to ten hours per day in isolation in their cells. The "Great Law" of William Penn and the Quakers advocated hard labor in place of capital punishment for those convicted of serious crimes.

Work was also the major component of the Auburn or "congregate" system. In contrast to the isolated work in the Pennsylvania system, inmates in Auburn prisons worked in group settings. The daily routine included congregate work in shops during the day, separation of prisoners into small cells at night, silence at all times, and lockstep marching formations. Silence was enforced because verbal exchanges between prisoners were believed to be contaminating. Advocates for the Auburn system argued that these prisons were cheaper to construct, offered better vocational training for the inmates, and produced more money for the state. The economic advantage is most likely one of the major reasons the congregate system was adopted in almost all American prisons. The development of prosperous prison industries was also a major concern of wardens (McKelvey, 1972).

The reformatory era brought in a new perspective on work and vocational training. The goal of the reformatories was to change youth so they would live crime-free lives after release. An important part of this reformation was preparing the youth for future employment. Academic education and vocational training were advocated as important components in the process of reformation. These ideas were later transferred to adult prisons.

Today, work, prison industries, and vocational education permeate the U.S. correctional system. A 1995 survey of all state and federal adult correctional facilities (1,500 in total) found that 94 percent of the facilities offered work programs (Stephan, 1997). Roughly a third of the facilities employed inmates in a prison industry and approximately half provided vocational training. Almost two-thirds of all inmates participated in a work program.

VARIED PURPOSES

Throughout history, work has served many purposes in U.S. corrections (Flanagan, 1989). Work has been used to reduce costs, supply governments with needed goods, keep inmates busy, rehabilitate inmates, and maintain the institution, and as retribution. The primacy of the various goals has waxed and waned over time. For example, from a retributive perspective, work was used as a form of punishment for crimes committed. Although this is less common than in the past, some states still sentence offenders to hard labor as punishment for their offense(s).

Inmate labor is also used to alleviate the cost of corrections. Prison farms are a good example of how inmate labor has been used to defray costs. Prisoners serve as laborers on the farms and produce the food for inmates. Inmates are also used for institutional maintenance tasks, which reduces the need to hire laborers and hence decreases the operating costs of prisons. They work in prison factories or industries where they produce goods such as furniture or license plates, thus diminishing the costs to the state. In addition, some inmate work programs are designed to provide payment of restitution to victims, reimburse the state for a portion of the costs of confinement, or help support dependents, thereby reducing welfare costs to the government.

Inmate labor also satisfies institutional-oriented goals. For example, work reduces inmate idleness and its attendant problems. Work also provides structure to the daily activities of offenders and limits the time inmates have to devise plans for escape, use the underground economy, or obtain contraband.

In contemporary correctional settings, some inmate labor is designed to benefit the inmate. Potential benefits of work include helping the delinquent or offender develop good work habits and improving life management skills. Work programs also provide inmates with income that can be used in the commissary while in prison or for "gate money" at release. From a rehabilitation perspective, work programs may give the offender real world work experience, job skills, and vocational training. Such experiences are expected to increase the likelihood of employment upon release and decrease the chances an inmate will return to criminal activity.

When the goal of inmate labor is to benefit society or the institution, there is often little interest in whether such work has an impact on future criminal activities. In fact, at times, these goals may actually conflict with individual level goals; for example, an intensive vocational educational program may remove inmates from institutional maintenance work. Victim restitution and dependent assistance diverts inmate earnings that might otherwise be used by the inmate for other purposes. However, many of the goals are compatible. For instance, products generated through prison industry may reduce costs to the state while at the same time giving inmates a chance to earn money. Work in prison may also help inmates learn good work habits and job skills that will enable them to find employment upon release. The focus of this chapter is on vocational education, prison industry, and work programs that are designed, at least in part, to reduce future criminal activity.

RATIONALE AS A CRIME REDUCTION TECHNIQUE

Research has consistently found an association between crime and unemployment (Farrington, 1986; Glueck & Glueck, 1930; Sampson & Laub, 1990; Wolfgang, Figlio, & Sellin, 1972). In comparison to the general public, offenders are less educated, have fewer marketable skills, and are more apt to be unemployed while in the community (Andrews & Bonta, (2003). Releasees from prison who continue to be involved with the criminal justice system have lower earnings and lower employment rates than those who desist (Needels, 1996). During periods when young adult males are unemployed, they have higher offending rates than when they are employed (Farrington, Gallagher, Morley, & St. Ledger, 1986; MacKenzie, Browning, Skroban, & Smith, 1999).

There are many theoretical explanations for the relationship between crime and unemployment (Bushway & Reuter, 1997; Fagan, 1995; Uggen, 2000). Some theorists argue that people make a rational choice between legal and illegal work based partly on the relative attractiveness of the two options. If legal work becomes more attractive, individuals will move into the legitimate labor force; when illegal work becomes more rewarding, they will turn toward that option. Others assert poverty may lead people into crime out of necessity. Relative deprivation theorists assert it is not poverty alone but rather the inequality of resources that leads people to crime. Yet others argue that crime and unemployment may be a lifestyle choice that some people make. Theorists in the control tradition suggest that employment may exert social control over individuals, thereby inhibiting criminal involvement (Sampson & Laub, 1990). People who participate in crime may also become stigmatized or labeled (by themselves or others) and denied opportunities because of these labels (Bushway & Reuter, 1997).

EFFECTIVENESS OF WORK AND VOCATIONAL PROGRAMS

Although there is theoretical and empirical evidence to suggest that unemployment is related to criminal offending, evidence of the effectiveness of vocational and work programs in reducing criminal activity is less clear (Bushway & Reuter, 1997; Gerber & Fritsch, 1995; Tracy & Johnson, 1994). Reviews of the research and meta-analyses suggest that some vocational education programs, multicomponent industry programs, and community employment programs may be effective in reducing the future criminal activities of offenders (Bouffard, MacKenzie, & Hickman, 2000; Wilson et al., 1999; Wilson et al., 2000).

Other transitional employment programs, community vocational training, work ethics, in-prison work programs, and halfway houses are not as successful.

Using meta-analytic techniques, my colleagues and I examined the effectiveness of education, vocation, and work programs in reducing recidivism of offenders (Wilson et al., 2000). After an intensive search, we identified twenty-six studies comparing vocational or work programs to nonprogram participation comparison groups. Studies included seventeen vocational education programs, four correctional industries programs, and five multicomponent or other work programs. Overall, the analysis indicated that vocational education programs work to significantly reduce recidivism. We estimated that if 50 percent of the comparison group recidivated, only 39 percent of those with vocational training would recidivate – an 11 percent reduction in recidivism as a result of program participation. There was no evidence that participation in correctional industries and other work programs significantly reduced recidivism; however, when the comparison group's recidivism was set to 50 percent, estimated recidivism rates for participants in prison industry and other work programs were 40 and 43 percent, respectively.

In the meta-analyses, we also examined whether employment programs had an impact on future employment (twelve studies reported information on employment). Analyses indicated that vocational training and other work programs significantly increased the future employment rate of the participants in comparison to nonparticipants. Programs that evidenced an effect on employment also tended to impact recidivism. One possible explanation for these results is that vocational training and other work programs increase employment opportunities, and this reduces future criminal activities. In other words, the programs increase employment, and employment, in turn, decreases recidivism. However, because many of these studies did not randomly assign nonparticipants and participants, it is impossible to rule out alternative explanations for the results. The most plausible alternative explanation is that the groups differed prior to program involvement and recidivism rates reflect these differences, not necessarily the impact of the program.

To review the effectiveness of work and vocational education programs, I divided the studies into three categories based on whether the major component of the program focused on (1) vocational education, (2) correctional industries, or (3) other work programs (e.g., work release). The studies are listed in Tables 6.1–6.3 along with the methods score, length of follow-up, and recidivism rates, and the related appendices provide a description of each study. The typical comparison group in these studies is a naturally occurring group of nonparticipants in the program of interest. Few studies randomly assigned subjects to the vocational education, industry, or work program. Many studies used a program-comparison contrast by post hoc matching of participants or a covariate adjusted analyses.

Vocational Education Programs

Vocational education is one of the most widely implemented educational programs in correctional settings because it addresses the high incidence of academic and employment failure among offenders. The type of program offered under the label of *vocational education* varies greatly. Programs include classroom-based education, job training, and apprenticeships in such areas as electrical and carpentry skills. The programs may also offer some life skills components to improve offenders' time management skills and work ethics.

Frequently, the programs begin with classroom instruction aimed at giving the inmates work-related knowledge such as basic math skills needed for automotive mechanics or construction tasks. Some programs such as the Wisconsin Department of Corrections offer accreditation to offenders who complete vocational education programs, enabling them to obtain a necessary trade license (Piehl, 1995). Other programs may offer more hands-on types of training such as the Home Builders Institute's Project Trade, which offers a series of construction job training programs for both juvenile and adult offenders (Home Builders Institute, 1996). Furthermore, through a partnership between the correctional institution and local tradespeople, postrelease employment possibilities are improved. That is, offenders can gain actual work experience in the community under the guidance of the Project Trade instructors.

TABLE 6.1. *Studies of vocational education treatment programs showing recidivism rates and length of follow-up*

Study (methods score)	Measure of recidivism	Recidivism				Follow-up period (in months)
		Experimental (%)	N	Control (%) #1/#2/#3	N	
Bloom et al., 1994 (5)	Self-report Rearrest	59.2	99	55.7	99	36
Lattimore et al., 1990 (5)	Rearrest	36.0	138	46.0*	109	24
Adams et al., 1994 (3)	Reincarceration	20.9	422	21.6/23.7	1,359/8,001	14–36
	Major Infractions	7.8		12.4/5.7		
Downes et al., 1989 (3)	Failure to Complete Parole	24.0	66	20.0	66	Unknown
Luftig, 1978 (3)	*State Reformatory:*		110		50	12
	Rearrest	37.3		66.0		
	Reincarceration	23.6		34.0		
	State Prison:	96		50		
	Rearrest	32.4		50.0		
	Reincarceration	24.0		40.0		
Saylor & Gaes, 1992 (3)	Parole Revocation	6.6	1,043	10.1*	3,070	12
Anderson, 1981 (2)	Parole Violation	20.4	98	36.4	140	Up to 36

Anderson, 1995a (2)	Reincarceration	30.1	630	31.3	N/A	24
Boudouris, 1985 (2)	Return to Prison[1]	25.0	251	41.0	305	48–96
	Rearrest/Parole Revocation	37.0	251	59.0	305	
Coffey, 1983 (2)	Reincarceration	46.0	116	41.0	116	Up to 24
Chown & Davis, 1986 (2)	Reincarceration		2,372		9,851	
		13.1		11.8		12
		26.1		22.5		24
		33.3		28.9		36
		36.9		33.2		48
		38.0		34.7		54
Hull, 1995 (2)	Reincarceration[1]	21.3	456	37.5/49.1	317/1,307	Up to 180
Maciekowich, 1976 (2)	Reincarceration	15.3	59	28.4	320	13–25
McGee, 1997 (2)	Reincarceration[2]	13.1	754	37.5	771	Up to 78
Piehl, 1995 (2)	Reincarceration[3]	35.0	431	43.9	545	36
Ryan, 1997 (2)	Parole Violation	25.0	323	41.0*	319	36–48
Schumacker et al., 1990 (2)	Rearrest, Technical Violation, or Conviction[2]	25.0	107	32.0	287	12
Winterton, 1995 (2)	Reincarceration[2]	21.0	47	36.0/36.5	47/30	12

[1] Numbers estimated from graphs.
[2] No significance tests reported.
[3] Calculated recidivism rate for nonparticipants from data in Table 3 of original study.
* Significantly different from experimental group, $p < 0.05$.

TABLE 6.2. *Studies of correctional industries programs showing recidivism rates and length of follow-up*

Study (methods score)	Measure of recidivism	Recidivism: Experimental (%)	N	Control (%) #1/#2/#3	N	Follow-up period (in months)
Maguire et al., 1988 (4)	Felony Arrest	29.0	399	34.0	497	Up to 54
Saylor & Gaes, 1992 (3)	Parole Violation	6.6	1,502	10.1*	1,829	12
Anderson, 1995b (2)	Reincarceration	24.6	744	29.9	7,839	Up to 24
Boudouris, 1985 (2)	Return to Prison[1]	9.0	254	41.0	305	48–96
	Rearrest/Parole Revocation	30.0		59.0		

[1] Numbers estimated from graphs.
* Significantly different from experimental group, $p < 0.05$.

A search of the literature turned up eighteen studies that examined the effectiveness of vocational education programs; however, only six were judged to be of sufficient scientific merit to warrant a score of three or better on the methods score (see Table 6.1). Two studies (Bloom, Orr, Cave, Bell, Doolittle, & Lin, 1994; Lattimore, Witte, & Baker, 1990) randomly assigned groups to treatment versus control. Bloom and colleagues studied male youth participating in the Job Training Partnership Act (JTPA). The programs operated in several states, and the content of the programs differed widely by site. For the most part, programs provided classroom training, job skills training, job search services, basic education, and work experiences. The programs did not specifically target offenders but did serve many young people with prior arrest records. As shown in Table 6.1, there were no significant differences between the two groups although participants in the treatment program recidivated at a higher rate than those in the control group.

In contrast, Lattimore and her colleagues (1990) found very different results in their study of an enhanced vocational education program for prison inmates. Participants in this study were very different from the JTPA study sample. The program included an assessment of vocational interest and aptitude, specific skills training, and postrelease employment assistance. Participants in the program had significantly lower arrest rates in the twenty-four months following release from prison than the control group. However, the participants in this program were most likely higher risk than participants in the JTPA programs. Therefore, the results may reflect the principle that intensive programs are most effective when participants are at higher risk for recidivism (Andrews, Zinger, et al., 1990; Cullen & Gendreau, 2000). Furthermore, it is worth noting that recidivism rates are difficult to compare because the JTPA study relied on self-reported recidivism whereas Lattimore and her colleagues used official records.

The remaining four programs that received a three on the research methods scale used previously existing groups in the analysis. That is, they compared participants to others who did not participate, had limited participation, or had participated in another program. The problem with these designs is that we can never be sure that the program participants did not differ from the nonparticipants before entering the vocational programs. For example, Saylor and Gaes (1992) found evidence that vocational education programs significantly reduced recidivism. They examined U.S. federal prison programs and used a recidivism measure that combined new criminal activities and technical violations. However, the treatment group consisted of a mixed-participant group who worked in prison industries only (57 percent), worked in prison industries and had vocational education or an apprenticeship (19 percent), or had vocational education and/or an apprenticeship (24 percent). The outcome data were not reported separately for the different groups so it is impossible to tell whether the reduction in recidivism was due to participation in vocational education, prison industries, apprenticeship, or some combination. The other three studies scored at level three reported no significant differences between the treated and comparison groups (Adams et al., 1994; Downes, Monaco, & Schreiber, 1989; Luftig, 1978).

As mentioned earlier, twelve studies were judged to be of such low scientific merit that they were not considered in making decisions about the effectiveness of vocational education programs. In the majority of these poorer quality studies, the participants had lower recidivism rates than comparison groups. However, because of the methods employed, it is unclear whether to attribute the results to the vocational education program or some other factor such as nonequivalent comparison groups.

Figure 6.1 presents the results of a meta-analysis of seven independent samples from six vocational education treatment studies [note: the study by Luftig (1978) includes more than one distinct sample]. The principal recidivism measures used to calculate effect sizes were rearrest (n = 4), reincarceration (n = 1), and parole revocation (n = 2). The effect size listed for Adams et al. (1994) was calculated by combining both control groups and taking the weighted mean of the groups' recidivism measures, producing a singular comparison measure. The most recent recidivism measures for each study were used, representing the longest follow-up period. Twelve of the studies included in Table 6.1 were excluded because of low methods scores.

As shown in Figure 6.1, the effect sizes of five of the studies favored the treatment group, and four of these effects were significant. Two effect sizes favored the control group, but these differences were not

Vocational Education Programs

Citation	Effect
Luftig, 1978 (reformatory)	3.27
Luftig, 1978 (prison)	2.10
Saylor & Gaes, 1992	1.59
Lattimore et al., 1990	1.49
Adams et al., 1994	1.16
Bloom et al., 1994	.85
Downes et al., 1989	.77
Mean Odds-Ratio (7)	**1.36**

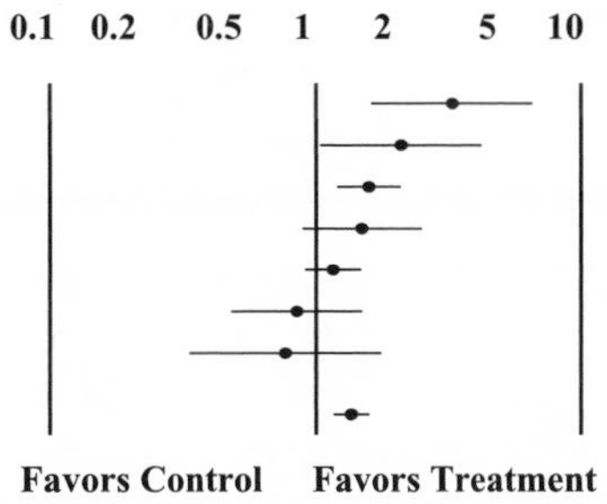

0.1 0.2 0.5 1 2 5 10

Favors Control Favors Treatment

Figure 6.1. Forest plot showing odds ratio and 95 percent confidence interval for studies of vocational education programs.

significant. The overall effect size indicated that the treatment group had significantly lower recidivism rates. Given these results, there is sufficient evidence at this point in time to conclude that vocational education programs are effective in reducing recidivism.

Correctional Industries Programs

Correctional industries is a term used to describe a wide range of employment-related activities occurring almost exclusively during an offender's term of incarceration. Although some industrial facilities are located outside of prison walls, correctional industry workers are typically serving time in some type of residential facility. The industries produce a wide range of products and services for government and private sector consumers including furniture, health technology, automobile parts, institutional and jail products, signs, printing products, textiles and apparel, traffic paint, and food. Inmates working in correctional industry differ from other prison inmates in that they are generally older, serving longer sentences, have better preincarceration employment records, and are less likely to be drug users (Flanagan, 1989).

Table 6.2 lists the methods score, length of follow-up, and recidivism rates of the four evaluations of correctional industries programs. Appendix 6.2 provides a description of each study. Given the large number of industry programs, it is surprising that so few have been evaluated. Most likely, this reflects the numerous goals of offender employment programs. That is, prison industry is designed to keep offenders busy while they are in prison, to provide goods and services, and to alleviate the costs of corrections. Hence, these goals appear to be more important than rehabilitation.

Maguire, Flanagan, and Thornberry (1988) examined prison industries programs in seven maximum-security facilities in New York. They found no significant differences between the treatment and control groups in their analysis of felony rearrests. In contrast, Saylor and Gaes (1992) found that participants in a federal prison industries program had significantly lower recidivism rates than comparison groups. Similar to Maguire et al., Saylor and Gaes statistically controlled for a range of factors that may have differentiated the groups prior to the study. Nevertheless, the number of subjects in the Saylor and Gaes analysis was very large and the difference in recidivism, although significant, was relatively small. Additionally, as previously noted in the Chapter 5, the treatment group in the Saylor and Gaes evaluation was composed of participants from a variety of programs, and the data from the different groups were not disaggregated; therefore, it is not possible to determine which program type (or which combination) produced the positive outcomes. The remaining two studies of state-run prison industry were judged to be so low in scientific rigor that they could not be used to make decisions about the effectiveness of industry programs (Anderson, 1995b; Boudouris, 1985).

Figure 6.2 presents the results from a meta-analysis of the two correctional industries programs that received a method score of three or higher. Figure 6.2 presents the results of a meta-analysis of two correctional industry program studies on offenders' recidivism rates. Effect sizes were calculated using the recidivism measures of felony arrest (n = 1) and parole violation (n = 1). The longest follow-up period for each study was used. Two studies from Table 6.2 were excluded from the plot because of low methods scores.

In both of the studies shown in Figure 6.2, those with prison industry experience had lower recidivism rates than the comparisons. The effect sizes favored the treated groups in both studies, but only the result from the Saylor and Gaes study was statistically significant. Furthermore, the overall mean effect size significantly favored the treatment group; however, this is due to the fact that the Saylor and

Correctional Industries Programs

Citation	Effect	0.1 0.2 0.5 1 2 5 10
Saylor & Gaes, (1992)	1.59	
Maguire et al., (1988)	1.26	
Mean Odds-Ratio (2)	**1.44**	
		Favors Control Favors Treatment

Figure 6.2. Forest plot showing odds ratio and 95 percent confidence interval for studies of correctional industries education programs.

Gaes study was more heavily weighted than Maguire et al. because of the large sample size.

It is noteworthy that one of the major flaws with these studies is the use of preexisting groups that are assumed to differ prior to the treatment. That is, those who volunteer and are selected to participate in industry work may be different from those who do not. Although the studies attempted to control for these differences in the multivariate statistical analysis, we cannot assume that all relevant factors were included. In addition, as mentioned previously, although the differences in recidivism rates in the Saylor and Gaes evaluation were significant, the absolute differences were relatively small (6.6 compared to 10.1) and most likely due to the large number of subjects in the study. Therefore, at this point, it is too early to make any definitive conclusions about the effectiveness of correctional industries programs; when the quality of the science, the results from the meta-analyses, the mixed group of participants, and the small substantive difference are considered, there is insufficient evidence to say these programs are promising.

Multicomponent and Other Work Programs

Multicomponent and work programs other than prison industries usually assist offenders in either obtaining employment or acquiring job search skills or provide other employment services. Frequently, correctional personnel supervise offenders in these programs when they are in the community. In some programs, the participants live in prerelease facilities in institutions, halfway houses, or other community residential facilities.

TABLE 6.3. *Studies of work and multicomponent programs showing recidivism rates and length of follow-up*

Study (methods score)	Measure of recidivism	Recidivism: Experimental (%)	N	Control (%) #1/#2/#3	N	Follow-up period (in months)
Clark et al., 1992 (5)	Program Misconduct	56.7	30	66.7	30	6
	M Days to Misconduct	125.2		81.8*		
	Return to Prison	13.3		33.0		
Uggen, 1997 (5)	Self-report Arrest	43.0	N/A[1]	43.0	N/A[1]	36
	Age ≤ 26	54.0		49.0		24
	Age > 26	26.0		36.0*		24
Turner & Petersilia, 1996 (4)	Rearrests	22.3	112	30.2	106	12
	Return to Prison	3.6		4.7		
Menon et al., 1992 (3)	Rearrest	48.0	N/A[1]	57.0	N/A[1]	12
	Reincarceration	23.0		38.0		
Milkman et al., 1985 (3)	Rearrest					
	Boston	71.0	216	66.0	162	24
	Chicago	64.0	278	67.0	251	
	San Diego	69.0	214	71.0	91	
	M Months to Rearrest					
	Boston	1.45		1.25		
	Chicago	1.33		1.25		
	San Diego	0.98		1.07		
Van Stelle et al., 1995 (3)	Rearrest	24.0	63	19.0/42.0*	36/200	9
	M Days to Rearrest	120		108/164		12
	Return to Prison	22.0		28.0/36.0		
Lee, 1983 (2)	Successful on Parole	75.0	140	50.0*/62.0*	94/136	32
Washington State	Rearrest	35.0	59	35.0	42	6
Department of Corrections,	Return to Jail/Prison	25.0		24.0		
1997 (2)	*M* Months to Violation	2.2		2.9		

[1] Sample size by group not reported for Uggen (1997) (total sample equals 2,276) or Menon et al. (1992) (total sample equals 6,539).
* Significantly different from experimental group, $p < 0.05$.

Work release programs allow offenders to leave the facility during their last few months in prison to seek employment or, more commonly, to participate in some type of work program (Turner & Petersilia, 1996). The goal of work release is to help inmates make the transition from institution to the community and to promote productive, stable employment following release. Work release has been part of many correctional systems for nearly eighty years. However, although forty-three states allow work release, only about one-third of these states actually operate such programs. Furthermore, fewer than 3 percent of all prison inmates participate in work release (Turner & Petersilia, 1996).

My colleagues and I located eight studies that examined the effectiveness of work or multicomponent programs (see Table 6.3 and Appendix 6.3). According to Table 6.3, six studies scored a three or more on the research methods scale. Four of the eight studies found no significant differences between groups on any measure of recidivism (Menon, Blakely, Carmichael, & Silver, 1992; Milkman, Timrots, Peyser, Toborg, Gottlieb, & Yezer, 1985; Turner & Petersilia, 1996; Washington State Department of Corrections, 1997). The remaining studies found some significant differences but not in all measures of recidivism (Clark et al., 1992; Lee, 1983; Uggen, 1997; Van Stelle et al., 1995). Furthermore, the direction of the differences did not always favor the treated group. For example, in their study of a training and employment demonstration project, Van Stelle and colleagues (1995) found that the treatment group (i.e., program graduates) had a higher prevalence of rearrest than one of the control groups (i.e., nonparticipants) but a significantly lower rate of rearrest than a second matched comparison group. Furthermore, there were no differences between the three groups in return to prison rates. Similarly, Clark, Hartter, and Ford (1992) found no significant differences between the treatment and control groups in rates of prison misconduct or return to prison (although this is most likely a result of the small sample sizes because the difference in return to prison rates was substantial: 13.3 percent versus 33 percent, respectively). Clark and colleagues did find, however, that on average controls were significantly more likely to engage in misconduct sooner than the treatment group. Finally, in one of the more rigorous studies conducted to date, Uggen (1997) found

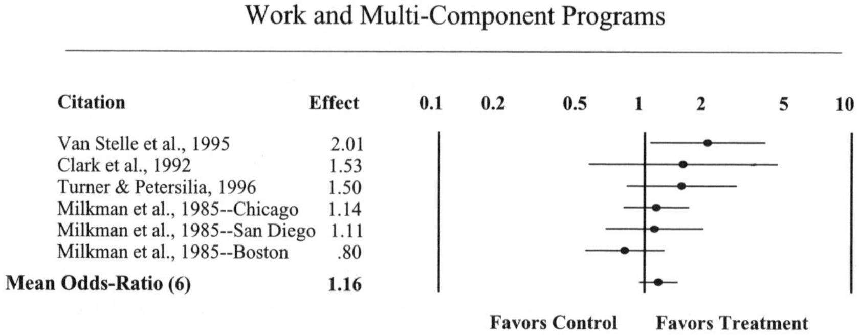

Work and Multi-Component Programs

Citation	Effect
Van Stelle et al., 1995	2.01
Clark et al., 1992	1.53
Turner & Petersilia, 1996	1.50
Milkman et al., 1985--Chicago	1.14
Milkman et al., 1985--San Diego	1.11
Milkman et al., 1985--Boston	.80
Mean Odds-Ratio (6)	**1.16**

0.1 0.2 0.5 1 2 5 10

Favors Control Favors Treatment

Figure 6.3. Forest plot showing odds ratio and 95 percent confidence interval for studies of work and multicomponent programs.

no significant differences in rearrests between offenders randomly assigned to participate in the National Supported Work Demonstration Project or the control group; however, when the groups were disaggregated by age, participation in work programs produced significantly lower rearrest rates for offenders aged twenty-seven and older, but this effect was not found for offenders aged twenty-six and younger.

Figure 6.3 presents the results of a meta-analysis of six independent samples from four studies of work and multicomponent programs. (Note: the study by Milkman et al. [1985] includes multiple distinct samples.) The primary recidivism measures used to calculate effect sizes were rearrest (n = 5) and program misconduct (n = 1). The studies by Menon et al. (1992) and Uggen (1997) were not included in the plot because these studies did not report sample size by groups. The effect sizes for Van Stelle and colleagues (1995) were calculated by combining both control groups used and taking the weighted mean of the groups' recidivism measures, producing a singular comparison measure. To represent the longest follow-up period, the most recent recidivism measure for each study was used. Two studies included in Table 6.3 were excluded because of low methods scores (Lee, 1983; Washington State Department of Corrections, 1997).

As shown in Figure 6.3, five of the effect sizes favor the treated group; however, only one of these is significant (Van Stelle et al., 1995). In addition, although the overall effect size favored the treatment group, the difference was not significant.

One difficulty in drawing conclusions about this group of studies is that there are large differences in the programs studied. For instance, programs vary in the types of employment services provided and the location of the programs (in prison, in the community, or both). Furthermore, inmates in some programs live in community residential programs (halfway houses, community work release facilities) whereas in others they do not. Nevertheless, taken as a whole, there is little evidence that these programs are effective in reducing recidivism.

CONCLUSION

The strong association between work and crime has led many people to hypothesize that if employment opportunities or work skills of offenders could be enhanced through programming, their future criminal activities would decline. My review of the different types of work and vocational programs suggests that this may be the case particularly if the program is some type of vocational education program. Disappointingly, there is little evidence that prison industries or other types of work programs are successful in reducing recidivism. At this point, I conclude that vocational education is effective in reducing recidivism but we do not know if prison industry or other work programs are effective.

APPENDIX 6.1. STUDY REFERENCE, DESCRIPTION, AND METHODS SCORES (IN PARENTHESES) OF VOCATIONAL EDUCATION TREATMENT PROGRAM STUDIES

Adams et al., 1994 **(3)**

Texas prison inmates admitted and released between March 1991 and December 1992 who participated in a vocational education program compared only to (1) participants in both academic and vocational education and (2) nonparticipants.

Anderson, 1981 **(2)**

Inmates paroled from the Vienna Illinois Correctional Center between 1972 and 1976 who received some type of vocational training certificate compared to those with no or lower levels of vocational training.

Anderson, 1995a **(2)**
Inmates released from Ohio prisons in FY 1992 who participated in a vocational education program compared to a control group of nonparticipants.

Bloom et al., 1994 **(5)**
Eligible male youth with prior arrest record in sixteen service delivery areas nationwide between November 1987 and September 1989 were randomly assigned to participate in the JTPA program or to the control group.

Boudouris, 1985 **(2)**
Inmates released from the Iowa State Penitentiary who participated in vocational education programs compared to a group of treated and untreated substance abusers.

Chown and Davis, 1986 **(2)**
Inmates paroled between January 1982 through July 1986 from the Oklahoma Department of Corrections who received vocational-technical training compared to inmates who did not receive training.

Coffey, 1983 **(2)**
Inmates paroled between January 1978 and June 1980 from the Kentucky Correctional Facility who received vocational training sufficient for entry-level employment compared to a random sample of parolees who had not received training.

Downes et al., 1989 **(3)**
Inmates in New Mexico prisons who participated in the Santa Fe Community College vocational education program between 1985 and 1987 were compared to a matched group of nonparticipants.

Hull, 1995 **(2)**
Inmates released between 1979 and 1994 who completed the Virginia Department of Correctional Education vocational education program compared to (1) vocational education program noncompleters and (2) nonparticipants.

Lattimore et al., 1990 **(5)**
Inmates between June 1983 and July 1986 at two North Carolina youth institutions randomly assigned to an enhanced vocational education program including postrelease placement or to a control group receiving routine services.

Luftig, 1978 **(3)**

Two separate study samples: (1) Youthful inmates paroled between 1970 and 1974 from the Minnesota State Reformatory who successfully completed vocational programming (e.g., upholstery, graphic arts) compared to nonparticipants and (2) adult inmates paroled between 1970 and 1974 from the Minnesota State Prison who successfully completed vocational programming (e.g., welding, office machine repair) compared to nonparticipants.

Maciekowich, 1976 **(2)**

Inmates released between 1973 and 1974 from Arizona prisons who enrolled in and completed a vocational education training program compared to nonparticipant inmates paroled in 1974.

McGee, 1997 **(2)**

Adult inmates in Illinois who completed requirements for an associate degree or postsecondary vocational certificate between July 1992 and June 1993 compared to inmates released between July 1991 and June 1995 who had not completed either of the programs.

Piehl, 1995 **(2)**

Male inmates released from WI Department of Corrections between October 1988 and August 1992 who completed vocational or educational programming compared to inmates who were eligible but did not participate.

Ryan, 1997 **(2)**

Inmates released between 1990 and 1994 who participated in the Pennsylvania Operation Outward Reach correctional education program compared to a random group of nonparticipants.

Saylor and Gaes, 1992 **(3)**

Federal Prison Industries' inmates who participated in industrial work for at least six months or had received vocational or apprenticeship instruction compared to nonparticipants.

Schumacker et al., 1990 **(2)**

Adults releasees from nineteen correctional institutions in a midwestern state who completed the vocational training program compared to releasees who did not enroll in training.

Winterton, 1995 **(2)**

Inmates at the New Hampshire State Prison participating in Transformations Technology Boot Camp, an intensive technical training program, compared to (1) an undescribed control group and (2) a shock control group.

APPENDIX 6.2. STUDY REFERENCE, DESCRIPTION, AND METHODS SCORES (IN PARENTHESES) OF CORRECTIONAL INDUSTRIES PROGRAM STUDIES

Anderson, 1995b **(2)**

Inmates released from the Ohio prison system in FY 1992 who participated in an Ohio Penal Industries job for more than ninety days compared to group of eligible nonparticipants.

Boudouris, 1985 **(2)**

Inmates released from the Iowa State Penitentiary who participated in industries, work farms, or vocational education programs compared to a group of treated and untreated substance abusers.

Maguire et al., 1988 **(4)**

Inmates employed in prison industry programs for at least six months between 1981 and 1982 in seven maximum-security New York State correctional facilities compared to inmates who did not meet the criterion for program participation.

Saylor and Gaes, 1992 **(3)**

Federal Prison Industries' inmates who participated in industrial work for at least six months or had received vocational or apprenticeship instruction were compared to nonparticipants.

APPENDIX 6.3. STUDY REFERENCE, DESCRIPTION, AND METHODS SCORES (IN PARENTHESES) OF WORK AND MULTICOMPONENT PROGRAM STUDIES

Clark et al., 1992 **(5)**

Inmates at a minimum-security residential program in Michigan randomly assigned to either the enhanced employment development condition or to the control condition, consisting of standard employment development services.

Lee, 1983 **(2)**

Wichita Work Release Program participants were compared to two separate groups of nonparticipants from two time periods.

Menon et al., 1992 **(3)**

Releasees participating in the Texas Employment Commission's Project RIO, an intensive employment service program including job preparation and job search assistance, compared to nonparticipants.

Milkman et al., 1985 **(3)**

Inmates released from adult correctional facilities in (1) Boston, (2) Chicago, and (3) San Diego who received both comprehensive employment-related services and follow-up services after placement compared to control group, who received normal services only.

Turner and Petersilia, 1996 **(4)**

Inmates who participated in the Washington State work release program in 1990 compared to a matched sample of inmates who completed their sentences in prison.

Uggen, 1997 **(5)**

Exoffenders from seven American cities referred to the National Supported Work Demonstration Project between March 1975 and July 1977 randomly assigned to either the employment program (i.e., minimum-wage subsidized job) or the control condition.

Van Stelle et al., 1995 **(3)**

Graduates between March 1993 and October 1994 of the prison-based Specialized Training and Employment Project at the Fox Lake Correctional Institute in Wisconsin were compared to (1) a control group of nonparticipants and (2) a matched comparison group of nonparticipants.

Washington State Department of Corrections, 1997 **(2)**

Work Ethic Camp (WEC) program participants (intensive work/educational/vocational programs) were compared to non-WEC participants in less intensive work/educational/vocational programs.

CHAPTER SEVEN

Cognitive Behavioral Therapy Programs

INTRODUCTION

Cognitive-behavioral treatments have become the dominant paradigm in clinical psychology (Dobson & Khatri, 2000). Based on cognitive-behavioral theory, these therapies represent a broad category of interventions that focus on human change through demonstrated behavioral outcomes. Changes in behavior are achieved through changes in the way an individual perceives, reflects, and thinks about their life (Dobson & Khatri, 2000). Theoretically, cognitive-behaviorism assumes that cognitions affect behavior, people can monitor and alter their cognitive activity, and changes in cognitions will lead to changes in behavior (Dobson & Craig, 1996). Therapy emphasizes the connection between cognitions and behavior. Dysfunctional behaviors are altered through changes in attitudes, beliefs, and thought processes (Porporino, Fabiano, & Robinson, 1991). In therapy, clients are made aware of their maladaptive thought processes, and they are encouraged to alter the way they think. These alterations in thinking are expected to alter the maladaptive behaviors being targeted by therapy.

The positive effects of cognitive-behavioral approaches to treatment have been a consistent theme in reviews of rehabilitation research (Cullen & Gendreau, 1989; Gendreau & Ross, 1987; Husband & Platt, 1993, Lipsy, 1992; Losel, 1995a). For example, in a meta-analysis of adult and juvenile correctional treatment programs, Andrews, Zinger, Hoge, Bonta, Gendreau, and Cullen (1990) identified cognitive-behavioral methods of therapy as one of the most critical aspects of effective correctional treatment. In another meta-analysis, Lipsy (1992) investigated delinquency outcomes in 443 studies and found that structured and focused treatment such as behavioral or skill-oriented programs had greater effects than other types of treatment.

Cognitive-behavioral therapies used with correctional populations characterize the type of changes targeted by the treatment with terms such as cognitive restructuring, coping skills, cognitive skills, problem solving, moral development, and reasoning (Henning & Frueh, 1996; Mahoney & Arnkoff, 1978). When applied to offender behavior, all assert that criminals think differently than noncriminals either because they have dysfunctional information processing and coping skills or a lower level of moral development. Each program has a slightly different focus.

The cognitive restructuring therapies emphasize the need to target maladaptive or dysfunctional thought processes in treatment. The mental health problems of typical offenders are thought to be the result of cognitive distortions, misperceptions of social settings, and faulty logic. The coping skills approach places more of an emphasis on improving deficits in the ability to adapt to stressful situations. The goal of therapy is to help offenders improve in interpersonal skills of problem solving, critical reasoning, and planning. Problem solving therapies view offenders as engaging in ineffective and maladaptive behaviors (Mahoney & Arnkoff, 1978) that can be changed by changing their ability to think about and solve problems.

Moral development therapies have a somewhat different theoretical basis when compared to the other cognitive-behavioral therapies (Arbuthnot & Gordon, 1988; Gendreau & Ross, 1981; Little & Robinson, 1988). From this perspective, offenders have deficits in their moral reasoning that affect their behavior. This is a stage theory of moral development based on the work of Piaget (1965) and Kohlburg (1976). According to these theories, as individuals grow older, they develop new ways of looking at the world. This growth can be understood as a series of stages through which the individual passes during development. Each stage must be mastered before the next in the sequence reached. One important developmental process is moral development. Individuals who are at higher levels of moral reasoning are more capable of choosing behavior that is socially defined as "right." However, problems in development leave offenders at lower stages of moral development. Thus, the goal of treatment is to raise the individual's moral reasoning to a higher level. As with the other cognitive-behavioral therapies, changes in reasoning are assumed to be associated with changes in behavior.

Cognitive-behavior treatment can be delivered in individual or group settings. Individualized one-on-one therapy by clinical psychologists or other mental health workers for those who are not seriously mentally ill appears to be impractical in most correctional settings. The cognitive-behavioral treatment programs common in many correctional systems in the United States and Canada today are highly structured programs provided to groups of offenders in classroom-type settings. Frequently, a detailed manual provides instruction on program delivery. The people trained to deliver the program come from a variety of backgrounds and have not necessarily had previous training in counseling or psychology. Those who developed the specific programs often provide training, and they may also have developed a system to ensure quality control. These programs are the focus of this chapter.

THE EFFECTIVENESS OF COGNITIVE-BEHAVIORAL PROGRAMS

My colleagues at the University of Maryland and I have conducted a narrative review of the moral reconation therapy (MRT) and reasoning and rehabilitation (R&R) research (Allen, MacKenzie, & Hickman, 2001) and a meta-analysis of cognitive-behavioral programs (Wilson, Allen, & MacKenzie, in press). Although our review and the meta-analysis examined somewhat different samples, our overall conclusions were similar. Cognitive-behavioral programs appear to be effective in reducing future criminal activities of offenders.

In the narrative review of cognitive-behavioral programs, we examined the effectiveness of the R&R program developed by Ross and Fabiano (1985) and the MRT program developed by Little and Robinson (1988). These are the two most frequently evaluated cognitive-behavioral programs. In the review, we identified twenty-one total studies, fourteen of MRT and seven of R&R (Allen et al., 2001).

The meta-analysis included evaluations of R&R, MRT, and other programs that were characteristic of the cognitive-behavioral programs offered by U.S. correctional systems. To be included in the analysis, studies had to evaluate a cognitive-behavioral model of treatment administered in a group setting with a structured or semistructured protocol designed to reduce criminal behavior. Study participants must have been under the supervision of or referred by the criminal or juvenile justice system. We excluded studies if the treatment consisted of individual counseling, focused only on social life skills or religious or spiritual concepts, or was provided primarily to sex offenders. Based on these criteria, we identified thirty-one articles reporting on twenty distinct studies, thirteen (or 65 percent) of which were evaluations of MRT and R&R and the remaining seven (or 35 percent) were studies representing various types of cognitive-behavioral programs. The narrative review included many studies that evaluated the same sample but reported on outcomes for different periods of time at risk, whereas the meta-analysis only included studies with independent samples.

The studies identified in the earlier narrative review and meta-analysis guided the selection of the final sample of studies for this evaluation of corrections-based cognitive-behavioral treatment programs. Tables 7.1 to 7.3 list the MRT, R&R, and other cognitive program studies with the methods score, recidivism outcome, and follow-up period. The accompanying Appendices 7.1 to 7.3 provide a description of each study.

MORAL RECONATION THERAPY (MRT)

MRT was developed by Little and Robinson (1988) based on a moral development model of offending. The goal of the program is to improve the social, moral, and behavioral deficits of criminal offenders. It is grounded in the theoretical ideas of Kohlberg's cognitive development theory of moral development. According to Kohlberg (1976) moral development progresses through six stages. Only a small percent of the adult population ever attains the highest level of moral reasoning. Higher levels of moral reasoning involve more abstract thinking and the ability to take the perspective of others. Individuals

TABLE 7.1. *Recidivism rates and length of follow-up of cognitive-behavioral studies using moral reconation therapy (MRT)*

Study (methods score)	Measure of recidivism	Recidivism: Experimental (%)	N	Control (%) #1/#2/#3	N	Follow-up period (in months)
Little et al., 1994 (3);	Arrest	65.5	1,052	77.8*	329	
Little et al., 1996 (3)	Incarceration	33.1		48.9*		36
	Incarceration	41.2		56.2*		
	Arrest (*M*)	2.70		3.27		600
Little et al., 1991a (2);	Arrest	61.0	70	70.0	82	36
Little et al., 1993b (3);	Incarceration	24.3		36.6		
Little et al., 1995b (3);	Arrest	73.0		77.0		60
Little et al., 1995a (3)	Incarceration	37.1		54.9*		
	Arrest	74.0		79.0		72
	Incarceration	42.9		58.5*		
	Incarceration	44.3		59.8*		84
Little et al., 1995b (3);	Arrest	20.0	115	27.6	65	12
Little et al., 1993a (3);	Arrest	39.1		46.2		24
Little et al., 1991b (2);	Incarceration	13.9		21.5		
Little et al., 1990 (2);	Arrest	45.2		61.5		36
Little & Robinson, 1989 (2)	Incarceration	22.6		36.9		
	Incarceration	31.3		39.7		42
	Arrest	61.0		73.8		72
	Incarceration	40.0		52.3		
Godwin, Stone, & Hambrock,	Incarceration	11.2	98	29.7*	5,119	12
1995 (3)	Incarceration	25.3		37.3*		24
Burnett, 1996 (2)	Arrest	10.0	30	20.0	30	12
	Incarceration	0.0		10.0*		
Krueger, 1997 (2)	Arrest	11.0	401	51.0	6,727	12
	Arrest	45.0	159	67.0*	25	48
	Arrest	62.0	82	95.0*	25	60

* Significantly different from experimental group, $p < 0.05$.

TABLE 7.2. *Recidivism rates and length of follow-up of reasoning and rehabilitation programs*

Study (methods score)	Measure of recidivism	Recidivism				Follow-up period (in months)
		Experimental (%)	N	Control (%) #1/#2/#3	N	
Porporino & Robinson, 1995 (4)	Conviction	13.0	446	23.0/14.0	104/207	9
	Low Risk	6.0	202	14.0/12.0	42/89	
	High Risk	18.0	244	29.0/14.0	62/118	
	Readmission	29.0	446	47.0/37.0	104/207	
	Low Risk	17.0	202	36.0/33.0*	42/89	
	High Risk	39.0	244	55.0/41.0	62/118	
Ross, 1995 (4)	Readmission	56.0	44	70.0	20	18
	Conviction	35.0		55.0		18
	Conviction	22.0		50.0		29
Ross, Fabriano, & Ewles, 1988 (4)	Conviction[1]	18.0	22	47.5/69.5	17/23	9
	Imprisonment[1]	0.0		11.0/30.0		9
Johnson & Hunter, 1995 (3)	Revocation	26.0	47	29.0/42.0	51/36	12
	Males Only	26.0		32.0/54.0		
Knott, 1995 (3) (comparison groups are listed within the study that may be included in the table)	Conviction[2]	44.0	130	40.0	100	12
	Incarceration[2] (on Reconviction)	37.0	57	27.0	40	
Porporino, Fabiano, & Robinson, 1991 (3) (see also Robinson, Grossman, & Porporino, 1991)	Readmission[1]	45.0	40	52.1	23	19
	New Conviction	20.0		30.4		
	W/out Conviction	25.0	12	21.7	5	19
	Readmission for New Conviction[1]		22		7	
	Low Risk	16.0		0.0		
	High Risk	18.0		42.0		
Raynor & Vanstone, 1996 (3)	Conviction	63.0	59	65.0[2]	164	24
	Incarceration	2.0		15.0		
Robinson, 1995 (3)	Technical Violation	24.8	1,444	25.3	379	12
	Conviction	19.7		24.8*		
	Readmission	44.5		50.1*		

[1] No significant tests reported.
[2] Adjusted to eliminate false positives.
* Significantly different from experimental group, $p < 0.05$.

TABLE 7.3. *Recidivism rates and length of follow-up of cognitive restructuring studies*

		Recidivism				
Study (methods score)	Measure of recidivism	Experimental (%) #1/#2/#3	N	Control (%) #1/#2/#3	N	Follow-up period (in months)
Baro, 1999 (4)	Assaults[1]	24.4	82	24.4	41	12
	Major Misconduct[1]	76.8		75.6		
Curulla, 1991 (3)	Court Charges[1]	6.3	16	27.8/24.4	18/33	6
Hamberger & Hastings, 1988 (3)	Repeat Spousal Violence	28.1	32	47.2	36	12
Henning & Frueh, 1996 (3)	New crime	50.0	28	70.8*	96	24
Kirkpatrick, 1996 (3)	Probation Violation and/or Arrest	35.7	277	61.3*	346	12
Marquis, Bourgon, Armstrong, & Plaff, 1996 (3)	Sample One					12
	Reincarceration	40.9	93	62.0	79	
	Sample Two					
	Reconviction	48.0/36.0/29.0	65/56*/14*	60.0	55	
Menton, 1999 (3)	Arrest	43.6	39	62.5	16	30
Moody, 1997 (3)	Recommitment	50.0	14	50.0	14	18
Siegel & Cole, 1993 (3) $n = 3{,}666$	Drug-Related Vehicular Offense	21.8	N/A[2]	28.6*	N/A[2]	12–24

[1] No significance tests reported.
[2] Sample size by group not reported for Siegel & Cole (1993), total sample equals 3,666.
* Significantly different from experimental group, $p < 0.05$.

at higher levels are less likely to harm others and, therefore, they are less likely to engage in typical criminal activity. Research has generally found support for this proposal. Juvenile delinquents and adult criminals tend to be at early stages of moral reasoning (Arbuthnot & Gordon, 1988).

Little and Robinson (1988) based the MRT program on a moral development model of offending; however, they recognize that criminal offenders have a large number of deficits that go well beyond delayed moral development. In their opinions, offenders who enter treatment are apt to have low levels of moral development as well as to be narcissistic and to have low ego strength, poor self-concepts, low self-esteem, an inability to delay gratification, and strong defense mechanisms. Thus, therapy must be designed to address these problems.

As with the other cognitive-behavioral programs, MRT draws a clear connection between thought processes and behavior. Treatment is highly structured and provided in a group setting. A manual outlines the series of exercises and lessons participants must complete, which are clearly described in the workbook that each participant receives. Furthermore, participants must complete each exercise in the proper sequence before being permitted to proceed to the next exercise. Sessions last one to two hours with approximately two sessions per week.

Table 7.1 shows studies of MRT with samples of offenders who were convicted of felony offenses, felony drug offenses, driving while intoxicated (DWI), and others. The first three groups of studies include one group of offenders (both comparison and experimental groups) showing the recidivism after different lengths of time at risk. For example, Little and colleagues (1991a, 1993b, 1995a, 1995b) examined the recidivism of felony drug offenders who participated in MRT (n = 70) compared to an untreated control group (n = 82) for times at risk of three, five, six, and seven years, respectively. As would be expected, recidivism rates grew larger with increased time at risk. For example, 24.3 percent of the felony drug offenders were reincarcerated after three years in the community; after seven years, the percent reincarcerated grew to 44.3. Little, one of the men who developed the MRT program, was the senior author in all of these studies. As shown in the table, six of the studies conducted by Little and his colleagues were scored a three on the research methods scale (Little et al., 1993a; 1993b; 1994; 1995a; 1995b; 1996). Furthermore, the majority of the studies that were scored a three in methods found significant differences when those who received MRT were compared with the controls. That is, felony offenders and felony drug offenders had significantly lower reincarceration rates than the comparisons. In no case was the recidivism of the treated group higher than the recidivism of the comparison group.

Additionally, Table 7.1 includes evaluations of MRT programs conducted with different samples of offenders from those in the Little and colleagues studies and in other settings. Although all of the studies found that MRT program participants had lower recidivism rates in comparison to the respective control groups, most of these studies are of low methodological rigor, with only the Godwin, Stone, and Hambrock (1995) study reaching a level three on the research methods score. Godwin and colleagues reported that participants receiving MRT as part of a prison-based substance abuse treatment program had significantly lower incarceration rates after both one and two years at risk in the community. In his series of studies (scored a two on the methods scale), Krueger (1997) found that inmates participating in MRT programming had significantly lower rates of rearrest than untreated controls after four and five years.

For the meta-analysis, we identified four independent samples from seven MRT program studies that scored a three on the research methods scale (note: only three distinct samples were identified from all of the studies conducted by Little and his colleagues). Figure 7.1 presents the results of a meta-analysis of four independent samples from seven cognitive-behavioral studies using moral reconciliation therapy. The primary recidivism measures used to calculate the effect sizes were incarceration ($n = 3$) and arrest ($n = 1$). The longest follow-up period for recidivism was used for each study. Four studies from Table 7.1 were excluded because of low methods scores. Overall, those who received MRT treatment had significantly lower recidivism in comparison to the control groups. In sum the research provides strong evidence that MRT programs are effective in reducing the recidivism of offenders.

Moral Reconation Programs

Citation	Effect
Little et al., 1995a	1.87
Little et al., 1996	1.84
Godwin et al., 1995	1.74
Little et al., 1995b	1.65
Mean Odds-Ratio (4)	**1.80**

0.1 0.2 0.5 1 2 5 10

Favors Control Favors Treatment

Figure 7.1. Forest plot showing odds ratio and 95 percent confidence interval for studies of MRT programs.

Reasoning and Rehabilitation (R&R)

Ross and Fabiano (1985) developed R&R based on the premise that offenders are delayed in the development of certain cognitive skills. They came to this conclusion after examining the correctional rehabilitation research literature and identifying a substantial number of studies that indicated significant reductions in recidivism (Gendreau & Ross, 1979; Ross & Gendreau, 1980). In their opinion, the fundamental difference between effective and ineffective programs was how criminal behavior was conceptualized. It was not that ineffective programs conceptualized criminal behavior based on some erroneous conceptual model but rather that they used a "seat of the pants" conjecture about what might work (Ross et al., 1988). In contrast, successful models of rehabilitation viewed offenders' behavior as a consequence of a variety of social, economic, cognitive, and behavioral factors shown by research to be functionally related to antisocial behavior and recidivism. Programs conceptualizing criminal behavior in this way focused on modifying clearly identified behaviors, attitudes, values, and thinking. The one program component common to almost every effective treatment program was some technique designed to change an offender's thinking.

Ross and Fabiano's (1985) review of the literature also led them to conclude that evidence exists to show that offenders have experienced developmental delays in the cognitive skills that are essential for social adaptation. As a result of these deficits, offenders have difficulties with interpersonal problem solving, coping skills, social perspective taking, and critical reasoning. They are apt to be impulsive, egocentric, and illogical and to have antisocial attitudes, values, and beliefs. Therefore, effective treatment should focus on modifying this defective thinking. The goal is to assist offenders in developing more effective problem solving and coping skills so they become more reflective and deliberate in thinking and less antisocial in attitudes, values, and beliefs.

R&R was developed to focus on changing the impulsive, egocentric, illogical, and rigid thinking of delinquents and offenders. They are taught to stop and think before acting, to consider the consequences of their behavior, to conceptualize alternative ways of responding to interpersonal problems, and to think how their behavior impacts other people. The program is designed to assist offenders in developing more effective problem solving and coping skills and more positive social attitudes, values, and beliefs (Ross & Fabiano, 1985; Porporino & Robinson, 1995).

From their knowledge of correctional programs, the developers of R&R assumed it would be impossible to have enough highly specialized staff such as psychiatrists, psychologists, or social workers (or money to hire such staff) to deliver a comprehensive program that would be widely available to delinquents and offenders. Therefore, they designed R&R to be delivered by line officers and other correctional staff. The R&R curriculum is divided into thirty-five sessions and, depending upon the number of sessions per week, runs eight to twelve weeks. The program occurs in a group setting of six to eight participants. A mixture of audio-visual presentations, games, puzzles, reasoning exercises, role playing, modeling, and group discussion techniques and strategies are also used (Ross et al., 1988; Porporino & Robinson, 1995).

Our search of the literature turned up the eight independent R&R studies listed in Table 7.2. A description for each study is provided in Appendix 7.2. Most of the studies used reconviction or reincarceration as the measure of recidivism. Two studies recorded technical violations. In contrast to the research of many other programs, none of the studies used arrest as a measure of recidivism; thus, it is difficult to compare these recidivism rates with the rates from studies examining other programs. Finally, the samples in the studies varied greatly: inmates incarcerated in federal prisons in Canada (Porporino et al., 1991;

Reasoning and Rehabilitation Programs

Citation	Effect
Ross et al., 1988	6.75
Ross, 1995	3.40
Johnson & Hunter, 1995	1.54
Robinson, 1995	1.35
Porporino et al., 1991	1.33
Raynor & Vanstone, 1996	1.12
Porporino & Robinson, 1995	1.09
Knott, 1995	.85
Mean Odds-Ratio (8)	**1.30**

0.1 0.2 0.5 1 2 5 10

Favors Control Favors Treatment

Figure 7.2. Forest plot showing odds ratio and 95 percent confidence interval for studies of R&R treatment programs.

Porporino & Robinson, 1995; Robinson, 1995; Ross, 1995), high-risk probationers in Canada (Ross et al., 1988), parolees in a specialized drug offender program (Johnson & Hunter, 1995), and probationers in the United Kingdom (Knott, 1995) and Wales (Raynor & Vanstone, 1996). Although none of the studies reached a research methods score of five, all of the R&R studies were scored three or four in research methods rigor, indicating relatively strong research designs and methods. Overall, the group receiving the R&R programming had lower recidivism rates than the control group; however, the rates were significantly different in only three of the comparisons.

Figure 7.2 shows the results of a meta-analysis of eight reasoning and rehabilitation programs on offenders' recidivism. The primary recidivism measure used in calculating effect sizes was conviction (n = 6), revocation (n = 1), and readmission (n = 1). The effect sizes for Porporino & Robinson (1995), Ross, Fabriano, and Ewles (1988), and Johnson and Hunter (1995) were calculated by combining both control groups used and taking the weighted mean of the groups' recidivism measures, producing a singular comparison measure. The most recent recidivism measures for each study were used, representing the longest follow-up period. The effect sizes favored the treatment group in all but one study (Knott, 1995). In some cases, there was a significant difference between groups (i.e., the confidence interval did not overlap one on the plot); however, it is noteworthy that several studies did not report significance tests. Yet, as a whole there is strong evidence that R&R is effective in reducing the future criminal activities of offenders.

The results are consistent with our conclusion from both our narrative review and meta-analysis that found R&R to be effective in reducing the recidivism of delinquents and offenders (Wilson et al., 2005; Allen et al., 2001). The meta-analysis illustrated in Figure 7.2 indicates that the overall mean effect size comparing the experimental to the control group was positive and statistically significant, or that R&R participants have lower recidivism than the comparison groups.

Cognitive Restructuring and Other Cognitive-Behavioral Programs

Two major theoretical perspectives underlie cognitive intervention programs: cognitive development and cognitive restructuring. Cognitive development interventions focus on deficits in moral reasoning, social skills, and problem solving that are viewed as delays in normal development. Cognitive restructuring programs focus on thinking distortions rather than deficits. That is, the perspective posits that offenders are not delayed in development but instead have developed faulty thinking patterns. Although the theoretical basis of R&R and MRT is cognitive development, in contrast most of the programs reviewed in this section consider offenders to have cognitive distortions; thus, treatment focuses on restructuring their thinking. Previous research has concluded that cognitive restructuring programs are effective in reducing criminal activities (Wilson et al., in press; Allen et al., 2001).

Table 7.3 lists the nine cognitive-behavioral programs along with the methods score, recidivism measures, outcomes, and follow-up period. Appendix 7.3 provides a description of each study. The nine cognitive-behavioral programs included in this section are varied in both the targeted treatment group and the theoretical perspective. All of the programs can be classified as cognitive-behavioral programs because, similar to R&R and MRT, the underlying assumption is that if thinking patterns are changed, a change in behavior will follow. Only one study (Baro, 1999) scored a four on the research methods score; the remaining studies had some research design problems and thus received a score of three on the research rigor scale.

Theoretical models for two commonly used cognitive restructuring programs are Yochelson and Samenow's errors in criminal thinking (1976) and Bush and Bilodeua's (1993) "Options." Kirkpatrick (1996) and Henning and Frueh (1996) examined programs that used Yochelson and Samenow's model of criminal thinking. Kirkpatrick evaluated a specialized program for drug offenders. The program, called Criminal Intervention, was based loosely on Yochelson and Samenow's errors in thinking model of cognitive change combined with a Christian faith-based component. Henning and Frueh also examined a cognitive restructuring program based on the Yochelson and Samenow's model of cognitive distortions and self-monitoring. In both studies, the treated group had significantly lower recidivism than the comparisons.

After an intensive search, I could only identify one study of the Bush and Bilodeua cognitive restructuring program. Baro (1999) examined the impact on disciplinary infractions including assaults of the Strategies for Thinking Productively (STP) program, an adaptation of Bush and Bilodeua's Options program. Phase I of the program teaches offenders principles of self-change in thinking patterns; Phase II focuses on practicing the skills learned. Prisoners attend fourteen lessons over an eight-week period. As in R&R and MRT, correctional officers, caseworkers, unit managers, and administrators deliver the program to offenders. Of the cognitive restructuring programs, this was the only study to score four in research methods rigor. Findings indicated that the male inmates participating in the program had significantly fewer assaults than the control group. It should be acknowledged that this study is very different from others in this chapter because the study focused on assaults and major misconducts in prison and not in the community.

Several of the cognitive restructuring programs reviewed here were designed to first assess the clients' needs and then provide individualized treatment programs. Thus, they differed in type of offender targeted or type of program provided but were based on a cognitive-behavioral model of treatment. For instance, Marquis, Bourgon, Armstrong, and Pfaff (1996) examined the effectiveness of a cognitive-behavioral program designed to target criminogenic factors such as substance abuse, violent behavior, and criminal attitudes. Participants attended the program for half a day four or five days a week for at least twenty days. The program placed a strong emphasis on anger management strategies. The researchers found very little difference between the treatment and control samples in reincarceration and reconviction rates.

The Weekend Intervention Program (WIP) studied by Siegel and Cole (1993) also begins with assessment followed by individualized treatment. WIP is an alternative to incarceration for people convicted in a municipal or county court of an alcohol- or drug-related vehicular offense. It is a three-day residential program focusing on changing the lifestyles and the role of drugs and alcohol in accomplishing those changes. In contrast to the Marquis et al. (1996) study, Siegel and Cole (1993) found a significant difference between program participants and the comparison group in recidivism rates. However, both studies examined a program that included assessment and individualized treatment, and both studies included offenders with substance abuse problems. Furthermore, participants in the Siegel and Cole (1993) study were permitted to complete a short-term (three-day) residential program in lieu of incarceration, whereas participants in the Marquis et al. (1996) study were placed in a longer-term residential facility. This raises the possibility that the studies examined very different types of offenders, and that accounts for the differing results in outcomes between the programs.

Two studies examined the effectiveness of cognitive-behavioral treatment for spousal batterers. Menton (1999) examined a domestic violence program that educated incarcerated male batterers about violence, anger, and power. The philosophy of the program is based on Lindsey, McBride, and Platt's book *Amend: Philosophy and Curriculum for Treating Batterers* (1993). The program curriculum consisted of twenty-seven hours of treatment divided into 1.5-hour sessions held twice per week during a nine-week period. Menton found that the treatment group had a lower rearrest rate than the comparison group, although this difference was not statistically significant and most likely attributable to the small sample size.

Hamberger and Hastings (1988) also studied a program for convicted male batterers; however, this program was community based rather than in an institution. The program consisted of a fifteen-week cognitive-behavioral skills training program. Similar to the program studied by Menton, the focus was on violence abatement. The authors found that after one year, repeated spousal violence was lower for those who completed the program in comparison to program dropouts.

Moody (1997) studied a juvenile "pair counseling" program designed to increase the moral reasoning and interpersonal relationships of juvenile delinquents with emotional problems. Pair counseling is based on Selman's work with emotionally disturbed children, which addresses their deficits in interpersonal understanding and social perspective taking (Selman & Schultz, 1990). However, rates of recommitment were identical for the treatment and comparison group.

Curulla (1991) studied a community-based aggression replacement training (ART) program for learning disabled misdemeanor offenders. The program consisted of social skills training, anger management, and moral education. The offenders participated in fourteen weeks of ART for two hours weekly. Two groups of participants were compared. One group received all three treatment phases, whereas the other group did not receive the moral education component. Both groups were compared to eligible offenders who did not receive the treatment program. Although the differences in recidivism appear to be large, there were no significant differences among groups. As with many of the studies in this review, most likely this was due to the small number of participants in the study. Overall, in almost all of the cognitive restructuring studies reviewed here, the treated group had lower recidivism rates in comparison to the control group. Furthermore, four of the studies found significant differences in recidivism favoring the treatment group (Henning & Frueh, 1996; Kirkpatrick, 1996; Marquis et al., 1996; Siegel & Cole, 1993). Figure 7.3 presents the results of a meta-analysis of nine independent samples from eight cognitive restructuring studies on offenders' recidivism [note: the study by Marquis et al (1996) includes multiple distinct samples]. The study by Siegel and Cole (1993) was excluded from the plot because the authors did not report sample sizes. Because the recidivism measures used in each study were not uniform, the following measures were used in calculating effect sizes: assaults (n = 1), court charges (n = 1), repeat spousal violence (n = 1), new crime (n = 1), probation violation and/or arrest (n = 1), recidivism (n = 1), rearrest (n = 1), recommitment (n = 1), and drug-related vehicular offense (n = 1). The effect size for Curulla (1991) was calculated using a singular comparison measure by combining both control groups and taking the weighted

Cognitive Restructuring Programs

Citation	Effect
Curulla, 1991	5.13
Kirkpatrick, 1996	2.84
Henning & Frueh, 1996	2.43
Marquis et al., 1996 (Sample One)	2.36
Hamberger & Hastings, 1988	2.29
Marquis et al., 1996 (Sample Two)	2.18
Menton, 1999	2.16
Moody, 1997	1.00
Baro, 1999	.93
Mean Odds-Ratio (9)	**2.37**

0.1 0.2 0.5 1 2 5 10

Favors Control Favors Treatment

Figure 7.3. Forest plot showing odds ratio and 95 percent confidence interval for studies of cognitive restructuring treatment programs.

mean of the groups' recidivism measures. The most recent recidivism measures were used, representing the longest follow-up period. The effect size in six of the studies favored the treated group (lower recidivism for treated group), two studies favored the comparison, and one found no difference. The overall mean effect size significantly favored the treated group with the confidence interval not overlapping one.

CONCLUSION

This chapter examined cognitive-behavioral programs of the type that operate in many correctional systems in the United States and Canada. These programs are based on cognitive-behavioral theory of human change. Cognitions are assumed to affect behavior and changes in cognitions can bring about changes in behavior. All of the programs attempt to change the thinking patterns of offenders and delinquents. The programs are usually relatively short term and highly structured and can be delivered by correctional officers and other staff not trained in psychology or social work. However, the programs differ in their views of the problems of offenders. MRT and R&R are based on the belief that offenders have cognitive deficits or developmental delays, whereas cognitive restructuring programs are based on the belief that offenders have developed faulty thinking patterns during development.

This review of the literature, as well as previous meta-analyses and narrative reviews, demonstrate that these programs are effective in reducing the criminal behavior of offenders. Using the criteria of the Maryland scale for scientific rigor, overall there are a sufficient number of studies ranking three or more that find significant differences to enable me to conclude that these cognitive-behavioral programs as a whole are effective. Also, the programs studied varied greatly in the type of participants (e.g., batterers, drug offenders, DWI, etc.) and where the program was held (e.g., prison, community, jail). The consistency of the results leads me to conclude that these programs are effective for adult offenders in a variety of settings. Only one study examined the effect of the program on juveniles (Moody 1997) and found no evidence that the program was effective.

Although these studies consistently demonstrated that those receiving any of the three types of cognitive-behavioral therapy had lower recidivism rates than the comparison group, there are some differences among the three programs examined. The results for the ten studies of R&R are not strong in the sense that only two studies found significant differences in recidivism, and when the effect sizes were compared, only two of the individual studies were significant. Overall, the effect size demonstrated a small but significant difference favoring the treated group. Although the results consistently demonstrated lower recidivism for the treated group, this difference was not always statistically significant.

The results for MRT programs show stronger support for the effectiveness of the programs. Significant differences favoring the MRT treated groups were found in the studies of felony offenders, felony drug offenders, and in the other settings. The effect sizes indicated that all of the effects favored the treated group, and the effects were significant for three of the studies. Overall, the mean effect was significant and favored the treated group. However, for both MRT and R&R, those who developed the programs conducted most of the evaluations. Hence, possibly, the researchers were able to guarantee the quality control of program delivery during the research. It is unclear whether the programs will continue to have positive effects in other contexts.

The results from the cognitive restructuring programs were also positive. Nine programs reached a level of three or greater on the methods score, four studies found significant differences, and the results in all but one of the studies favored the treated group. The effect sizes indicated a significant overall effect, and three of the individual studies had significant effects. However, it is noteworthy that these studies varied greatly in type of offender studied and location of treatment.

In summary, cognitive-behavioral programs are successful in reducing the future criminal activities of offenders. The programs appear to be effective in a variety of settings and for a variety of offenders. It would be interesting in the future for researchers to examine differences in effectiveness based on these differences in settings and offenders. For example, there is little research examining the effectiveness of these programs for juveniles. Furthermore, given that Little and his colleagues found significant differences in recidivism for felony offenders and felony drug offenders but not for DWI offenders, this suggests that the effectiveness of the program may differ by type of offender. Similarly, although one R&R study found large differences between the treated and untreated samples in reconvictions for high-risk probationers (Ross et al., 1988), in another study (Porporino & Robinson, 1995) the low risk group appeared to be more affected by the program than the high risk group. In sum, studies examining for whom the programs are effective and in what settings will be a valuable addition to the literature.

APPENDIX 7.1. STUDY REFERENCE, DESCRIPTION, AND METHODS SCORES (IN PARENTHESES) OF MORAL RECONATION TREATMENT FOR OFFENDERS

Burnett, 1996 (2)

Postincarcerated offenders who received MRT treatment between February and September 1994 in three Washington State counties were compared to untreated controls.

Godwin et al., 1995 (3)

Voluntary participants receiving MRT between January 1993 and December 1993 as part of a prison-based substance abuse treatment program in Lake County, Florida, Detention Center compared to untreated controls.

Little et al., 1994 (3); Little et al., 1996 (3)

Voluntary participants receiving MRT-based programs as part of the drug therapeutic community at Shelby County Correction Center in Tennessee compared to untreated controls.

Little et al., 1991a (**2**); Little et al., 1993b (**3**); Little et al., 1995b (**3**); Little et al., 1995a (**3**)

Felony drug offenders treated with MRT and released between 1987 and 1988 from the Shelby County Correction Center compared to untreated controls.

Little et al., 1995b (**3**); Little et al., 1993a (**3**); Little et al., 1991b (**2**); Little and Robinson, 1990 (**2**); Little and Robinson, 1989c (**2**)

Felons treated with MRT and released between 1987 and 1988 from the Shelby County Correction Center who were multiple DWI offenders compared to untreated DWI offenders.

Krueger, 1997(**2**)

MRT program implemented in April 1992 at the Wayne County Jail in Wooster, Ohio. Approximately eighty inmates participated in the program each year in the ongoing, open-ended group. Most inmates serve nine months or less at the facility, and no incentives were offered for inmate participation. In the one-year follow-up, MRT-treated inmates who had been released for a year or more (n = 401) were compared to all jail inmates (n = 6,727). In the four-year follow-up, MRT-treated inmates who had been released for four years (n = 159) were compared to a random sample of untreated inmates who had been released for equivalent amount of time (n = 25). In the five-year follow-up, MRT-treated inmates who had been released for five years (n = 82) were compared to untreated controls (n = 25).

APPENDIX 7.2. STUDY REFERENCE, DESCRIPTION, AND METHODS SCORES (IN PARENTHESES) OF REASONING AND REHABILITATION TREATMENT FOR OFFENDERS

Johnson and Hunter, 1995 (**3**)

Colorado parolees beginning in January 1991 participating in the Specialized Drug Offender Program randomly assigned to receive treatment with cognitive components compared to (1) program participants without cognitive component and (2) regular probation.

Knott, 1995 (**3**)

Probationers participating in Straight Thinking on Probation (STOP) R&R program in the United Kingdom beginning in 1991 compared to a control group of probationers.

Porporino and Robinson, 1995 **(4)**
Adult male offenders in Canadian federal system were randomly assigned to R&R or to a waiting-list control group. Program completers compared to (1) dropouts and (2) wait-list controls. Additional comparisons made for groups classified into high and low risk categories.

Porporino et al., 1991 **(3)** (see also Robinson, Grossman, & Porporino 1991)
Canadian incarcerated male offenders who completed the Cognitive Skills Training Program and had been released into the community compared to offenders who volunteered but did not participate. Additional comparisons made for groups classified into high and low risk categories.

Ross, 1995 **(4)**
Adult male offenders in Canadian federal system were randomly assigned to R&R or the waiting-list control group.

Ross et al., 1988 **(4)**
Canadian high risk male probationers assigned to the Cognitive Training group (including critical thinking, assertiveness training, and structured learning theory) compared to (1) regular probation plus life skills training and (2) regular probation only.

Raynor and Vanstone, 1996 **(3)**
Probationers participating and completing the STOP R&R program in Wales compared to those referred to a custodial comparison group.

Robinson, 1995 **(3)**
Participants who completed a Canadian Cognitive Skills Training program compared to a waiting-list control group.

APPENDIX 7.3. STUDY REFERENCE, DESCRIPTION, AND METHODS SCORES (IN PARENTHESES) OF COGNITIVE RESTRUCTURING TREATMENT FOR OFFENDERS

Baro, 1999 **(4)**
Male offenders in the Michigan Reformatory who completed Phase I and offenders who completed Phase I and began Phase II of a cognitive restructuring and relapse prevention program compared

to inmates receiving other self-help programs (e.g., AA, NA, religious/cultural, education).

Curulla, 1991 **(3)**

Learning-disabled offenders through the Northeast District Court in the state of Washington receiving Aggression Replacement Training (ART) in the community with moral education compared to (1) ART without moral education and (2) eligible learning-disabled offenders with no treatment.

Hamberger and Hastings, 1988 **(3)**

Convicted male batterers in the community completing a fifteen-session cognitive behavioral violence abatement program including cognitive restructuring compared to treatment dropouts.

Henning and Frueh, 1996 **(3)**

Male offenders released between June 1988 and September 1993 from the medium-security Northwest State Correctional Facility completing cognitive self changes therapy and cognitive monitoring with group and individual therapy compared to offenders in same facility receiving no treatment.

Kirkpatrick, 1996 **(3)**

Male offenders placed under community supervision between November 1992 and October 1994 who were court mandated to participate in Criminal Intervention, a cognitive restructuring treatment program by the Allen County Community Corrections Project in Fort Wayne, Indiana, compared to a group of offenders placed in community supervision in the same time period who did not receive treatment.

Marquis et al., 1996 **(3)**

Sample One: Offenders in a residential facility in Canada who participated in some form of substance abuse relapse prevention programming during 1991–1992 compared to eligible group housed in same facility on the waiting list for treatment.

Sample Two: Offenders in a residential facility in Canada who participated in some form of (1) substance abuse relapse prevention programming, (2) substance abuse programming and anger management programming, and (3) an anger management program during 1993–1994 compared to eligible group housed in same facility on the waiting list for treatment.

Menton, 1999 **(3)**

Convicted male batterers between July 1994 and December 1996 released into the community participating in cognitive restructuring (completers and dropouts) through the Domestic Violence Program at Norfolk County Sheriff's Office and Correction Center in Massachusetts compared to group released at same time who chose not to participate in treatment.

Moody, 1997 **(3)**

Male juveniles incarcerated at North Carolina training school who voluntarily participated in pair counseling that incorporated social skills and moral reasoning compared to group of juveniles in the same institution who received no treatment.

Siegel and Cole, 1993 **(3)**

Offenders adjudicated in eleven Ohio counties between March 1983 and July 1984 with drug- or alcohol-related vehicular conviction who completed the WIP, a three-day intensive residential program with cognitive restructuring and relapse prevention, in lieu of incarceration compared to offenders placed in jail or receiving a fine.

PART THREE

TARGETING SPECIFIC TYPES OF OFFENDERS

CHAPTER EIGHT

Sex Offender Treatment

INTRODUCTION

The term *sex offender* includes various types of offenders. From the perspective of the criminal justice system, sex offenders are usually classified into two categories: (1) people who have committed forcible rape and (2) people who have committed sexual assault (this includes statutory rape; sodomy; incest; offenses against chastity, common decency, and morals; unwanted sexual contact; and fondling). According to the FBI UCRs, the number of reported forcible rapes of females in the United States in 2004 was 63.5 for every 100,000 females in the population (Federal Bureau of Investigation, 2004). However, accurate estimates of the incidence of sexual crimes are extremely difficult to obtain because many victims fail to report such offenses.

Of the approximately 5 million people under some type of correctional supervision in the United States in 1994, only 4.7 percent were convicted of a sexual offense (the most serious crime of conviction). Almost 60 percent of the convicted sex offenders are in the community. Many of those in prison will also be returned to the community. Furthermore, offenders convicted of either rape or sexual assault receive sentences averaging 12.5 and 8.5 years, respectively (Greenfeld, 1997). Although the sentence lengths have not changed in the past decade, the amount of time these offenders actually spend in prison has increased because they serve a larger percentage of their sentence in prison. The length of stay for rape convictions has increased from 3.5 years to 5 years, and the length of stay for sex assault convictions increased from 2 to 3 years (Greenfield, 1997).

Figure 8.1 shows the percentage of convicted sex offenders under different types of correctional supervision (Greenfield, 1997). As seen, convicted sex offenders make up a relatively small percentage of the correctional population. Also, these percentages differ greatly by the jurisdiction being examined. Most imprisoned sex offenders are males (approximately 99 percent) who have previously been convicted of a felony (60 percent); 10 to 15 percent have previously been convicted of a sex offense. According to estimates from the Bureau of Justice Statistics (Greenfield, 1997), within three years of release from prison, approximately 50 percent of sex offenders will be rearrested for a new sex offense and 34 percent will be reconvicted. Thus, although sex offenders are a relatively small percentage of the total correctional population, the severity of their crimes and the high recidivism rates makes them a serious concern for corrections.

THEORETICAL PERSPECTIVES

Researchers and clinicians who study and treat sex offenders have two different philosophies about the assessment, etiology, and treatment of sex offenders. One group believes that sex offenders with sexual disorders must be distinguished from other offenders who may be convicted of a sex offense but do not have a disorder. Those who hold this view believe that sex offenders diagnosed with sexual disorders should be targeted for specialized treatment, whereas other types of generalized treatment programs may be more appropriate for offenders without such disorders. The second perspective holds that there are no fundamental differences within the sex offender population or between sex offenders and other types of offenders. Instead, typologies or classification systems are developed for subtypes of sex offenders, based typically on behavior and motive for the offense. Thus, treatment is designed to address the specific criminogenic characteristics of the different classes, much like one would with violent or drug offenders. According to advocates of this perspective, sex offenders have some problems directly related to sex offending and these need to be addressed in treatment; however, many of their problems are similar to those of other types of offenders. For this reason, general treatment programs designed for other types of offenders may also be appropriate for sex offenders.

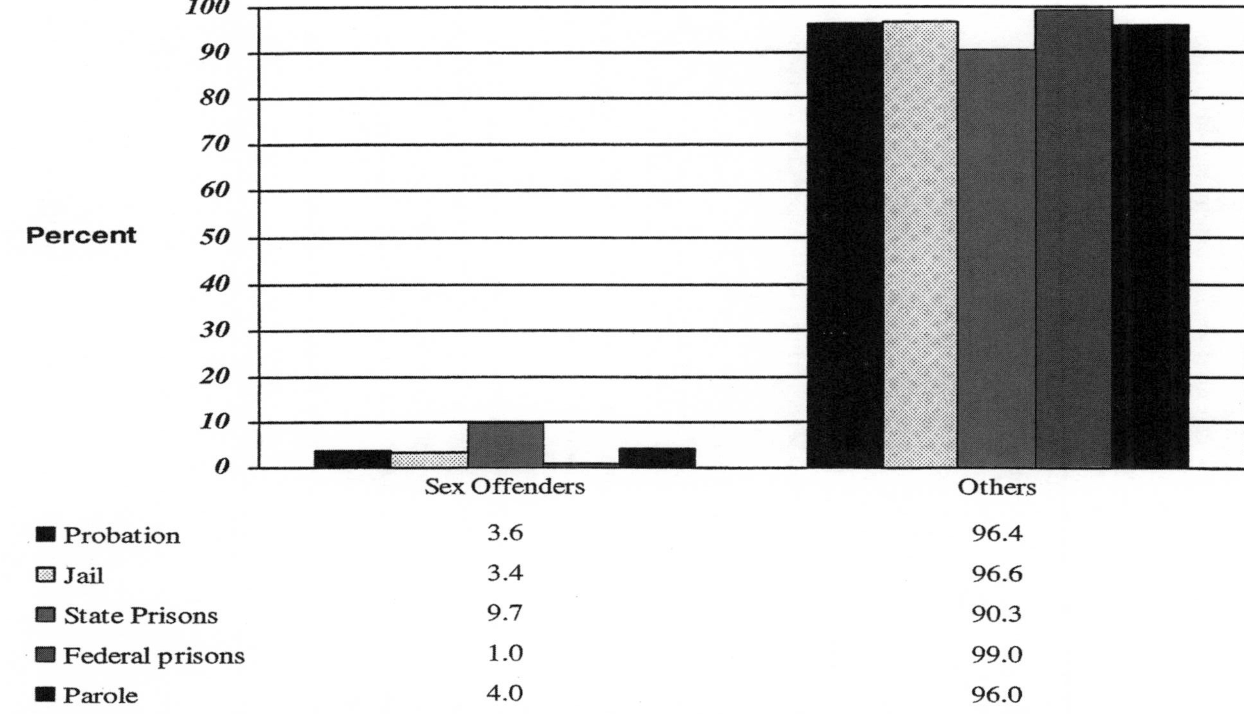

Figure 8.1. Percentage of convicted offenders under correctional supervision who are sex offenders.

Sex Offenders with Sexual Disorders

From the perspective of the criminal justice system, sex offenders are offenders who are convicted of sex offenses (i.e., rape and sexual assault). However, many psychologists, psychiatrists, and clinical social workers would not consider that all of these offenders suffer from sexual disorders. For example, if a man breaks into a house to commit a burglary, finds a woman alone in bed, and decides to rape her, the criminal justice system will define him as a sex offender. However, from a mental health perspective, although he may have other cognitive deficits and problems that led to his illegal behavior, he may not necessarily be suffering from an abnormal mental condition related to his sexual makeup. His behavior would not be classified as a disease but would be instead considered criminal. It is possible to come up with many other examples of sex offenses committed by someone who does not have a sexual disorder.

Those who make this distinction between sex offenders with and without sexual disorders believe that sex offender treatment should focus on the offenders with sexual disorders. The offenders with sexual disorders are predisposed to misbehave sexually because there is something fundamentally different about their sexual makeup. Many people who have worked with individuals with sexual disorders believe that as people mature, they discover the nature of their own sexual orientation and interests (Berlin, 2000). These individuals do not consciously choose of their own volition to be different; they discover their differences as they develop.

The ways individuals differ from each other sexually can be described in one of four ways (Berlin, 2000). First, people differ in the behaviors they find sexually arousing. Arousing behaviors vary from the conventional (e.g., missionary position during intercourse) to behaviors that are usually labeled deviant by society such as sadomasochism. The second way people differ is in the kind of partners toward whom they are sexually attracted. The majority of the adult population is attracted primarily to adults of the opposite sex; however, many adults have homosexual attractions. A small percent, pedophiles, are attracted to children. Third, people differ in the strength of their sexual drive. That is, they differ in the degree of intensity of sexual desire, the extent to which their sex drive motivates their behavior, and the difficulty they have in trying to resist sexual temptations. Many sex offenders with sexual disorders have difficulty resisting their erotic temptations. Finally, people differ in attitudes about sexual behavior and whether sexual temptations should be resisted. For example, some people believe that sexual intercourse should be delayed until marriage. A pedophile may believe that there is nothing wrong with having sexual intercourse with children.

Differences in these four characteristics help to explain sexual disorders or paraphilias as defined by the *Diagnostic and Statistical Manual of Mental Disorders* (DSM-IV; American Psychiatric Association, 1994). According to most psychiatric textbooks, a paraphilic disorder is characterized by intense, recurrent, erotically arousing fantasies and urges involving inappropriate objects or coercive sexual activities. These are typically directed toward (1) nonhuman objects, (2) suffering or humiliation, or (3) children or other nonconsenting people (American Psychiatric Association, 1994). Individuals may have intense and recurrent erotically arousing fantasies about behaviors such as cross-dressing (transvestitic fetishes) or exhibitionism. Others have recurrent cravings for sexual partners such as animals (zoophilia) or children (pedophilia).

Many researchers and clinicians who work directly with sex offenders believe that specialized treatment is needed for sex offenders with these sexual disorders. Treatment of sex offenders begins with an assessment of the offender to identify whether the behavior is the result of an abnormal sexual makeup. This must be distinguished from behavior that reflects other deficits or problems such as impulsiveness or antisocial personality (Berlin, 2000). That is, paraphilic behavior does not simply reflect a character issue, lack of self-control, or misuse of power; therefore, offenders diagnosed with a sexual disorder should receive specialized treatment designed for sex offenders. Other types of treatment programs such as cognitive skills or victim awareness may be useful for offenders convicted of sex offenses who are not identified as suffering from a sexual disorder but exhibit other problems. However, treatment programs offered within the criminal justice system or used to treat offenders do not always make the distinction between offenders convicted of sex crimes with and without a sexual disorder.

Etiology of Sexual Disorders

We do not know what causes sexual disorders. Research suggests that sexual orientation and disposition are related to biology and are relatively stable and that signs of sexual disorder show up early in life (Buhrich, Bailey, & Martin, 1991; Collaer & Hines, 1995). There appears to be something fundamentally and biologically different about the sexual makeup of people with sexual disorders that predisposes them to commit sexual offenses (Berlin, 2000). As they mature, individuals with sexual disorders discover their sexual aberrations; it is not a conscious choice.

Both life experiences and constitution play a role in determining sexual makeup. There is little evidence that sexual disorders result from genetic abnormalities alone. For example, in studies of males whose sexual organs had been damaged during infancy, Money (1980) found genetic males changed through surgery and hormone therapy who were raised as girls had female gender identities and were attracted to males. Conversely, researchers comparing people with paraphilic disorders to others who have conventional interests have found that a significant majority of those with sexual disorders had biological abnormalities such as chromosomal anomalies, abnormal testosterone levels, or pathological electroencephalograms (Berlin, 2000). From this work, Berlin concludes that there may be an association between certain kinds of biological abnormalities and unconventional kinds of sexual interests.

Another factor that seems to be associated with sexual disorders is a history of childhood sexual abuse. Although most children who experience abuse do not grow up to have sexual disorders, many individuals with sexual disorders had been abused by adults when they were children. In these instances, sexual abuse during childhood appears to have a negative impact on subsequent sexual development that predisposes the individual to have abnormal sexual cravings as an adult (Groth, 1979; Money, 1980). Hence, those who believe in the importance of separating those with sexual disorders from other sex offenders argue that a history of childhood abuse and biological abnormality are risk factors that increase the probability that an individual will have a sexual disorder.

Similarities Between Sex Offenders and Other Offenders

The second perspective on sex offenders and their treatment is that sex offenders are not fundamentally different from other offenders and so a different approach to theory, assessment, and treatment is not required (Andrews & Bonta, 2003). From this perspective, sex offenders have many of the same dynamic risk factors that nonsexual offenders have; therefore, treatment should focus on changing these factors.

Evidence in support of this perspective comes from research examining the criminal behavior of sex offenders. Convicted sex offenders engage in many types of criminal activities, not only deviant sexual activity. Studies of sex offenders in both institutions (Weinrott & Saylor, 1991) and outpatient clinics (Maletzky, 1991) demonstrate that many of them have a history of nonsexual offending. Weinrott and Saylor (1991) found this was true of rapists and also of child molesters, who are often considered to limit their deviance to children. Furthermore, longitudinal studies have found that many sex offenders go on to commit future sexual and nonsexual crimes (Bench, Kramer, & Erickson, 1997; Hanson & Bussiere, 1998). For example, in a meta-analysis, Hanson and Bussiere found an average nonsexual recidivism rate of 12.2 percent after 4.5 years.

Not only do sex offenders commit many nonsexual crimes, but those factors found to predict nonsexual offending also predict sex offending (Andrews & Bonta, 1998). For example, antisocial personality and antisocial cognitions have been found to be the major dynamic risk factors for recidivism for both sex offenders and other types of offenders (Andrews & Bonta, 1998; Hanson & Bussiere, 1998).

Another similarity between sex offenders and other types of offenders is their association with other offenders. That is, future offending by nonsexual offenders can be successfully predicted as a function of their association with other antisocial individuals. There is also some evidence that sex offenders associate with each other. In support of this, Hanson and Scott (1996) found that child molesters reported knowing other child molesters and rapists knew other rapists, but nonsexual offenders did not report any sex offender associates.

In attempts to understand and appropriately treat sex offenders, some clinicians and researchers have proposed classification schemes for rapists (Groth, 1979; Knight & Prentky, 1990) and pedophiles (Groth, 1978; Knight, 1988). The Groth (1979) typology classified anger, power, and sadistic rapes based on the presumed motivations and aims of rapists. Knight and Prentky (1990) classify rapists into opportunistic, pervasively angry, sexual, or vindictive depending upon the behaviors and motives involved in rape. Pedophiles are classified as immature, regressed, exploitative, or aggressive/sadistic based on the behaviors and motives involved in the crime. It should be noted that these schemes are designed to include all sex offenders and not only those with sexual disorders. However, researchers have not examined differences in the effectiveness of treatment based on a match between the proposed sex offender classification and type of treatment.

TREATMENT APPROACHES

Designing treatment for sex offenders depends upon a number of factors, including contemporary perspectives on the underlying causes of the behavior, the training of treatment providers, the available resources, the voice of victim advocates, and the climate within the correctional system. A number of treatment components are used today, and a few are particularly distinctive in both theory and practice. Broadly defined, these treatment types include behavioral, cognitive-behavioral, and medical (General Accounting Office, 1996). However, less clearly delineated treatment strategies include an amalgamation of a number of treatment elements not specific to sex offenders, such as individual and family psychotherapy, victim awareness, and sex education. Many of these treatment programs do not distinguish between sex offenders with sexual disorders and others.

In the early and middle twentieth century, sex offenders were viewed as suffering from a sickness. This viewpoint was highly compatible with the larger positivist perspective in which offenders and their behaviors were thought to be the result of an individual's illness or societal troubles. Professionals were optimistic that this malady, among others, could be reversed with intensive psychotherapy. Although this approach gave way in the 1950s and 1960s when tenets from behaviorism and conditioning emerged as the dominant conceptualization

(Laws, 1995), psychotherapy remains a popular component in treatment packages.

The idea that sex offenders suffer from poor mental health is evident in today's approaches. In the less clearly identifiable treatment category, which will be referred to as generalized psychosocial treatments, a number of components are used alone or in combination to remedy the offenders' poor mental health and to bolster their ability to function normally. In a survey of juvenile sex offender treatment programs at state-operated correctional institutions, Sapp and Vaughn (1990) reported that sex education and victim empathy, among other treatment modalities, were offered by 90 percent of the institutions. Social skills training is yet another popular treatment component. McFall (1990) concluded, however, that social skills training is not based on a coherent theory; that is, there is no coherent theoretical basis for inferring that sex offenders are generally lacking social skills.

The one guiding principle behind these approaches is that sex offenders suffer from poor mental health and any program that improves mental health and well-being should also help reduce future rates of sexual offending. This is clearly the assumption of the common practice of referring sex offenders to nonspecific community-based psychotherapy. Competent psychologists, psychiatrists, or social workers are likely to adopt the therapeutic modality under which they were trained, be it psychodynamic, eclectic, or rational emotive. Unless they have specialized training in the treatment of sex offenders, it is highly unlikely that they will provide treatment tailored to the needs of the sex offender. However, the correctional treatment literature is at odds with this approach, generally concluding that theoretically derived and focused interventions prove more fruitful than combinations of miscellaneous treatment approaches (Andrews, Bonta, & Hoge, 1990; Andrews, Zinger, et al., 1990; MacKenzie, 1997).

Psychotherapy

Psychodynamic theory assumes that people ordinarily develop conventional erotic attractions toward age-appropriate partners of the opposite sex; however, unhealthy early life experiences may interfere with this normal process of maturation. Using a process of introspection, therapy is directed toward identifying what went wrong during development. It is assumed that understanding the problems will facilitate the correction of the problem. Therapy may be either in individual or group settings.

Chemical or Surgical Castration

Hormonal and medical treatments reflect a biological perspective on the causes of sex offending. These treatments seek to lower the physiological drive of offenders through hormone manipulation (Marshall, Eccles, & Barbaree, 1991). Testosterone is thought to be the most important hormone influencing sexual behavior in human males, and thus it is theorized that lowering testosterone will reduce sexual offending. Testosterone can be lowered through surgical castration or by using various medications, often called chemical castration. Surgical castration is the removal of the testes (not the penis) because the testes are the major source of testosterone production in the body.

Today, testosterone levels are usually lowered pharmacologically. The most often used drug is medroxyprogesterone acetate (MPA) or Depo-Provera (Berlin, 2000; Money, Wideling, Walker, & Gain, 1976). The drug can be injected intramuscularly once per week. Blood tests confirm that MPA decreases serum testosterone levels significantly. The goal is to reduce the intensity of the sexual cravings among those with sexual disorders.

Hormonal treatment is often administered in concert with other forms of treatment, most typically psychotherapy. Using a combination of biological and psychological perspectives, this hybrid approach reflects the view that physiological factors are not solely responsible for sexual offending. The hybrid approach attempts to reduce the sexual cravings of the offender while simultaneously improving their cognitive ability to control their sexual behavior. Self-deception is also a characteristic of many individuals with sexual disorders, particularly pedophiles. They rationalize that their activities with children are not damaging to the child and that the child enjoys the relationship. Psychotherapy attacks this self-deception to help offenders stop rationalizing their activities and to help them resist their urges.

Behavioral Treatment

Behavioral approaches, based on the theories of behaviorism, have been designed specifically for sex offenders. The goal is the reduction of sex offending through the modification of inappropriate sexual preferences (Quinsey & Earls, 1990). Behavioral therapists are less concerned about whether the individual has an underlying disorder and are more concerned with changing the observed behavior. Researchers have repeatedly found that sex offenders frequently report ruminating over sexual fantasies involving the types of behaviors in which they engage. Furthermore, the relative amount of sexual arousal elicited by deviant and nondeviant cues in phallometric assessment consistently differentiates sex offenders such as child molesters, rapists, and sadists from other males (Quinsey, 1986). Therefore, behavioral therapy focuses on changing inappropriate sexual interests.

Behavioral treatment usually begins by assessing the offenders' sexual preferences through self-report, criminal history, or phallometric measures. Phallometric assessments or penile plethysmography uses physiological monitors to measure penile tumescence. The monitor is attached to the penis and measures erections in response to various stimuli. Phallometric measures are considered more objective indicators of arousal than self-report; however, even these measures are susceptible to error (Quinsey & Chaplin, 1988). With the phallometric assessment procedure, it is assumed that the client acts in accord with the identified preferences. When the phallometric assessment demonstrates that the offender prefers an inappropriate stimulus (e.g., child, forced sex) or has poor discrimination between appropriate and inappropriate stimulus categories, the inappropriate sexual interest is targeted for intervention. Because decreases in deviant sexual interests do not necessarily increase appropriate sexual interests, therefore, some therapists provide follow-up treatment designed to increase nondeviant arousal. As of yet, there is little research examining the effectiveness of this strategy.

Three commonly used behavioral treatment techniques are aversion therapy, covert sensitization, and satiation. Aversion therapy couples a negative stimulus with a paraphilic stimulus or with sexual arousal in the presence of a paraphilic stimulus. For example, the offender may receive a mild shock to the arm with the presentation of a slide of a nude female child (a classical conditioning paradigm) or the client may be shocked when some criterion of penile tumescence increase occurs during an audiotaped description of a violent rape, but not when consenting sex is depicted (a signaled punishment paradigm).

Covert sensitization, which requires clients to imagine aversive events associated with a paraphilic stimulus, has recently become more popular than electrical aversion. Satiation is another behavioral technique that has been used to reduce inappropriate sexual interest. This technique requires offenders to masturbate while fantasizing aloud about sexually appropriate themes and continue to masturbate after switching to a very detailed description of a paraphillic fantasy. This is continued for a lengthy period designed to produce boredom. Offenders receiving behavioral treatment are frequently taught to use a variety of strategies, and treatment is often extended into the community.

Cognitive-Behavioral Treatment

Cognitive-behavioral treatment is concerned with teaching offenders the mental skills necessary for controlling their own behaviors. This form of treatment reflects the philosophy that sexual offending is a choice made by the offender, over which he or she has cognitive control, albeit limited, and reflects a social learning or cognitive-behavioral theoretical model (e.g., Bandura, 1977). The focus of treatment is on the cognitive distortions and dysfunctional thought processes of the sex offender. The cognitive-behavioral perspective downplays the emphasis on the underlying roots of the behavior in favor of identifying the high risk situations that may support it (Laws, 1995). Treatment is concentrated on the pragmatic goal of altering the behavior through teaching offenders the skills of self-reinforcement and the monitoring of their internal dialogue through "various forms of modeling and cognitive restructuring" (Laws, 1995:42).

Since the 1980s, this treatment has been widely adopted by the correctional field and touted as among the most promising. The success of this treatment often is attributed to its structured and focused nature (Izzo & Ross, 1990; MacKenzie, 1997). Encompassed within this category is the popular relapse prevention approach, which provides offenders with training in the identification of relapse warning signs and coping methods necessary to derail the chain of events leading to sexual offending (Guarino & Kimball, 1998; Laws, 1995; Nicholaichuk, 1996).

These treatments have been offered to a wide variety of sex offenders, ranging from inhibited exhibitionists to violent predatory rapists. This indicates a lack of consensus as to whether different sex offending behaviors should be considered as falling within a spectrum of general sex offending or whether the categories of sex offending should be considered as a true typology.

EFFECTIVENESS OF SEX OFFENDER TREATMENT

Previous literature reviews and meta-analyses examining the effectiveness of sex offender treatment have shown little consistency in their conclusions. For example, after reviewing the literature, Furby, Weinrott, and Blackshaw (1989) and Quinsey, Harris, Rice, and Lalumiere (1993) concluded that there is no convincing evidence that treatment reduces future sexual offending. However, Hall (1995), in a meta-analysis, and Marshall, Jones, Ward, Johnston, and Barbaree (1991) and Blanchette (1996), in literature reviews, concluded that research does show the benefit of treatment.

Our search of the literature turned up twenty-eight documents with twenty-five independent studies meeting the study's eligibility criteria. Studies were considered eligible for the review if they evaluated a treatment program for adolescent or adult sex offenders, were written in English language, had a measure of sexual reoffending as an outcome, and had a comparison group of nontreated offenders or that was not specific to sex offenders. Only evaluations of treatment programs delivered after 1970 were included because treatment prior to 1970 may have been characteristically different from current treatment practices. All of the evaluations reviewed here were completed after 1975.

Subjects in the studies were exclusively males. There were a variety of sex offender types, and many studies included several different types participating in the same program. Most often the studies included pedophiles (64 percent of the studies) and rapists (52 percent of the studies). Additionally, a variety of recidivism measures were reported: rearrests (n = 10), reconvictions (n = 6), charged or reconvictions (n = 2), reoffending (n = 2), relapse (n = 2), self-report recidivism (n = 1), new arraignment (n = 1), rearrest including self-report (n = 1), recidivism (n = 1), reoffending/relapse (n = 1), and rearrests/convictions/technical violations (n = 1).

The methods scores, recidivism measures, outcomes, and follow-up period of the studies are listed in Tables 8.1–8.4. The accompanying

TABLE 8.1. *Studies of cognitive-behavioral treatment with relapse prevention for sex offenders showing recidivism rates and length of follow-up*

		Recidivism				
Study (methods score)	Measure of recidivism	Experimental (%)	N	Control (%) #1/#2/#3	N	Follow-up period (in Months)
Borduin et al., 1994 (5)	Reoffending		8		8	$M = 37.2$
	Sex	12.5		75.0*		
	Nonsex	25.0		50.0		
	Arrests (*M*)					
	Sex	0.12		1.62*		
	Nonsex	0.62		2.25		
Nicholaichuk et al., 1995 (4)	Reconvictions		296		283	70.8 for Treatment Group
	Sex	14.5		33.2*		
	Non-Sex	32.1		35.0		
	Return to Fed Prison					
	Sex	6.1		20.5*		87.6 for Comparison Group
	Nonsex	7.8		7.1		
Hanson et al., 1993 (4)	Reconvictions		106		31/60	$M = 108$, $M = 336$, and $M = 240$ Respectively
	Sex/Violent	44.0		48.0/33.0		
Marques et al., 1994 (4)	Rearrests		98		97/96	$M = 34.8$
	Sex	8.2		13.4/12.5		
	Other Violent	8.2		17.5/ 9.4		
Marshall et al., 1991 (3)	Charged or Reconvicted		17		23/21	48
	Sex	23.6		39.1/57.1*		
Guarino & Kimball, 1998 (3)	New Arraignments	30.3	44	48.0	31	12
McGrath et al., 1998 (3)	Arrests		71		32/19	$M = 62.4$
	Sex	1.4		15.6/10.5		
	Nonsex	1.4		3.1/15.7		
	Nonviolent	7.0		15.6/36.8		
	Probation Violation	25.4		28.1/47.3*		

Huot, 1999 (2)	Rearrests		65		159/27	72 (approx.)
	Sex	14.0		20.0/22.0		
	Person Offense	9.0		21.0/19.0		
	Any	11.0		18.0/4.0		
Oregon DOC, 1994 (2)	Recidivism	N/A	253	N/A	425	24
Song & Lieb, 1995 (2)	Rearrests		119		159	Up to 84
	Sex	11.0		12.0		
	Violent	1.0		3.0		
	Felony	5.0		6.0		
Alaska DOC, 1996 (2)	Rearrests (*M*)	4.4	411	4.9/4.7/7.0	74/86/100	12
Gordon & Nicholaichuk, 1996 (2)	*Comparison 1*		257		1,16	60 for Treatment Group
	Reconvictions				4	
	Sex	4.7	80	6.2		36 for Comparison Group
	Nonsex	7.8		13.6	116	
	Comparison 2					
	Reconvictions	6.0		14.6*		
	Sex	8.6		14.6		
	Nonsex					
Studer et al., 1996 (2)	Rearrests		120		100	$M = 38.4$
	Sex	3.3		10.0*		
	Nonsex	12.5		27.0*		
Hildebran & Pithers, 1992 (2)	Reoffense/Relapse	6.0	50	48.0*	40	72
Nicholaichuk, 1996 (2)	Rearrest/Conviction/ Technical Violation		26		35	$M = 30$
	Sex	11.0		3.0		

* Significantly different from experimental group, $p < 0.05$.

TABLE 8.2. *Studies of behavioral treatment for sex offenders showing recidivism rates and length of follow-up*

Study (methods score)	Measure of Recidivism	Recidivism: Experimental (%)	N	Control (%) #1/#2/#3	N	Follow-up period (in months)
Marshall & Barbaree, 1988 (4)	Rearrests	13.2	68	34.5	58	Up to 132
	Self-Report (*M*)					
	Sex Offense	1.44		1.6		
Davidson, 1984 (3)	Convictions		101		101	60
	All	16.0		36.0		
	Assault	11.0		23.0		
	Sex	7.0		13.0		
	Charges					
	Sex	22.0		14.0		
Marshall et al., 1991 (3)	Charged or Reconvicted		23		21	108
	Sex	39.1		57.1		
Rice et al., 1991 (2)	Convictions		29		29	72 (Approx.)
	Sex	37.9		31.0		

Significantly different from experimental, $p < 0.05$.

TABLE 8.3. *Studies of hormonal medication and surgical castration for sex offenders showing recidivism rates, length of follow-up and sample characteristics*

Study (methods score)	Measure of Recidivism	Recidivism				Follow-up period (in months)
		Experimental (%)	N	Control (%) #1/#2/#3	N	
McConaghy, Blasczynski, & Kidson 1988 (5)	Relapse		10		10/9	24–60
	Self-Reported Behavior/Urges	10.0		40.0/11.0		
Fedoroff, Wisner-Carlson, Dean, & Berlin, 1992 (4)	Relapse (*M*)		27		19	84
	Self-Report of Inappropriate Sex Behavior	.33 (14.8)		1.5 (68.4)		
Maletzky, 1991 (3)	*Current Tx Group*		100		100	4.6
	Reoffense					
	(Self-Report and/or Official)	0.0		2.0		
	Person/Sex Offense					
	Previous Tx Group					
	Reoffense	9.0	100	6.0	100	36
	(Self-Report and/or Official)					
	Person/Sex Offense					
Wille and Beier, 1989 (3)	Arrests		99		35	120
	Sex Offense	3.0		46.0[2]		
	Nonsex Offense	25.0		43.0		
Langevin et al., 1979 (2)	Recidivism (Self-Report)		5		12	Up to 24
	Sex	20.0		50.0		
Meyer et al., Cole, & Emory, 1992 (2)	Rearrest (Includes Self-Report)[1]	18.0	40	58.0/35.0	21/29	Up to 144

[1] Significance tests not reported.
[2] Significantly different from experimental group, $p < 0.05$.

TABLE 8.4. *Studies of general psychosocial treatment for sex offenders showing recidivism rates and length of follow-up*

Study (methods score)	Measure of recidivism	Recidivism: Experimental (%)	N	Control (%) #1/#2/#3	N	Follow-up period (in months)
Lab et al., Shields, & Shondel, 1993 (2)	Reconvictions		46		109	8–15
	Sex	2.2		3.7		
	Nonsex	24.0		18.0		
Minnesota DOC, 1987 (2)	Rearrest		64		73	10
	Sex	2.0		3.0		
	Assaultive	0.0		1.0		
	Nonperson	0.0		3.0		
Song & Lieb, 1995 (2)	Rearrests			14.0/31.0*	306/160	Up to 84
	Sex	11.0	321	13.0[1]/12.0		
	Violent	2.0		25.0[1]/32.0		
	Felony	7.0				

[1] Significantly different from experimental group, $p < 0.05$.

Appendices 8.1–8.4 provide descriptions of each study. Table 8.1 lists fifteen cognitive-behavioral/relapse prevention studies with their methods score, corresponding recidivism rates, and follow-up period. Seven of the fifteen studies received a score of three or higher on the methods scale. The majority of the studies report arrest (n = 6) and conviction (n = 3) as the primary recidivism outcomes; the remaining studies use new arraignment (n = 1) and reoffending/relapse (n = 1), charged/reconviction (n = 1), reoffending (n = 1), rearrests/convictions/technical violations (n = 1), and recidivism (n = 1). Seven of the fifteen studies found significant differences between treatment and comparison groups, and the direction of the differences consistently favor the treated group (Borduin, Henggeler, Blaske, & Stein, 1994; Nicholaichuk, Gordon, Andre, & Gu, 1995; Marshall et al., 1991; McGrath, Hoke, & Vojtisek, 1998; Gordon & Nicholaichuk, 1996; Studer, Reddon, Roper, & Estrada, 1996; Hildebran & Pithers, 1992).

Behavioral therapy studies are shown in Table 8.2 along with their methods score, measure of recidivism, and follow-up time. Only one of the four behavioral therapy studies received a methods score of two (Rice, Quinsey, & Harris, 1991). Two studies reported significant differences between treatment and comparison groups (Marshall & Barbaree, 1988; Davidson, 1984); however, the direction of the differences did not always favor the treatment group. Specifically, Davidson found that in terms of any subsequent conviction and any subsequent assaultive conviction (which included conviction for sex offenses), the treated group showed a lower rate of recidivism than did the control group; however, in terms of sex charges, the treated group was significantly charged more frequently than the control group. Also, it should be noted that the sex charges against the treated group did not result in more convictions (i.e., the charges were either dropped or the man was acquitted), whereas all of the charges against the control group led to convictions.

Hormonal medication and surgical castration studies with their methods score, measure of recidivism, and follow-up period are listed in Table 8.3. Four of the six studies received a score of three or higher on the research methods scale. Relapse (n = 2), reoffending (n = 1), rearrests (n = 1), self-report recidivims (n = 1), and rearrests including self-report (n = 1) were reported as the main recidivism outcome in these studies. The treated group in most of the hormonal medication and surgical castration studies consisted of sex offenders treated with the antiandrogen hormone MPA, whereas the control group included sex offenders who were not treated with MPA. Only one study (Wille & Beier, 1989) found significant differences between treatment and comparison groups, and the direction of the difference favored the treated group.

Table 8.4 lists three general psychosocial studies along with their methods score, corresponding recidivism rates, and follow-up time. None of the general psychosocial studies reached a score of three or higher on the research methods scale. One study found significant differences between groups and the direction of the differences favored the treated group (Song & Lieb, 1995). The study by Lab and colleagues (1993) examined a court-based, offense-specific psychosocial education program established for juvenile sexual offenders. Lab and his colleagues report that although there were no significant differences between treated youths and control youths in terms of committing a further sex offense or any further offense, in terms of committing any further offense, treated youths tended to recidivate slightly more than control youths.

My colleagues and I at the University of Maryland have completed several narrative reviews and meta-analyses to examine the effectiveness of treatment for sex offenders (the studies examined are listed in Tables 8.1–8.4, separated by treatment modality, and descriptions are provided in Appendices 8.1–8.4). In three separate reviews, we examined the effectiveness of adult sex offender treatment using the quality of the research design (e.g., methods score) and the significance and direction of the results to draw conclusions about what works in sex offender treatment (MacKenzie, 2000; MacKenzie & Hickman, 1998; Polizzi, MacKenzie, & Hickman, 1999). We separated programs into those that were provided within the criminal justice setting (prison based) from those that were provided in hospital or hospital-based outpatient settings (nonprison based). Descriptions of the setting of the treatment for each study are provided in Appendices 8.1–8.4.

Of the eight studies of the criminal justice setting that we examined in our assessment (Huot, 1999; Alaska Department of Corrections,

1996; Gordon & Nicholaichuk, 1996; Nicholaichuk et al., 1995; Song & Lieb, 1995, two studies; Oregon Department of Corrections, 1994; Hanson, Steffy, & Gauthier, 1993), only two received a score three or higher on the methodology rigor (Hanson, Steffy, & Gauthier, 1993, and Nicholaichuk et al., 1995). Furthermore, only the study by Nicholaichuk and colleagues found significant differences between the treatment and the controls. Nicholaichuk and colleagues found significant differences between groups for sex offense reconvictions (but not for nonsexual offenses) and for readmission rates (see Table 8.1). The remaining six studies received a two on the research methods scale because they were judged too inadequate in scientific methodology to be used to determine effectiveness. From this review, we concluded that the sex offender treatment provided within prison or community corrections was promising but at this point there is insufficient evidence to conclude that the treatment is effective.

Our assessment of hospital-based settings included five studies (Marques, Day, Nelson, & West, 1994; Marshall, Eccles, & Barbaree, 1991, 2 studies; Rice, Quinsey, & Harris, 1991; Marshall & Barbaree, 1988). Overall, studies in hospital settings were of higher methodological quality than the criminal justice setting studies; four of the five studies in hospital settings received a score of three or higher on the methods assessment (Marques et al., 1994; Marshall & Barbaree, 1988; Marshall et al., 1991, 2 studies). The study by Rice, Quinsey, and Harris (1991) was judged too low in scientific merit to draw conclusions about the effectiveness of sex offender treatment. Two of the scientifically stronger studies found lower recidivism rates for the treated group compared to the untreated group (Marshall & Barbaree, 1988; Marshall et al., 1991). Marshall and Barbaree found child molesters treated with behavioral therapy had significantly lower recidivism rates than those who did not receive treatment. Marshall et al. found exhibitionists given cognitive-behavioral treatment had lower recidivism rates than those who received behavioral therapy or no treatment. Furthermore, in comparison to the no-treatment group, the behavioral therapy group had significantly lower recidivism. From this assessment of the research, we concluded that hospital-based sex offender treatment was effective in reducing recidivism.

Although we concluded that sex offender treatment was generally effective, we could not determine whether these results were dependent on the characteristics of the offender or of the treatment provided because the studies differed in the type of sex offender treated and the treatment offered. Differences between the prison-based treatment and the non-prison-based settings may be the result of the quality of the studies. For instance, only two prison-based studies were rated three or greater on the methods scale whereas four of the non-prison-based studies received a score of three or higher on the methods assessment. Another possibility is that treatment provided in hospital-based settings operated under a different theoretical perspective; thus, it is expected that they would be more apt to focus on identifying and treating sex offenders with sexual disorders. Furthermore, such offenders may be more amenable to treatment or, alternatively, because the treatment is more focused on their specific problems, it may be more effective.

Accordingly, the studies judged to be so low in scientific merit that we did not use them to draw conclusions about effectiveness most often suffered from a poor comparison group. Many used dropouts or "unmotivated" individuals from the programs as the comparison. There is every reason to believe that these individuals differed prior to the treatment, so we cannot tell from the research whether the programs had an effect or whether differences in recidivism were a result of these initial differences.

We extended the work examining the effectiveness of sex offender treatment using meta-analytic techniques (Gallagher, Wilson, Hirschfield, Coggeshall, & MacKenzie, 1999; Gallagher, Wilson, & MacKenzie, 1999). We included the twenty-eight evaluations listed in Tables 8.1–8.4 in our meta-analysis. The standardized mean difference or Cohen's *d* (Cohen, 1988) was used to calculate the effect sizes. This represents the contrast between the treatment and control group in units of the standard deviation (Lipsey & Wilson, 1993). Some of the studies from the MacKenzie and Hickman (1998) and Polizzi et al. (1999) were excluded from the meta-analysis because the control groups received alternative sex offender treatment (e.g., the comparison groups received treatment; there was *no* comparison group with *no* treatment).

Sex Offender Cognitive-Behavioral Treatment Programs

Citation	Effect
Borduin et al., 1994	21.00
McGrath et al., 1998	8.24
Marshall et al., 1991	4.33
Nicholaichuk et al., 1995	2.93
Guarino & Kimball, 1998	2.24
Marques et al., 1994	1.67
Hanson et al., 1993	.78
Mean Odds-Ratio (7)	**2.04**

0.01 0.1 1 10 100

Favors Control **Favors Treatment**

Figure 8.2. Forest plot showing odds ratio and 95 percent confidence interval for studies of sex offender cognitive-behavioral treatment programs.

The meta-analyses included information reflecting potential substantive (e.g., treatment type, offender type, program length, and location of treatment) and methodological (e.g., similarity of treatment and control groups, follow-up length, type of recidivism, scientific methods score, subject attrition) differences among the studies. Although our interest focused on the effectiveness of treatment, information on these other variables enabled us to examine whether the results could be explained on the basis of differences in the substantive or methodological characteristics of the studies.

Overall, the results indicated the treated group had lower sexual recidivism than the control group as indicated by the positive and statistically significant mean effect size (Cohen's $d = 0.48$). The average estimated recidivism was 12 percent for the treated group and 22 percent for the comparison group. According to Cohen's rule of thumb (1988), the mean effect size would be considered evidence of a moderate effect. Most of the differences favored the treated group although many of the differences were not significant in the individual studies. There were large differences in effect sizes across studies, meaning that the significant results of the meta-analysis could not be generalized to all sex offender treatment programs. For this reason, we examined substantive and methodological characteristics of the studies to identify where the differences existed.

Figures 8.2–8.4 present the effect sizes of those studies scored three or greater on the methods score, categorized according to treatment type: cognitive-behavioral/relapse prevention (n = 7), behavioral

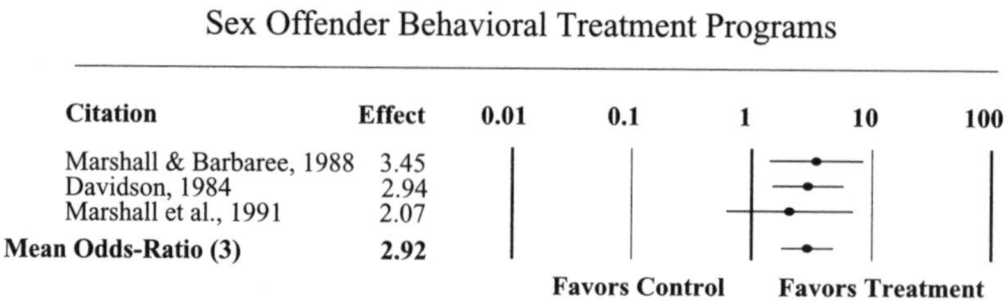

Sex Offender Behavioral Treatment Programs

Citation	Effect	0.01	0.1	1	10	100
Marshall & Barbaree, 1988	3.45					
Davidson, 1984	2.94					
Marshall et al., 1991	2.07					
Mean Odds-Ratio (3)	**2.92**					

Favors Control **Favors Treatment**

Figure 8.3. Forest plot showing odds ratio and 95 percent confidence interval for studies of sex offender behavioral treatment programs.

(n = 3), and hormonal medication (n = 4). (Note: none of the general psychosocial studies received a score of three or higher.)

Figure 8.2 represents the results of seven cognitive-behavioral treatment studies for sex offenders on the offenders' sex offense recidivism. The recidivism measures used in calculating effect sizes were rearrest for sex offense (n = 2), charged or reconvicted for a new sex offense (n = 3), new arraignment (n = 1), and reoffending sex offenses (n = 1). The effect sizes for Hanson et al. (1993), Marques et al. (1994), Marshall et al. (1991), and McGrath et al. (1998) were calculated by combining both control groups for each study and taking the weighted mean of the groups' recidivism measures, producing a single comparison measure. The most recent recidivism measures were used, representing the longest follow-up period. Eight of the studies included in Table 8.1 were excluded because of low methods scores.

Figure 8.3 presents the results of three behavioral treatment studies for sex offenders on the offenders' sex offense recidivism. The recidivism measures used in calculating effect sizes were rearrest(n = 1), conviction (n = 1), and charge/reconviction (n = 1). The most recent recidivism measures were used, representing the longest follow-up period. The study by Rice et al. (1991) was excluded because of low methods scores.

Figure 8.4 presents the results of four hormonal medication and surgical castration treatment studies for sex offenders on the offenders' sex offense recidivism. The recidivism measures used in calculating effect sizes were rearrest (n = 1), relapse (n = 2), and reoffense (n = 1). The effect size for Maletzky (1991) was calculated using a

Sex Offender Hormonal Treatment Programs

Citation	Effect
Wille & Beier, 1989	26.95
Fedoroff et al., 1992	12.46
McConaghy, 1988	3.21
Maletzky, 1991	.65
Mean Odds-Ratio (4)	**4.01**

0.01 0.1 1 10 100

Favors Control **Favors Treatment**

Figure 8.4. Forest plot showing odds ratio and 95 percent confidence interval for studies of sex offender hormonal treatment programs.

singular comparison measure by combining both treatment groups and taking the weighted mean of the groups' recidivism measures. The most recent recidivism measures were used, representing the longest follow-up period. Two studies from Table 8.3 were excluded because of low methods scores.

Based on the overall effect sizes presented in the three plots, cognitive-behavioral and behavioral treatment and hormonal medication significantly reduced the sexual offense recidivism of treated offenders relative to the control group.[1]

Using estimates from the meta-analysis, we calculated the expected percentage recidivating after treatment assuming the comparison group recidivated at 15 percent. In comparison, these calculations estimated the recidivism rates for those who received behavioral or cognitive-behavioral treatment or chemical castration as somewhere between 5 and 7 percent. Table 8.5 shows the estimated average sexual reoffending rates for treatment and comparison groups for the twenty-five studies that reported dichotomous recidivism data. There were substantial differences between the treatment and comparison groups for all treatment types except general psychosocial. However, the meta-analysis indicates that only the cognitive-behavioral treatment and the hormonal medication were significantly different.

[1] Note that in the Gallagher and colleagues meta-analysis, surgical castration had the largest overall mean effect size; however, extreme caution is warranted in interpreting this finding because the effect size was based on a single study conducted in Germany. No further discussion of surgical castration follows in this chapter because it is not an option currently used in the United States.

TABLE 8.5. *Estimated mean recidivism rates from studies of four different types of sex offender treatment programs*

Treatment type	Number of studies	Estimated mean recidivism (percent)	
		Treatment	Comparison
Behavioral	4	28	39
Cognitive-Behavioral/ Relapse Prevention	13	9	21
General Psychosocial	3	7	8
Hormonal Medication	5	12	30
Total	25	12	22

Source: Gallagher et al., 1999.

In addition, there were no significant differences based on treatment length, whether the treatment was provided by a criminal justice agency, or whether treatment was within an institution. Studies assessed at a low level of methodological rigor were included in the meta-analyses. The studies that scored higher on the methods score had larger effect sizes, suggesting that the finding of an overall positive effect for treatment cannot be attributed to the inclusion of methodologically weak studies in the meta-analysis.

We found some consistent differences between types of treatment programs that make it difficult to draw comparisons between them. For instance, studies differed in the type of outcome measures used. All of the cognitive-behavioral/relapse prevention studies used official measures of recidivism. In contrast, many of the hormonal castration studies used composite measures, including both self-report and official measures of recidivism. The hormonal studies were all offered in non–criminal justice settings, and many of the samples included exhibitionists and pedophiles. However, the cognitive-behavioral studies were mostly criminal justice based, took place in institutional settings, and were more apt to include rapists. Thus, the studies do not give sufficient information to draw conclusions about the type of offender who will benefit most from the treatment or whether the results depended upon a match between the offenders and treatment philosophy (e.g., hormonal treatment limited to those identified to have with sexual disorders).

CONCLUSION

The review of sex offender programming along with the prior assessments and the meta-analyses by my colleagues and myself clearly indicate that sex offender treatment programs using cognitive-behavioral therapy/relapse prevention and chemical castration/psychotherapy are effective in reducing recidivism. There is some evidence that treatment in hospital-based settings is more effective than treatment provided in prisons. However, any conclusions about these differences are limited because of other differences in the programs and the samples of offenders used in the studies in the different settings.

APPENDIX 8.1. STUDY REFERENCE, DESCRIPTION, AND METHODS SCORES (IN PARENTHESES) OF COGNITIVE-BEHAVIORAL TREATMENT FOR SEX OFFENDERS

Alaska Department of Corrections, 1996 **(2)**
Prison-based, treated through the Hiland Mountain Sex Offender Treatment Program between January 1987 and August 1995 compared to untreated (1) motivated sex offenders, (2) unmotivated sex offenders, and (3) nonsexual offenders.

Borduin et al., 1994 **(5)**
Sixteen juvenile sexual offenders who had participated in a larger study of delinquency in July 1983 and July 1985; randomly assigned to multisystemic or individual therapy conditions.

Gordon and Nicholaichuk, 1996 **(2)**
(1) Prison-based, varied sex offenders who completed the Clearwater sex offender treatment program between 1981 and 1994 were compared to a national sample of sex offenders released from service institutions in 1988. **(2)** Prison-based, high risk sex offenders from the first treatment group were compared to the national sample.

Guarino and Kimball, 1998 **(3)**
Assaultive male juvenile sex offenders committed to Division of Youth Services (MASS) between 1993 and 1994 who were referred to DYS secure classification panel; sex offender treatment group compared to nonspecialized treatment group.

Hanson et al., 1993 **(4)**
Child molesters who received prison-based treatment in Ontario between 1965 and 1973 compared to (1) child molesters from the same institution as the treatment group, but prior to the treatment program being offered, and (2) nonparticipants.

Hildebran and Pithers, 1992 **(2)**
Non-prison-based, varied sex offenders in the Vermont Treatment Program for Sexual Aggressors over seven years compared to dropouts.

Huot, 1999 **(2)**
Sex offenders in the Minnesota Department of Corrections who successfully completed prison-based treatment compared to (1) those who never entered treatment and (2) dropouts.

Marques et al., 1994 **(4)**
Child molesters and adult rapists in a non-prison-based Sex Offender Treatment and Evaluation Project through the California Department of Corrections were randomly assigned to three groups: (1) volunteer treatment group, (2) volunteer control, and (2) nonvolunteer control.

Marshall et al., 1991 **(3)**
Study 2: Exhibitionists at the Kingston Sexual Behavior Clinic between 1976 and 1984, non–prison based, treated compared to (1) Study 1 treated with aversive behavior therapy and (2) untreated.

McGrath et al., 1998 **(3)**
Convicted male adult sex offenders in community correctional supervision for at least three months in rural Vermont between 1984 and 1995 who received comprehensive outpatient cognitive-behavioral and relapse prevention treatment compared to (1) less specialized treatment group and (2) group with no treatment.

Nicholaichuk et al., 1995 **(4)**
High risk sex offenders who volunteered for and completed the Clearwater Sex Offender Treatment Program between 1981 and 1996, compared to stratified matched sample of offenders incarcerated in the prairie region of the Correctional Service of Canada from 1983 to 1996; matched on age of index offense, date of index offense, and prior criminal history.

Nicholaichuk, 1996 (2)
Child molesters in Saskatchewan, mostly first-time offenders, prison-based, completed relapse prevention program compared to (matched) untreated group.
Oregon DOC, 1994 (2)
Prison-based, intensive residential (CTP) compared to outpatient treated (CTS).
Song and Lieb, 1995 (2)
Washington state sex offenders who completed the prison-based Sex Offender Treatment Program at the Twin Rivers Correctional Center by March 1993, compared to incarcerated untreated group.
Studer et al., 1996 (2)
Dischargees from the Phoenix Program, an in-patient sexual offender treatment program at the Alberta Hospital Edmonton (psychiatric hospital), between July 23, 1987, and December 18, 1992, who completed the sex offender treatment program compared to noncompleters.

APPENDIX 8.2. STUDY REFERENCE, DESCRIPTION, AND METHODS SCORES (IN PARENTHESES) OF BEHAVIORAL TREATMENT FOR SEX OFFENDERS

Davidson, 1984 (3)
Offenders treated with prison-based sex offender program in a Canadian penitentiary between 1974 and 1982 compared to matched untreated group.
Marshall and Barbaree, 1988 (4)
Child molesters (nonfamilial) at the Kingston Sexual Behavior Clinic between 1978 and 1985 treated in a non-prison-based setting compared to untreated group.
Marshall et al., 1991 (3)
Study 1: Exhibitionists at the Kingston Sexual Behavior Clinic treated with non-prison-based aversive behavior therapy compared to untreated group.
Rice et al., 1991 (2)
Child molesters who were released from a maximum-security psychiatric institution before December 31, 1983, and were treated with

behavioral therapy in addition to the regular institution activities compared to matched untreated group who only received the regular institution regime.

APPENDIX 8.3. STUDY REFERENCE, DESCRIPTION, AND METHODS SCORES (IN PARENTHESES) OF HORMONAL MEDICATION AND SURGICAL CASTRATION TREATMENT FOR SEX OFFENDERS

Fedoroff et al., 1992 **(4)**

Outpatient treatment at the Johns Hopkins Sexual Disorders Unit of individuals with paraphilic sexual disorders who completed five years of treatment prior to December 31, 1989, treated with MPA compared to non-MPA group.

Langevin et al., 1979 **(2)**

Male exhibitionists voluntarily treated with assertion therapy with provera compared to therapy alone.

Maletzky, 1991 **(3)**

(1) Sex offenders in an outpatient sexual abuse clinic currently treated with MPA compared to a matched non-MPA group.

(2) Sex offenders in an outpatient sexual abuse clinic previously treated with MPA compared to a matched non-MPA group.

McConaghy, 1988 **(5)**

Inpatient program at the Behavior Therapy Unit at the Prince of Wales Hospital; sex offenders using MPA therapy plus imaginal desensitization compared to (1) desensitization alone and (2) MPA alone.

Meyer et al., 1992 **(2)**

Offenders referred to the Rosenberg Clinic in Texas using MPA compared to those who (1) refused and (2) who stopped taking medication.

Wille and Beier, 1989 **(3)**

Male offenders in the Federal Republic of Germany between 1970 and 1980 that received voluntarily surgical castration compared to noncastrated group.

APPENDIX 8.4. STUDY REFERENCE, DESCRIPTION, AND METHODS SCORES (IN PARENTHESES) OF GENERAL PSYCHOSOCIAL TREATMENT FOR SEX OFFENDERS

Lab et al., 1993 **(2)**

Juveniles from a large metropolitan county in the midwest in court-based Sexual Offender Treatment, an offense-specific psychosocial education program, between January 1, 1988, and April 30, 1991, compared to traditional non-offense-specific treatment group (assigned to group by risk).

Minnesota Department of Corrections, 1987 **(2)**

Offenders in prison-based and aftercare Transitional Sex Offender Program in Minnesota between 1978 and 1983 compared to untreated, unselected group.

Song and Lieb, 1995 **(2)**

Washington state sex offenders convicted of a felony sex offense between January 1985 and April 1986 who were treated through the Special Sex Offender Sentencing Alternative program compared to incarcerated (1) eligible nonparticipants and (2) ineligible nonparticipants.

Juvenile Delinquents

THE JUVENILE JUSTICE SYSTEM

The first juvenile court in the United States was established more than one hundred years ago in Chicago. Prior to this, children as young as seven were processed the same as adults. They could stand trial in criminal court and be sentenced to prison or death. The juvenile court reflected a change in the philosophy toward juveniles. The new courts focused on the welfare of the child. The delinquent child was viewed as in need of benevolent intervention from the court. Juvenile courts sought to rehabilitate delinquents so they would become productive members of society. By 1925, all but two states had established either juvenile courts or probation services for juveniles. During the next fifty years, juvenile courts in most states had exclusive jurisdiction over all youth under age eighteen who were charged with violating criminal laws.

As occurred with adult offenders in the United States, attitudes toward the rehabilitation of juveniles changed during the 1970s. There was less support for rehabilitation. The public perceived that serious juvenile crime was increasing and that the system was too lenient with juvenile delinquents. In response, many states passed more punitive laws. Some of these laws removed young lawbreakers from the juvenile system and required that they be tried in adult criminal courts. During the 1990s, all but three states passed laws designed to crack down on juvenile crime. These laws expanded eligibility for criminal court processing and adult correctional sanctioning and reduced confidentiality protections for juveniles.

JUVENILE CRIME STATISTICS

During the late 1980s and the early 1990s, there was some justification for the public's perception that serious juvenile crime was increasing. From 1988 through 1994, juvenile violent crime arrests increased substantially. In contrast, juvenile property crime arrests stayed relatively stable. The UCR Violent Crime Index (including murder, forcible rape, robbery, and aggravated assault) for juveniles rose from approximate 300 arrests per 100,000 juveniles in 1988 to more than 500 arrests per 100,000 in 1994.

In 1994, arrests of juveniles for both violent and property crimes began to decline. Between 1994 and 2002, violent crimes declined 47 percent. The juvenile Violent Crime Index arrest rate in 2002 was the lowest since 1980. Property crime arrests also dropped during this time. Between 1994 and 2002, juvenile property crime rates dropped 43 percent.

PROGRAMS FOR JUVENILE DELINQUENTS

Many of the chapters in this book examine rehabilitation and intervention programs for both juvenile delinquents and adult offenders. The chapters on vocational education, cognitive-behavior treatment, sex offenders, drug courts, drug treatment, and boot camps all include studies of juveniles and adults. Data for juveniles are examined and/or discussed separately where appropriate. Additionally, juvenile samples are identified in the appendices of the tables. In this chapter, I examine research and programs that are designed specifically for juvenile delinquents that have not been included in other chapters of this book.

Deterrence and Increased Control Programs

Many of the programs offered to juvenile delinquents are similar to programs offered in the adult correctional system. Additionally, similar to adult corrections, many of the programs developed during the 1980s and 1990s were based on the control philosophy using deterrence and incapacitation as the theoretical rationales. For example, although they often began later than adult programs, boot camps, intensive supervision, and electronic monitoring programs grew during this period (see Chapters 13 and 14 in this volume). One type of deterrent program, designed specifically designed for juveniles, was Scared Straight.

Scared Straight. The program began in the 1970s when a New Jersey state prison designed a program to "scare" at-risk or delinquent children from a future life of crime. The program, known as Scared Straight, was run by inmates serving life sentences. The inmates gave an aggressive presentation to juveniles who visited the prison. They described life in adult prisons and included exaggerated stories of rape and murder (Finckenauer, 1982). The program received favorable media attention, and this led to replication in more than thirty jurisdictions in the United States. Today, the original harsh presentations have changed to include less confrontation and more educational components; however, the programs still focus on a deterrent model for reducing crime. The programs have also spread to other nations. According to Petrosino, Turpin-Petrosino, and Buehler (2003), similar programs have been used in Australia, the United Kingdom, Norway, Germany, and Canada.

Petrosino, Turpin-Petrosino, and Buehler (2003) completed a systematic review and meta-analysis of Scared Straight and other juvenile awareness programs as a pilot test for the newly formed international Campbell Collaboration (see Chapter 4 of this volume for a description of the Collaboration). Studies included in the review had to have a randomized design, involve juveniles, and have an outcome measure of subsequent criminality. They screened more than five hundred citations and identified nine randomized trials for the analysis. The nine studies were conducted in eight different states in the United States (two studies were done in Michigan). The researchers reviewed the studies to see if there were any implementation problems that would restrict the generalizations from the studies. They concluded "the kids received what they were designed to receive."

Results from the meta-analysis indicated that the intervention *increased* the crime or delinquency outcomes for those who received the program. From the data, they estimate that for every 1 control participant who offends, 1.7 treated kids (e.g., those who received Scared Straight) offend. Further statistical tests demonstrated that these results could not be attributed to methodological problems in the data. According to the researchers, the program led to an overall negative impact on subsequent offending. Not only are Scared Straight programs *not* effective, they appear to have a detrimental effect.

Interventions for Serious Juvenile Offenders

Lipsey and Wilson (1998) conducted meta-analyses examining the impact of interventions for serious juvenile offenders. They analyzed a subset of the data Lipsey (1992, 1995) used in his original meta-analysis of delinquency interventions (see Chapter 4, this volume). They focused on studies in which the majority of the juveniles were adjudicated delinquents, in which referrals to the program had been made by a juvenile justice source, and/or in which most or all of the juveniles under study had demonstrated an aggressive history. Two hundred studies met these criteria and were included in the analysis.

Overall, they found that the programs for the serious juvenile offenders were effective in reducing recidivism. From their results, they estimate that effect size indicated a 44 percent recidivism rate for the treated juveniles compared to a 50 percent rate for the untreated control group. However, they found large variability in the effect sizes. Some studies reported effects much larger than the overall effect size, and other studies reported smaller effects. They explored the nature of this variability in a series of analyses. Some of the differences in effects were due to methodological differences among the studies, so these factors were controlled in the analyses examining the impact of treatment variables.

To examine what types of programs were most effective, Lipsey and Wilson (1998) divided the studies into interventions with noninstitutionalized juveniles (n = 117) and studies of interventions with institutionalized juveniles (n = 83). For each intervention, they examined the characteristics of the juveniles, the general program characteristics, the treatment type, and the amount of treatment (i.e., dosage).

Noninstitutional Programs. Lipsey and Wilson's meta-analysis (1998) of noninstitutionalized serious juvenile offenders revealed that the effects of treatment were larger for more serious juveniles (e.g., had more prior offenses, had more person offenses) than for less serious offenders. This is consistent with Andrews et al.'s risk principle (1990) – treatment will be more effective with offenders who are at higher risk for recidivism. The results from dosage effects were unclear with contradictory relationships. Difficulties with treatment delivery and implementation were associated with smaller effects. In addition, stronger effect sizes were associated with researcher involvement in the design, planning, and delivery of treatment.

Differences were also found in effects depending upon the type of treatment offered to noninstitutionalized serious juveniles. The most effective programs were personal skills training, individual counseling, and behavioral programs. The next most effective programs were multiple services (e.g., service brokerage, multimodal service) and restitution programs for juveniles on probation or parole. Programs that were ineffective in reducing recidivism were wilderness/challenge programs, early release from probation or parole, deterrence programs, and vocational programs (not including those involving paid employment). The results from one group of programs were ambiguous: employment-related academic programming, advocacy/social casework, group counseling, family counseling, and reduced caseloads on probation/parole. According to the researchers, no conclusions about the effectiveness of these programs can be determined at this point in time.

Institutional Programs. Results from Lipsey and Wilson's meta-analysis (1998) of the institutionalized juvenile programs differed from the results for the noninstitutionalized juvenile programs. First, treatment was more effective when provided by mental health personnel (in contrast, primarily, to juvenile justice personnel). Second, programs that had been in operation longer, were monitored for quality control, and were of longer duration were more effective than programs that were newer, less monitored, and shorter, respectively. No significant differences were found in the effectiveness of programs depending upon the characteristics of the juveniles (i.e., prior offenses or seriousness of prior offenses did not make a difference in the analysis).

The most effective types of treatment for the institutionalized juveniles were interpersonal skills programs (similar to the results for the noninstitutionalized programs) and the teaching family home program. Also effective but less consistent in results were multiple service programs, community residential programs (mostly non–juvenile justice), and a miscellaneous category of other treatments not classified elsewhere. No effects were found for milieu therapy, drug abstinence programs, wilderness/challenge programs, and employment-related programs. Finally, results were ambiguous for behavioral programs, individual and group counseling, and guided group interactions. The researchers concluded that overall the research demonstrates that interventions for serious delinquents can be effective.

Therapeutic Wilderness and Challenge Programs

Wilson and Lipsey (2003) recently completed another meta-analysis examining wilderness and challenge programs for juveniles. It is important to note that programs included in the analyses had to be designed to reduce or prevent antisocial or delinquent behavior using treatment that included both physical challenge and an interpersonal therapeutic component. For this reason, I refer to these programs as "therapeutic wilderness and challenge" programs. To be included in the analysis, the programs had to target youth between ten and twenty-one years of age and be directed toward changing antisocial or delinquent behavior. Youth in the programs could be either at risk for delinquency or delinquent. Thus, this sample includes more at-risk (and not necessarily delinquent) youth than the other evaluations examined in this book. The study also had to include an outcome measuring antisocial or delinquent behavior.

Wilson and Lipsey found the programs reduced the recidivism rates (including antisocial and delinquent behavior) of the participants. They estimate the recidivism rates for participants at 29 percent could be compared to the 37 percent rate for the comparison subjects. Wilson and Lipsey found that programs with relatively more intense physical activities or with greater therapeutic enhancements led to the largest reduction in delinquent behavior. The effectiveness of the therapeutic enhancements is consistent with findings from other evaluations – that human service–type programs are most effective.

The finding that intense physical activity is also associated with a reduction in delinquent behavior is more surprising. Other evaluations of programs with intense activity are not necessarily found to be effective (see, for instance, the chapter on boot camps in this volume). However, there are several possible reasons for this finding. First, because all the programs had to include a therapeutic component to be included in the meta-analysis, the results reflect intense physical exercise combined with human service programs. This combination may be important. Second, the samples were not all delinquents nor did the outcome measures in this meta-analysis measure delinquency so the subjects and their behavior may be less criminal than those examined in most studies in this book. The sample group may be less delinquent than other samples because the subjects include both at risk and delinquent youth. Furthermore, the outcome measures include both antisocial and delinquent behavior.

MULTISYSTEMIC THERAPY

In preparation for writing this chapter, I reviewed the programs included in the Blueprints for Violence Prevention. The Blueprints Initiative began at the Center for the Study and Prevention of Violence as an initiative of the state of Colorado. The project was originally designed to identify model violence prevention programs and to implement them in Colorado. Later, it was supported by the Office of Juvenile Justice and Delinquency Prevention (OJJDP) and became a national violent prevention initiative.

The major goals of the Blueprint Initiative are (1) to identify effective, research-based programs and (2) to assist jurisdictions to replicate these effective programs. Programs included as Blueprint models must have demonstrated significant impacts on problem behavior (violence, aggression, delinquency, and/or substance abuse) using a strong research design. This effect must be sustained for at least one year beyond intervention, and the program must be replicated in at least one other site.

The Blueprints Initiative has identified eleven model programs. Most of the programs are directed at preventing juveniles from becoming involved in criminal behavior and are therefore not directly relevant to the population of juveniles examined in the book. For example, both the Life Skills Training (LST) and the Promoting Alternative Thinking Strategies (PATHS) model programs are designed to be delivered to children in schools. Only one of the model programs focuses on juvenile delinquents – Multi-Systemic Therapy (MST).

MST was developed to provide cost-effective, community-based treatment to youth with serious behavior disorders who are at high risk for out-of-home placement. The theoretical foundation of MST is found in Henggeler and Bourdin's work (1990), *Family Therapy and Beyond.* From their perspective, individuals must be viewed within a complex social network encompassing the individual, family, and extrafamilial groups such as peer, school, and neighborhood. Behavioral problems can stem from any place within the social network. MST targets the multiple factors that can contribute to antisocial behavior. The strengths in each individual's social network are used to promote positive change in behavior. MST helps parents deal effectively with the youth's problems and helps the youth cope with family, peer, school, and neighborhood problems. The goal is to reduce or eliminate the need for out-of-home placements.

In MST, a team of professionals including a therapist or case manager and other practitioners is assigned to individual juveniles. The team is available twenty-four hours a day, seven days a week. The team not only assists the juvenile but also provides help to the family. Interventions include strategic family therapy, structural family therapy, behavioral parent training, and cognitive-behavioral therapies. The family interventions may seek to promote the parents' capacity to monitor and discipline their children. Peer interventions remove the youth from deviant peer groups and help them to develop relationships with prosocial peers. School/vocational interventions improve the youth's chance for future employment and financial success. Treatment usually last approximately four months and includes approximately sixty hours of face-to-face contact with the family.

The program is highly structured; activities such as homework, household chores, community services, and family outings are carefully planned. Parents, teachers, siblings, neighbors, or professionals in the community monitor the activities of the youth. A great deal of structure is provided in the early stages of the program, and this gradually diminishes as the juveniles and their families develop prosocial knowledge and skills to structure their lives.

Multi-Systemic Treatment Programs

Citation	Effect	0.01	0.1	1	10	100
Bourdin et al., 1990 (Sex Offenses)	21.00					
Henggeler et al., 1991	5.43					
Bourdin et al., 1990 (Non-Sex Offenses)	3.00					
Henggeler et al., 1993	2.70					
Mean Odds-Ratio (4)	**3.90**		**Favors Control**		**Favors Treatment**	

Figure 9.1. Forest plot showing odds ratio and 95 percent confidence interval for studies of MST programs.

I identified eight evaluations of MST. Scherer and Brondino (1994) conducted a randomized trial (which scored a five in methods rating). They reported were no significant differences between groups, but they did not report recidivism rates. For this reason, their study is not included in further discussion and is omitted from tables and plots. As shown on Table 9.1, six of the remaining studies were scored five on research methods. The recidivism rates were lower for the experimental groups in all of the evaluations; in four evaluations the differences were significant.

Figure 9.1 presents the results of four independent samples of three juvenile MST studies on recidivism. The recidivism measure used for calculating effect sizes was rearrest (n = 4). The most recent recidivism measures were used, representing the longest follow-up. Lastly, studies that only reported means (n = 3) were excluded from the plot. As shown, the overall log-odds were significant. The large number of randomized trials combined with the results showing lower recidivism rates provides strong evidence that MST is effective in reducing recidivism.

A strong positive aspect of this research is that the large proportion of the studies were randomized trials. The major disadvantage is that all of the strongly designed studies were conducted by the people who developed the program, Henggeler and his colleagues. The question is whether these results can be generalized to other jurisdictions and successfully implemented by other people.

Despite the fact that my review of MST as well as many other reviews have concluded that MST is an effective program, a recent systematic

TABLE 9.1. *Studies utilizing MST for juvenile offenders showing recidivism rates and length of follow-up*

Study (methods score)	Measure of recidivism	Recidivism				Follow-up period (in months)
		Experimental (%)	N	Control (%) #1/#2/#3	N	
Bourdin, Henggler, Blaske, & Stein, 1990 (5)	Rearrest		8		8	$M = 37.2$
	Sex Offenses	12.5		75.0*		
	Nonsex Offenses	25.0		50.0		
Bourdin et al., 1995 (5)	Rearrest (*M*) (SD)	1.71 (1.04)	92	5.43 (3.62)*	84	48
Henggeler et al., 1991 (5)	Substance-Related Arrest	3.0	92	15.0*	84	48
Henggeler, Cligempeel, Brondino, & Pickrel, 2002 (5)	Self-Report Delinquency Scale		43		37	48
	Aggressive Crimes (*M*) (SD)	0.61 (0.90)		1.36 (2.21)*		
	Property Crimes (*M*) (SD)	0.89 (2.01)		1.26 (2.39)		
Henggeler et al., 1997 (5)	Self-Report Delinquency Scale		82		73	19
	General Delinquency	0.58 (0.57)		0.75 (0.62)		
	Index Offenses	0.11 (0.25)		0.23 (0.34)		
Henggeler, Melton, Smith, Schoenwald, & Hanley, 1993 (5)	Arrest[1]	61.0	43	80.0	41	28.8
Willman & Chun, 1973 (2)	Recidivism	20.8	178	42.7	75	12–24

[1] No significance tests reported.

* Significantly different from experimental group, $p < 0.05$.

review conducted by Littell (2005) raises some questions about the research. Littell carefully examined the MST studies over time. Many of the studies had multiple reports (per study) and multiple outcomes per report. When she examined the research over time she found problems related to randomization procedures, sample sizes, unyoked designs, unstandardized observation periods within studies, and systematic omission of those who refused treatment or did not complete MST. When she controlled for these problems in a meta-analysis she concluded that the effectiveness of the programs was not well established, although she found no evidence that MST had harmful effects or was less effective than other services. Thus, this is a cautionary note about the effectiveness of MST.

RESIDENTIAL PROGRAMS

I identified eight evaluations of residential programs for juveniles (see Table 9.2). Most of the programs included in the evaluations were wilderness programs (n = 6). Only Greenwood and Turner (1993) and Gottfredson and Barton (1993) did not examine wilderness programs. When compared to the control groups, the juveniles in the programs studied had lower recidivism rates in six of the evaluations; three of these studies found significant differences (Baer, Jacobs, & Carr, 1975; Kelly & Baer, 1971; Gottfredson & Barton, 1993). Two of the significant evaluations were completed in the 1970s and studied wilderness programs (Baer et al., 1975; Kelly & Baer, 1971). Furthermore, the Baer et al. study was rated only two on research methods. The Gottfredson and Barton study examined the recidivism of juveniles placed in a traditional training school compared to community placement. The residential placement groups had significantly lower recidivism rates.

The experimental groups in the Castellano and Soderstrom (1992) and Deschenes, Greenwood, and Marshall (1996) studies had higher recidivism than the control groups. Both of these studies were rated four in research methods. Deschenes et al. studied the Nokomis Challenge program that utilized wilderness adventure and aftercare. Castellano and Soderstrom studied the Spectrum Wilderness program. The study conducted by Deschenes and her colleagues reported

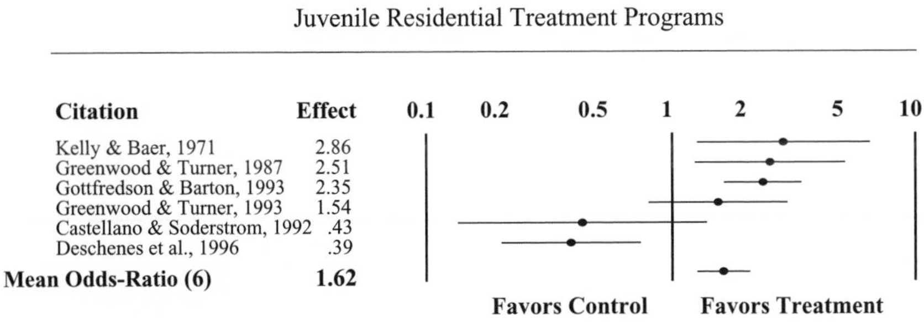

Juvenile Residential Treatment Programs

Citation	Effect
Kelly & Baer, 1971	2.86
Greenwood & Turner, 1987	2.51
Gottfredson & Barton, 1993	2.35
Greenwood & Turner, 1993	1.54
Castellano & Soderstrom, 1992	.43
Deschenes et al., 1996	.39
Mean Odds-Ratio (6)	**1.62**

Figure 9.2. Forest plot showing odds ratio and 95 percent confidence interval for studies of juvenile residential treatment programs.

significant differences between the groups. In the Castellano and Soderstrom study, despite the large differences in recidivism rates (80 compared to 63.4), the differences were not significant; however, the number of subjects in the groups was quite small (n = 30).

Figure 9.2 represents the results on recidivism of six studies utilizing residential treatment for juvenile offenders. The recidivism measures used for calculating effect sizes were rearrest (n = 5) and return to juvenile or adult institution (n = 1). Furthermore, the most recent recidivism measures were used, representing the longest follow-up period. Two studies from Table 9.2 were excluded because of low methods scores (Baer et al., 1975; Willman & Chun, 1973). As shown in Figure 9.2, the overall effect size favored the treated group and was significant. Effect sizes significantly favored the treated groups in three evaluations: Kelly and Baer (1971), Gottfredson and Barton (1993), and Greenwood and Turner (1987b). Effect sizes favored the control group in the Deschenes et al. (1996) study.

In summary, recidivism results are very varied for these residential programs for juveniles. Some studies have found reduced recidivism for those released from residential programs, others find the exact opposite. Many evaluations examined wilderness programs, and the results from the wilderness programs were inconsistent. Two wilderness programs found significant differences in favor of the residential programs, two found the opposite results. For this reason, it is impossible to say at this point in time that residential programs for juveniles are effective. I believe the differences are most likely due to the type of treatment and therapy offered to juveniles in the residential programs;

TABLE 9.2. *Studies utilizing residential treatment for juvenile offenders showing recidivism rates and length of follow-up*

Study (methods score)	Measure of recidivism	Recidivism: Experimental (%)	N	Control (%) #1/#2/#3	N	Follow-up period (in months)
Greenwood & Turner, 1993 (5)	Rearrest		73		75	12
	Any	50.7		61.3		
	Robbery	6.8		8.0		
	Assault	2.7		8.0		
	Burglary	9.6		12.0		
	Theft	17.8		26.7		
	Weapons	5.5		1.3		
	Drugs	4.1		6.7		
	Miscellaneous	19.2		29.3		
	Parole Violation	26.0		24.0		
	Reincarceration					
	Any	23.3		29.3		
	Robbery	2.7		5.3		
	Assault	0.0		1.3		
	Burglary	6.8		4.0		
	Theft	6.8		13.3		
	Drugs	2.7		1.3		
	Miscellaneous	2.7		6.7		
	Parole Violation	5.5		10.7		
Castellano & Soderstrom, 1992 (4)	Rearrest		30[2]		30[2]	18–41
	Any	80.0		63.4		
	Violent	40.0		26.7		
	Readjudication	53.3		50.0		

Deschenes et al., 1996 (4)	Rearrest		97		95	24
	Felony	30.9		19.0*		
	Any Other	8.2		1.0*		
	Any Drug	3.1		1.0		
	Any Property	12.4		11.6		
	Any Person	7.2		5.3		
	Reconviction	15.5		5.3*		
	Reincarceration	11.3		1.0*		
Greenwood & Turner, 1987b (3)	Rearrest[1]		89		79	18
	Any	63.0		81.0		
	Safety	33.0		37.0		
	Reconviction[1]					
	Any	49.0		57.0		
	Safety	16.0		24.0		
	Replacement[1] (Prison or CYA)	18.0		8.0		
Kelly & Baer, 1971 (3)	Recidivism (Return to Juvenile or Adult Institution)	20.0	60	41.7*	60	12
Baer et al., 1975 (2)	Recidivism (Reinstitutionalization)	30.0	50	90.0*	10	60
Willman & Chun, 1973 (2)	Recidivism	20.8	178	42.7	75	12–24

[1] No significance tests reported.

[2] Rates given in this table for both the experimental and control groups are for individuals representing a combination of "successes" and "failures."

* Significantly different from experimental group, $p < 0.05$.

however, there is insufficient information about the details of the programs to make this comparison. More research needs to be completed before conclusions can be drawn about the effectiveness of residential programs for juveniles.

COMMUNITY SUPERVISION

I identified nine programs examining community supervision of juveniles (see Table 9.3). These nine programs yielded ten independent study samples [the Greenwood et al. (1993) study includes two independent samples]. All of the juveniles in the experimental groups were given some type of intensive supervision in the community. Some were immediately placed in the community (n = 5), whereas others served some time in a facility and the supervision was considered aftercare (n = 4). Experiences of the comparison groups also varied; seven of the comparison groups had been released after serving time in facilities. The control groups in the other two studies were on probation or regular supervision. Many of the studies (n = 7) had a small number of subjects in the groups (i.e., fifty or fewer).

Recidivism for the experimental groups was lower in six of the studies; however, only one of these differences was significant. The significant study was rated five (Sontheimer & Goodstein, 1993) on research methods. They studied male delinquents released from a development center. The youth were randomly assigned to intensive supervision or traditional aftercare. The experimental groups had higher recidivism in four studies, but none of these differences were significant.

Figure 9.3 presents the results of seven independent samples of six juvenile community supervision studies on recidivism. Although the principal recidivism measure for the majority of the studies are rearrests (n = 3), for those studies that do not have a measure of rearrest, readjudication (n = 1) and recorded incidences of offenses or charges (n = 3) are used to calculate the effect sizes. Furthermore, studies that only reported means (n = 1) or were given a methods score of two (n = 2) are excluded from the plot.

As shown in the plot, there is no overall significant difference between the treated and comparison groups. Effect sizes for the Sontheimer and Goodstein (1993) evaluations significantly favored

TABLE 9.3. *Studies utilizing community supervision for juvenile offenders showing recidivism rates and length of follow-up*

Study (methods score)	Measure of recidivism	Recidivism: Experimental (%)	N	Control (%) #1/#2/#3	N	Follow-up period (in months)
Elrod & Minor, 1992 (5)	Criminal Offenses	68.2	22	66.7	21	24
	Status Offenses	45.5		61.9		
Greenwood et al., 1993 (5)	*Detroit*		50		49	12
	Rearrest					
	Any	22.0	46	18.4	41	
	Person	6.0		6.1		
	Property	4.0		8.2		
	Drugs	8.0		2.0		
	Other	4.0		2.0		
	Reconviction	14.0		14.3		
	Pittsburgh					
	Rearrest					
	Any	47.8		48.8		
	Person	8.7		17.1		
	Property	23.9		21.9		
	Drugs	10.9		7.3		
	Other	2.2		2.4		
	Reconviction	34.8		46.4		
Sontheimer & Goodstein, 1993 (5)	Rearrest		44		46	$M = 11$
	Misdemeanor or Felony	50.0		74.0*		
	Felony	25.0		41.0		
Barton & Butts, 1990 (4)	Readjudication[1]	78.0	326	53.0	18	24
	Weighted Charges (M)[2]	5.41	326	4.05	5	
	Weighted Criminal Charges (M)[3]	3.69		3.58	160	

(continued)

TABLE 9.3 *(continued)*

Study (methods score)	Measure of recidivism	Recidivism				Follow-up period (in months)
		Experimental (%)	N	Control (%) #1/#2/#3	N	
Land & Williams, 1990 (4)	Delinquent Offenses[1]	18.3	49	28.1	57	N/A
	Status Offenses[1]	18.3		21.0		
Minor & Elrod, 1990 (4)	Status Offenses (*M*)		22		23	18
	During ISP	0.50		0.44		
	After ISP	0.41		0.84		
	Criminal Offenses (*M*)					
	During ISP	0.19		0.13		
	Delinquency (Self-report) (*M*)	3.24		3.46		
Wiebush, 1993 (3)	Charges		81		76	18
	Any	81.5		82.9		
	Felony	50.6		56.6		
	Misdemeanor	46.9		38.2		
	Status	13.6				
	Probation/Parole Violation	60.5		46.1		
	Readjudication					
	Any	76.5		77.6		
	Felony	46.9		53.9		
	Misdemeanor	34.6		35.3		
	Status	7.4		5.3		
	Probation/Parole Violation	56.8		31.6		
Rickards, 1987 (2)	Referral to juvenile intake services[1]	30.0	10	33.0	21	8
Troia, 1994 (2)	Reinstitutionalization[1]	17.2/46.6	105/43	32.2	606	12

[1] No significance tests reported.
[2] Adjusted to compensate for case difference in months at large.
* Significantly different from experimental group, $p < 0.05$.

Juvenile Community Supervision Treatment Programs

Citation	Effect
Sontheimer & Goodstein, 1993	2.83
Land et al., 1990	1.73
Wiebush, 1993	1.10
Greenwood et al., 1993 (Pittsburgh)	1.04
Elrod & Minor, 1992	.93
Greenwood et al., 1993 (Detroit)	.80
Barton & Butts, 1990	.32
Mean Odds-Ratio (7)	**.66**

Figure 9.3. Forest plot showing odds ratio and 95 percent confidence interval for studies of juvenile community supervision treatment programs.

the treated group. Overall, there is insufficient evidence to conclude that community supervision for juveniles is effective in reducing recidivism.

CONCLUSION

In this chapter, I examined three interventions for juvenile delinquents: (1) MST, (2) residential programs, and (3) community supervision. Only MST was found to be effective in reducing recidivism. Most of the evaluations of MST used random assignment of subjects to the treatment or control group. Therefore, the results provide strong evidence for the effectiveness of MST. The only limiting factor was that all the strong studies were conducted by Henggeler and his colleagues who designed the MST program. Thus, there is some concern about whether the results will generalize to new jurisdictions where researchers and program operators differ.

There was insufficient evidence to conclude that residential programs for juveniles were effective in reducing delinquent or criminal activity. Six of the seven residential programs were wilderness programs. Two of these studies were rated two on research methods. Of the four remaining wilderness evaluations, only the evaluation by Kelly and Baer (1971) found significant differences between groups in favor of the group who attended the wilderness program. Deschenes et al. (1996) found the opposite – the comparison group had significantly lower recidivism. Only one study, the Greenwood and Turner (1993) evaluation of the Paint Creek Youth Center, examined a program that was not a wilderness program. They did not report significance tests for the results; however, the effect size analysis indicated that the difference between groups was not significant. Thus, although results were somewhat mixed, there was not enough evidence to conclude that these programs were effective in reducing recidivism.

Many of the residential programs I examined were wilderness programs. A question that arises is, Why do the results differ from the meta-analysis Wilson and Lipsey (2003) completed on wilderness and challenge programs for juveniles? Several explanations are possible. First, there are major differences between the systematic reviews in (1) the programs included in the analysis, (2) the samples, and (3) the outcomes. Wilson and Lipsey focused on therapeutic wilderness and challenge programs, the samples were at-risk youth, and the outcomes included both antisocial and delinquent behavior. In contrast, the programs I examined did not necessarily have a therapeutic focus, the samples were delinquent youth, and the outcomes were limited to criminal or delinquent behavior. Any one of these differences could explain the differences in conclusions about the effectiveness of the programs.

The results from the examination of the community supervision programs for juveniles led me to conclude that these programs were not effective in reducing recidivism. This is similar to the findings for adult offenders (see Chapter 14); supervision programs that often focus on increasing the control over offenders are not effective in reducing recidivism.

APPENDIX 9.1. STUDY REFERENCE, DESCRIPTION, AND METHODS SCORES (IN PARENTHESES) OF MST PROGRAMS FOR JUVENILE OFFENDERS

Bourdin et al., 1990 (5)

Sixteen juvenile sexual offenders who had participated in a larger study of delinquency in July 1983 and July 1985 were randomly assigned to MST or individual therapy (using a blend of psychodynamic, humanistic, and behavioral approaches) conditions.

Bourdin et al., 1995 **(5)**

One hundred seventy-six families with a twelve- to seventeen-year-old adolescent offender were randomly assigned to MST or individual therapy (using a blend of psychodynamic, client-centered, and behavioral approaches that focused on the individual adolescent rather than the systems in which the adolescent was embedded). The analyses compared (1) completers and dropouts combined and (2) completers only.

Henggeler et al., 2002 **(5)**

Eighty of 118 substance-abusing juvenile offenders from a previous study conducted in the mid-1990s who were randomly assigned to MST or usual community services were analyzed in this four-year follow-up. The usual community services included community-based substance abuse treatment.

Henggeler et al., 1997 **(5)**

Violent or chronic juvenile offenders from two different sites within the South Carolina Department of Juvenile Justice and their primary caregivers were randomly assigned to MST or usual services. The groups were temporally yoked to control for historical and related threats to validity.

Henggeler et al., 1993 **(5)**

Eighty-four juvenile offenders at imminent risk of out-of-home placement resulting from serious criminal activity were randomly assigned to receive family preservation using MST or usual services provided by the Department of Youth Services.

Henggeler et al., 1991 **(5)**

Adolescent offenders and their families who participated in the Missouri Delinquency Project were randomly assigned to MST or individual counseling (blend of psychodynamic, client-centered, and behavioral approaches). The analyses compared (1) completers and dropouts combined and (2) completers only.

Scherer and Brondino, 1994 **(5)**

Fifty-five serious and chronic juvenile criminal offenders and their mother figures from two sites in South Carolina were randomly assigned to multi-systemic family preservation therapy or the Department of Juvenile Justice Program usual services.

APPENDIX 9.2. STUDY REFERENCE, DESCRIPTION, AND METHODS SCORES (IN PARENTHESES) OF RESIDENTIAL TREATMENT PROGRAMS FOR JUVENILE OFFENDERS

Baer et al. 1975 **(2)**

Male delinquents committed to the Massachusetts Division of Youth Service during the spring of 1966 who volunteered to participate in the Outward Bound wilderness program were studied. Those youths receiving a certificate of completion and merit for the program are compared to youths who participated but did not receive a certificate.

Castellano and Soderstrom, 1992 **(4)**

Youths who participated in the Spectrum wilderness program between January 1987 and December 1988 are compared to a matched comparison group of delinquents that did not participate in Spectrum but matched the treatment group on relevant demographic variables; Spectrum participants possessed a more serious arrest history and were more likely to engage in repetitive delinquency than the comparison group.

Deschenes et al., 1996 **(4)**

Participants in the Nokomis Challenge Program between January 1991 and November 1991 through the Michigan Department of Social Services, which utilizes wilderness adventure and aftercare, are compared to delinquents who were eligible for the program but were not placed either because of physical problems or judges' discretions.

Gottfredson and Barton, 1993 **(4)**

Delinquents who (1) received treatment at and were released from the Montrose Training School prior to its closing and (2) received treatment at the Montrose Training School as well as various other settings after the school's closing are compared to a group of delinquents who would have probably been committed to Montrose but were referred to Division of Juvenile Services after the school's closing and spent little or no time in an institution.

Greenwood and Turner, 1987 **(3)**

Male youths who participated in the VisionQuest wilderness program are compared to delinquents that were housed at San Diego

County Probation Department's camp at West Fork (YCC); the VisionQuest group possessed a more serious delinquent history than the YCC group.

Greenwood and Turner, 1993 **(5)**

Male delinquents committed to the Ohio Division of Youth Services for a class 1 or 2 felony between February 1986 and April 1988 who were randomly assigned to participate in the Paint Creek Youth Center (PCYC) are compared to youths eligible for PCYC but who were randomly assigned to receive treatment at the Training Institute for Central Ohio or Riverview training schools.

Kelly and Baer, 1971 **(3)**

Male youths were selected from the Reception Center, Lyman School for Boys, and Industrial School for Boys in Massachusetts. Voluntary participants in the twenty-six-day wilderness adventure program, Outward Bound (in Colorado, Minnesota, or Maine), are compared to youths who were either institutionalized or paroled through the Massachusetts Division of Youth Service.

Willman and Chun, 1973 **(2)**

Male youths participating in the Homeward Bound wilderness program in East Brewster, Massachusetts, are compared to male youths adjudicated during the same time who were housed at the Lyman School for Boys (a traditional reform/training school) in Westboro, Massachusetts.

APPENDIX FOR TABLE 9.3. STUDY REFERENCE, DESCRIPTION, AND METHODS SCORES (IN PARENTHESES) OF COMMUNITY SUPERVISION TREATMENT PROGRAMS FOR JUVENILE OFFENDERS

Barton and Butts, 1990 **(4)**

Relatively serious and chronic male offenders recommended for commitment to the state between February 1983 and March 1985 in Wayne County, Michigan. Those randomly assigned to intensive supervision (either Intensive Probation Unit, Comprehensive Youth Training and Community Involvement Program, or Michigan Human Service, Inc.) are compared to those that were committed to the state for placement.

Elrod and Minor, 1992 **(5)**

Offenders randomly assigned to participate in the second wave of the community Intensive Supervised Probation (ISP Project Explore in Michigan; these offenders are compared to delinquents who were released to standard probation.

Greenwood et al., 1993 **(5)**

The Skillman Intensive Aftercare Program

Detroit, Michigan: Male youths returning to families in the Detroit area from a training school run by the Department of Social Services (DSS). Participants in the Skillman Aftercare Program, averaging twenty long contacts per month, are compared to youths who received minimal attention and services from their regularly assigned caseworkers.

Pittsburgh, Pennsylvania: Male youths returning to homes in the Pittsburgh area after completing a placement in VisionQuest. Participants in the Skillman Aftercare Program, averaging one hundred short contacts per month, are compared to youths who received minimal attention and services from their regularly assigned caseworkers.

Land and Williams, 1990 **(4)**

A largely female group of delinquents who were adjudicated undisciplined in the North Carolina evaluation sites after November 1, 1987. Delinquents randomly assigned to participate in intensive protective supervision are compared to those who were assigned to regular protective supervision.

Minor and Elrod, 1990 **(4)**

Offenders randomly assigned to participate in the community ISP Project Explore in Michigan; these offenders are compared to delinquents who were released to standard probation.

Rickards, 1987 **(2)**

Youths participating in Kenosha County's Intensive Aftercare Program (IAP) between January and August 1987 with electronic monitoring implemented in the beginning phases of the project are compared to youths also participating in the IAP but without the electronic monitoring aspect.

Sontheimer and Goodstein, 1993 **(5)**

Male delinquents committed to the Bensalem Youth Development Center (YDC) by Philadelphia Family Court and who were released from the YDC between December 1988 and January 1990. Youth randomly assigned to IAP were compared to those randomly assigned to traditional aftercare probation.

Troia, 1994 **(2)**

Youths participating in a Wisconsin IAP pilot program during fiscal years 1991 and 1992 from (1) Kenosha, Rock, Waukesha, and Vilas/Oneida Counties and (2) Racine County were compared to youths from the sixty-five other Wisconsin counties who did not have IAP available to them; the individuals from Racine County exhibited a more serious prior arrest history than other IAP youth.

Wiebush, 1993 **(3)**

Felony offenders who were originally sentenced to Division of Youth Services (DYS). Those diverted to the Lucas County Ohio Intensive Supervision Unit (ISU) between October 1987 and May 1989 are compared to offenders that met the initial screening criteria for the ISU but were not accepted into the program (DYS) and were paroled by May 1989.

CHAPTER TEN

Domestic Violence Offenders

INTRODUCTION

Estimates of the occurrence of domestic violence differ depending upon the survey used to collect the data; however, it is clear that this phenomenon affects a large part of the population. According to the 1992 NCVS, more than 1 million women were victimized by intimate partners, a category that includes boyfriends, girlfriends, spouses, and former spouses, in that year (Andrews & Bonta, 2003; Healey, Smith, & O'Sullivan, 1998). According to the Bureau of Justice Statistics (BJS), approximately 840,000 women were assaulted, raped, or robbed by intimate partners in 1996 (Greenfeld et al., 1998). Estimates from the National Violence Against Women Survey indicate approximately 1.8 million women and 1 million men were raped, physically assaulted, or stalked by an intimate partner in the past twelve months (Tjaden & Thoennes, 2000). Straus, Gelles, and Steinmetz (1980) estimated that 2 million women were victimized each year by their husbands and further speculated that if ex-husbands and boyfriends were included in the calculations, the estimate could be as high as 4 million.

Whichever figure is used, it is clear that domestic violence affects a large number of women sometime in their life. Physical violence can have far reaching effects on women and can continue long after surface injuries have healed. Research has shown that women who suffer domestic assault at the hands of an intimate partner are more likely to show increased rates of depression, suicide, anxiety, post-traumatic stress syndrome, low self-esteem, and substance abuse problems (Tjaden & Thoennes, 2000). Other detrimental effects of this violence include disproportionate risks of rape, miscarriage, and abortion; increased rates of general mental illness; subsequent high rates of medical complaints; and rates of suicide five times higher than that of the general population (Buzawa & Buzawa, 1996b). In addition, approximately 525,000 women will suffer serious injury as the result of rape, physical assault, or stalking by an intimate partner in their lifetime (Tjaden & Thoennes, 2000). Also, a large number of these women will seek out medical treatment for their injuries, having a significant impact on scarce hospital resources. Given that domestic violence is quite pervasive and has immense social and economic costs to this society, the criminal justice system has recently begun to recognize intimate partner violence as a criminal act punishable by law.

Up until about the 1970s, domestic violence was seen as a family matter between a man and his wife or significant other in which the government should not intervene. As a result, police were afforded large amounts of discretion in deciding whether to arrest suspects in domestic abuse incidents (Fagan, 1996). This began to change in the 1970s with the rise of the feminist movement and victim advocates pushing for legislators and the criminal justice system to recognize domestic abuse as a significant social problem. As a result, much of the research on spousal assault or intimate partner violence has been completed only in the past thirty years because it is only in this time that the criminal justice system has recognized it as a criminal act (2003).

The significance of the women's movement in bringing the issue of domestic violence to the public's attention is no coincidence. Research has clearly demonstrated that women are more likely to be the victim of intimate partner violence at the hands of a male partner than men being victimized by a female partner (Tjaden & Thoennes, 2000). Although there is evidence that males are also victims of domestic violence and do sustain injury as the result of assaults by female partners, the numbers indicate that domestic violence directed at women is a far greater problem (Tjaden & Thoennes, 2000). Specifically, in 1996, females accounted for approximately 85 percent of those victimized in intimate relationships, according to the BJS (Greenfeld et al., 1998). The National Violence Against Women Survey also found that women were significantly more likely than men to report being raped, physically assaulted, and/or stalked by an intimate partner

(Tjaden & Thoennes, 2000). The survey indicated that approximately 25 percent of women compared to just less than 8 percent of men surveyed had been the victim of rape or physical assault by a current or former spouse, cohabiting partner, boyfriend/girlfriend, or date in their lifetime (Tjaden & Thoennes, 2000). The prevalence rates for the past twelve months showed a similar trend, with 1.5 percent of women versus 0.9 percent of men reporting victimization (Tjaden & Thoennes, 2000).

Although males are more likely than females to be the victim of violent crime (e.g., homicide, robbery, and aggravated assault), females are more likely to be victimized by people they know, and a large share of this violence is inflicted by an intimate (Craven, 1997). The National Violence Against Women Survey found that, of the women assaulted or raped, 76 percent were victimized at the hands of an intimate (Tjaden & Thoennes, 2000). More specifically, research has found that women in the United States are at greater risk of being assaulted, injured, raped, and murdered by a current or past *male partner* than all other types of assailants combined (Wyatt, Axelrod, Chin, Vargas-Carmona, & Burns-Loeb, 2000). Furthermore, the majority of domestic assailants are men (Healey et al., 1998).

The evidence presented attests that domestic violence against women, in particular intimate violence perpetrated by a male partner, is a substantial problem. For this reason, research has focused on trying to understand why men commit these violent acts and what interventions can be used to prevent male batterers from continuing to assault intimate partners. As a result, the batterer treatment programs and criminal justice strategies examined in this chapter are limited to those dealing with male batterers.

DEFINING DOMESTIC VIOLENCE

There is no clear, all-inclusive definition for the behaviors that should be labeled domestic violence, and as a result, researchers have adopted their own. The most comprehensive definition is given in a National Institute of Justice report where domestic violence is defined as

> a constellation of physical, sexual, and psychological abuses that may include: physical violence, intimidation, threats, isolation, emotional

> abuse, sexual abuse, manipulation using children, total economic control, and assertion of male privilege (such as making all major family decisions and expecting the woman to perform all household duties). (Healey et al., 1998:1)

In addition to this, Wiehe (1998) describes intimate partner violence as the physical, emotional, or sexual abuse of a wife by her husband or by someone else with whom she is cohabiting. More generally, domestic violence has been defined as a general pattern of assaultive or coercive behaviors, including sexual, physical, or psychological abuses (Healey et al., 1998; Wiehe, 1998). Whichever definition is used, the critical component underlying the various descriptions is offender motivation: the principal motivation behind the batterer's behavior is an attempt to control the victim, whether by fear, intimidation, or physical, sexual, or emotional abuse (Postmus, 2000).

Other, more broad definitions have characterized domestic violence as occurring when one person victimizes another in an intimate relationship, the infliction of a single incidence of violence against one's intimate with or without provocation, or any act of physical aggression against an intimate. The general concepts that all these definitions incorporate are that an act of aggression needs to occur, and this act must be against another adult with whom the abuser has an intimate, interdependent relationship (Feldman & Ridley, 1995).

THEORETICAL PERSPECTIVES

Social learning theory stresses that people learn by observing those around them in their immediate environment. In particular, domestic violence theory is concerned with the exposure to violence in childhood and how this impacts future violence in adulthood (Feldman & Ridley, 1995; Milhalic & Elliott, 1997; Wiehe, 1998). The view is that violence can be learned and modeled by children and that the effects of constantly observing a parent abuse others as a way to deal with family issues causes the child to internalize violence as a valid coping strategy to be used later in life. The child is then more likely to grow up and utilize violence in his own family in times of stress or simply as a means of conflict resolution (Milhalic & Elliott, 1997). As a result, a child who observes violence in his childhood will be at a greater risk for exhibiting these behaviors later in life. However, the social learning perspective does not say that all children, or even a majority of children who witness or experience violence, will become batterers but rather that the use of violence in later life will only occur if it becomes functional to that individual. This is how research attempts to explain why only about 40 percent of abused children grow up to become abusive parents and/or partners (Dutton, 1998).

A large group of individuals who have witnessed violence in their life never see the need or opportunity to imitate these behaviors and therefore do not engage in violence toward their significant others. Nevertheless, numerous studies have found that male batterers are far more likely to have been abused as children and to have witnessed parental violence when compared to nonabusive males (Dutton, 1998; Milhalic & Elliott, 1997). Estimates from various research studies suggest that approximately 60–80 percent of abusive males come from violent homes (Feldman & Ridley, 1995).

The feminist-based theory can be seen as an extension of the social learning perspective, developed to more critically deal with domestic violence as a societal issue. Feminist theory was first developed in the 1970s as the women's movement gained full momentum and domestic violence was first recognized as a legitimate social and criminal problem. This perspective was designed and developed by women, mainly in an effort to put a stop to intimate partner violence and to raise social consciousness about the need to treat battered women. Feminist theory defines domestic violence as the use of coercive behavior to gain power and control over another person. These behaviors can incorporate any or all of those discussed earlier. By centering around the gender analysis of power, this theory seeks to provide explanations as to why the majority of batterers are men and not women (Healey et al., 1998).

According to feminist theory, violence is a means for maintaining a patriarchal organization in the family and asserting male dominance in situations where it is perceived to be threatened. Men legitimize their use of violence because it is viewed as a necessary means to maintain order in the household. In addition, this violence occurs when the man feels that his wife or significant other is failing to give him the respect to which he is entitled as a male (Healey et al., 1998). In the 1995 Canadian Violence Against Women Survey, patriarchal views were found to be significantly correlated with abuse, including jealousy and the use of control over women (2003).

MANAGEMENT AND TREATMENT APPROACHES

Most male batterers try to avoid taking responsibility for their actions, and as a result, one of the key goals of any intervention strategy is to increase accountability (Babcock & La Taillade, 2000; Pence, 1989). An effective intervention must encourage a batterer to acknowledge his violence and how it has adversely affected others around him (Healey et al., 1998). The most widely used and empirically supported intervention approaches are based in feminist theory and cognitive-behavioral approaches. However, in the past two decades, experiments have been conducted with a new approach that attempts to utilize criminal justice sanctions (e.g., arrest, citations, prosecution) as a deterrent to future violence.

Feminist Treatment

The feminist approach is by far the most prominent type of clinical intervention used with batterers today. This approach focuses on the sexist attitudes adopted by men that are thought to encourage the use of violence toward women (Sonkin, 1995). Feminist theory views domestic violence as a criminal behavior, not as a result of any underlying personality disorder. Its main goal is to get the abuser to accept responsibility for his actions and not blame these actions on past abuse experiences or as a reaction to provocation by a partner. Third, these programs focus on re-educating men rather than providing therapy, because the thrust of feminist theory is on the idea that violence is learned in a social context and can therefore be unlearned, not on the psychopathology of the batterer. This results in programs stressing the end of the abusive behavior and protection of the victim, rather than focusing on healing the batterer (Babcock & La Taillade, 2000; Pence, 1989).

Cognitive-Behavioral Treatment

Cognitive-behavioral approaches focus on modifying thinking and behaviors in current situations to allow the batterer to control his own actions (Healey et al., 1998). Psychologists usually guide these interventions with the primary focus aimed at stopping the violence. Similar to the feminist perspective, cognitive-behavioral approaches are based on the idea that violent behavior is learned and that therefore nonviolence can also be learned. Domestic assault is seen as a behavior of choice that can be controlled if batterers are taught that it is an inappropriate response in all situations. Cognitive-behavioral theory recognizes the difficulties in this because it assumes the use of violence by batterers is an adaptive response, whether as a coping mechanism for conflict resolution, as a stress reliever, or simply as a method to maintain dominance and control (Babcock & La Taillade, 2000). Furthermore, abuse may be positively reinforced through victim compliance, enabling the batterer to get what he wants (Healey et al., 1998). As a result, cognitive-behavioral interventions first recognize the pros and cons of violence but then focus on skills training and anger management techniques to curb violent behavior before it begins or escalates (Babcock & La Taillade, 2000).

Central to this approach is the cognitive or thinking aspect. The thoughts and feelings of the batterer just prior to a violent incident are examined so that he can see the irrationality of his thought processes. Most often, the pattern that emerges is that of developing irrational negative thoughts toward a partner and then getting angry as a result (Healey et al., 1998). Treatment then focuses on teaching these men to recognize these dangerous thought patterns and to interrupt them before they become violent, replacing these thoughts with positive coping statements. In conjunction with this, anger management and stress relaxation classes help the batterer to reduce his physiological arousal after he has successfully avoided the use of violence (Babcock & La Taillade, 2000; Healey et al., 1998; Sonkin, 1995).

Criminal Justice Sanctions

The use of sanctions as treatment may seem like a large divergence from feminist and cognitive-behavioral approaches, but in reality, they share a common link. Criminal justice sanctions (e.g., arrest, prosecution) and batterer treatment programs are not mutually exclusive. In many cases, a batterer may have been mandated to participate in treatment by the court system as a result of arrest and/or as a condition of probation. Hence, in many situations, arrest is a confounding factor in research examining the effectiveness of the treatment strategy being used. This is one of the reasons researchers began to examine the impact of arrests. By isolating the effects of arrest from formal treatment, researchers hoped to determine whether this highly utilized police strategy may in fact help decrease domestic violence in and of itself.

The implications of this relatively new research are far reaching given that arrest is one of the most utilized criminal justice strategies and that domestic violence is the most frequent form of violence that police encounter, more common than all other forms of violence combined (Sherman, 1992). In fact, Buzawa and Buzawa (1996a) suggest that police departments may be the most logical agencies to deal with domestic violence for many reasons: police are usually the ones who have the initial contact with the perpetrator and victim, are highly visible authority figures, provide free service, maintain a central dispatch system, and are the only agency that can provide twenty-four-hour rapid assistance to victims. Furthermore, police are much more accessible to victims of domestic assault when compared to other agencies that may be helpful in domestic assault cases (e.g., medical services, social welfare; Buzawa & Buzawa, 1996a).

CRIMINALIZATION OF DOMESTIC VIOLENCE

As discussed in the introduction, domestic violence has only recently been viewed and punished as a criminal act. For most of this country's history, violence toward women has been accepted as a method to maintain the family unit. Although the Massachusetts Body of Laws and Liberties passed laws to make domestic violence illegal dating back to 1641, these written laws did not supercede the cultural norm of acceptance of violence toward women (Buzawa & Buzawa, 1996a). As a result, a general acceptance of a husband's right to inflict harm on his wife to maintain the family unit prevailed. Evidence of this is found in an eighteenth-century codification. The well-known "rule of thumb" law allowed a husband to beat his wife with a rod or stick no thicker than his thumb. Additionally, a husband could punish his wife with physical violence as long as no permanent marks were left by the assault (Buzawa & Buzawa, 1996a).

Police culture up until the mid-twentieth century viewed intimate assaults as private, family matters in which officers had no right or obligation to intervene, and hence these incidents almost never resulted in arrest. In fact, in 1967 the International Association of Chiefs of Police manual stressed that arrest should only be used as a last resort in these family disputes (Sherman, 1992). Officers were encouraged to focus their efforts on arresting more serious, felony offenders because these cases would more likely result in a conviction (Buzawa & Buzawa, 1996a). In addition, police were reluctant to arrest in domestic cases because many perceived the threat of danger to themselves as very high if they tried to arrest the batterer (Buzawa & Buzawa, 1996b).

In the 1970s, women's rights advocates and feminist groups lobbied for changes in legislation to provide greater protection for women victims. Simultaneously, several women filed lawsuits against police departments because they felt they were not being adequately protected from a violent partner (Jaffe, Hastings, Reitzel, & Austin, 1993). As a result, many substantive changes have been made in the laws to increase the use of arrest and encourage the development of mediation, counseling, and treatment programs for both batterers and victims (Buzawa & Buzawa, 1996b). However, these changes were slow to come, and police first developed alternate strategies to avoid arrest such as conflict resolution, mediation, or counseling (Jaffe et al., 1993).

Unfortunately, the adoption of these approaches by the police did not add much protection for women because they continued to stress the avoidance of arrest and treated the domestic incident as a no fault, noncriminal act. Feminist groups continued to campaign for a less social work–oriented perspective toward domestic cases and to adopt a more rigid, criminal perspective (Sherman & Berk, 1984). According to a 1975 police guide, *The Function of the Police in Crisis Intervention and Conflict Management*, officers were instructed to avoid arrest at all costs and in situations where an arrest seemed inevitable, they should try to dissuade arrest by cautioning the victim about all the negative effects an arrest can bring (Jaffe et al., 1993).

As the 1980s approached, police culture gradually began to adopt an increased use of punishment in domestic incidents. By 1980, domestic violence legislation had been passed in forty-seven states, mandating such policies as changes in protection orders, allowing for warrantless arrest for misdemeanor assaults, and recognizing a history of abuse and threat as part of a legal defense for battered women who killed their abusive husbands (Fagan, 1996).

EFFECTIVENESS OF INTERVENTIONS

Of great importance is the evaluation of the treatment programs and criminal justice sanctions designed to reduce domestic violence. One of the main problems with assessing the effectiveness of male batterer interventions has been the study methodology employed. This review of the literature includes both a quantitative assessment of each study as well as an analysis of the direction and significance of the results. Furthermore, the full ranges of interventions for the male batterers including feminist-based, cognitive-behavioral, and criminal justice sanctions are assessed.

The twenty-one studies assessed in this research were divided into three distinct categories based on the nature of the intervention used. Feminist and cognitive-behavioral interventions involve many overlapping concepts, and therefore classification into one of these two categories was subjective, based on an overall conclusion of the general theoretical approach guiding the intervention. Six studies were classified as feminist-based interventions, six as cognitive-behavioral studies, and nine studies were classified as legal interventions. The studies are listed by category in Tables 10.1–10.3 along with the methods score, length of follow-up, and recidivism rates. The related appendices (10.1–10.3) provide a description of each study.

Feminist-Based Interventions

In reviewing the available literature, two recent reviews of treatment programs were found. Davis and Taylor (1999) and Babcock and La Taillade (2000) examined interventions grounded in feminist and

TABLE 10.1. *Recidivism rates and length of follow-up of feminist-based studies of domestic violence interventions*

Study (methods score)	Measure of recidivism	Recidivism: Experimental (%)	N	Control (%) #1/#2/#3	N	Follow-up period (in months)
Saunders, 1996 (5)	Arrest for Battery	23.2	56	20.3	64	18–54
	Any Crime	26.8		28.1		
Chen et al., 1989 (4)	Charges/Domestic	5.0	120	10.0	101	14–16
	Charges/Other	8.3		16.8		
Babcock & Steiner, 1999 (3)	Police Report	16.9	284	61.8	55	24
Edleson & Syers, 1991 (3)	Victim or Self-Report of Violence	36.4	19	21.1	22	18
Palmer et al., 1992 (3)	Physical Abuse or Threats in Police Records	10.0	30	31.0*	26	12–24
Edleson & Grusznski, 1989 (2)	Partner Report of Violence	41.6	84	48.6	37	12
	Threat of Violence	35.7		29.7		

* Significantly different from experimental group, $p < 0.05$.

TABLE 10.2. *Recidivism rates and length of follow-up of cognitive-behavioral studies of domestic violence interventions*

Study (methods score)	Measure of recidivism	Recidivism				Follow-up period (in months)
		Experimental (%)	N	Control (%) #1/#2/#3	N	
Feder & Dugan, 2002 (5)	Rearrest	24.2	227	23.2	168	12
Dunford, 2000 (4)	Arrest for Battery	3.6	168	4.0	150	12
Dobash & Dobash, 2000 (3)	Arrest/Domestic	7.0	35.0	10.0	30.0	18
Gondolf, 1999 (3)	Victim Report of Domestic Assault					15
	Severe/Any	12.0/27.0	210	23.0/35.0	210	
	Any Assault[1]	22.0	129	35.0	114	
Dutton et al., 1997 (2)	Arrest/Assault	23.2	156	28.0/21.0	167/91	62.4
	Wife Assault	17.9		22.2/16.5		
Hamberger & Hastings, 1988 (2)	Police or Self-Report Domestic Violence	28.1	32	47.2	36	12

[1] Ns are approximation.

* Significantly different from experimental group, $p < 0.05$.

TABLE 10.3. *Recidivism rates and length of follow-up of arrest studies of domestic violence offenders*

Study (methods score)	Measure of recidivism	Recidivism				Follow-up period (in months)
		Experimental (%)	N	Control (%) #1/#2/#3	N	
Berk et al., 1992 (5)	Crime	19.3	421	19.4	1158	?
Dunford et al., 1990 (5)	Arrest	11.9	109	11.3/8.7	106/115	6
	Victim Complaint	17.4		17.9/14.8		
Dunford, 1992 (5)	Arrest	21.1	109	14.0	221	12
	Victim Complaint	27.5		22.2		
Dunford, 1990 (5)	Arrest/6 Months	5.4	111	11.8	136	6
	Victim Complaint	14.4		22.1		
	Victim Report of Injury	16.2		30.1*		
	Arrest/12 Months	10.8		20.6*		12
	Victim Complaint	25.2		31.6		
	Victim Report of Injury	19.0		34.6*		
Hirschel & Hutchinson, 1992 (5)	Arrest	18.2	214	19.2/11.8	224/212	6
	Victim Report of Repeat Incident	58.9	112	65.3/59.8	124/102	

Pate & Hamilton, 1992 (5)	Offense Report of Assault		537		370[1]	6
	Employed	6.2		12.3		
	Unemployed	16.7		7.1*		
Sherman & Berk, 1984 (5)	Arrest	10.0	136	19.0/24.0	89/89	6
	Victim Report of Repeat Incident	19.0		37.0/33.0		
Sherman et al., 1991 (5)	Hotline Report of Violence	27.0	324	27.0/26.0	300/297	6
	Arrest	20.0		21.0/23.0		
	Victim Report of Violence	35.0		30.0/31.0		
Sherman et al., 1992 (5)	Hotline Report of Violence		324		300/297	6
	Employed	20.0		17.0/28.0		
	Unemployed	28.0		31.0/26.0		
	Married	17.0		15.0/26.0		
	Not Married	28.0		28.0/27.0		

[1] Ns are approximation.

* Significantly different from experimental group, $p < 0.05$.

cognitive-behavioral theory, and both concluded that domestic violence interventions do indeed have a moderate beneficial effect on reducing recidivism. Babcock and La Taillade also examined the effect sizes for feminist and cognitive-behavioral approaches separately and concluded that feminist interventions were approximately three times as effective at reducing recidivism when compared to cognitive-behavioral interventions. Furthermore, research conducted by Feldman and Ridley (1995) agrees that batterer treatments do significantly reduce the level of physical violence, but they suggest that more subtle forms of abuse, such as psychological and emotional, are not altered by treatment.

Table 10.1 describes the six studies identified as feminist interventions. The research found lower rates of recidivism for the treatment group in three of the studies (Babcock & Steiner, 1999; Chen, Bersani, Myers, & Denton, 1989; Palmer, Brown, & Barrera, 1992); however, only one study found statistically significant differences favoring the treatment group over the comparison group (Palmer, Brown, & Barrerra, 1992). In contrast, Saunders (1996), the only study employing the "gold standard" of a randomized design that assigned male batterers to either feminist or psychodynamic treatment, found a slightly higher recidivism rate for the feminist treatment versus the comparison group.

Figure 10.1 presents the results of a meta-analysis of five feminist-based studies of domestic violence interventions. The recidivism measures used in calculating effect sizes were arrest for battery (n = 1), charges/domestic (n = 1), police report (n = 1), victim or self-report of violence (n = 1), and physical abuse or threats in police records. The most recent recidivism measures were used, representing the longest follow-up period. The study by Edleson and Grusznski (1988) was excluded from the analysis because of its low methods score. Only one study significantly favored the treatment over the control group (Babcock & Steiner, 1999).

Briefly, the studies in this category suffered from a few different methodological problems that raise questions as to whether their results should inform policy. For example, Saunders (1996) used a randomized design but only treatment completers were included in

Domestic Violence Feminist-Based Treatment Programs

Citation	Effect
Babcock & Steiner, 1999	7.96
Palmer et al., 1992	4.00
Chen et al., 1989	2.23
Saunders, 1996	.84
Edleson & Syers, 1991	.50
Mean Odds-Ratio (5)	**2.82**

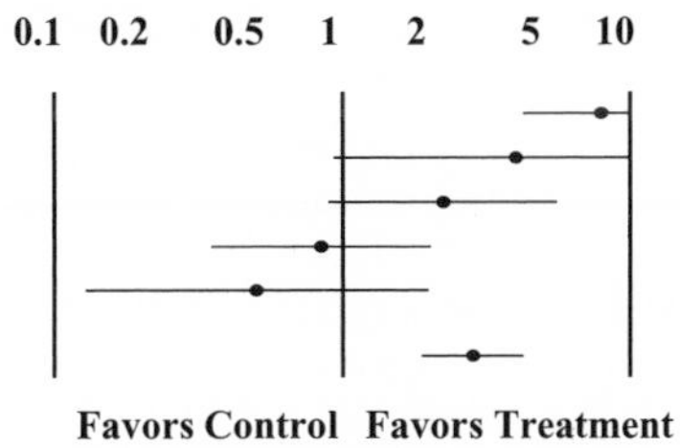

0.1 0.2 0.5 1 2 5 10

Favors Control **Favors Treatment**

Figure 10.1. Forest plot showing odds ratio and 95 percent confidence interval for studies of domestic violence feminist-based treatment programs.

the analysis when feminist treatment was compared to psychodynamic approaches. It is possible that research designs comparing program completers to dropouts end up evaluating two noncomparable groups. That is, people who complete treatment are likely to be more motivated than those who drop out and hence will likely show more positive results. This was the major methodological flaw of the research done by Edleson and Grusznski (1988). Also, many batterers fail to complete the treatment program, and attrition is a large problem in much of the research. Another flaw is that recidivism analyses are often done on very small groups of men, leading researchers to question the generalizability of these findings.

Cognitive-Behavioral Interventions

Of the six studies of cognitive-behavioral programs included in this review, four studies were rated as level three or higher on the methods score (Dobash & Dobash, 2000; Dunford, 2000; Feder & Dugan, 2002; Gondolf, 1999; see Table 10.2). Although most of the cognitive-behavioral studies examined here found lower rates of recidivism for the treatment group, none of these differences were statistically significant except for Gondolf (1999). Gondolf found significant reductions in severe posttreatment assaults among batterers when a very intensive treatment was compared to a short-term, nonintensive treatment; however, Gondolf did not find significant results between the groups in overall recidivism. Furthermore, the one study employing random

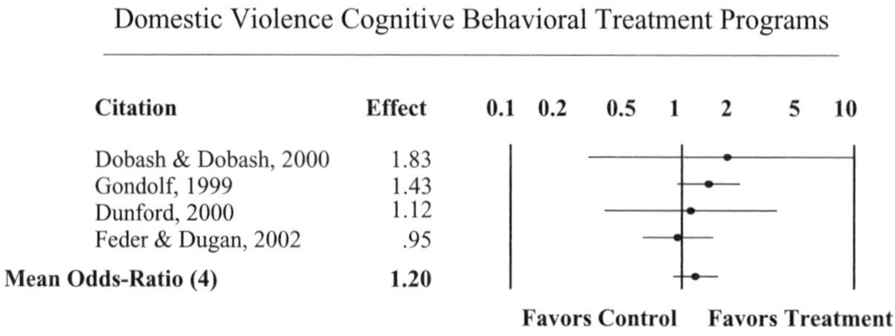

Domestic Violence Cognitive Behavioral Treatment Programs

Citation	Effect
Dobash & Dobash, 2000	1.83
Gondolf, 1999	1.43
Dunford, 2000	1.12
Feder & Dugan, 2002	.95
Mean Odds-Ratio (4)	**1.20**

0.1 0.2 0.5 1 2 5 10

Favors Control **Favors Treatment**

Figure 10.2. Forest plot showing odds ratio and 95 percent confidence interval for studies of domestic violence cognitive-behavioral treatment programs.

assignment to treatment or control found no differences in rates of rearrest among male batterers convicted of misdemeanor domestic violence (Feder & Dugan, 2002).

Figure 10.2 presents the results of a meta-analysis of four cognitive-behavioral studies of domestic violence interventions. The recidivism measures used in calculating effect sizes were rearrest (n = 1), arrest for battery (n = 1), arrest/domestic (n = 1), and victim report of domestic assault (n = 1). The most recent recidivism measures were used, representing the longest follow-up period. Two studies were excluded from the analysis because of low methods score. Results of the meta-analysis reveal no significant differences in recidivism rates as indicated by the overall mean effect size.

Overall, the research on cognitive-behavioral interventions suggests they can decrease recidivism; however, the failure to find statistically significant reductions cautions against reaching any definitive conclusions. Attention must be given to the methodological flaws inherent in many of the studies in the cognitive-behavioral category. Two studies suffered from the treatment completer versus dropout design noted for the feminist interventions, and therefore findings must be interpreted cautiously (Dutton, Bodnarchuk, Kropp, Hart, & Ogloff, 1997; Hamberger & Hastings, 1988). Although the remaining four studies were more methodologically sound, incorporating generally acceptable designs with a valid control group, only one produced statistically significant reductions in future domestic violence in the treatment versus the comparison group (Gondolf, 1999).

Criminal Justice Sanctions

The Spouse Assault Replication Program (SARP), as it is commonly referred to in the literature (Garner, Fagan, & Maxwell, 1995), constitutes the bulk of the research investigating the use of sanctions in domestic violence incidents (see Table 10.3). The Minneapolis Domestic Violence Experiment (Sherman & Berk, 1984) was the first study and was subsequently replicated in five other cities with two separate replications conducted in Omaha, thus resulting in seven replications in total: Omaha, Nebraska; Charlotte, North Carolina; Milwaukee, Wisconsin; metro-Dade (Miami), Florida; and Colorado Springs, Colorado (Berk, Campbell, Klap, & Western, 1992; Dunford, Huizinga, & Elliott, 1990; Dunford, 1990; 1992; Hirschel & Hutchinson, 1992; Pate & Hamilton, 1992; Sherman et al., 1991).[1] None of the studies of sanctions employed treatment programs for male batterers but instead investigated the effects of intervention by the police (e.g., through arrest, police response to calls).

When the SARP was undertaken, certain critical research design characteristics were implemented across the studies. These included the use of random assignment to arrest (treatment) or alternate (control) conditions and the measurement of the primary outcome, criminal recidivism, using victim interviews and official records. In addition, eligibility criteria were also standardized across studies such that cases were only considered for inclusion in the study if they constituted a misdemeanor spouse assault (Garner, Fagan, & Maxwell, 1995). The evaluations that resulted from the SARP are therefore viewed as the strongest test of the effect of arrest on male batterers.

There are two different ways that the Minneapolis study and its seven published replications must be examined to determine the effect of arrest on deterring subsequent domestic violence. First, when examining the general results, without looking at any characteristics of the batterers, four of the studies showed a deterrent effect for arrest (Berk et al., 1992; Dunford, 1990; Sherman & Berk, 1984; Sherman et al.,

[1] The study by Sherman and Smith (1992) was a re-analysis of data from the Milwaukee replication and therefore cannot be included in the primary evaluation because it would result in double counting. In addition, another study was not included in the primary evaluation of effectiveness because of its poor design (Murphy, Musser, & Maton, 1998).

Domestic Violence Criminal Justice/Arrest Interventions

Citation	Effect
Sherman & Berk, 1984	2.37
Dunford, 1990	2.14
Pate & Hamilton, 1992	1.20
Sherman et al., 1991	1.12
Sherman et al., 1992	1.08
Berk et al., 1992	1.01
Hirschel & Hutchinson, 1992	.83
Pate & Hamilton, 1992	.83
Dunford, 1992	.61
Mean Odds-Ratio (9)	**1.06**

0.1 0.2 0.5 1 2 5 10

Favors Control **Favors Treatment**

Figure 10.3. Forest plot showing odds ratio and 95 percent confidence interval for studies of domestic violence criminal justice/arrest interventions.

1991). These studies were conducted in Colorado Springs, Omaha (offender absent), Minneapolis, and Milwaukee, respectively. One caveat must be noted: in the Colorado Springs replication, the authors found that arrest deterred re-offending only when measured by victim reports for which there was a very low response rate; as such, the generality of those results is questionable. However, replications in the cities of Omaha (offender present) and Charlotte both found an escalation in future domestic violence following arrest when compared to other responses by the police (Dunford, 1992; Hirschel & Hutchinson, 1992, respectively).

Figure 10.3 presents the results of nine criminal justice/arrest-based treatment studies on recidivism with regards to domestic violence offenders. The principal recidivism measure in each study involves a return to violence for the offenders; this is evidenced by rearrest (n = 7), offense report of assault (n = 1), and hotline report of violence (n = 1). To generate the best possible measure of recidivism, the longest follow-up period available is used to calculate the effect sizes. Please note that the recidivism measure used to calculate the effect sizes reported for Pate and Hamilton 1992 and Sherman et al. 1992 is an average taken for the employed and unemployed groups.

At first glance, it appears these results are inconclusive given that four studies revealed positive, deterrent effects for arrest whereas two studies showed that arrest produces an escalation in violence (a final study showed no difference in recidivism between comparison groups; Dunford et al., 1990). However, the second manner in which this data has been examined involves focusing on how arrest operates for different types of offenders. Specifically, evaluations have distinguished offenders according to their stake in conformity and found this to condition the deterrent effect of arrest. When stake in conformity was measured by marriage and employment status, the Colorado Springs, Miami metro-Dade, and Milwaukee studies found arrest serves as a deterrent for offenders with a high stake in conformity (i.e., married, employed), whereas arrest leads to an escalation in violence for offenders with a low stake in conformity (i.e., unmarried, unemployed; Berk et al., 1992; Pate & Hamilton, 1992; Sherman et al., 1992, respectively). These findings suggest that a number of important implications must be considered if criminal justice sanctions are used to curb domestic violence.

The critical analysis by Garner et al. (1995) provides a comprehensive assessment of the methodological problems surrounding the SARP. Garner et al.'s main criticism centers around the appropriateness of comparing the data across the cities given the subtle differences in the studies. First, although there was an agreement that criminal recidivism was the outcome of interest and that it should be measured using official records and victim reports, there was considerable variation in how researchers operationalized the construct. For example, some studies used reports of subsequent domestic violence whereas others focused on any type of violence, and some studies relied on prevalence measures whereas others looked at frequency rates. Second, some cities incorporated a design comparing arrest to no arrest (Miami metro-Dade), whereas others included comparisons of up to four treatments (Colorado Springs), making comparisons across the studies more difficult. In addition, follow-up periods were not identical in all cities, leading to more time at risk to re-offend for some groups of offenders compared to others. Although these criticisms are indeed valid, the research methods employed in SARP are far superior to those used in evaluations of both the feminist and cognitive-behavioral treatment programs and therefore provide the strongest evidence yet when addressing the effectiveness of domestic violence intervention approaches.

CONCLUSION

In assessing the three types of domestic violence interventions, it is necessary to address the level of scientific rigor incorporated in the specific studies. Clearly, the feminist and cognitive-behavioral treatment studies lack the sound methods used in the SARP studies; thus, more weight can be placed on conclusions drawn from the arrest approach compared to the treatment programs themselves.

What Works?

Using the Maryland criteria, none of the interventions examined in this analysis show strong evidence that they work to reduce domestic violence. Neither of the two types of treatment programs, feminist or cognitive-behavioral, produced two studies with clear significant results favoring the treatment group over the control group. Furthermore, although the evaluations of criminal justice sanctions were scientifically rigorous, the results for the direct effect of arrest were contradictory, thereby undermining any definitive conclusions regarding effectiveness.

What Is Promising?

Based on the Maryland criteria, feminist interventions were shown to be promising. One study found that batterers attending psychoeducational treatment classes had significantly lower recidivism rates when compared to a probation group of abusers (Palmer et al., 1992). In conjunction with this, the preponderance of the evidence supported feminist-based approaches with three studies finding lower (albeit not significant) recidivism rates for the treatment compared to the control group (Babcock & Steiner, 1999; Chen et al., 1989; Edleson & Grusznski, 1988).

The cognitive-behavioral approach is also classified as promising. Gondolf (1999) found that an intensive nine-month program that included counseling, extensive clinical evaluations, and substance abuse treatment significantly reduced recidivism when compared to a less intensive three-month program consisting of counseling and referral to substance abuse programming. The preponderance of the evidence also supports cognitive-behavioral approaches as promising as evidenced by the three studies finding lower (although not significant) rates of recidivism for the treatment group (Dobash & Dobash, 2000; Hamberger & Hastings, 1988; Dutton et al., 1997).

The use of criminal justice sanctions to deter violence was also labeled promising rather than as definitively working, given the contradictory nature of the results for the direct effect of arrest. That is, although two studies found a significant deterrent effect of arrest, three replications showed a nonstatistically significant escalation of violence following arrest. Criminal justice sanctions were also shown to have promising results when used with specific groups of offenders. Three studies found a deterrent effect for arrest among offenders with a high stake in conformity, but only one of these studies (Miami metro-Dade) produced statistically significant differences in subsequent domestic assault (Pate & Hamilton, 1992). The replication in Miami metro-Dade found significant reductions in future violence among employed batterers who were arrested and an escalation in violence among unemployed batterers who were arrested. In addition, the Milwaukee and Colorado Springs replications both detected reductions in postarrest violence among those with a high stake in conformity, but these differences were not significant.

When Sherman and Berk (1984) undertook the Minneapolis study, they likely did not anticipate its far reaching effects. By examining the arrest decision as treatment, the response of the criminal justice system could be isolated and examined without confounding sanctions and treatment programming effect. This study and the others in the SARP set the stage for how law enforcement would manage male batterers. Their research was largely responsible for moving officers away from the mediation model and toward the criminalization of the offense. This research also investigated how arrest and other alternative police strategies have differential effects on different types of offenders. Treatment programs are only recently using batterer typologies to determine which types of treatments work best for which types of offenders.

It is crucial for investigators to continue to examine the use of arrest and prosecution approaches with male batterers. Arrest is now a commonly used sanction by police officers dealing with domestic cases and often results in court-mandated treatment for the abuser. Researchers interested in isolating the independent effect of clinical interventions such as feminist or cognitive-behavioral treatments must therefore account for the impact of the arrest experience in either deterring or escalating subsequent violence. The only clear result from the arrest data so far is that it appears to deter offenders who possess strong social bonds within their community. Treatment program developers would be well advised to heed these results in considering how to provide differential treatment strategies to offenders with different characteristics.

APPENDIX 10.1. STUDY REFERENCE, DESCRIPTION, AND METHODS SCORES (IN PARENTHESES) OF FEMINIST INTERVENTION TREATMENT FOR DOMESTIC VIOLENCE OFFENDERS

Babcock and Steiner, 1999 **(3)**

Convicted male abusers court mandated to attend treatment program through the King County Probation Department (Washington) in July 1992 compared to batterers incarcerated in lieu of treatment.

Chen et al., 1989 **(4)**

Convicted male abusers, court referred to the Time Out treatment program between October 1983 and June 1985, completing at least 75 percent of the program compared to control group of nonreferred abusers receiving no treatment.

Edleson and Grusznski, 1989 **(2)**

Male batterers referred by community agency, partner, or court to attend treatment; psychoeducational, open-ended, self-help group treatment completers compared to treatment dropouts.

Edleson and Syers, 1991 **(3)**

Male batterers seeking treatment services by reporting to an agency were randomly assigned to a feminist-based education program compared to self-help program modeled after Alcoholics Anonymous' twelve-step program or a combination program. Each program also looked at different amounts of treatment, comparing twelve sessions to thirty-two sessions.

Palmer et al., 1992 (3)

Convicted wife abusers court mandated between February 1987 and June 1988 to participate in psychoeducational and anger management classes and placed on probation compared to control group receiving probation and no treatment.

Saunders, 1996 (5)

Male batterers assessed and accepted for treatment were randomly assigned to receive feminist cognitive-behavioral treatment compared to process psychodynamic treatment. Comparisons were made using program completers (as defined by the program policy as sixteen out of twenty sessions).

APPENDIX 10.2. STUDY REFERENCE, DESCRIPTION, AND METHODS SCORES (IN PARENTHESES) OF COGNITIVE-BEHAVIORAL TREATMENT FOR DOMESTIC VIOLENCE OFFENDERS

Dobash and Dobash, 2000 (3)

Convicted male batterers court referred to cognitive-behavioral treatment involving conflict resolution and anger management classes through Britain's CHANGE program and Lothian Domestic Violence Probation Project compared to male batterers attending no treatment but given a fine or court sanction.

Dunford, 2000 (4)

Navy men convicted of wife assault who received different types of cognitive skills training and anger management treatment compared to navy men who received no treatment services.

Dutton et al., 1997 (2)

Convicted male spouse abusers court referred to attend the Vancouver Assaultive Husbands Program in Canada between June 1982 and December 1992; program completers compared to (1) dropouts and (2) no shows.

Feder and Dugan, 2002 (5)

Male batterers convicted of misdemeanor domestic violence in Broward County, Florida, in a five-month period in 1997 were randomly assigned to treatment and control groups; those sentenced to twelve months of probation and twenty-six weeks of counseling are compared those sentenced to twelve months of probation only.

Gondolf, 1999 **(3)**

Group 1: Male batterers court ordered to attend treatment; participants in Denver's highly specialized, intensive treatment program compared to batterers attending the short-term, nonintensive program at Pittsburgh.

Group 2: Same as mentioned but limited to batterers who completed at least three months in the Denver and the Pittsburgh programs.

Hamberger and Hastings, 1988 **(2)**

Male spouse abusers completing court ordered cognitive-behavioral therapy program including a skills training component, communication/assertiveness component, and a relaxation component compared to treatment dropouts.

APPENDIX 10.3. STUDY REFERENCE, DESCRIPTION, AND METHODS SCORES (IN PARENTHESES) OF CRIMINAL JUSTICE TREATMENT FOR DOMESTIC VIOLENCE OFFENDERS

Berk et al., 1992 **(5)**

Colorado Springs Spouse Abuse Experiment: Males involved in misdemeanor domestic violence randomly assigned to arrest with an emergency protection order compared to (1) emergency protection order coupled with immediate crisis counseling for suspect, (2) emergency protection only, and (3) police restoring order at scene.

This data compares "good risk" suspects (employed in labor force or military; n = 1,080) compared to "bad risk" (unemployed; n = 499) and whether or not they were arrested.

Dunford et al., 1990 **(5)**

Omaha Police Experiment (Offender Present): Males accused of misdemeanor domestic assault randomly assigned to arrest by police compared to (1) males who were separated from their partner by police and (2) mediation by police to settle conflict.

Dunford, 1992 **(5)**

Omaha Police Experiment (Offender Present): Reanalysis of Dunford et al. (1990) with longer follow-up period and comparison groups combined.

Dunford, 1990 **(5)**

Omaha Police Experiment (Offender Absent): Males accused of misdemeanor assault who were absent when the police arrived at the scene and were issued a warrant compared to those who did not receive a warrant for their arrest.

Hirschel and Hutchinson, 1992 **(5)**

Charlotte Spouse Assault Experiment: Males accused of misdemeanor domestic assault between August 1987 and June 1989 randomly assigned to arrest compared to (1) issuance of a citation to the offender to appear in court on specific charges and (2) advisement and separation of couple.

Pate and Hamilton, 1992 **(5)**

Metro-Dade Spouse Assault Experiment: Males who were randomly assigned to arrest for domestic assault compared to those who received no arrest between 1987 and 1989.

Sherman and Berk, 1984 **(5)**

Minneapolis Domestic Violence Experiment: Males accused of simple misdemeanor domestic assault between March 1981 and August 1982 randomly assigned to arrest by police compared to (1) males who were separated from their partner by police and (2) couples who were simply advised, which could include mediation.

Sherman et al., 1991 **(5)**

Milwaukee Domestic Violence Experiment: Males accused of misdemeanor domestic assault between June 1987 and August 1988 randomly assigned to full arrest procedure (twelve hours) compared to those (1) receiving short arrest (three hours) and (2) issued a warning.

Sherman et al., 1992 **(5)**

Milwaukee Domestic Violence Experiment: Reanalysis of Sherman et al. (1991) with focus on interaction between treatment condition and offender characteristic (e.g., employment and marital status).

PART FOUR

MANAGEMENT AND TREATMENT OF SUBSTANCE ABUSERS

CHAPTER ELEVEN

Drug Courts

A Strategy for Managing Drug-Involved Offenders

INTRODUCTION

Drug courts are a management strategy designed to use the authority of the courts to reduce crime by changing defendants' drug-using behavior. Drug-involved defendants are diverted to drug courts in exchange for the possibility of dismissed charges or reduced sentences. Judges preside over drug court proceedings and monitor the progress of the defendants. Working in collaboration with prosecutors, defense attorneys, treatment providers, probation agents, and others, judges proscribe sanctions for noncompliance with program requirements and rewards for compliance.

In comparison to traditional courtrooms, the drug court model is less punitive and more healing and restorative in nature. Courtroom procedures are more informal. Direct exchanges between the participant and the judge are common, and interactions between the state and defense are nonadversarial. A new working relationship occurs between the criminal court and health and treatment systems (Goldkamp, 1999). The role of the judge galvanizes the treatment process into a more powerful and accountable form of rehabilitation than previously available in the criminal justice system. The focus is not on the disposition of criminal cases but instead on rehabilitating drug-involved offenders.

The major goals of most drug courts are to reduce drug use and criminal activity. These goals are accomplished by engaging and retaining drug-involved offenders in supervision and treatment programs. Expertise about drug cases is concentrated in a single courtroom.

Advocates of the drug courts argue that use of one courtroom increases the effectiveness of both clinical assessment of defendants' needs and case management.

The drug court model usually involves several components. Defendants in need of treatment must be identified and referred to the court as soon as possible after arrest. In most drug courts, the defendant must agree to certain conditions before being accepted into the drug court. Defendants are usually required to submit to mandatory periodic drug testing. There is usually some reward for successful participation such as dismissal of charges (in the diversion or presentence models) or reduced sentences (in the postsentence model). The judge in the drug court supervises structured community-based supervision and treatment. Typically, defendants are required to complete a treatment program to graduate from the drug court.

The central component of all drug court programs is attendance at regularly scheduled status hearings where the judge monitors the progress of the participants. The purpose of these hearings is to provide continuing court supervision and to keep the offender in treatment. Treatment providers and/or supervising agents prepare reports documenting such things as drug testing results and attendance at counseling sessions. These are reported at the status hearings. The judge rewards progress and sanctions noncompliance.

Rewards and sanctions vary by court, judge, and participant. The judge may reward positive behavior by reducing the frequency of status hearings. Sanctions for noncompliance with conditions of the court vary from a verbal warning to return to an earlier phase of the program, short terms of incarceration, or more frequent status hearings, treatment sessions, or drug tests. Many programs use graduated sanctions, increasing the severity of the sanctions with each subsequent violation of the rules. Some programs respond to violations of the rules by increasing the intensity of the treatment. For instance, offenders who have been attending outpatient treatment may be required to attend a residential program. From this perspective, sanctions are not designed to simply punish inappropriate behavior but also to address the offender's needs. Offenders who fail drug tests or do not attend treatment sessions are assumed to have a more severe addiction that needs to be addressed with more intensive treatment.

History of Drug Courts

The number of drug courts has rapidly grown since the first one started in 1989 in Dade County, Florida. By May 2001, 688 drug courts were operating in the United States (American University, 2001). Another 432 were in the planning process. These included 483 adult, 158 juvenile, 38 family, and 9 combination (adult/juvenile/family) courts.

It should be noted that some drug courts existed before the Dade County drug court. These earlier drug courts were designed to expedite drug cases and not to link drug-involved offenders to treatment. For a time, the new drug courts were referred to as drug treatment courts because the new courts focused on providing treatment to drug-involved offenders. Although most of the time today people use the term *drug courts* to refer to this new type of drug court, some people continue to refer to the current drug courts as drug treatment courts to distinguish them from the early case-expediting drug courts.

Some have argued that drug courts are one of the major justice reforms of the twentieth century in the United States (Goldkamp, White, & Robinson, 2000). Drug courts represent a paradigm shift away from the punitive orientation toward drug-related crime that had been so prominent during the 1980s in the United States. The "war on drugs" exemplified this perspective. The expansion of criminal sanctions for drug crimes began in the 1970s but picked up speed in the 1980s with the declaration of the "war on drugs" and the passage of the anti-Drug Abuse Acts of 1986 and 1988. From the perspective of the crime control strategy, it was thought that increasing arrests and punishment for drug offenses would be effective in reducing illegal drug use and sales. The problem was that many of the offenders caught in the net of control were users and addicts. The increased use of imprisonment and longer terms of imprisonment did nothing to address the offenders' problems. Drug courts represent a major change from the crime control perspective because they recognize that many of the offenders have serious needs that must be addressed if they are to live crime-free lives.

As the concept of drug courts spread to other jurisdictions, numerous aspects of the original Dade County drug court model have been changed. The new courts differed from the original model in many ways, including the population targeted, selection procedures, and sentencing policies. Furthermore, the drug court concept has been adapted to other problems faced by the criminal justice systems. The more active hands-on judicial philosophy has been referred to as problem solving or problem-oriented courts (Goldkamp, 2000). Problem solving courts based on the drug court philosophy have begun for domestic violence, mental health, and family issues. However, these courts are so new that little research is available to give us any information about their effectiveness.

Differences From Traditional Management Strategies

The drug court model differs from other types of programs for drug-involved offenders in several important ways. As in other courts, the judge oversees the legal and procedural issues of the case. However, in the drug courts, the judge also functions in a more proactive role by immediately rewarding or sanctioning defendants. Also, in contrast to other programs, components of the criminal justice system and the treatment system work together to use the coercive power of the court to promote abstinence, treatment attendance, and other prosocial behavior. Rather than the usual adversarial relationship among actors in the court (defense attorneys, prosecutors), drug courts attempt to promote close-working relationships among everyone involved, with the primary focus being a reduction in defendants' drug use and criminal activity.

In the past, the typical offender targeted by the drug courts would most likely have been sentenced to probation or a short jail sentence. With such sentences, defendants would have received little drug treatment or close community supervision. Drug court procedures increase the intensity of supervision and the amount of drug treatment. In comparison to other forms of community supervision, court appearances, drug tests, supervision, and treatment contacts are much more frequent in drug courts (Belenko, 1998b).

There have been other attempts to coerce defendants into treatment while they are under the supervision of the courts or corrections. Programs such as Treatment Alternatives to Street Crime (TASC), diversion programs, and conditions of probation and intermediate sanctions have been tried. A major problem with many of these programs was the fact that supervision of treatment often rested on several agencies. As a result, it was difficult to monitor treatment progress and compliance with conditions of supervision. Treatment providers were often hesitant to report noncompliance because supervising agents would use criminal justice sanctions against the offender, and these would not necessarily increase the offender's access to treatment. From the perspective of the treatment providers, some relapse in drug use is expected during treatment, and this may indicate the need for changes in the treatment regime. In contrast, criminal justice personnel frequently viewed relapse as a failure deserving of punishment.

Another problem with traditional methods of managing drug-involved offenders was the length of time it took to sanction offenders for misbehavior. When agents reported violations of conditions of supervision, it often took a long time before a hearing occurred or sanctions were imposed. Drug courts attempt to rectify these problems by using the power of the court to immediately respond to positive or negative behavior. At the regularly scheduled status hearings, after hearing reports from treatment providers and supervising agents, the judge sanctions misbehavior and rewards program compliance. These rewards and punishments do not have to be delayed as they would in other types of programs.

Drug courts may also hold treatment providers more accountable for the treatment provided. For example, differences among treatment programs in success rates may be more transparent in the drug court model. Judges can contract with and assign defendants to the more successful programs. Furthermore, from the perspective of treatment providers, criminal justice clients are often not ideal candidates for treatment programs. As a result, under other treatment models, it was often difficult to find treatment slots for drug-involved offenders, or there was a long delay between identification of the need for treatment and program initiation. Treatment providers may also view the drug courts as more supportive of the treatment perspective because sanctions for misbehavior often increase the amount or level of treatment. In addition, as a result of the status hearings, all actors in the system, from defense attorneys to treatment providers and probation agents, know what the defendant has done and how the court has responded.

Differences Among Drug Courts

Although there are basic commonalities among the different drug court programs, there are large differences in the approaches used, participant eligibility and characteristics, type of treatment, and sanctions and rewards. For example, some drug court programs defer prosecution of offenders who enter the programs (diversion programs), some allow offenders to enter on a trial basis after entering a plea, and others allow offenders to enter the program after their case has been adjudicated. For instance, in a survey conducted by the Government Accounting Office (GAO, 1997), the researchers found that 44 percent of the programs deferred prosecution of offenders if they agreed to enter a drug treatment program, approximately 38 percent allowed offenders to enter the program after adjudication, and the remaining 18 percent used a combination of approaches or some other approach.

Diversion drug courts offer defendants the opportunity to obtain treatment and avoid the possibility of a felony conviction. Shortly after being charged, defendants waive their right to a speedy trial and enter a treatment program. Those who fail to complete the treatment program have their charges adjudicated. Defendants who complete the treatment program and graduate from the drug court program are not prosecuted further or have their charges dismissed.

Although all drug courts have a treatment component as part of their overall program, the type and extent of the treatment provided varies greatly among programs. The drug courts themselves are a management strategy for offenders. The actual type of treatment used in the drug courts varies greatly across jurisdictions.

Most drug court participants are adult, nonviolent offenders with a substance addiction; however, the characteristics of the participants differ among programs. Programs report targeting various populations such as adults, women, juveniles, nonviolent and violent offenders, offenders with and without a substance addiction, first-time and repeat offenders, and probation violators. In the survey conducted by the GAO (1997), the researchers found that 16 percent admitted juveniles, 6 percent accepted offenders with a current conviction for a violent offense, 16 percent accepted offenders with a prior conviction for a violent offense, 17 percent accepted offenders without a substance addiction, 78 percent accepted repeat offenders, and 63 percent accepted probation violators.

Review of client characteristics described in qualitative and quantitative evaluations have found drugs of choice of clients in drug courts also vary greatly across the courts (Belenko, 1998b, 1999). For example, a large majority (87 percent) of the clients in Baltimore City Drug Court reported using heroin, in Polk County court the majority preferred methamphetamines (67 percent for white males, 81 percent for white females), and in Roanoke, VA, Syracuse, NY, and Lackawanna County, NY, it was cocaine or crack. Several drug courts reported that marijuana was the primary drug of choice and the Cumberland County Drug Court reported alcohol as the primary drug.

EFFECTIVENESS OF DRUG COURTS

In comparison to many other strategies and programs, a relatively large number of studies have examined drug courts. Table 11.1 shows the recidivism rates from thirty-two drug court evaluations. Twenty-seven of the studies were scored at three or greater on the methods scale. Not only are there a large number of studies examining drug courts but also the quality of these studies is high. Two studies used random assignment and were scored a five on methods, eight were scored four, and seventeen were scored three. The remaining studies (n = 5) were scored two.

Most of the studies (n = 30) examined the effectiveness of adult drug courts. Only one study (Miller, Scocas, & O'Connell, 1998) examined a juvenile program, and another studied a program that admitted both adults and juveniles (McNeece & Byers, 1995). Twenty of the programs studied were diversion programs, eight were postadjudication, and the remaining included both. The severity of the charges or convictions of the participants differed greatly in the various courts. Some limited participation to first-time offenders charged with possession, under the influence, or misdemeanor drug offenses. Other jurisdictions admitted much more serious offenders. The comparison subjects in most of the studies received standard probation.

Rearrests were used as a measure of recidivism in most of the studies (n = 27). The five remaining studies used reconvictions (n = 2),

TABLE 11.1. *Drug court studies showing recidivism rates and length of follow-up*

Study (methods score)	Measure of recidivism	Recidivism: Experimental (%)	N	Control (%) #1/#2/#3	N	Follow-up period (in months)
Deschenes et al., 1995 (5)	Rearrest	31.3	176	32.6	454	12
	Technical Violation	39.8		46.3		
	Technical Violation/Drug	10.0		26.0*		
	Reincarceration	9.0		23.0*		
Gottfredson et al., 2003 (5)	Rearrest	66.2	139	81.3*	96	24
	Reconviction	48.9		53.2		
Deschenes et al., 1999 (4)	Rearrest	21.6	236	33.8	234	12–33
	Rearrest/Drug	14.0		26.5		
	Reconviction	15.7		23.5		
Finigan, 1998 (4)	Rearrest[1] (M)	0.59	300	1.53	150	24
	Rearrest[1]/Serious Offenses (M)	0.42		1.17		
	Rearrest[1]/Drug Offenses (M)	0.22		0.78		
	Reconviction[1] (M)	0.48		1.11		
Granfield et al., 1998 (4)	Rearrest (M) (SD)	1.4 (7.24)	100	1.5 (7.24)	200	12
	Revocation[2]	22.0		14.5		
Johnson, Formichella, & Bowers, 1998 (4)	Rearrest[3]		224		181	
	6 months	41.1		41.4		6
	12 months	61.3		69.2*		12
	18 months	71.2		79.9		18
	Any Charges[4]	58.5		82.9*		Unknown
Miethe, Lu, & Reese, 2000 (4)	Court Appearances	26.2	301	15.9	301	12
	Court Appearances/Drug	11.0		6.3		

Peters & Murrin, 2000 (4)	Arrests/Escambia	48.0	81	63.0*	81	30
	Arrests/Okaloosa	26.0	31	55.0*	31	
Sechrest, Shichor, Artist, & Briceno, 1998 (4)	Rearrest	14.7	102	25.5*	243	12–30
Spohn, Piper, Martin, & Frenzel, 2001 (4)	Rearrest	42.1	392	60.8*	326	12
	Reconviction	20.7		28.9*		
Bavon, 2001 (3)	Rearrest	12.7	157	16.8	107	12
Brewster, 2001 (3)	Rearrest	5.4	184	21.5	51	Unknown
	Reconviction	5.4		29.4		
Cosden, Crothers, & Peerson, 1999 (3)	Rearrest (M) (SD)	1.24 (1.29)	235	1.31 (1.29)	66	12
	Reconviction (M) (SD)	0.39 (0.72)		0.47 (0.72)		
	New Charges/Drug (M) (SD)	1.73 (2.56)		1.98 (2.56)		
Ericson, Welter, & Johnson, 1999 (3)	Rearrest	21.5	466	16.9	473	9
	Rearrest/Felony	12.2		11.6		
	Rearrest/Drug	0.08		0.09		
Goldkamp & Weiland, 1993 (3)	Rearrest	33.0	326	47.0	302	18
	Failure to Appear	55.0		9.0*	3,763	
Goldkamp et al., 2000 (3)	Rearrest					
	Multnomah	37.0	692	49.0	401	12
	Clark	53.0	499	65.0	510	12
	Rearrest/Drug					
	Multnomah	22.0		32.0		
	Clark	26.0		52.0		
Gottfredson, Coblentz, & Harmon, 1996 (3)	Rearrest					
	District	22.6	84	27.1	351	6
	Circuit	26.5	34	30.4	125	
	VOP	18.5	27	30.2	53	

(continued)

TABLE 11.1 *(continued)*

Study (methods score)	Measure of recidivism	Recidivism: Experimental (%)	N	Control (%) #1/#2/#3	N	Follow-up period (in months)
	Reconviction					
	District	7.1		7.7		
	Circuit	3.0		4.0		
	VOP	0.0		11.3		
Harrell, Roman, & Sack, 2001 (3)	Arrests	28.6	283	35.1	114	24
Harrell, Hirst, Mitchell, Marlowe & Merrill, 2001 (3)	Rearrest	24.9	250	55.3	137	12
	Self-Reported/Drug Use	17.0	213	26.0		1
	Self-Reported/Arrest	16.0	245	26.0		6
Johnson & Latessa, 2000 (3)	Rearrest	28.7	226	38.2*	230	15.3
	Rearrest/Multiple Times	29.7		46.5*		
	Convicted for Initial Rearrest	26.0		31.1		
Miller et al. 1998 (3)	Rearrest					
	3 months	14.8	144	21.1	90	3
	6 months	24.2		32.2		6
	9 months	38.1		43.3		9
	12 months	33.3		51.1		12
M M Bell Inc., 1998 (3)	Rearrest	17.4	304	33.0	200	3–38
Roehl, 1998 (3)	Felony Arrests/Drug	32.5	40	47.1	51	12–18
	Felony Convictions/Drug	30.0		27.5		
Santa Clara County Courts, 1997 (3)	A. Rearrest[5]					12

A. Compared to (1) Eligible Defendants Who	(1)	3.0	136	57.0	101	
Declined to Participate; (2) Eligible	(2)			60.0	151	
Defendants Who Were Not Referred to Drug Court	B. Positive Drug Specimen Results[5]					
B. Compared to Probationers on (1)	(1)	5.4		10.2		
Electronic Monitoring Supervision; (2)	(2)			13.2		
Intensive Supervision; (3) General Supervision	(3)			24.5		
Stageberg, Wilson, & Moore, 2001 (3)	Reconviction[5]	47.6	124	54.6	188	10.86
Terry, 1999 (3)	Rearrest	19.0	221	28.0	69	12
Vito & Tewksbury, 1998 (3)	Reconviction	48.4	217	55.4	74	12
Anspach & Ferguson, 1999 (2)	Drug Relapse	33.3	6	75.0	12	12
	New Criminal Charges	33.3		66.7		
Godley Dennis, Funk, Siekmann, & Weisheit, 1998 (2)	Rearrest[6] (M) (SD)	0.4	104	0.5	150	12
Harrison, Parsons, Byrnes, & Sahami, n.d. (2)	Felony Booking (M) (SD)	1.06	158	3.2	26	Unknown
McNeece & Byers, 1995 (2)	Rearrest	0.03	62	15.4	91	6
Terry, 1995 (2)	Rearrest	38.7	788	30.0	300	24–36

1 Per 100 clients; no standard deviation was reported.

2 Significance testing was not conducted for revocation.

3 Rates unadjusted for time elapsed since contact with the court.

4 Significance testing not reported.

5 No standard deviation was reported.

* Significantly different from experimental group, $p < 0.05$.

court appearances (n = 1), drug relapse (n = 1), and felony booking (n = 1) as recidivism measures. Nine studies reported reconvictions and/or technical violations as well as arrests. Ten studies reported recidivism measured specifically related to drug offenses. Most of the recidivism measures were the proportion of unsuccessful cases; however, five studies report mean number of recidivist events instead of proportions.

Both studies that were scored a five found significant differences in recidivism between participants and nonparticipants (Deschenes, Turner, & Greenwood, 1995; Gottfredson, Najaka, & Kearley, 2003). In the Deschenes et al. study, the participants had significantly fewer technical violations for drug use and fewer reincarcerations; however, there were no significant differences in rearrests or technical violations. In the Gottfredson et al. study, the drug court participants had significantly fewer rearrests and fewer reconvictions.

Twenty-one of the twenty-five studies scored at levels three or four found the drug court sample had lower recidivism than comparison groups. However, only six of the twenty-five found significant differences in recidivism.

Three of the twenty-five level three or four studies found mixed results. There was no consistency in their findings nor could I identify why the results from these three studies differed from the other twenty-one studies. Specifically, in the Granfield, Eby, and Brewster (1998) study, the participants and comparisons had approximately the same mean number of arrests (1.4 compared to 1.5) in a one-year follow-up period but the participants had more revocations. Goldkamp and Weiland (1993) found that participants had fewer rearrests but a much larger number failed to appear. Roehl (1998) reported only drug-related felony arrests or convictions. The drug court participants had fewer arrests but slightly more convictions.

Figure 11.1 illustrates the meta-analysis's results of twenty-four drug court studies from Table 11.1. Studies that received a method score of two or less (n = 5) and studies that reported means and standard deviations for their recidivism measure (n = 3) were not included in the analysis. Rearrest rates were the primary measure employed in calculating the effect sizes (n = 21), but reconviction rates (n = 2) and court appearances (n = 1) were utilized for those studies that did not

Drug Court Programs

Citation	Effect
Santa Clara County, 1997	48.21
Brewster, 2001	4.79
Harrell et al., 2001	3.78
M M Bell, Inc., 1998	2.33
Peters & Murrin, 2000	2.14
Spohn et al., 2001	2.13
Miller et al., 1998	2.09
Sechrest et al., 1998	1.99
Deschenes et al., 1999	1.85
Roehl, 1998	1.85
Goldcamp, 1993	1.79
Goldcamp et al., 2000	1.78
Johnson et al., 1998	1.65
Terry, 1999	1.62
Johnson & Latessa, 2000	1.53
Bavon, 2001	1.39
Harrell et al., 2001	1.35
Gottfredson et al., 1996	1.33
Vito & Tewksbury, 1998	1.33
Stageberg et al., 2001	1.31
Cosden et al., 1999	1.10
Deschenes et al., 1995	1.06
Granfield et al., 1998	1.04
Ericson et al., 1999	.75
Miethe et al., 2000	.53
Gottfredson et al., 2003	.45
Mean Odds-Ratio (26)	**1.55**

0.01 0.1 1 10 100

Favors Control **Favors Treatment**

Figure 11.1. Forest plot showing odds ratio and 95 percent confidence interval for studies of drug court programs.

have a measure of rearrest. In cases where there were more than one experimental or control group (n = 3), the average of the groups was plotted. Finally, for those studies that had more than one follow-up period for their recidivism measure (n = 2), only the longest period was included.

The plot shows a more favorable effect than the significance tests alone. The effect sizes in twenty-two of the studies favored the drug court participants and one-half of these show significant differences between the participants and the nonparticipants. Only two of the effect sizes favor the nonparticipants, and only one of these is significant. The three level three or four studies not shown on the plot used number of rearrests or reconvictions as the measures of recidivism.

These studies did not find any significant differences between groups.

In sum, there is very strong evidence that drug courts reduce the future criminal activities of offenders. Almost all of the studies found the drug court participants had lower recidivism than the comparisons. Seven of the studies found these differences to be significant. The effect size analysis found eleven significant differences.

CONCLUSIONS

According to this review, drug courts are effective in reducing recidivism. Drug courts are a management strategy that involves aspects of both rehabilitation and deterrence. Thus, it is difficult at this point to identify exactly what aspects of the courts lead to the positive outcomes. To answer this question Goldkamp et al. (2000) examined the impact of treatment exposure, sanctions, and appearance before the drug court judge on outcomes from courts in Las Vegas and Portland. Controlling for participant risk, they found all three factors (treatment, sanctioning, and attendance at drug court sessions) were significant predictors of reoffending in Las Vegas. This was not the case in Portland, where only sanctioning with time in jail predicted the outcome. More research is needed to identify exactly which components of the drug courts are important in reducing recidivism.

APPENDIX 11.1. STUDY REFERENCE, DESCRIPTION, AND METHODS SCORES (IN PARENTHESES) OF DRUG COURT STUDIES

Anspach and Ferguson, 1999 **(2)**

Project Exodus Drug Court Program in Cumberland County, Maine. A minimum of nine months is required to successfully complete the program. Program completers between January 1998 and December 1998 were compared with program expelled.

Bavon, 2001 **(3)**

Tarrant County DIRECT Project designed for minor drug offenders (ages seventeen and older) charged with possession of less than

3 grams of controlled substance, or possession of more than 4 oz. but less than 1 lb. of marijuana, or obtained or attempted to obtain a controlled substance by fraud. Program participants whose cases closed in FY 1995–1996 and 1997–1998 were compared to those eligible for the program but who opted not to participate.

Brewster, 2001 (**3**)

Chester County Pennsylvania Drug Court. Program participants between October 1997 and January 1999, nonviolent offenders charged with nonmandatory drug offenses, were compared to offenders placed on probation prior to the drug court and who would have met the drug court's eligibility requirements.

Cosden et al., 1999 (**3**)

Ventura County Drug Court for defendants charged with a misdemeanor drug charge who had histories of drug problems and who were viewed as appropriate to receive treatment. Program participants were compared to individuals eligible for the program but who were unable to participate and thus received normal criminal processing.

Deschenes et al., 1995 (**5**)

Maricopa County Arizona First Time Drug Offender Program. This is a postadjudication, probation enhancement program for probationers with a first-time felony conviction for drug possession. Randomly assigned drug court participants were compared to a matched group of routine probationers, all sentenced in 1992 or 1993.

Deschenes et al., 1999 (**4**)

Orange County Drug Court Program for nonviolent drug offenders charged with felony possession who showed signs of drug addiction. Drug court participants between March 1995 and December 1998 were compared to offenders sentenced to formal probation during the same time period.

Ericson et al., 1999 (**3**)

Hennepin County Drug Court for all felony-level drug offenders except those charged with felony person offenses and/or stand alone weapon offenses. Drug court participants in 1997 were compared to felony drug offenders convicted in the year immediately preceding the start of the drug court (1996).

Finigan, 1998 **(4)**

Multnomah County Sanction Treatment Opportunity Progress Drug Diversion Program for defendants charged with possession of a controlled substance but no distribution or manufacturing charges. Program participants between 1994 and 1995 were compared to defendants eligible for the program but who chose not to participate.

Godley et al., 1998 **(2)**

Madison County Assessment and Treatment Alternative Court in Illinois. Nonviolent adult drug offenders diagnosed with an alcohol or drug dependency were compared with those eligible for the program but who declined to participate between January 1996 and January 1997.

Goldkamp and Weiland, 1993 **(3)**

Miami Drug Court for felony defendants; defendants assigned to Diversion and Treatment Program (DATP) between August 1, 1990, and September 30, 1990, were compared to (1) a sample of felony defendants entering the district court prior to establishment of the drug court and to (2) a cohort of felony defendants contemporaneously processed through circuit court.

Goldkamp et al., 2000 **(3)**

Multnomah County Drug Court for felony drug defendants charged with level I or II drug possession offenses under Oregon statutes. Program participants between 1991 and 1997 were compared to offenders who attended the drug court orientation but never entered the program.

Clark County Drug Court for defendants charged with felony drug possession and "under the influence" offenses. Drug court participants between 1993 and 1997 were compared to offenders who did not enter the drug court and whose cases were processed in the normal manner.

Gottfredson et al., 1996 **(3)**

Baltimore Drug Court Treatment program (BDCT) for nonviolent male and female offenders with drug abuse problems. Offenders between 1994 and 1995 assigned to BDCT were compared to a randomly selected group of those in traditional parole and probation services. BDCT was broken down into district court, circuit court, and violation of probation.

Gottfredson et al., 2000 **(5)**

Baltimore City Drug Treatment Court. Offenders randomly assigned between February 1997 and August 1998 to one of four treatment modalities – intensive outpatient, methadone maintenance, inpatient, and transitional housing – were compared to offenders incarcerated or supervised as usual.

Granfield et al., 1998 **(4)**

Random sample of all narcotic criminal filings in Denver District Court between December 1994 and March 1995; group assigned to standard individual/group counseling and frequent urine testing for various drugs was compared to group assigned to standard counseling and sporadic urine testing mandated by court. The drug court participants were compared to two pre–drug court control cohorts, one from 1992–1993 and one from 1993–1994.

Harrell et al., 2001 **(3)**

Brooklyn Treatment Court (BTC) program. Women offenders between June 1997 and January 1999 with no prior arrests but with reported drug-use histories assigned to drug court were compared to women arrested on drug felony charges who were not referred to BTC.

Harrell et al., 2001 **(3)**

Birmingham Alabama Breaking the Cycle program. Felony drug offenders recruited for the program between October 1998 and May 1999 were compared to felony drug offenders selected prior to the full implementation of the program.

Harrison et al., n.d. **(2)**

Salt Lake County Drug Court in Utah. Adult felons charged with drug offenses between July 1996 and September 1998 who had at least one prior drug conviction were compared to similar offenders eligible for the program but who chose not to participate.

Johnson and Latessa, 2000 **(3)**

Hamilton County Drug Court program in Ohio. The treatment program is community based and includes three phases: inpatient, outpatient, and aftercare. Drug-involved nonviolent offenders who participated in the program were compared to offenders who refused to participate or were refused by the treatment facility, all between January 1997 and October 1998.

Johnson et al., 1998 (**4**)

Drug Court Program in Mobile County, Alabama. Conducted on an outpatient basis; designed to last twelve months; treatment components include urine testing, acupuncture services, individual and group counseling, maintenance of sobriety, development of life skills, and so forth. Participants were compared to a no-treatment group.

McNeece and Byers, 1995 (**2**)

Hillsborough County Drug Court in Florida. Program participants, consisting of young adult offenders whose primary problem was cocaine, were compared to other young adult drug offenders in comparison programs (Broward County Substance-Abuse Outpatient Treatment Program and Monroe County Pretrial Substance-Abuse Services Program).

Miethe et al., 2000 (**4**)

Las Vegas Drug Court designed primarily for first-time offenders charged with possession or under the influence of a controlled substance (mainly cocaine or methamphetamine). Marijuana users were also allowed to participate but they were personally responsible for the entire treatment fee ($1,200). Program participants in 1995 were compared to a proportionate, stratified random sample selected from the non–drug court cases processed in the general district courts during the same time period.

Miller et al., 1998 (**3**)

Delaware Drug Court Diversion Program for juveniles with no prior criminal records arrested for misdemeanor drug charges. Juveniles admitted into the diversion program by midsummer 1997 were compared with a random group of juveniles with equivalent criminal histories prior to the implementation of the drug court in the first half of 1995.

M M Bell, Inc., 1998 (**3**)

King County Drug Court for defendants charged with possession of schedule I or II drugs with no prior adult convictions for sex or violent offenses. Drug court participants were compared to eligible offenders who did not participate between August 1994 and July 1997.

Peters and Murrin, 2000 **(4)**

Drug court programs in Escambia and Okaloosa Counties in Florida. Drug court participants between June 1993 and June 1995, nonviolent offenders with limited history of involvement in the criminal justice system, were compared to a group of regular probationers between June 1993 and October 1995 matched on county of residence, gender, race/ethnicity, and offense type.

Roehl, 1998 **(3)**

Monterey County Drug Court for offenders charged with simple possession of a controlled substance or being under the influence of a controlled substance who had no prior violent felony/misdemeanor convictions and drug trafficking/sales convictions. Drug court participants between July 1995 and December 1996 were compared to randomly selected offenders arrested for drug possession or under the influence of an illegal substance in the year prior to the establishment of the drug court (July 1994–June 1995).

Santa Clara County Courts, 1997 **(3)**

One-year drug court treatment program (March 1996–March 1997) based on the needs of the participants. Severely addicted nonviolent, hard-core addicts assigned to treatment were compared to (1) defendants eligible but who declined to participate, (2) defendants eligible but who were not referred to the program, (3) probationers under electronic monitoring supervision, (4) probationers on intensive supervision, and (5) probationers under general supervision.

Sechrest et al., 1998 **(4)**

Riverside County Drug Court in California (ROC Program). Felony drug offenders assigned to the program between January 1996 and March 1997 were compared to drug offenders arrested in 1995 (prior to the drug court) who could have been candidates for the drug court.

Spohn et al., 2001 **(4)**

Douglas County drug court for nonviolent offenders with medium to high risk. Drug court participants were compared to (1) felony drug offenders assigned to the Douglas County Attorney's Diversion Program prior to 1997 and (2) individuals arrested for felony drug offenses between January 1997 and March 1998 and who were traditionally adjudicated. Subjects were matched on most serious offense, gender, race/ethnicity, and age.

Stageberg et al., 2001 **(3)**

Polk County Drug Court program in Iowa. Drug court participants prior to October 1998 (had to be nonviolent offenders, with a risk score of twelve or higher and a history of drug or alcohol abuse) were compared to (1) offenders referred to the drug court and who were formally screened and rejected by the program prior to October 1998 and (2) "target population" identified prior to drug court development in 1996.

Terry, 1995 **(2)**

Broward County Drug Court in Florida for first-time cocaine offenders. Program participants were compared with those eligible for the program but who did not participate between July 1991 and June 1992.

Terry, 1999 **(3)**

Broward County Drug Court for felony drug offenders charged with the possession and/or purchase of any controlled substance as defined by Florida Statute 893.03. Drug court participants between 1991 and 1992 were compared to offenders eligible for the program but who declined to participate.

Vito and Tewksbury, 1998 **(3)**

Drug court program in Jefferson County, Kentucky. First-time, nonviolent offenders were voluntarily diverted into this twelve-month community treatment program that encompasses acupuncture and the development of social and educational skills. Program participants were compared with offenders eligible for the program but who declined to participate.

CHAPTER TWELVE

Drug Treatment Programs for Offenders

INTRODUCTION

The United States declared a "war on drugs" in the early 1980s. This "war" was based on a control philosophy of corrections and focused on the use of deterrence and incapacitation to try to reduce drug use and drug-related crimes. Severe penalties for drug-involved offenders were expected to reduce drug use and its related criminal activities. These policies resulted in a tremendous increase in the number of drug-involved offenders in prisons. For example, according to a 1997 survey of incarcerated offenders, 57 percent of the state inmates and 45 percent of federal inmates reported drug use in the month prior to their offense. Surveys of state inmates in Texas and Ohio reported that 56 percent and 51 percent, respectively, were diagnosed to need drug treatment. Many of these offenders were convicted of drug crimes (Lo & Stephens, 2000; Peters, Greenbaum, Edens, Carter, & Ortiz, 1998).

During the 1990s, it became obvious that the war on drugs was not having the desired effect. Federal, state, and local law enforcement agencies had responded to the drug crisis by targeting drug suppliers and users. Severe penalties for such drug-involved offenders were expected to keep the offenders in prison for longer periods of time and deter others from dealing or using drugs. These tactics proved to be ineffective in reducing the supply of drugs in most communities. Drug-involved offenders continued to be a problem for criminal justice systems. Overloaded court dockets, increased populations in prisons and community corrections, soaring costs for building and operating jails and prisons, and early release of violent felons were just some of the problems. As a result, policy makers and criminal justice system professionals searched for alternative strategies to address the drug crisis.

As several issues became well known, interest in addressing the drug problem increased. First, the relationship between drugs and crime was well documented (e.g., Ball, Shaffer, & Nurco, 1983; Davis & Lurigio, 1996; Inciardi, 1974; Tonry & Wilson, 1990; Wish & Johnson, 1986). Although the correlational relationship between drug use and crime is not necessarily causal, the assumption is that a reduction in drug use will mean a corresponding decrease in criminal activities. Second, drug-involved offenders were an overwhelming financial drain on the U.S. criminal justice system. Third, these offenders posed threats to themselves and others. Those who injected drugs were at high risk for spreading HIV infections through risky sexual activities and needle-sharing practices. If drug-dependent offenders could be given treatment, their drug use might be reduced or eliminated, and this, in turn, might decrease their criminal activity, lower criminal justice system costs, and reduce the spread of HIV. Such thinking served as the philosophical basis for establishing drug intervention strategies in criminal justice settings.

An advantage of intervening while offenders were in criminal justice settings was that treatment could take place in a variety of settings using various modalities. Programs could be voluntary or coerced and could take place in the community or in facilities. Although the benefits associated with intervening in the cycle of drug abuse and crime via treatment interventions are clear, the effectiveness of these drug treatment programs is much less so. The need to examine the effectiveness of these programs is especially important in light of current federal and state budget deficits and continuous skepticism regarding the efficacy of correctional rehabilitation programs. This chapter examines evidence on the effectiveness of drug treatment programs that are provided to offenders in (1) the community and (2) when they are incarcerated in jails and prisons.

TREATMENT FOR DRUG-INVOLVED OFFENDERS

Various treatment modalities are used to assist drug-involved offenders. Modality refers to the traditional approaches used to treat drug dependence in the United States. The major treatment modalities are detoxification, methadone maintenance, outpatient drug-free programs involving counseling, and therapeutic communities (TCs). Treatment using any of these modalities can occur in the community or in a correctional facility. Detoxification may be in the community or in jail but most offenders are past the detoxification stage when they arrive at prison. Methadone maintenance is seldom used in jails or prisons. When offenders attend treatment interventions in the community, they are often mixed with others who are not offenders. In correctional facilities, offenders can participate in TCs or outpatient-type programs. Inmates in outpatient-type programs in facilities live in cells or dormitories with other inmates but participate in the drug program when it is offered (day or evening). The number of hours offenders spend in outpatient programs per week varies greatly in both community settings and in jails or prisons.

Although programs can be classified into one of the modalities discussed earlier, it must be realized that there are wide variations within each modality. Differences exist in program characteristics, structure, philosophy, funding sources, and services offered. Furthermore, the characteristics of the participants vary greatly between and within modalities.

Alcoholic Anonymous (AA) and Narcotic Anonymous (NA) programs (also referred to as twelve-step programs) are common in communities and jail and prison settings. Offenders are sometimes required to attend such programs. For example, AA or NA may be a condition of probation or parole. In some locations, these programs are considered treatment. However, most experts in the field of drug treatment do not consider them treatment, although they may consider them to be an important adjunct to treatment.

Some programs use acupuncture combined with drug treatment. In one study of acupuncture, Russell, Sharp, and Gilbertson (2000) found clients who had a combination of treatment and acupuncture stayed in treatment longer than those who just received treatment. However, there were no significant differences between the groups in arrests.

Detoxification

Detoxification refers to the facilitation of drug withdrawal. The primary objective of detoxification is to provide symptomatic relief for drug addicts while treatment staff work to eliminate their physical dependence on drugs. This process can occur with or without the assistance of drugs or chemicals. For example, antagonists, substances that block or counteract the effects of opiates, are sometimes used to help heroin addicts detoxify. Similarly, the antihypertension drug clonidine has been used to help relieve symptoms connected with opioid withdrawal (Abadinsky, 2001). It is important to note that besides referrals to other treatment services, detoxification does not necessarily include subsequent therapeutic services.

Methadone Maintenance

Methadone, a wholly synthetic narcotic, has the capability of reproducing the same analgesic and sedative effects as heroin. Methadone was initially used in hospitals after World War II to help detoxify people addicted to opiates. The use of methadone to treat heroin addicts in a dramatically new way (i.e., through maintenance) was advanced by Vincent Dole and Marie Nyswander of Rockefeller University (1965). They proposed that it be used to maintain heroin addicts, not just as a short-term detoxification tool.

Methadone maintenance is generally recommended for drug addicts who are unable to function normally without chemotherapeutic support. Under federal regulations, methadone is provided for drug-dependent individuals at stable dosage levels as an oral substitute for heroin or other morphine-like drugs for durations exceeding twenty-one days. Treatment goals of methadone maintenance often do not include complete opiate abstinence; instead, they focus on improvement of other aspects of social functioning that are believed to help the addicts in living a socially conforming and productive life. Given that methadone itself is addictive, program participants are usually kept in the programs as long as they follow rules and guidelines and if there is sufficient program funding (Anglin & Hser, 1990).

Most studies of the effectiveness of methadone maintenance have focused on examining whether the programs successfully reduce drug use and not whether there is an impact on recidivism (Ball & Ross, 1991; Magura, Nwakeze, Kang, & Demsky, 1999). In general, results indicate the programs do appear to successfully reduce the use of drugs while people are in the program.

Outpatient Drug-Free Programs

Perhaps the most common approach to the treatment of drug addiction is outpatient drug-free programs. This treatment modality has been estimated to serve about 60 percent of drug abusers in treatment (Sandhu, 1981). The outpatient drug-free approach is an intervention that employs a wide variety of nonmaintenance (i.e., without drugs) programs. Although outpatient drug-free programs do not utilize any chemical agents or medications in their treatment, prescription drugs may serve as an adjunct to treatment or be used to treat medical symptoms (Anglin & Hser, 1992).

Outpatient drug-free programs vary widely, ranging from very demanding daytime therapeutic community-type meetings to relaxed programs of activities. The primary focus of outpatient drug-free treatment is to counsel and train drug abusers so they can improve their social skills. Hence, the goals of outpatient drug-free programs are to help drug abusers refrain from using licit and illicit drugs as well as to recognize life circumstances that foster their drug use (Anglin & Hser, 1992).

Therapeutic Communities

TC is a generic term referring to residential-based, self-help, drug-free treatment programs. These programs are premised on the belief that effective treatment for drug abusers must occur in a twenty-four-hour residential living environment. It is assumed that stable recovery from drug addiction depends upon the successful integration of a variety of social and psychological goals. Hence, the goals of TCs are to change the lifestyle of drug addicts to help them remain abstinent from illicit substances, eliminate their antisocial activity, increase their employability, and instill in them prosocial attitudes and values (De Leon, 1986).

In TCs, drug abuse is viewed as deviant behavior resulting from impeded personality development and/or chronic deficits in social, educational, and economic skills. Moreover, a large proportion of drug addicts come from socially and economically disadvantaged backgrounds, where drug abuse is more of a social response than a psychological disturbance. Accordingly, the TC treatment perspective posits that the problem is the person, not the drug, and the addiction is only a symptom and not the essence of the disorder (Nielson & Scarpitti, 1997).

The model of all TCs is believed to have originated in 1958 by the Synanon Foundation (Platt & Labate, 1976). The founder of the Synanon Foundation, Charles E. Dederich, was a former alcoholic who was a participant in and advocate of the AA approach to substance abuse. TCs are generally characterized by a strict hierarchy and an insistence on rigid adherence to norms. Ex-addicts serve as treatment staff. It is important to note that although the Synanon model calls for a lifetime commitment, contemporary models of TCs have either abandoned or modified this aspect of the Synanon model (Abadinsky, 2001).

Drug Treatment Effectiveness

Prior meta-analyses examining the effectiveness of drug treatment programs have found mixed results; although most find TCs to be effective, the results vary when evaluations of other modalities are studied. For example, Pearson and Lipton (1999) examined the impact of programs for drug-involved offenders in prison, jail, or other residential settings. They examined studies of TCs (n = 7), group counseling (n = 7), and boot camps (n = 6) for drug-involved offenders. In their analysis, only the TCs were effective in reducing recidivism. From the results of the analysis, they estimated a 56.7 percent success rate for the TC group compared with 43.4 percent success for the comparison group. The recidivism measure (effect size) in the analysis combined both return to drug use and return to crime so caution should be taken in generalizing these percentages to recidivism measures alone.

The evaluations included in the meta-analysis by Pearson and Lipton (1999) included drug treatment evaluations conducted between 1968 and 1996. In addition to the analysis of TCs, counseling, and boot camps, they attempted to examine the effectiveness of methadone maintenance, substance abuse education, twelve-step programs, and cognitive-behaviorial therapy treatments. However, they were unable to draw conclusions about the effectiveness of these treatments because there were too few evaluations to meta-analyze.

Another meta-analysis, conducted by Prendergast and his colleagues (Prendergast, Podus, Chang, & Urada, 2002), examined drug treatment studies completed during approximately the same time period as the studies examined by Pearson and Lipton (i.e., 1965–1996). They focused on interventions directed toward changing future drug use and/or criminal activity. Seventy-eight studies examined the impact of the programs on drug use; twenty-five examined the impact on crime. The studies included in the analysis compared the impact of the treatment to no treatment or minimal treatment. On average, they found that clients who participated in treatment had better outcomes (less drug use and fewer crimes) than the comparisons. Results were significant for both drug use and crime. They translated the effect sizes into estimates of a 57 percent success rate for treated groups compared to 42 percent for comparison groups for the drug use outcome and 53 percent (treated group) compared to 47 percent (comparison) for crime. Overall, drug treatment in their analysis was effective; however, they did not find any significant differences for the different treatment modalities.

Gender- and Race/Ethnic-Specific Programming

Recently in the United States, there have been heated debates about the importance of gender- and race-specific programming, particularly in substance abuse programs. Some people believe that most treatment programs have been designed for white, male participants and such programs do not adequately address the needs of women and different racial/ethnic groups. Conversely, others argue that the programs are designed to meet the needs of substance abusers and the techniques are appropriate for men, women, and various racial/ethnic groups. At this point in time, there is little empirical data to support either side of this argument.

In their meta-analysis, Prendergast and his colleagues (2002) examined whether gender made a difference in their overall results. They did not find any gender differences in treatment effectiveness. However, it is important to note that the gender variable in this study refers to the mix of males and females in a given study sample. Thus, results showed that programs with a large percent of female participants in the study were no more or less effective than those with a large percent of male participants.

In this chapter, I examine two different types of drug treatment for offenders: (1) treatment provided in community settings and (2) treatment provided in jails or prisons. There were too few studies examining the impact of gender- or race/ethnicity-specific treatment to enable any conclusions in regard to the debates about treatment focused on these groups.

Drug Treatment in the Community

Drug treatment for offenders in the community resulted from coordinated efforts by some states to divert drug-abusing offenders out of the criminal justice system and into community-based treatment. The inability of many criminal justice settings to provide adequate treatment for drug-involved offenders combined with encouraging evaluation findings from early community-based drug treatment programs provided the incentive for this movement. During the 1980s, when control became the philosophy of corrections, interest moved to programs that required offenders to participate in outpatient drug treatment as a condition of probation or parole. This became particularly popular when it was shown that offenders stayed in treatment longer and did as well as others even if they were coerced to attend treatment programs (Anglin & Hser, 1992). Prior to this many people believed that treatment would be effective only if substance abusers voluntarily joined programs. The finding that treatment could be effective if coerced provided a good rationale for requiring offenders to participate in treatment as part of their sentence.

Criminal justice system decision makers have had difficulties ensuring that offenders received treatment. One problem faced by many probation and parole offices is the limited number of treatment slots available for offenders in the community. Often, offenders are not considered preferred clients for the programs, and/or the treatment programs have long waiting lists. Even if offenders were required to attend treatment as a condition of probation or parole, it was often impossible to find a program that was willing and able to accept them (this may be one of the advantages of drug courts where the treatment slots are contracted by the court; see Chapter 11).

A large number of sentenced offenders are required to attend drug treatment while they are under the jurisdiction of the criminal justice

Outpatient Drug Treatment Programs

Citation	Effect
Rosner (n.d.)	2.72
Goldkamp & Weiland, 1993	2.29
Moon & Latessa, 1994	1.68
Rhodes & Gross, 1997--OR	1.31
Rhodes & Gross, 1997--DC	1.21
Oregon DOC, 1994	1.11
Mean Odds-Ratio (6)	**1.54**

0.1 0.2 0.5 1 2 5 10

Favors Control Favors Treatment

Figure 12.1. Forest plot showing odds ratio and 95 percent confidence interval for studies of outpatient drug treatment programs.

system. According to research by the U.S. Bureau of Justice Statistics (1997), drug or alcohol treatment was a condition of sentencing for 41 percent of adults on probation. Thirty-seven percent of these had received treatment. Furthermore, 17 percent of all probationers reported having participated in a drug treatment program during their probation sentence. This percentage rose as the severity of prior drug use increased. Of those with any past drug use, 25 percent had received treatment, and the percentage grew to 42 percent for those using drugs in the month before the offense. A majority of those using drugs at the time of their offense reported participation in drug treatment during their current sentence. However, it is important to note that the type of treatment referred to in these statistics includes a wide variety of different types of treatment interventions including self-help groups (AA and NA), drug rehabilitation, and outpatient clinics (Bureau of Justice Statistics, 1997).

Effectiveness of Community Drug Treatment. We located seven studies of outpatient treatment programs for offenders. (There are other studies but they do not report necessary information about offenders and recidivism.) Shown in Table 12.1 are the studies and the recidivism rates. Figure 12.1 presents the results of five outpatient treatment studies on recidivism, with six samples being represented (two samples from the Rhodes and Gross study). The measures of rearrest (n = 2), admitted criminal behavior (n = 2), revocations (n = 1), and general criminal record (n = 1) are used to calculate the effect sizes for the

TABLE 12.1. *Studies of outpatient drug treatment programs for offenders showing recidivism rates and length of follow-up*

Study (methods score)	Measure of recidivism	Recidivism				Follow-up period (in months)
		Experimental (%)	N	Control (%) #1/#2/#3	N	
Rhodes & Gross, 1997 (5)	*DC*					6
	Admitted Criminal Behavior	10.0	199	15.0	185	
	Rearrest	18.0	229	21.0	221	
	OR					
	Admitted Criminal Behavior	22.0	191	27.0*	185	
Oregon DOC, 1994 (4)	Revocations[1]	58.4	327	56.0	327	24
Goldkamp & Weiland, 1993 (3)	Rearrest	33.0	326	53.0*	301	18
Moon & Latessa, 1994 (3)	Rearrest	21.0	274	31.0	103	20
Rosner, 1988 (3)	"General Criminal Record"	9.9	420	21.3*	47	30
Falkin, Strauss, & Bohen, 1999 (2)	Rearrest	39.0	1009	52.5*	613	12
Van Stelle, Mauser, & Moberg, 1994 (2)	Rearrest	43.0	111	74.0*	148	18

[1] Significance tests not reported.

* Significantly different from experimental group, $p < 0.05$.

samples included in the figure. Although Table 12.1 presents the results of seven studies of treatment, two of these studies were excluded from the figure because of low methodology ratings (Falkin, Strauss, & Bohen 1999; Van Stelle, Mauser, & Moberg, 1994). The longest follow-up periods available for each study were also used to calculate the effect sizes.

As shown in Table 12.1 and Figure 12.1, five of the studies with methods scores three or greater found effects favoring the group given drug treatment. However, only the Rosner (1988) and Goldkamp and Weiland (1993) studies found significant differences between groups. The Rhodes and Gross (1997) studies did not have significant effect sizes but the difference for one of the samples (Oregon) is significant according to their analysis. Overall, the combined effect size demonstrated that outpatient drug treatment significantly reduced recidivism when the performance of the treated group was compared to the control group.

The two studies that found significant differences in effect sizes between the treatment and control group examined very different programs. The Goldkamp and Weiland (1993) study examined an outpatient treatment for felons in drug court, so these results are not surprising given the findings of the drug court studies (see Chapter 11 in this volume). The second study finding a significant difference was an all-male drinking-driver program for first time offenders (Rosner, 1988).

The programs that favored the treated group but were not significant in the effect size analysis also varied. Moon and Latessa (1994) studied probationers, Rhodes and Gross (1997) studied intensive case management, and Oregon DOC (1994) studied the corrections treatment services (CTS). From the information given in the evaluation reports, it is difficult to identify what specific mechanisms might be affecting the results.

Taken as a whole, the results indicate that outpatient drug-free treatment programs provided to offenders in the community are effective in reducing the future criminal activities of offenders. Because the programs differ dramatically, it is difficult to draw any conclusions about the specific type of outpatient treatment that is most effective or for whom (which type of offender) the treatment works best.

Considering the large number of drug-involved offenders who are being supervised in the community and who report having attended drug treatment, it is shocking that we could identify only a small number of studies examining outpatient treatment for offenders in the community. My investigation of the effectiveness of this type of treatment does suggest that the programs can be effective. However, this conclusion should be very cautiously generalized to other community drug treatment programs. First, I assume the quality control for evaluated programs is higher compared to other programs offered to offenders. Furthermore, the large differences in the programs and in the participants in these studies prohibit any conclusions about the mechanisms that might be influencing the results or the type of drug-involved offender/delinquent who would benefit from the treatment. Thus, at this point in time, I think it would be a mistake to generalize to outpatient treatment programs commonly offered to offenders in the community.

Incarceration-Based Drug Treatment

The period when an offender is locked up represents an opportune time to break the cycle of drug abuse and crime. Incarceration-based drug treatment programs encompass drug intervention programs that take place in jail, detention facilities, and prisons. Roughly 65 percent of all prisoners have a history of regular illicit drug use but less than 15 percent receive any form of systematic or intensive drug treatment while in prison (Mumola, 1999). The level of treatment provided to incarcerated individuals in the United States is far short of the level needed (Belenko, 1998a).

There have been ongoing discussions in the fields of substance abuse and corrections about incarceration-based rehabilitation strategies. On one side is the belief that correctional institutions are hostile environments that impede treatment attempts and, therefore, treatment efforts should be reserved for offenders serving their sentences in the community. On the other side, evidence has been cited to show that incarceration-based substance abuse intervention could help reduce posttreatment drug use as well as control recidivism (Wexler, Williams, Early, & Trotman, 1996; Wexler, Falkin, & Lipton, 1990; Anglin & McGlothlin, 1988; Simpson, 1988).

An overwhelming proportion of all offenders in the United States are substance abusers. According to a report released by the National Institute of Justice in April 2003, 52 to 80 percent of male arrestees in major urban areas test positive for drug use (National Institute of Justice, 2003). Without effective interventions, the likelihood of these offenders returning to their patterns of illicit drug use and criminal offending is almost certain. Hence, the need to develop effective treatment programs for substance abusers while they are under correctional supervision is apparent.

There are many reasons why incarceration-based drug treatment programs can be effective. First, correctional facilities are believed to possess the capability to coerce treatment for offenders who would not otherwise participate. Second, the correctional environment helps reduce the availability of illicit substances that eventually facilitates detoxification. Third, because the location of many prison-based substance abuse treatment programs are removed from the larger correctional environment, treatment programs may allow participants to receive treatment in a safe and clean environment (Mitchell, MacKenzie & Wilson, in press).

Treatment in Jails and Detention Facilities. A large number of jail inmates are drug involved. According to a report by the Bureau of Justice Statistics (2000), more than 70 percent of local jail inmates had used drugs regularly or had committed a drug offense. Approximately 36 percent were under the influence at the time of arrest. The most serious offense was a drug crime for 22 percent of the convicted jail inmates (not including drinking while driving and drunkenness). Hence, jails could provide an opportunity to help inmates recognize the negative consequences of drug abuse, motivate them to address their problem through treatment, and encourage their participation in community substance abuse services during incarceration or following discharge.

In 1998, about 43 percent of jail jurisdictions provided substance treatment, and 68 percent provided other programs for drug-involved offenders. Self-help groups (such as AA, NA, or other peer group counseling) were the most common substance abuse program (64 percent) provided in jails. About 30 percent of the jails had education or awareness programs. Overall, 12 percent of jail jurisdictions provided all types of programs and treatment and about 22 percent had only AA, NA, or other self-help programs. In 1996, more than half the jail inmates surveyed who said they had ever used drugs or who used regularly had participated in substance abuse treatment or programs in the past. Among convicted inmates in jails, 58 percent of those who had used drugs in the month before the offense and 61 percent of those who had used drugs at the time of the offense had participated in some type of substance abuse treatment or program. Thus, although many inmates in local jails are participating in treatment, a fairly substantial percent are not. Furthermore, what is considered to be drug treatment varies greatly and many times includes only AA, NA, or education and awareness programs (Bureau of Justice Statistics, 2000).

Treatment in Prison. Similar to jail inmates, many state and federal prison inmates in the United States are drug involved. According to the Bureau of Justice Statistics (1999), 75 percent of state and 80 percent of the federal prisoners may be characterized as alcohol- or drug-involved offenders. Offenders convicted of drug crimes make up 21 percent of state prison inmates and 60 percent of the federal inmates.

Many prisoners report participation in drug treatment (loosely defined) in the past but few report participating while they are in prison. For example, a third of the state prisoners reported past participation in an alcohol or drug abuse program such as time spent in a drug treatment residential facility, professional counseling, detoxification, or use of a maintenance drug (Bureau of Justice Statistics, 1999). However, only about 12 percent of the state prisoners had participated in these types of treatments since admission to prison. When treatment is defined to also include education and awareness programs as well as peer group counseling such as NA and AA, a larger percent (28 percent) report receiving treatment. Despite the fact that a large percent of the prison inmates can be characterized as drug involved, a relatively small number actually receive treatment. Given the potential associated with implementing corrections-based drug intervention strategies, knowledge of the effectiveness of these programs is critical (Bureau of Justice Statistics, 1999).

Effectiveness of Incarceration-Based Treatment. Incarceration-based drug treatment programs embrace a variety of treatment approaches such as group and individual psychotherapy, twelve-step programs, and methadone maintenance as well as punitive measures such as boot camps. Despite the many types of treatment approaches, evaluations of incarceration-based drug treatment programs have primarily examined TCs and group counseling programs (Mitchell, MacKenzie, & Wilson, in press).

The first corrections-based TC was established in 1962 in Nevada state prison. In 1967, the Federal Bureau of Prisons implemented a TC in its Danbury, Connecticut, institution. From the 1970s through the mid-1980s, however, corrections-based TCs appeared to come and go reportedly because of prison crowding, state budget deficits, staff burnout, and conflicts between custodial officials and TC staff. Yet, a few TC programs, most notably the Stay'N Out TC that was established in New York in 1974, continued to operate. This program served as the protocol for subsequent corrections-based TCs (Camp & Camp, 1990).

Contemporary incarceration-based TCs are modeled after the Stay'N Out TC and are generally located in total treatment environments. Participants are housed in units segregated from the general inmate population. Treatment usually lasts from six to nine months. The majority of the treatment staff are former drug abusers who themselves were rehabilitated in TCs. The protocol of TC programs includes individual and group counseling, a system of explicit rewards that reinforce the value of earned achievement, and specific rules and regulations that guide the behavior of residents and program management (Inciardi, 1996).

Recently my colleague, Ojmarrh Mitchell, and I completed a meta-analysis examining the effectiveness of prison-based drug treatment for a Campbell Collaboration systematic review (Mitchell & MacKenzie, 2003; see also Mitchell, MacKenzie, & Wilson, 2005). The studies included in the analysis had to meet the following eligibility requirements: intervention conducted in a correctional facility, delivered since 1979 (to increase similarity to current programs), quasi-experimental or experimental design (comparison group of no treatment or minimal treatment), and criminal behavior outcome

Incarceration-Based Drug Treatment Programs

Citation	Effect
Field, 1985	6.94
Inciardi et al., 1997 (KEY-CREST)	3.84
Wexler et al., 1999	3.53
Pelissier et al., 1998	2.95
Taxman & Spinner, 1996	1.76
Inciardi et al., 1997 (CREST)	1.54
Smith, 1996	1.50
Wexler et al., 1990 (male)	1.40
Peters et al., 1993	1.23
Wexler et al., 1990 (female)	1.14
Gransky & Jones, 1995 (DGSAT)	1.04
Knight et al., 1999	1.02
Tunis et al., 1995 (New)	.99
Tunis et al., 1995 (SAID)	.93
Sealock et al., 1997	.90
Inciardi et al., 1997 (KEY)	.89
Zhang, 2000 (Mod 1)	.86
Eisenberg & Fabelo, 1996	.75
Dugan & Everett, 1998	.69
Shaw & MacKenzie, 1992	.59
Little et al., 1991	.56
Tunis et al., 1995 (JET)	.47
Tunis et al., 1995 (REACH)	.46
Tunis et al., 1995 (DEUCE)	.46
Mean Odds-Ratio (24)	**1.23**

0.1 0.2 0.5 1 2 5 10

Favors Control Favors Treatment

Figure 12.2. Forest plot showing odds ratio and 95 percent confidence interval for studies of incarceration-based drug treatment programs.

(including drug use). Overall, the meta-analysis indicated that drug treatment programs were modestly effective in reducing recidivism. Seventy-nine percent of the recidivism effect sizes favored the treated group. Assuming a 50 percent recidivism rate for the comparison group, the treated group's recidivism rate was estimated at 45 percent. However, there were differences in the effectiveness of treatment based on the treatment modality. The TC programs had the largest positive (and significant) effect size; assuming a 50 percent recidivism rate for the comparison group, the mean recidivism rate for TC programs would be 43 percent. The effect size analysis for the group counseling programs was also significant but the magnitude of the effect was small.

Shown in Table 12.2 are the recidivism rates for twenty-nine studies examining incarceration-based drug treatment programs. Two of the studies reported separate recidivism rates for males and females (Wexler, Falkin, & Lipton, 1990; Magura, Rosenblum, & Joseph, 1993) and two studies reported results from two or more independent samples (Tunis, Austin, Morris, Hardyman, & Bolyard, 1995; Oregon Department of Corrections, 1994). Ten of the studies were rated two on the methods score. Figure 12.2 presents the results of twenty-four samples utilized in the seventeen incarceration-based treatment studies on recidivism with methods scores greater than two. Although twenty-nine studies are originally included in Table 12.2, the outcomes from studies reporting in means only (n = 2) and those from studies with a methods score of two (n = 10) are excluded from the plot. The principal recidivism measure in each sample for calculating effect size involves a return to the criminal justice system for the offenders; this is evidenced by rearrest (n = 13), reincarceration (n = 3), reconviction (n = 6), technical violations (n = 1), and general recidivism (undefined; n = 1). To generate the best possible measure of recidivism, the longest follow-up period available is used to calculate the effect sizes.

As shown in Figure 12.2, eleven of the effect sizes favored the treated group; eight of these differences were significant. Eleven effect sizes favored the comparison group, and three of these were significant. Two effect sizes did not favor either the treated or comparison group. Overall, the analysis indicated a significant difference between groups with the treated group having significantly lower recidivism.

Drug treatment in a prison setting was examined in seventeen of the studies (including studies scoring two on the methods scale). Of these, twelve studied TCs and the remaining five examined group therapy in an outpatient-type model. Effect sizes are shown in Figure 12.2 for twenty-four independent samples. Six of the eight studies finding significant differences between the treated and comparison groups were prison TCs, one was an outpatient/group therapy-type program, and one program was given to jail inmates. Inciardi, Martin, Butzin, Hooper, and Harrison (1997) studied the in-prison TC (Key) as well as the impact of a TC work release program (Crest) and the combination

TABLE 12.2. *Studies of incarceration-based drug treatment programs for offenders showing recidivism rates, length of follow-up, and sample characteristics*

Study (methods score)	Measure of recidivism	Recidivism				Follow-up period (in months)
		Experimental (%)	N	Control (%) #1/#2/#3	N	
Wexler, DeLeon, Thomas,	Reincarceration	40.2/8.2	194/97	49.7	290	12
Kressel, & Peters, 1999[2] (5)	Reincarceration	48.8/14.0	80/43	67.1	85	24
Dugan & Everett, 1998 (4)	Recidivism (*M* & std. dev.)	4.5 (6.3)	61	3.4 (5.2)	56	24
Inciardi et al., 1997 (4)	Key				184	18
	Rearrest	57.0	37	54.0		
	Drug Use	88.0	38	84.0		
	Crest					
	Rearrest	43.0	179	54.0*		
	Drug Use	69.0	183	84.0*		
	Key-Crest					
	Rearrest	23.0	43	54.0*		
	Drug Use	53.0		84.0*		
Pelissier et al., 1998 (4)	Rearrest	70.0	899	87.3*	967	6
	Rearrest or Revocation	95.3		82.6*		
Sealock et al., 1997 (4)	Rearrest	74.0	298	72.0	222	18
	Alleged Offenses (*M* & std. dev.):					
	All	1.90 (1.92)	297	1.79 (1.96)		
	Person	0.41 (0.81)		0.41 (.73)		
	Property	0.82 (1.23)		0.86 (1.28)		
	Drug	0.41 (0.77)		0.22 (.59)*		
	Readjudication	53.0	298	48.0		
	Offenses involved (*M* & std. dev.):					
	All	1.11 (1.41)	297	0.91 (1.33)		
	Drug	0.31 (0.66)		0.12 (0.40)*		

Shaw & MacKenzie, 1992 (4)	Rearrest		74		182	12
	All	37.8		26.6		
	Drug	9.5		4.9		
	Reincarceration/Revocation	28.4		18.9		
	Positive Drug Screen	13.5		5.0		
Smith, 1996 (4)	Rearrest		250		246	36
	Any	64.1		72.8*		
	"Other"	10.8		15.4		
	Drug Offenses	38.1		48.0*		
	Property Offenses	28.8		37.8*		
	Violent Offenses	28.8		37.8*		
	Reconvictions					
	Any	45.9		53.4		
	"Other"	1.8		2.4		
	Drug Offenses	28.6		35.2		
	Property Offenses	15.1		19.4		
	Violent Offenses	14.8		19.0		
Taxman & Spinner, 1996 (4)	Rearrest		296		232	24
	Any	55.1		68.1*		
	New Offense	38.5		48.7*		
	Technical Violation	16.6		19.4		
Zhang, 2000 (4)	*(M) and std. dev.*		427		427	(*M*) = 51
	Rearrest	3.54 (3.05)		3.28 (3.47)		
	Sustained Petitions	1.41 (1.52)		1.53 (1.59)		
	Probation Violations	0.16 (0.44)		0.10 (0.50)		
Eisenberg & Fabelo, 1996 (3)	Reincarceration	14.1	672	19.0	395	12
	Rearrest	23.5		29.0		
Field, 1985[1] (3)	Reincarceration	29.2	144	74.1	27	36
	Reconviction	45.8		85.2		

(continued)

TABLE 12.2 *(continued)*

Study (methods score)	Measure of recidivism	Recidivism: Experimental (%)	N	Control (%) #1/#2/#3	N	Follow-up period (in months)
Gransky & Jones, 1995[1] (3)	Reincarceration for Technical Violation	41.1	168	42.1	247	24
Hughey & Klemke, 1996[3] (3)	Rearrest (*M*)		226		34/134	12
	All	3.3		5.4*/4.0*		
	Substance Abuse	0.4		0.9*/0.6*		
	Reconvictions (*M*)	1.7		2.9*/2.2*		
	Probation Violations	1.5		2.7*/1.6		
Knight, Simpson, & Hiller, 1999[4] (3)	Reincarceration	1.3	169	16.6/6.5	122/103	12
	Reincarceration	11.7		48.6/29.1		24
	Reincarceration					
	All	24.9		63.6*/42.0*		36
	Parole Revocation	18.9		41.3/22.3		
	New Offense	6.0		22.0*/19.0*		
Little et al., 1991a (3)	Arrest Followed by a Conviction	24.3	70	36.6	82	(*M*) = 38
Magura et al., 1993[2] (3)	*Males*		116		33	~6.5
	Recidivism:					
	Property Offenses (*M*)	54		51		
	Illegal Income (within past week)	64.0		58.0		
	Drug Injection (past month)	66.0		64.0		
	Heroin Use (past month)	69.0		79.0		
	Heroin or Cocaine Use (past month)	76.0		82.0		
	Females					
	Recidivism:					
	Property Offenses (*M*)	83		46		

	Illegal Income (Within Past Week)	71.0		76.0		
	Drug Injection (Past Month)	48.0		52.0		
	Heroin Use (Past Month)	68.0		76.0		
	Heroin or Cocaine Use (Past Month)	76.0		91.0		
Peters, Kearns, Murrin, Dolente, & May, 1993 (3)	Rearrest	63.0	168	68.0	252	12
	(*M* & std. dev.)	1.1 (1.1)		1.5 (1.6)		
	Drug-Related Rearrest (*M* & std. dev.)	0.52 (0.71)		0.48 (0.77)		
Tunis et al., 1995 (3)	Reconviction (Any Crime)					12
	Santa Clara County	18.0	102	31.0	90	
	Contra Costa County	12.0	192	23.0	148	
	Los Angeles County	12.0	135	22.0	98	
	New York City	19.0	202	20.0	256	
	Westchester County	21.0	91	21.0	114	
	All Samples Combined	16.0	722	22.0	706	
	Reconviction (Drug Crime)					12
	Santa Clara County	4.0	102	13.0	90	
	Contra Costa County	5.0	192	13.0	148	
	Los Angeles County	6.0	135	15.0	98	
	New York City	10.0	202	11.0	256	
	Westchester County	9.0	91	3.0	114	
	All Samples Combined	11.0	722	11.0	706	
Wexler, Falkin, & Lipton, 1990 (3)	*Male*		435			34–42
	Rearrest	26.9		34.6*/39.8*/40.9*	573/261/	
	Positive Parole Discharge	58.1		52.6/52.7/60.6	159	
	Female		247			30–35
	Rearrest	17.8		29.2*/23.7		
	Positive Parole Discharge	77.2		68.2/52.9	113/38	

(continued)

TABLE 12.2 *(continued)*

Study (methods score)	Measure of recidivism	Recidivism				Follow-up period (in months)
		Experimental (%)	N	Control (%) #1/#2/#3	N	
Eisenberg, 2001 (2)	Reincarceration	31.0	1506	32.0	3098	24
Field, 1989[1] (2)	Rearrest	77.8	144	92.0	65	36
	Reconviction	66.7		89.0		
	Reincarceration	46.4		85.0		
Gransky & Jones, 1995[1] (2)	Reincarceration		739		3,350	24
	All	31.5		28.6		
	New Offense	18.1		26.4		
	Technical Violation	13.4		2.2		
Hartmann, Wolk, Johnston, & Colver, 1997 (2)	Rearrest	14.6	161	28.0	125	3
Oregon DOC, 1994[1] (2)	*CTP*	120		120	24	
	Revocations	42.5		44.2		
	CTS	327		327		
	Revocations	41.6		44.0		
Prendergast et al., 1996[2] (2)	Return to Custody	15.8/17.4	19/23	22.7	22	12
	In Prison (at Time of Interview)	15.8/30.4		50.0		
	Reason for Return to Custody					
	Technical Violation	66.6/54.5		50.0		
	New Term	33.3/45.5		50.0		
Siegal, Wang, Falck, Rahman, & Carlson, 1997 (2)	Rearrest					
	All	14.1				
	Selected Offenses (Violent & Drug)	4.6				
	Drug	0.8				

Washington State DOC 1988 (2)	Recidivism	21.1	436	28.75	240	24
	New Conviction	9.4		13.3		
	Parole Violation	11.7		15.4		
Wexler, Graham, Koronkowski, & Lowe, 1995 (2)	Return to CDC prison		108/61		73	12
	All	42.6/26.2		63.0*		
	SATCU	2.8/8.2		9.6		
	Parole Violation	18.5/8.2		26.0		
	Pending Revocation	4.6/0.0		5.5		
	New Term	16.7/9.8		21.9		
Zhang, 2000 (2)	*(M) and std. dev.*		100		100	12
	Rearrest	1.05 (1.31)		1.37 (1.68)		
	Sustained Petitions	0.26 (0.5)		0.36 (0.59)		
	Probation Violations	0.18 (0.52)		0.18 (0.59)		
	Self-report delinquency:					
	Status Offenses	1.22 (1.11)		1.02 (1.03)		
	Vandalism	0.24 (0.51)		0.18 (0.5)		
	Theft	1.02 (1.67)		0.61 (1.15)[5]		
	Violent Offenses	0.65 (1.07)		0.50 (0.79)		
	Nondrug Offenses	3.13 (3.35)		2.31 (2.54)[5]		
	Drug Use	1.68 (1.02)		1.35 (1.05)[5]		
	Drug Sale	0.20 (0.47)		0.13 (0.42)		
	All Drug Offenses	1.88 (1.27)		1.48 (1.23)[5]		

1 Significance tests were not reported.
2 Significance tests were not reported for individual measures.
3 Standard deviations were not reported.
4 Significance tests were not reported for the measures at twelve and twenty-four months.
5 Cannot tell percentages for comparison group.
* Significantly different from experimental group, $p < 0.05$.

of in-prison and aftercare work release (Key-Crest). They found the TC work release, Crest, and the combination of in-prison and aftercare, Key-Crest, were effective but the in-prison, Key, alone was not.

Only two studies examined drug treatment for detained juveniles (Sealock, Gottfredson, & Gallagher, 1997; Zhang, 2000). In both studies, the control group had lower recidivism but the results were not significant. Zhang's juvenile study (2000) examined the impact of drug treatment provided in a boot camp for juveniles. The two other studies of boot camps examined programs for adult drug-involved offenders (Shaw & MacKenzie, 1992; Gransky & Jones, 1995). Consistent with other research on boot camps, none of the three studies of boot camps for drug-involved offenders found significant differences between groups (see Chapter 13).

There are nine different effect sizes in Figure 12.2 for studies examining drug treatment in jails [note: the Tunis et al. (1995) study had five separate independent samples]. Only the study by Taxman and Spinner (1996) found a significant difference between groups in favor of the drug treatment group. The program they studied had an aftercare component.

Overall, the majority of the programs that found significant differences in favor of the treated groups had an aftercare component. Of the studies showing significant differences in effect sizes, only the study by Wexler, Falkin, and Lipton (1990) did not. Thus, follow-up aftercare may be a particularly important component of successful programs.

Another commonality among effective incarceration-based programs is the modality – the majority of the effective programs were TCs (n = 6 of eight on Figure 12.2). As with aftercare, this appears to be an important aspect of successful programs.

CONCLUSIONS

Overall, drug treatment is effective in reducing the recidivism of drug-involved offenders. Treatment in both community settings and facilities is effective. There are some characteristics of incarceration-based treatment that appear to be necessary components for effective treatment. Effective incarceration-based programs use a TC treatment modality and provide an aftercare component. Although the results for community treatment programs for offenders and for outpatient treatment met my criteria for being considered effective, there are problems is drawing conclusions about the characteristics of effective programs. Overall, the impacts of the community and outpatient treatments are small, and little can be said about the characteristics of the effective programs. As a result, it is difficult to advise program developers about how to implement an effective program.

What is disappointing in this research is the number of poorly designed studies. Drug treatment researchers continually make the mistake of omitting the noncompleters from the analyses or of examining the completers compared to either dropouts or those who do not volunteer. These are faulty research designs because those who drop out of or refuse to volunteer for a program most likely differed from the completers prior to the treatment. The comparison may show us differences in the two groups, but nothing can be said about the impact of the treatment because the groups differed prior to treatment. A comparison of the dropouts or the nonvolunteers to the completers ruins the experimental design. Nothing can be said about the effect of the treatment in these designs because it is impossible to rule out alternative explanations for the results.

Given the large number of offenders who are drug involved, future research should use rigorous research designs to examine the effectiveness of various modalities. The poor research designs currently in use often prohibit us from eliminating alternative explanations for the outcomes. It is impossible to say whether the treatment made a difference in recidivism or whether the groups differed prior to the treatment and that this is what resulted in any observed differences in recidivism.

More information is also needed about the intensity of the treatment protocols and the specific components of effective programs. Although some programs are effective, there are also many that are not. More detailed information about the treatment integrity of the different programs would help us draw conclusions about the specific components that appear to be beneficial.

The research also suffers from clear definitions of what is meant by treatment. Surveys such as those by the Bureau of Justice Statistics often include NA, AA, or drug education in their definition of treatments. Research has failed to examine whether these interventions are effective. The danger is that this systematic review of the literature on drug treatment in which I conclude that drug treatment is effective will be interpreted by some to mean that NA, AA, or drug education alone are effective in reducing recidivism. There is no evidence supporting this perspective.

APPENDIX 12.1. STUDY REFERENCE, DESCRIPTION, AND METHODS SCORES (IN PARENTHESES) OF COMMUNITY TREATMENT STUDIES

Falkin et al., 1999 **(2)**

Probationers admitted to treatment through New York City's Central Placement Unit, which is contracted with nine outpatient drug-free treatment programs, are compared to probationers referred to treatment but not admitted.

Goldkamp and Weiland, 1993 **(3)**

Participants in Dade County's Felony Drug Court, which emphasizes a community-based outpatient treatment focus, are compared with a 1987 sample of felony 2 and 3 drug offenders that were processed before the implementation of the drug court.

Moon and Latessa, 1994 **(3)**

Participants of the Chemical Offender Program between September 1990 and May 1992, which focuses on treatment through acupuncture and traditional group counseling and therapy, are compared to a group of similar probationers between 1989 and 1992 that received "some form of drug treatment."

Oregon DOC, 1994 **(4)**

Participants receiving outpatient treatment between 1989 and 1991 through CTS are compared to a statistically matched group of offenders who did not receive treatment and were incarcerated between 1989 and 1991.

Rhodes and Gross, 1997 **(5)**

Two samples: Washington, D.C., and Portland, Oregon, arrestees. A program of intensive case management, designed to increase utilization of substance abuse treatment among arrestees through supplementary intervention and program materials, was implemented. Samples were randomly assigned to the full case management model, provided with a referral guide and a supplementary video, or provided with a referral guide, supplementary video, and had one counseling and referral session with a specialist (comparable to no treatment conditions).

Rosner, 1988 (3)

Participants between January 1981 and June 1982 of an all-male drinking-driver rehabilitation program for first-time offenders are compared to offenders that qualified and applied for the program but did not attend for various reasons.

Van Stelle et al., 1994 (2)

Completers of the Wisconsin Treatment Alternative Programs between June 1990 and May 1991, a case management model utilizing offender-appropriate substance abuse treatment, are compared to offenders that began the treatment but dropped out because of various circumstances.

APPENDIX 12.2. STUDY REFERENCES, DESCRIPTION, AND METHODS SCORES (IN PARENTHESES) OF INCARCERATION-BASED TREATMENT FOR OFFENDERS

Dugan and Everett, 1998 (4)

Eligible inmates screened for chemical dependency were randomly assigned to either participate in treatment involving seventy-two hours of group therapy in a jail based upon Glasser's "reality therapy" or receive no treatment.

Eisenberg, 2001 (2)

Participants in the Substance Abuse Felony Punishment program in a Texas jail in FY 1996–97 were compared to a comparison group with similar characteristics. Program completers were also compared to program noncompleters.

Eisenberg and Fabelo, 1996 (3)

Male and female program completers of the In-Prison Therapeutic Community (IPTC) in Texas between 1992 and 1993 were compared to noncompleters and a comparison group of individuals who met the IPTC selection criteria but were not selected because they were released from prison prior to program selection.

Field, 1985 **(3)**

Graduates (1976–79) of Oregon's Cornerstone Therapeutic Community Program coupled with a six-month community-based aftercare are compared to dropouts of the same program that received less than thirty days of treatment.

Field, 1989 **(2)**

Participants (1983–85) of Oregon's Cornerstone Therapeutic Community Program coupled with a six-month community-based aftercare are compared to dropouts of the same program that received less than sixty days of treatment.

Gransky and Jones, 1995 **(3)**

Dwight Gateway Substance Abuse Treatment Program: Female offenders participating in a TC program during the FYs 1990–92 are compared to female offenders at traditional prisons, who were eligible for the program but unable to be placed, matched to treatment group on basis of substance abuse history, age, race, and sentence time remaining.

Gransky and Jones, 1995 **(2)**

Impact Incarceration Program: Nonviolent offenders incarcerated for the first time who were housed in a residential boot camp treatment program in FY 1992–93 were compared to inmates housed in traditional facilities that met the eligibility requirements but did not participate in the program.

Hartmann et al., 1997 **(2 or 3)**

Prison inmates who were graduates of the Ozarks Correctional Center Drug Treatment Program (OCCDTP) between September 1995 and March 1996 were compared to a control group from the Missouri Department of Corrections, who had been released within the same time period, were matched on the eligibility criteria for OCCDTP, and had an alcohol or drug problem based on the Prison Inmate Inventory.

Hughey and Klemke, 1996 **(3)**

Jail inmates graduating from Linn County Florida's Inmate Recovery Program (IRP) utilizing day treatment and aftercare between January 1991 and December 1993 were compared to (1) IRP noncompleters and (2) a matched inmate control group that received no treatment; subjects had prior histories of substance abuse and/or alcohol/drug arrest.

Inciardi et al., 1997 **(4)**

Delaware drug offenders receiving no treatment were compared with similar offenders receiving (1) prison-based TC treatment (Key) (2) work-release TC treatment (Crest) followed by aftercare, and (3) prison-based followed by work-release TC treatment (Key-Crest) and aftercare.

Knight et al., 1999 **(3)**

Offenders (both low and high severity) admitted to the Texas In-Prison Therapeutic Community between June 1993 and January 1994 and completing treatment followed by community-based residential aftercare and up to a year of outpatient counseling were compared with similar offenders who (1) participated in the program but dropped out during aftercare and (2) were recommended for the program but received no treatment because of various factors.

Little et al., 1991a **(3)**

Male offenders who began MRT during their incarceration at the Shelby County Correction Center and were released between 1987 and 1988 were compared to a control group of male inmates who applied for treatment during the same time but did not receive treatment because of a limited number of funded program spots.

Magura et al., 1993 **(3)**

Heroin addicts with an extensive criminal history incarcerated at Riker's Island receiving methadone maintenance treatment through the Key Extended Entry Program between November 1988 and April 1990 are compared with a similar group of offending heroin addicts from Riker's Island who were detoxified only.

Oregon Department of Corrections, 1994 **(2)**

Corrections Treatment Program: Six-to-eighteen-month intensive residential treatment for chronic addicts with long criminal histories, followed by six months of transitional services after parole. Participants treated between 1989 and 1991 are compared to those that received no treatment and were incarcerated at the same time.

Corrections Treatment Services: Outpatient drug and alcohol treatment (generally for two hours per week over a six-to-twelve-month period), including individual and group counseling and workshops. Participants treated between 1989 and 1991 were compared to those that received no treatment and were incarcerated at the same time.

Pelissier et al., 1998 **(4)**

Nine-to-twelve-month Drug Abuse Treatment Program (DAP) emphasizing treatment community within prison and aftercare component. Participants that volunteered for the program through several sites were compared to a mixed group of offenders who either did not volunteer for DAP or were located at non-DAP sites but were similar to treatment group with regards to other demographic variables.

Prendergast et al., 1996 **(2)**

All-female sample with expected parole release date between December 1993 and June 1994: Participants of Forever Free at the California Institute for Women, a prison-based substance abuse program, (1) who completed the program and entered an optional community-based residential program and (2) who completed the program but did not enter the residential program, were compared to offenders who applied to Forever Free but were not admitted.

Peters et al., 1993 **(3)**

Offenders who participated in the Hillsborough County Sheriff's Office Substance Abuse Jail Program in Florida between June 1988 and January 1991, utilizing TC as well as cognitive-behavioral group psychotherapy approaches, are compared to offenders identified as having a substance abuse problem who did not participate.

Sealock et al., 1997 **(4)**

Juvenile offenders: Drug-involved youths committed by the judge to participate in a two-month residential substance abuse treatment program were compared to similar drug-involved youths who were assigned by the judge to probation.

Shaw and MacKenzie, 1992 **(4)**

Participants of a two-phase shock incarceration program including a 90- to 180-day regimen modeled after military training and a period of intense parole supervision between October 1987 and October 1988 are compared to offenders with regular parole and probation sentences who were legally eligible for the shock incarceration but were not recommended.

Siegal et al., 1997 (2)

Inmates receiving therapeutic community treatment for substance abusers in Ohio prisons were compared to inmates that declined participation in the program; lack of relevant historical information for the groups. Subjects were interviewed between January 1991 and December 1995.

Smith, 1996 (4)

Participants receiving treatment with the Civil Addiction Program involving inpatient educational treatment in prison coupled with outpatient aftercare were compared with offenders receiving no treatment matched to the treatment group with respect to age, race, offense, county, and number of commitment convictions.

Taxman and Spinner, 1996 (4)

Participants of the Jail Addiction Services Project in Montgomery County, Maryland, between November 1991 and May 1993 were compared to randomly selected offenders entering the Montgomery County Detention Facility during the same time period with a reported drug/alcohol problem and similar criminal history but receiving no treatment.

Tunis et al., 1995 (3)

Male participants discharged from the Jail Education and Treatment (JET) program in Santa Clara County between August 1991 and October 1992 were compared to a sample of jail inmates released between January 1991 and December 1991 who were matched on race, age, primary offense, and sentence length.

Participants in the DEUCE program in Contra Costa County between June 1992 and September 1992 were compared to a group of jail releases between January 1991 and December 1991 who were matched on race, age, gender, primary offense, and sentence length.

Program participants in the Rebuilding, Educating, Awareness, Counseling and Hope (REACH) program (females only) in Los Angeles County admitted between March 1992 and September 1992 were compared to a group obtained from four different samples of female inmates at Sybil Brand Institute, which does not provide drug treatment, who matched the REACH participants on offense, sentence status, sentence length, security level, and motivation for treatment.

Participants who voluntarily entered the Substance Abuse Intervention Diversion (SAID) program in New York City between March 1992 and February 1993 were compared to a group of inmates who had been recruited for SAID but not placed in the program because of facility issues (i.e., overcrowding) and inmates placed in non-SAID minimum security dorms.

Male and female inmates housed in the New Beginnings program (Westchester County) between February 1991 and December 1992 who voluntarily participated in the study were compared to a group of inmates made up of those who were recommended for the program but opted not to participate, inmates who volunteered for New Beginnings but were ineligible because of sentence length or some other factor, and inmates rejected by the program because of poor behavioral record.

Washington State Department of Corrections, 1988 **(2)**

Washington state's substance abuse program included skills training, substance abuse education, and counseling; program participants between March 1984 and September 1986 were compared with nonparticipants who were released for parole between December 1983 and March 1984.

Wexler et al., 1999 **(5)**

Random assignment from a voluntary waiting list to treatment and nontreatment groups; completers receiving (1) treatment with the Amity Prison Therapeutic Community Substance Abuse Program and (2) completers receiving treatment with the Amity Prison Therapeutic Community Substance Abuse Program as well as voluntarily receiving aftercare at a residential facility were compared to nonparticipants receiving no treatment.

Wexler et al., 1990 **(3)**

Male only: Participants of the Stay'n Out Therapeutic Community Program are compared to (1) participants of a non-TC milieu drug treatment program and (2) participants receiving counseling drug treatment and (3) offenders who volunteered for the TC but never entered the program. Subjects terminated treatment between 1977 and 1984 or had been placed on the waiting list.

Female only: Participants of the Stay'n Out Therapeutic Community Program are compared to (1) participants receiving counseling drug treatment and (2) offenders who volunteered for the TC but never entered the program. Subjects terminated treatment between 1977 and 1984 or had been placed on the waiting list.

Wexler et al., 1995 **(2)**

Participants paroled from the California Department of Corrections beginning in April 1992 receiving (1) treatment with the Amity Prison Therapeutic Community Substance Abuse Program and (2) participants receiving treatment with the Amity Prison Therapeutic Community Substance Abuse Program as well as aftercare at a residential facility were compared to nonparticipants receiving no treatment; no information was provided as to the demographic characteristics of the samples.

Zhang, 2000 **(4)**

Module 1: Los Angeles County Drug Treatment Boot Camp (DTBC) for drug-involved juvenile offenders; the program emphasized military atmosphere, drug treatment, and educational programs. Graduates who completed the program between April 1992 and December 1993 were compared to a matched sample of juvenile offenders participating in other boot camp programs that did not utilize a paramilitary atmosphere but were active during the same time period.

Zhang, 2000 **(2)**

Module 2: Los Angeles County DTBC for drug-involved juvenile offenders; the program emphasized military atmosphere, drug treatment, and educational programs. Graduates who completed the program between December 1995 and March 1997 were compared to juvenile offenders completing other boot camp programs during 1996 that did not utilize a paramilitary atmosphere, unsuccessful match with DTBC on ethnicity and age.

PART FIVE

CONTROL, DISCIPLINE, AND PUNISHMENT

CHAPTER THIRTEEN

Correctional Boot Camps

INTRODUCTION

Correctional boot camps are short-term incarceration programs modeled after military basic training (MacKenzie & Parent, 1992; MacKenzie & Hebert, 1996). Since their inception in the adult correctional systems in the United States in 1983 in Georgia and Oklahoma, the programs have rapidly grown, first within adult correctional systems and later in local jails and in juvenile institutions. Boot camps for juveniles were developed after the adult camps; however, they developed rapidly during the 1990s and by 2000 there were seventy juvenile camps in the United States (Koch Crime Institute, 2001). Today, correctional boot camps exist in the United States in federal, state, and local adult jurisdictions, and in state and local juvenile facilities. Correctional boot camps have also been opened in Canada and England.

There are some similarities among most of the correctional boot camps. As in military basic training, inmates often enter the camps in squads or platoons. There may be an elaborate intake ceremony where inmates are immediately required to follow the rules, respond to staff in appropriate ways, stand at attention, and have their heads shaved. While in the program, participants are required to follow a rigorous daily schedule of activities including physical exercise, drill, and ceremony. They arise early each morning and are kept active for most of the day. Staff are addressed by military titles. Punishment for misbehavior is immediate and swift and frequently involves some type of physical activity such as push-ups. A graduation ceremony marks successful completion of the program. Family members and others from the outside public are often invited to attend the graduation ceremony.

Boot camp programs differ greatly in the amount of emphasis placed on rehabilitation versus physical training and hard labor (MacKenzie & Hebert, 1996). Some programs devote a relatively large amount of time in the daily schedule to therapeutic programming such as academic education, drug treatment, or cognitive skills. In other camps, inmates may spend the majority of their time in physical training, drill, and work. Following graduation, some programs provide aftercare or re-entry programs to assist participants with adjustment to the community. Programs also differ in whether they are designed as alternatives to probation or prison and whether inmates must volunteer.

CONTROVERSY OVER BOOT CAMPS

Boot camps remain controversial. Advocates argue that the atmosphere of the camps is conducive to positive growth and change (Clark & Aziz, 1996). From their perspective, the camps provide a positive atmosphere that will force participants to confront past misbehavior, admit the errors of their ways, and change in ways that will result in less criminal activity in the future. The strict discipline is expected to assist inmates in learning how to make decisions. Inmates are expected to learn to delay gratification and thus be less impulsive, a characteristic that is associated with criminal behavior. The close relationship that arises between the drill instructors and inmates is also expected to have a positive impact on the inmates. The drill instructor is viewed as a role model. Inmates are expected to want to model staff's positive social behavior.

Critics of the camps take a very different view of the effect of the military basic training atmosphere. They argue that many of the components of the camps are in direct opposition to the type of relationships and supportive conditions that are needed for quality therapeutic programming (Andrews, Zinger, et al., 1990; Gendreau, Little, & Groggin, 1996; Morash & Rucker, 1990; Sechrest, 1989). According to them, the confrontational atmosphere of the camps is antithetical to constructive therapy. Behavioral therapy and the use of rewards and punishments to change behavior require substantial clinical knowledge and training.

Few boot camp staff have the prerequisite training and experience, and so they will not be able to develop programs that successfully change the behavior of inmates. Furthermore, the confrontational interactions may be damaging to some inmates. For example, such interactions may be reminiscent of previous abusive situations for those who have been abused in the past. They may respond with extreme stress or helplessness – reactions that may inhibit their participation in therapeutic programs even if such programs are provided within the boot camp.

THEORETICAL PERSPECTIVES

Correctional boot camps were not developed based on a coherent theoretical model. In many cases, the initial impetus for the camps came from policy makers who believed young offenders would benefit from the regimentation and rigorous discipline of the military basic training. In an era of "tough on crime" perspectives in the United States, boot camps were also important because they were not soft on criminals. Most theoretical discussions regarding the camps are based on suppositions about how or why the camps might have an impact.

Some have argued that the camps may have an impact on the impulsiveness of offenders. According to the social control perspective, although all people have the propensity to commit crime, most do not because their behavior is regulated by a set of internal and external control mechanisms (Gottfredson & Hirschi, 1990). Offenders are more impulsive and do not have the same control over their behavior as other people do. Boot camps may help offenders change by teaching them skills that enable them to control their behavior (Kempinen & Kurlychek, 2003). The strict rules and discipline may provide the external social control mechanisms that coerce the offenders into making changes in their behavior.

In their examination of life course development and crime, Sampson and Laub (1990) propose that offending patterns can change as a result of a critical life event. Furthermore, the effect of the life event may depend on its ability to build and foster ties to society. Boot camps may be such a critical life event for some inmates. Participants' life trajectories may be leading them down a path of crime and delinquency.

The shock of the rigorous boot camp atmosphere may be a critical life event that serves as a turning point in their lives, turning them away from drugs and crime toward more positive social activities (Sampson & Laub, 1990). The question is whether such an experience results in closer ties to family, employment, or other prosocial bonds. Such ties have been found to be associated with reduced criminal activities (MacKenzie et al., 1999; Horney, Osgood, & Marshall-Ineke, 1995).

Social learning is another theoretical perspective that may be used to hypothesize why boot camps may have an impact on recidivism. Inmates in the camps may learn basic life skills that help them to live in the community without becoming involved in crime. In the camps, they are expected to learn and practice positive social activities such as exercising, rising early each morning, taking care of their clothes and bedding, polite responses to others, and impulse control. The staff may also be effective models of positive behavior that inmates learn to emulate. However, whether these experiences are sufficient to lead to a noncriminal lifestyle still remains the question.

POTENTIAL IMPACTS OF THE BOOT CAMPS

Research has focused on many potential impacts of the camps. Some research has examined whether the camps change participants' attitudes, attachments to the community, or impulsivity while participants are in the facilities (MacKenzie, Wilson, Armstrong, & Gover, 2001; MacKenzie & Shaw, 1990; MacKenzie & Souryal, 1995). In general, participants in the boot camps appear to make more positive changes than inmates in traditional facilities. Boot camp inmates report that they have changed in positive ways. In support of a social learning perspective, the antisocial attitudes of the boot camp inmates are reduced while they are in the camps (MacKenzie et al., 2001; MacKenzie & Souryal, 1995). This is an important change because such attitudes have continually been found to be associated with criminal activities (Andrews & Bonta, 2003).

On one hand, the positive changes inmates make during the programs, however, may be due to other aspects of the environment and not just the military atmosphere (MacKenzie et al., 2001). For example, participants in the boot camps may be carefully selected from those who are entering the correctional system. The atmosphere of such camps may be better because offenders are less violent and create fewer problems in the institution. Inmates in the camps may not have to interact with the more aggressive inmates who are incarcerated in traditional institutions. Furthermore, inmates selected to enter the boot camps may differ in other ways. They may be more motivated to change or have other characteristics that improve their chances for positive change.

On the other hand, aspects of the environment of the camps may lead to positive changes and positive attitudes toward the program. The atmosphere may create a camaraderie among the participants or a strong mentoring relationship may develop between the officers and the participants, and factors such as these may lead to positive changes.

Other research has focused on the impact of the programs on prison crowding and the need for prison beds (MacKenzie & Piquero, 1994; MacKenzie & Parent, 1991). There is evidence that the camps have the potential to reduce the need for prison beds. However, in few jurisdictions do the camps actually reduce the need for prison beds. The small size of most boot camps combined with the fact that many camps draw participants from those who would have received a sentence of probation results in little reduction in the need for prison beds.

Although there is an interest in positive changes the offenders make while they are in the programs and the impact of the programs on prison crowding, most interest appears to focus on whether the camps are effective in reducing the recidivism of participants. For instance, state correctional officials reported five major goals for the boot camps: deter future crime, protect the public, rehabilitate the offender, reduce costs, and lower recidivism (Gowdy, 1996). Thus, except for reducing the costs, all of the major goals are associated in some way with recidivism reduction.

IMPACT ON RECIDIVISM

Adult Boot Camps

Shown in Table 13.1 are fourteen studies examining the impact of adult boot camps on recidivism. The accompanying Appendix 13.1

TABLE 13.1. *Boot camp programs for adult offenders showing recidivism rates and length of follow-up*

Study evaluated (methods score)	Measure of recidivism	Recidivism: Experimental (%)	N	Control (%) #1/#2/#3	N	Follow-up period (in months)
Austin, Jones, & Bolyard, 1993 (4)	Rearrest[1]	47.3	528	44.3	205	Up to 14
Burns & Vito, 1995 (4)	Tech. Probation Violation	6.6	153	7.6	170	12
	New Offense Conviction	7.9		7.5		
	Reincarceration	14.4		15.3		
Camp & Sandhu, 1995 (4)	Any Conviction	34.0	254	37.0	254	Unknown
Flowers, Carr, & Ruback, 1991 (4)	Return to Prison[1]	49.9	375	57.4	701	60
Harer & Klein-Saffran, 1996 (4)	Return to Prison from Halfway House	43.6	150	32.9	160	$M = 48$
	Rearrest or Revocation (Postrelease)	56.3		77.0		
Jones and Ross, 1997 (4)	Arrest		331		369	$M = 37.7$
	All Offenses	50.8		32.5*		
	Violent/Felony	14.6		15.7		
	Property	29.6		24.9		
	Drug	17.2		10.3*		
	Other	12.4		6.8*		
Jones, 1998 (4)	*Sample 1*		1,388		5,609	36
	Reincarceration for a New Crime	25.0		35.0		
	Reincarceration for a Technical Violation	13.0		2.0		
	Sample 2		2,688		9,414	36
	Reincarceration for a New Crime	26.0		36.0		
	Reincarceration for a Technical Violation	8.0		2.0		

	Sample 3		1,593		4,439	24
	Reincarceration for a New Crime	17.0		23.0		
	Reincarceration for a Technical Violation	11.0		4.0		
	Sample 4		1,646		4,214	12
	Reincarceration for a New Crime	6.0		11.0		
	Reincarceration for a Technical Violation	6.0		4.0		
Kempinen & Kurlychek, 2003 (4)	Failure (New Crimes and Technical Violations)	44.0	508	38.0	532	24–36
	New Crimes	12.0		15.0		
	Technical Violations	32.0		24.0		
MacKenzie, Brame, McDowall, & Souryal, 1995[1] (4)	*Florida*		180		109	12
	Arrest	54.0		65.8		
	New Crime	9.7		22.4		
	Technical Violation	11.4		12.3		
	Georgia		79		85	
	New Crime	16.6		5.2		12
		41.4		14.6		24
	Technical Violation	5.0		3.7		
		11.0		3.7		
	Illinois		196		98	12
	New Crime	7.5		12.7		
	Technical Violation	11.8		2.6		
	Louisiana		291		251	
	Arrest	29.0		42.1		12
		43.8		58.1		24
	New Crime	15.4		23.0		
	Technical Violation	19.3		22.8		

(continued)

TABLE 13.1 *(continued)*

Study evaluated (methods score)	Measure of recidivism	Recidivism: Experimental (%)	N	Control (%) #1/#2/#3	N	Follow-up period (in months)
	New York		191		95	12
	Arrest	53.5		57.0		
	New Crime	8.1		10.3		
	Technical Violation	7.9		8.2		
	Oklahoma		241		70	24
	Revocation for New Crime or Technical Violation	11.4		13.6		
	South Carolina – "Old"		84		69	12
	Arrest	63.4		50.1		
	New Crime	13.8		15.4		
	Technical Violation	14.5		18.6		
	South Carolina – "New"		84		64	12
	Arrest	40.3		43.2		
	New Crime	1.3		5.7		
	Technical Violation	2.1		5.5		
Marcus-Mendoza, 1995 (4)	Violation of Parole or Return to Prison					30
	Females	13.2	332	14.0	409	
	Males	20.3	1,403	28.7*	2,258	
Jones & Ross, 1997 (3)	Arrest		309		331	$M = 38$
	All Offenses	46.9		69.2*		
	Violent/Felony	15.2		23.3*		
	Property	28.5		48.1*		
	Drug	16.8		28.8*		
	Other	12.0		19.1*		

State of New York DOC Division of Parole, 2000[1] (3)	*Sample 1*		20,778		22,375	36
	Return to Prison	40.0		41.0		
	Return to Prison for a New Crime	19.5		21.0		
	Return to Prison as a Rule Violator	20.5		20.0		
	Sample 2		3,246		2,567	24
	Return to Prison	22.0		28.0		
	Return to Prison for a New Crime	15.7		9.0		
	Return to Prison as a Rule Violator	20.0		19.0		
	Sample 3		3,266		2,388	12
	Return to Prison	10.5		13.0		
	Return to Prison for a New Crime	4.3		3.0		
	Return to Prison as a Rule Violator	6.3		10.0		
Wright & Mays, 1998[1] (3)	New Sentence	31.3	560	14.3	1,377	$M = 30$
	Violation of Probation or Parole	4.3		4.3		
Jones, 1996 (2)	Revocation for New Crime, Technical Violation, or Absconding From Supervision	59.0	33	61.0	123	$M = 115$ Days

[1] No significance tests were conducted.

* Significantly different from experimental group, $p < 0.05$.

provides a description of each study. The table shows the results for independent samples and for different measures of recidivism. Ten of these studies scored a four on the methods scales, three scored a three, and one scored a two. The scores of four were generally a result of researchers using quasi-experimental designs matching subjects or controlling for differences in the statistical analysis. So far, no study of adult boot camps has used random assignment to treatment and control conditions.

There are few significant differences when the recidivism rates of these boot camp releasees are compared with control groups. Excluding the findings for technical violations for the moment, a comparison of the results of the studies demonstrates varied and conflicting results. For example, Jones and Ross (1997) and Marcus-Mendoza (1995) found significantly lower recidivism rates for the experimental groups for some measures of recidivism. In contrast, Jones (1997) found significantly lower recidivism for the control group on some measures. MacKenzie, Brame, McDowall and Souryal (1995) found mixed results when control variables were added to the analysis. In some states the control group had lower recidivism, in others the boot camp releasees did. The remaining studies did not find significant differences or did not complete or report significance tests.

Another way to examine these data is to calculate effect sizes and standard deviations for recidivism rates. These are shown in the forest plot in Figure 13.1. Effect sizes were calculated for the same study (e.g., MacKenzie et al., 1995) if the samples were independent (e.g., Georgia samples, South Carolina samples). Figure 13.1 presents the results of nineteen adult boot camp studies (twenty-five samples) on recidivism. Although the principal recidivism measure for the majority of the studies is rearrests (n = 8), for those studies that do not have a measure of general rearrest, reconvictions for new offense (n = 3), return to prison (n = 4), revocation for new crime/technical violation (n = 1), reconviction (n = 1), parole violation/return to prison (n = 2), general recidivism (n = 2), rearrest/revocation (n = 1), parole violation/new sentence (n = 1), new crime/technical violations (n = 1), and reincarceration for a new crime (n = 1) are used to calculate effect sizes. The measures represented by MacKenzie and Souryal (1995) in Table 13.1 are not used in the forest plot because

Adult Boot Camp Programs

Citation	Effect
Harer & Klein-Saffran, 1996	2.61
Jones & Ross, 1997	2.54
Mackenzie et al., 1995 (LA)	1.80
Mackenzie et al., 1995 (IL)	1.68
Mackenzie et al., (FL) 1995	1.67
Marcus-Mendoza, 1995 (Male)	1.58
Jones, 1998	1.42
NYDOC, 2000 (re 1996-97)	1.38
Flowers et al., 1991	1.35
Mackenzie et al., 1995 (OK)	1.32
NYDOC, 2000 (re 1997-98)	1.27
Jones, 1996	1.15
Jones, 1995	1.15
Mackenzie et al., 1995 (NY)	1.15
Camp & Sandhu, 1995	1.15
Mackenzie et al., 1995 (SC-new)	1.14
Marcus-Mendoza, 1995 (Female)	1.06
NYDOC, 2000 (re 1988-1996)	1.04
Burns & Vito, 1995	.97
Austin et al., 1993	.89
Kempinem & Kurlychek, 2001	.78
Mackenzie et al., 1995 (SC-old)	.60
Wright & Mays, 1998	.47
Jones, 1997	.47
Mackenzie et al., 1995 (GA)	.23
Mean Odds-Ratio (25)	**1.15**

Figure 13.1. Forest plot showing odds ratio and 95 percent confidence interval for studies of adult boot camp programs.

MacKenzie et al. (1995) denotes the same information. In addition, the effect size of Jones (1998) represents a combination of the four sample groups reported in Table 13.1. It should also be noted, in general, that the longest follow-up periods available for each study were used to calculate the effect sizes.

As shown in Figure 13.1, the results are similar to the significance test results with some of the effect sizes favoring the boot camp programs and some favoring the comparisons. The standard deviation for the odds ratios overlaps one in most of the studies, meaning that there is no significant difference between the groups. According to this plot, the combined results of the research suggest that there is a small reduction in recidivism for those who participate in boot camps.

As occurred with recidivism rates, the results for the technical violations also vary. Nine of the comparisons for technical violations find

Juvenile Boot Camp Programs

Citation	Effect
Florida DOJJ, 1997a	2.29
Florida DOJJ, 1997c	1.96
Farrington et al., 2001 (HIT)	1.66
Mackenzie et al., 1997	1.57
Aloisi & LeBaron, 2001	1.52
Farrington et al., 2001 (MCTC)	1.40
T3 Associates, 2000	1.32
Florida DOJJ, 1996a	1.17
Peters, 1996a	1.11
Zhang, 2000	1.09
Peters, 1996b	.87
Florida DOJJ, 1997d	.75
Florida DOJJ, 1996c	.67
Florida DOJJ, 1996b	.66
Boyles et al., 1996	.63
CYA, 1997	.49
Florida DOJJ, 1997b	.43
Thomas & Peters, 1996	.39
Mean Odds-Ratio (18)	**1.07**

0.1 0.2 0.5 1 2 5 10

Favors Control Favors Treatment

Figure 13.2. Forest plot showing odds ratio and 95 percent confidence interval for studies of juvenile boot camp programs.

lower rates for the control groups whereas six find in favor of the boot camp groups. Few of the contrasts were significant.

Juvenile Boot Camps

Shown in Table 13.2 are seventeen studies of juvenile boot camps. The accompanying Appendix 13.2 provides a description of each study. In comparison to the studies of the adult programs, these studies are scored higher in research methods. Three studies used random assignment of juveniles to the boot camps and comparison facilities and thus received a method score of five (Peters, 1996a; 1996b; Thomas & Peters, 1996), ten were scored a four in research methods, and the remaining four studies were scored a three (Aloisi & LeBaron, 2001; Boyles, Bokenkamp, & Madura, 1996; Farrington, Hancock, Livingston, Painter, & Towl, 2000; Zhang, 2000). Seven of the studies, conducted by the Florida Department of Juvenile Justice, examined boot camps located in different Florida counties.

Figure 13.2 presents the results of seventeen of the juvenile boot-camp studies (eighteen samples) on recidivism. Although the principal recidivism measure for the majority of the studies are rearrests (n = 8), for those studies that do not have a measure of general rearrest, reconvictions (n = 3), adjudicated new offenses (n = 1), new convictions/pending charges (n = 1), arrest/recommitment (n = 1), new referrals/arrest (n = 1), new court filing/arrest (n = 1), and arrest for new charges/recommitment (n = 1) are used to calculate effect sizes. The arrest/recommitment measure representing the Mackenzie, et al. study that was used in the forest plot is a combination of both the "early" and "late" groups' recidivism. It should also be noted, in general, that the longest follow-up periods available for each study were used to calculate these effect sizes.

The results for the studies of juvenile boot camps are very similar to the findings for the adult programs. Few of the studies found any significant differences between boot camp participants and comparison groups in recidivism. The results for each study are surprisingly consistent for different measures of recidivism and different follow-up times. For example, T3 Associates (2000) calculated recidivism rates at six, twelve, and twenty-five months for new convictions, pending charges, and the combination (convictions and charges). In all but one of the comparisons, the boot camp participants had lower recidivism. Conversely, in the Department of Youth Authority study Bottcher (1997) calculated recidivism for twelve, eighteen, and twenty-four months for arrests, law violations, and return to custody. The comparison samples had lower recidivism on all measures and at all time periods. Thus, although there are many different contrasts, there is consistency for the seventeen studies.

Eight of the studies found control groups had lower recidivism rates for most of the measures of recidivism at almost all follow-up times. Two of these studies reported significant differences favoring the control groups (Bottcher, 1997; Boyles et al., 1996). A similar number of studies (eight) found the comparison groups had lower recidivism. Two of these studies reported significant differences favoring the boot camp participants (MacKenzie, Souryal, Sealock, & Bin Kashem, 1997; Aloisi & LeBaron, 2001).

One study by Farrington, Ditchfield, and Hancock (2002) found differences in the two comparison samples – one favored the boot camp participants, one favored the comparisons. This study may be

TABLE 13.2. *Boot camp programs for juvenile offenders showing recidivism rates and length of follow-up*

Study evaluated (methods score)	Measure of recidivism	Recidivism: Experimental (%)	N	Control (%) #1/#2/#3	N	Follow-up period (in months)
Peters, 1996a (5)	Conviction for a New Offense	28.1	160	31	174	$M = 28$
	Conviction for a Technical Offense	28.1		29.3		
Peters, 1996b (5)	Adjudication/Adult Conviction for Criminal Offense[1]	38.8	80	35.5	107	28
Thomas & Peters, 1996 (5)	Court Adjudicated New Offenses[1]	71.8	170	50	172	6–24
Bottcher, 1997 (4)	Arrest	84.7	313	77.8	243	12
		89.9	296	84.2*	203	18
		93.7	223	87.9*	149	24
	Arrest for Technical Violation	24.0		19.8*		
		12.0		19.2		
		20.2		16.1		
	Arrest for Law Violation	69.7		58.0*		
		67.9		65.0		
		73.5		71.8		
	Return to Custody	3.6		3.2		
		6.5		5.8		
		9.1		8.6		
Florida Department of Juvenile Justice, 1996a (4)	New Referrals or Adult Arrest	71.0	63	75.0	63	12
	Readjudication/Reconviction	59.0		67.0		
	Commitment/Reincarceration	14.0		19.0		

Florida Department of Juvenile Justice, 1996b (4)	Rearrest[1]	74.0	58	66.0	58	12
	Readjudication/Reconviction[1]	60.0		50.0		
	Recommitment to the Dept. of Juvenile Justice[1]	28.0		12.0		
Florida Department of Juvenile Justice, 1996c (4)	Arrest	65.0	52	56.0	52	12
	Readjudication/Reconviction	56.0		50.0		
	Recommitment to the Dept. of Juvenile Justice	19.0		12.0		
Florida Department of Juvenile Justice, 1997a (4)	Arrest	69.0	55	84.0	55	12
	Readjudication/Reconviction	58.0		67.0		
	Recommitment to the Dept. of Juvenile Justice	15.0		13.0		
Florida Department of Juvenile Justice, 1997b (4)	Arrest	36.0	28	21.0	26	6
	Readjudication/Reconviction	21.0		18.0		
	Recommitment to the Dept. of Juvenile Justice	18.0		7.0		
Florida Department of Juvenile Justice, 1997c (4)	Arrest	62.0	64	77.0	64	12
	Readjudication/Reconviction	50.0		61.0		
	Recommitment to the Dept. of Juvenile Justice	28.0		30.0		
Florida Department of Juvenile Justice, 1997d (4)	Arrest	64.0	59	58.0	59	12
	Readjudication/Reconviction	49.0		49.0		
	Recommitment to the Dept. of Juvenile Justice	19.0		15.0		

(continued)

TABLE 13.2 *(continued)*

Study evaluated (methods score)	Measure of recidivism	Recidivism				Follow-up period (in months)
		Experimental (%)	N	Control (%) #1/#2/#3	N	
Mackenzie et al., 1997 (4)	Arrest or Recommitment to Juvenile Facility					
	"Early" Group	79.0	207	83.3*	461	24
	"Late" Group	74.1	162	83.9*	275	
T3 Associates Training and Consulting, 2000 (4)	Overall Recidivism (New Convictions or Pending Charges)	18.4	87	19.8	86	6
		39.0	59	50.0	60	12
		37.3	110	43.9	107	25
	New Convictions	13.8		16.3		
		28.8		31.7		
		20.9		23.4		
	Pending Charges	5.7		3.5		
		11.9		18.3		
		23.6		28.0		
Aloisi & LeBaron, 2001 (3)	Recommitment to JCC/Commitment to DOC		323		286	
		17.3		19.9		6
		25.2		30.1		12
		32.6		37.5		18
		36.9		50.0		24
	New Adjudication/Conviction	25.7		33.9*		
		41.5		53.2*		
		55.8		68.1*		
		68.0		76.4		

	New Court Filing/Arrest	36.5		49.7*		
		55.0		71.8*		
		72.4		79.9		
		80.3		86.1		
Boyles et al., 1996 (3)	Arrest for New Charges	42.4	177	30.4*	138	6
	Commitment	22.2		13.0*		12
Farrington et al., 2001 (3)	Reconviction					12
	TC HIT	34.7	176	55.1*	127	
	CMCTC	29.5	61	30.9	97	
	Reconviction					24
	TC HIT	65.1	175	75.6	127	
	CMCTC	44.3	61	52.6	97	
Zhang, 2000 (3)	*Sample 1*		427		427	48
	Arrest	85.0		86.0		
	Probation Violation	13.3		6.1		
	Sustained Petitions or Convictions	67.0		67.0		
	Sample 2		100		100	12
	Arrest	53.0		56.0		
	Probation Violation	22.0		22.0		
	Sustained Petitions or Convictions	23.0		30.0		

[1] No significance tests reported.

* Significantly different from experimental group, $p < 0.05$.

important in helping us to interpret the findings from these studies. They examined two boot camps and compared the participants to comparison groups. In one boot camp the participants spent a large amount of time in therapeutic activities, and in the other camp the participants did not. The participants from the therapeutic boot camp had lower recidivism than the comparison group; the participants from the other boot camp did not. Thus, differences between studies may be due to differences in the boot camp programs. That is, therapeutic boot camps may be effective in reducing recidivism whereas boot camps that focus on military drill and ceremony may not be as effective as other options.

A SYSTEMATIC REVIEW AND META-ANALYSIS

To examine the impact of the boot camps and the components of the programs, my colleagues and I completed a meta-analysis of boot camp and boot camp–like programs for juvenile and adult offenders (MacKenzie, Wilson, & Kider, 2001). The meta-analysis permitted us to compare the results when we controlled for differences among programs and in the research methods employed for the studies. All of the programs included in the analysis were residential programs with militaristic environments. Studies were included in the meta-analysis if they included a comparison group who were convicted or adjudicated and reported a postprogram measure of recidivism. Experimental and quasi-experimental designs were included in the analysis. We identified forty-four different independent boot camp comparisons. The effect sizes ranged from large reductions to large increases in the risk of recidivating when the boot camp participants were compared to control groups. Overall, we found that the odds of recidivating for the two groups were almost identical (as in the forest plot in Figures 13.1 and 13.2). That is, if the comparison group recidivism rate was set at 50 percent, the estimated recidivism rate for the boot camp participants was estimated to be 49.4 percent. Of the forty-four studies included in the analysis, nine studies observed a statistically significant positive benefit of boot camps, eight observed a negative benefit, and the remaining twenty-seven found no difference between the groups.

We investigated whether the differences in the results from these studies resulted from methodological variables, offender characteristics, or program differences. We did not find any changes in the results when methodological variables were added into the analysis nor were any of the methodological variables significant. Thus, it did not matter whether the studies used random assignment, controls for sample differences, matching, or some other methodology; the overall findings of no differences between groups held.

Disappointingly, very little information regarding the characteristics of the offenders and the programs was reported in the studies. Therefore, it was not possible to use many variables related to offender characteristics or program differences in the analyses. We could classify programs as juvenile or adult programs and whether offenders or delinquents who were adjudicated for violent crimes were permitted to enter the boot camps. These individual characteristics made no differences in the results.

Many of the studies did not report even the genders of the samples. We could identify three all-female samples and four with mixed genders. We found no differences based on gender. However, there was insufficient data to adequately explore whether boot camps are differentially effective for males and females as hypothesized by some theorists (Morash & Rucker, 1990). There was also insufficient information given in the studies to permit us to examine either differential impacts of racial/ethnic makeup or offender risk level.

We also examined whether the results differed depending upon program components such as aftercare, academic or vocational education, drug treatment, counseling, or manual labor. Only an aftercare component for adult programs made a significant difference. Boot camp participants in adult programs that had an aftercare component did significantly better than comparison groups. However, it should be noted that information on the intensity and frequency of different types of treatment in the facilities was not available for the majority of studies. Most likely, there were large differences in the type of treatment provided by various boot camp programs, and the information was not available in the manuscripts. Thus, we could not really answer the question of whether boot camps that incorporated "appropriate" treatment were more successful than comparison facilities.

CONCLUSION

At this point in time, there is no evidence that correctional boot camps are effective in reducing the future criminal activities of adults or juveniles. Compared to other correctional programs, there is a fairly large body of research examining the boot camps (n = 31 studies). Furthermore, most of the studies were scored three or greater on the methods scale. The combination of the number of studies and the quality of the studies leads me to conclude that the military atmosphere of the boot camps is not effective in changing offender behavior. The fact that the information reported in the studies was not detailed enough to enable us to examine in the meta-analyses whether different components of the program are important is disappointing. The meta-analyses suggested that an aftercare component for adult offenders may be associated with reduced recidivism. The problem is we have little information about the type of aftercare that was provided. For example, did offenders participate in drug treatment or employment programs or was the aftercare limited to only more intensive supervision by the probation or parole agents? The lack of information in the studies about the specific components of the boot camps and comparison facilities meant that we could not identify why the recidivism of some boot camp participants was lower than comparisons or, conversely, why in some studies the comparison group had lower recidivism.

If the major goal of the boot camps is to reduce recidivism, then there is little reason to continue to use these programs in correctional settings. However, if the programs are designed to meet other correctional goals such as reducing the need for bed space and/or providing an acceptable mechanism for early release, then more work needs to be done to examine whether the therapeutic components within a boot camp would be effective in reducing recidivism. The most fruitful direction for future research is to examine the question of whether these camps are a better or worse way to provide treatment. That is, in comparison to intensive treatment alone, do the boot camps with intensive treatment programs have a greater impact on recidivism?

APPENDIX FOR 13.1. STUDY REFERENCE, DESCRIPTION, AND METHODS SCORES (IN PARENTHESES) OF BOOT CAMP TREATMENT FOR OFFENDERS

Austin et al., 1993 (4)

Los Angeles Regimented Inmate Diversion (RID) program for young adult males; RID participants between September 1990 and June 1991 were compared to a group of RID-eligible offenders who served their time in a county jail or prison.

Burns and Vito, 1995 (4)

Alabama Disciplinary Unit boot camp graduates were compared to a group of offenders who were placed on probation or had a split sentence.

Camp and Sandhu, 1995 (4)

Oklahoma Female Offender Regimented Treatment Program. Caucasian and African American participants admitted to the program between 1991 and 1994 were compared to a group of prison releasees who had served in ODOC prison.

Flowers et al., 1991 (4)

Georgia's Special Alternative Incarceration program for males; boot camp graduates admitted between December 1983 and December 1986 were compared to a group of prison releasees who had served in a GDOC prison.

Harer and Klein-Saffran, 1996 (4)

Lewisburg Pennsylvania Intensive Confinement Center boot camp for male federal offenders; ICC participants were compared to a eligible federal prison inmates who were released from prison before the program began.

Jones, 1996 (2)

Houston, Texas, Harris County's Court Regimented Intensive Probation Program (CRIPP) boot camp for probationers; male and female boot camp graduates who also completed Super Intensive Probation Program (SIPP) aftercare successfully were compared to a group of probationers who only completed SIPP successfully.

Jones and Ross, 1997 (4)

Male boot camp participants in the Intensive Motivational Program of Alternative Corrections (IMPACT) in North Carolina were compared to a stratified random sample of prisoners released between 1992 and 1993 from NCDOC, who were previously matched as closely as possible to the boot camp sample on prior arrests, current offense, race, and marital status.

Jones, 1998 **(4)**

Illinois' Impact Incarceration Program (IIP); four samples of IIP graduates over different time periods of release were compared to a respective comparison group of offenders who were IIP eligible but served their time in an IDOC prison. Sample 1: released 1991–93; Sample 2: released 1994–95; Sample 3: released 1996; Sample 4: released 1997.

Jones and Ross, 1997 **(3)**

IMPACT participants who did not participate in electronic house arrest (EHA) probation after release were compared to a group of high risk offenders who completed EHA as a condition of probation.

Kempinen and Kurlychek, 2003 **(4)**

Pennsylvania's Quehanna Motivational Boot Camp for males and females; boot camp graduates released between 1996 and 1997 were compared to a group of eligible offenders released during the same period who completed a traditional prison term.

MacKenzie et al., 1995 **(4)**

Florida's shock incarceration graduates and dropouts, males, eighteen to twenty-five, with no previous felonies or incarceration, compared to prison releasees who were matched on demographics, criminal history, and supervision level and were eligible for boot camp.

Georgia's boot camp graduates, male, first-time incarcerated offenders, sentenced to program as condition of probation, were compared to probationers who were eligible for boot camp and matched on demographics, criminal history, and supervision level.

Illinois' shock incarceration graduates, male and female, with no prior adult felony conviction or incarceration, were compared to prison releasees who were eligible for the program and were matched on demographics, criminal history, and supervision level.

Louisiana's IMPACT graduates and dropouts, male and female, with voluntary participation, were compared to prison releasees and probationers who were eligible and matched on demographics, criminal history, and supervision level.

NYDOC's male and female participants, aged sixteen to twenty-nine, with voluntary participation, were compared to prison releasees who were eligible for the program and matched on demographics, criminal history, and supervision level.

Oklahoma's RID participants, males aged seventeen to twenty-five, were compared to prison releasees who were eligible for the program but no space was available at the time of prison sentence, matched on demographics, criminal history, and supervision level.

SCDOC's "old" shock incarceration, male and female participants aged seventeen to twenty-four, were compared to probationers from SCDOC who were eligible for the program, matched on demographics and criminal history.

SCDOC's "new" shock incarceration, male and female participants aged seventeen to twenty-four, who were sent to the program as an alternative to prison were compared to prison releasees from SCDOC who were eligible for the program, matched on demographics and criminal history.

Marcus-Mendoza, 1995 **(4)**

Oklahoma's Shock Incarceration Program (SIP) for males and females. The female sample consisted of shock participants since 1991 compared to a group of prison releasees serving a traditional sentence in the same prison facility prior to the existence of SIP. The male sample consisted of shock participants since 1991 compared to a group of prison releasees serving a traditional sentence in the same prison facility prior to the existence of SIP.

New York Department of Corrections, 2000 **(3)**

New York's Shock Program; three samples of shock participants (graduates and a removal group who finished sentence in prison) over different time periods of release were compared to a respective comparison group for each who were shock eligible but served their time in an NYDOC prison. Sample 1: released 1988–1996; Sample 2: released 1996–97; Sample 3: released 1997–98.

Wright and Mays, 1998 **(3)**

Oklahoma's Regimented Inmate Discipline (RID) for males; RID graduates between 1989 and 1991 were compared to a group of offenders who completed a term in a traditional prison or were placed on probation during the same time period.

APPENDIX 13.2. STUDY REFERENCE, DESCRIPTION, AND METHODS SCORES (IN PARENTHESES) OF BOOT CAMP TREATMENT FOR JUVENILE OFFENDERS

Aloisi and LeBaron, 2001 **(3)**

Males; graduates from the Wharton tract residential phase of the Stabilization and Reintegration Program (SRP) in New Jersey between February 1997 and August 1999 compared to males with no boot camp experience, no first-degree offenses, and no sex or arson offenses committed by the Juvenile Justice Commission and released from other facilities to supervision by the commission's aftercare/parole services.

Boyles et al., 1996 **(3)**

Boot camp for males and females between the ages of eleven and eighteen; boot camp graduates through the Colorado Juvenile Regimented Training Program serving probation afterward between August 1994 and December 1995 were compared to a group of juvenile offenders who served time in traditional residential facilities followed by a period of probation during same time period as the boot camp group.

Bottcher, 1997 **(4)**

Boot camp for males and females; participants were screened eligible for boot camp and then randomly assigned to boot camp or an alternate California Youth Authority (CYA) residential institution; this study compared boot camp participants to this comparison group.

Farrington et al., 2001 **(3)**

Two samples: males, eighteen to twenty-one, not absconding risk, no sex offenses, and mentally and physically capable, with six months to serve in (1) Thorn Cross High Intensity Training and (2) Colchester

Military Corrective Training Centre compared to males from prisons in the area that met criteria (some did not meet psychological criteria) but chose not to participate.

Florida Department of Juvenile Justice, 1996a (4)

Leon County, Florida's boot camp for males; boot camp graduates were compared to a group of juvenile offenders who served time in traditional residential facilities, at the same risk level, and released at the same time period.

Florida Department of Juvenile Justice, 1996b (4)

Manatee County, Florida's boot camp for males; boot camp graduates were compared to a group of juvenile offenders who served time in traditional residential facilities, at the same risk level, and released at the same time period.

Florida Department of Juvenile Justice, 1996c (4)

Pinellas County, Florida's boot camp for males; boot camp graduates were compared to a group of juvenile offenders who served time in traditional residential facilities, at the same risk level, and released at the same time period.

Florida Department of Juvenile Justice, 1997a (4)

Martin County Sheriff's Office Boot Camp for males in Florida; boot camp graduates between August 1994 and February 1995 were compared to a group of juvenile offenders who served time in one of five Department of Juvenile Justice traditional residential facilities, at the same risk level, and released at the same time period; matched on race, commitment history, commitment offenses category, number of prior felony referrals, and age at time of first delinquency referral.

Florida Department of Juvenile Justice, 1997b (4)

Polk County, Florida's boot camp for females; boot camp graduates were compared to a group of juvenile offenders who served time in traditional residential facilities, at the same risk level, and released at the same time period.

Florida Department of Juvenile Justice, 1997c (4)

Polk County, Florida's boot camp for males; boot camp graduates between February 1994 and December 1995 were compared to a group of juvenile offenders who served time in Department of

Juvenile Justice traditional residential facilities, at the same risk level, and released at the same time period; matched on race, commitment history, commitment offenses category, number of prior felony referrals, and age at time of first delinquency referral.

Florida Department of Juvenile Justice, 1997d **(4)**

Bay County, Florida's boot camp for males; boot camp graduates were compared to a group of juvenile offenders who served time in traditional residential facilities, at the same risk level, and released at the same time period.

Mackenzie et al., 1997 **(4)**

New York State's Sergeant Henry Johnson Youth Leadership Academy (YLA) boot camp for males; boot camp participants were compared to a group of eligible juvenile offenders who served time in traditional residential facilities. Two samples were compared: (1) "early" boot camp participants to comparison group; and (2) "late" boot camp participants to comparison group (post–March 1993 when the program changed).

Peters, 1996a **(5)**

Boot camp for males; boot camp graduates were compared to a group of eligible offenders placed in other Division of Youth Services facilities.

Peters, 1996b **(5)**

Boot camp for males; boot camp graduates were compared to a group of eligible offenders placed in other DYS facilities.

Thomas and Peters, 1996 **(5)**

Boot camp for males and females; all adjudicated youths screened eligible for boot camp were randomly assigned to boot camp or an alternate Youth Department of Corrections facility. This study compared boot camp graduates to this comparison group.

T3 Associates Training and Consulting, 2000 **(4)**

Project Turnaround for males; boot camp participants between March 1998 and June 2000 were compared to a group of eligible juvenile offenders placed in traditional juvenile custody facilities.

Zhang, 2000 **(3)**

Two samples: males, sixteen to eighteen years old, documented or alleged drug users with sustained petitions from juvenile court for nonviolent, nonsexual offenses, who completed the Los Angeles

County Drug Treatment Boot Camp between April 1992 and December 1993 compared to offenders, sixteen to eighteen on entry, with no prior camp experience, nonviolent, nonsexual offenders, from four juvenile camps in the area with similar confinement, matched on gender, age, ethnicity, and prior arrest history.

CHAPTER FOURTEEN

Intermediate Sanctions

Intensive Supervision Programs and Electronic Monitoring

INTRODUCTION

During the 1980s,in response to the record numbers of convicted offenders and widespread prison crowding, correctional officials in the United States expanded the range of sentencing options for convicted offenders (Morris & Tonry, 1990; Cullen, Wright, & Applegate, 1996; Tonry & Lynch, 1996; Byrne, Lurigio, & Petersilia, 1992; Harland, 1996; Smykla & Selke, 1995). Prior to this, there were few sentencing options for punishing criminals. Offenders were either incarcerated or given standard probation. In some jurisdictions, ordinary probation often equated with perfunctory supervision. The problem was that the range of severity of crimes did not fall neatly into these two categories of punishments. For many offenders, prison was often too severe a punishment whereas probation was too lenient.

To remedy the situation, many states began to develop alternatives. These alternatives, variously labeled intermediate sanctions, correctional options, alternative punishments, or community corrections, were designed to be punishments somewhere between prison and routine probation with respect to harshness and restrictiveness. Rather than being limited to a choice of either prison or ordinary probation, offenders could be given one of a variety of sanctions that ranged between prison and probation in severity. Numerous different types of intermediate sanctions were developed including house arrest, electronic monitoring, intensive supervision, boot camps, split sentences, day reporting centers, fines, and community service.

As a result of the disillusionment with the effectiveness of rehabilitation and the focus on justice and incapacitation, intermediate sanctions were proposed as an ideal way to provide a range of sanctions between probation and parole (Morris & Tonry, 1990; Tonry, 1996a). Theoretically, these sanctions could be scaled in severity to be proportionate to the severity of the crimes committed. The intermediate sanctions developed during the late 1970s and 1980s reflected the philosophy of the times. Conservative attitudes prevailed, and war was declared on drugs and crime. Many people considered rehabilitation programs as coddling criminals. Intermediate punishments could be argued as tough on crime and criminals.

Not only did these punishments hold the possibility of scaling for severity, but they also were expected to deter offenders from future criminal acts and restrict them so they would not have the opportunity to reoffend. In a sense, the sanctions might be referred to as *semi-incarceration* because the increased surveillance and control were expected to reduce offenders' ability to commit crimes. Theoretically, increasing the surveillance and control over offenders in the community would prevent criminal activities by reducing both their capacity and their opportunity to commit crimes.

The punitive nature of the sanctions were expected to act as a specific deterrence to reduce the offenders' future criminal activity, and the threat of the sanctions were expected to act as a general deterrence to reduce potential criminals from committing crimes. From this perspective, the sanctions would change offenders' perceptions of the costs of crime. Offenders were thought to be able to assess the positive and negative consequences of their actions and, following this assessment, act in their own self-interest. The profit of the crime is assumed to push people toward criminal activities; the pain of the punishment pushes them away from it. Instead of ordinary probation, the more severe sentencing options were expected to increase the costs of crime and thereby reduce criminal activity.

INCREASED CONTROL AND SURVEILLANCE

House arrest, intensive supervision, curfew, day reporting, and other intermediate sanctions fulfill many purposes. They provide graduated punishments that may be more appropriate than either probation or prison for some offenses, and they maintain a higher level of offender restraint and accountability than does standard probation or parole supervision. In addition, intermediate sanctions may provide enhanced levels of treatment or services for problems that are common among criminal offenders, such as drug abuse, low education levels, and unemployment. Finally, when used in lieu of confinement, intermediate sanctions may reduce prison or jail populations and associated costs.

This chapter examines sanctions that increase control over offenders in the community and studies assessing the effectiveness of this control in reducing criminal activity. The term control is used to refer to activities such as contacts with agents, urine testing, and employment verification that represent control over offenders and increased accountability. It is the control aspects of the sanctions and not the rehabilitation that is the primary focus of the research; thus, this section examines whether such control-focused sanctions are effective in preventing the future criminal activities of these offenders.

Throughout the 1980s and 1990s, the federal government under the sponsorship of the National Institute of Justice, U.S. Department of Justice, funded a wide range of evaluations of different correctional alternatives. There is now a body of research that permits us to draw some conclusions about the crime prevention effectiveness of these programs. This chapter reviews the literature and research on two of the major alternative sanctions: intensive supervision programs and electronic monitoring. The focus of most of these studies has been the recidivism rates of offenders who are given sanctions that increase the degree of control and surveillance over their activities. In the majority of cases, no significant differences are found between offenders placed in alternative sanctions and the comparison groups. Except in a few instances, there is no evidence that these alternatives are effective in reducing crime as measured by official record data. The problem is that most of these alternatives increase the probability of detection. It is unknown whether the actual offense rates change. That is, the increased probability of detection may mean that the intensively supervised offenders are at higher risk of being caught when a criminal act is committed, compared to the comparison offenders, who may commit crimes much more frequently.

We conducted a self-report study of probationers to examine the impact of probation on the criminal activity of offenders (MacKenzie et al., 1999). When compared with the year before arrest, fewer offenders committed crimes, and those who did commit crimes were less active. Thus, it appeared that probation did reduce criminal offending. Furthermore, violations of probation were correlated with criminal activity. We concluded that violations of probation may be warnings that the offender is criminally active. If this is the case, increased violations may signal a return to criminal activity. From this perspective, the finding that intensive supervision is associated with increased probation violations may mean that the probationers who are most apt to be involved in criminal activity are correctly being identified.

Most of the research on intermediate sanctions uses official data, and such data have major limitations. One of the major difficulties with official data is that criminals are arrested and convicted of relatively few of the crimes they commit. For example, in our probation study, we found only 2.1 percent of the self-reported person crimes and only 1.5 percent of the property crimes resulted in arrests during the year before probation (MacKenzie, Browning, Priu, Skroban, & Smith, 1998). This increased slightly during probation but the percentages were still relatively low with 6.8 percent arrests for self-reported person crimes and 11.1 percent for property crimes.

The most helpful sign from the research on intermediate sanctions programs is in the exploratory research following most of the evaluations. Much of the exploratory research focuses on alternative sanctions that increase the treatment and therapeutic aspects of the programs and compares the effectiveness of such programs with similar alternatives that do not include treatment or therapy. The findings suggest that if sanctions include appropriate treatment, the recidivism of the offenders receiving the treatment may be reduced. From this perspective, it is not the increased control that is effective in reducing the criminal activities of the offenders, but rather the rehabilitation programs they receive during the intermediate sanction program.

INTENSIVE SUPERVISION PROGRAMS

Compared to regular probation and parole services, intensive community supervision, usually called intensive supervised probation or parole (ISP), was designed to provide increased control of offenders in the community (Lurigio & Petersilia, 1992; Petersilia & Turner, 1993; Cullen et al., 1996; Tonry & Lynch, 1996). ISP programs can be classified as institutional diversion, probation enhancement ISP, and early release ISP. Diversion programs, also called "front-end" ISP, are efforts aimed at alleviating prison overcrowding by diverting low risk offenders to ISP programs in the community as a substitute for a prison term. Probation enhancement ISP, on the other hand, is implemented for offenders whose needs and problems are seen as being inadequately addressed with routine probation. Hence, offenders who are placed in probation enhancement programs usually have either failed standard routine supervision or committed offenses deemed to be too serious for supervision on routine caseloads. Finally, early release programs, also known as "back-end" ISP, provide a mechanism for releasing offenders already in prison as a means to conserve prison resources and save money (Clear & Dammer, 2000).

History of ISP

The concept of ISP can be traced as far back as fifty years ago. Specifically, from 1954 to 1964, the Probation and Parole Department of California implemented a Special Intensive Parole Unit experiment to deal with offenders who were high risk recidivists or in need of special rehabilitation services. The experiment involved reducing probation and parole officers' caseload sizes to a minimum of fifteen and a maximum of thirty-five for the purpose of more intensive supervision and monitoring. Evaluative results of these programs, however, revealed that smaller caseloads accomplished very little except for greater detection of technical violations (Glaser, 1969).

ISP programs became very common and popular in the late 1980s. In fact, by 1990, ISP programs were found in jurisdictions in all fifty states (Petersilia & Turner, 1993). The popularity and wide acceptance of ISP programs, especially intensive supervision probation, is believed to lie in their potential for cost savings and capacity for accommodating large numbers of offenders entering the criminal justice system.

Nonetheless, ISP programs have been criticized as an ill-conceived response to jail and prison overcrowding that lacks empirical and evaluative supports (Clear, Flynn, & Shapiro, 1987). The goal of ISP programs to divert offenders into community-based corrections who would otherwise be incarcerated has also been questioned. For example, in a study in Tennessee, the authors found that although some offenders were being diverted away from prison, many more offenders who would have normally been placed in regular probation were being sentenced to ISP (Whitehead, Miller, & Myers, 1995). Similarly, in another study conducted in Florida, the authors uncovered that judges sentenced probation-eligible offenders to prison and offenders who would receive probation in any event to ISP (Baird & Wagner, 1990). Likewise, in Colorado, a study of ISP revealed no significant differences between cases recommended for ISP and those not recommended, with the authors' conclusion that the implemented program was not a prison-diversion program based on state guidelines (Reichel & Sudbrack, 1994).

Studies of ISP do indeed reveal that there are increased direct contacts between the offenders and the supervising probation or parole agent. Many programs combine other options such as electronic monitoring and/or home confinement with the increased agent-offender contacts. Furthermore, indirect methods of observation are also frequently combined with the ISP programs. Many times, offenders are required to report for more frequent urine testing or agents may conduct regular employment verification. In all, these direct and indirect observations provide substantially increased levels of control within probation and parole programs. However, the type and level of demands placed on offenders differ enormously by jurisdiction. Offenders are often required to pay fines, keep a mandatory curfew, or provide community service, and these additional requirements also differ by jurisdiction.

Impact on Recidivism

ISP programs grew dramatically in the 1980s, and by 1990, virtually every state in the nation had developed some type of ISP program. In part, this was the result of the initial research examining the programs in New Jersey and Georgia, where the findings suggested that

ISP led to a significant decrease in reincarceration (in Georgia, see Erwin, 1986) and rearrests (in New Jersey, see Pearson, 1987). However, critical reviews of the research demonstrated that the data did not support the initial unqualified conclusions about the ability of the ISP programs to reduce crime. Recognizing the limitations of the prior research, Petersilia and Turner (1993) used an experimental design to evaluate fourteen ISP programs in nine states. This experimental design with random assignment of offenders to ISP and control groups eliminated many of the past methodological problems of the earlier studies. Recidivism was measured using both arrests and technical violations. When ISP participants were compared to the control group, there were no significant differences in arrests. At the end of the one-year study period, about 37 percent of the ISP participants and 33 percent of the control offenders had been arrested, a difference that was not significant. In comparison, the researchers found a significant difference when the technical violation rates were examined. The average ISP violation rate was found to be 65 percent for ISP participants compared with 38 percent for the controls. In summary, although there was no evidence that the increased surveillance in the community deterred offenders from committing crimes, it did appear that this additional control increased the probability that technical violations would be detected.

As shown in Table 14.1, there is a fairly substantial body of research now available on ISP. Table 14.1 lists the sixteen ISP studies along with the methods score, corresponding recidivism rates, and follow-up time. The accompanying Appendix 14.1 provides a description of each study. We identified fourteen studies that scored three or greater on the methods scoring system, and several of these contained multiple samples. However, few of the studies found statistically significant differences between ISP participants and comparisons, and the direction of the differences between the ISP groups and the comparison groups varied, sometimes favoring ISP, sometimes favoring the alternative. Thus, there is no evidence that recidivism is reduced by increasing the surveillance and other control over offenders on ISP. In fact, the increased surveillance may be associated with increases in technical violations.

Figure 14.1 represents the results of a meta-analysis of thirty-one independent samples from thirteen intensive probation and parole treatment programs [note: the studies by Latessa (1991; 1993a),

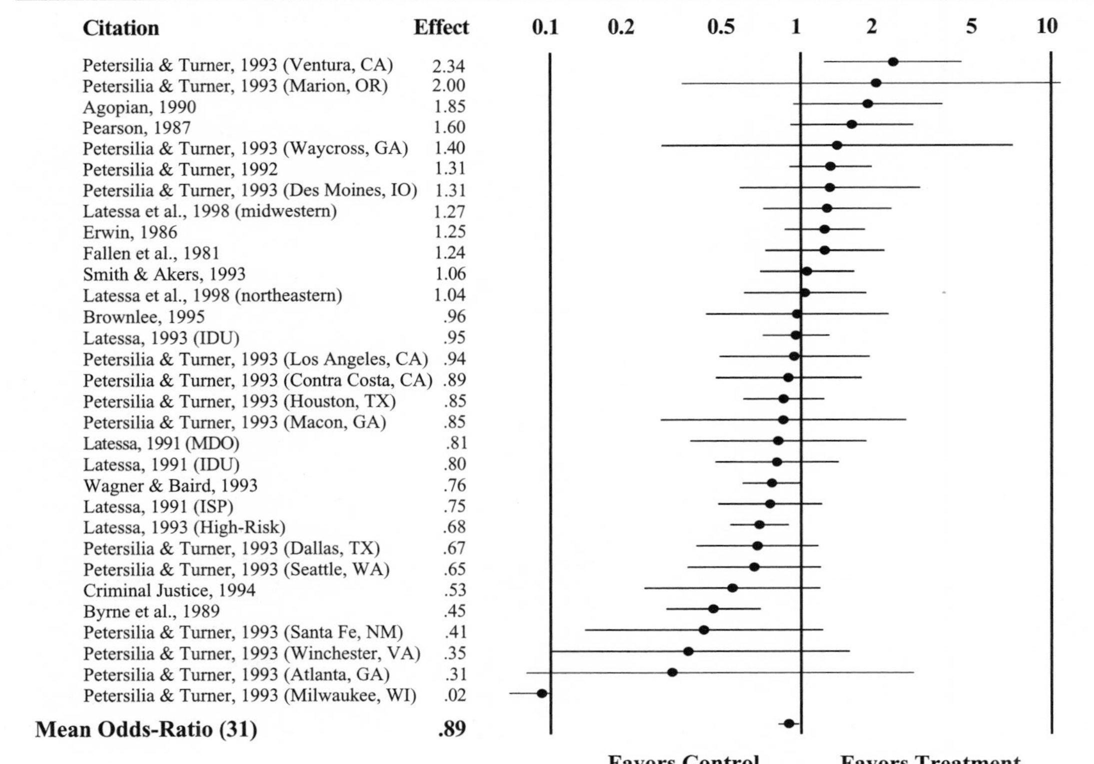

Intensive Supervision Parole and Intensive Supervision Probation Programs
Citation
Effect
0.1
0.2
0.5
1
2
5
10
Petersilia & Turner, 1993 (Ventura, CA) 2.34
Petersilia & Turner, 1993 (Marion, OR) 2.00
Agopian, 1990 1.85
Pearson, 1987 1.60
Petersilia & Turner, 1993 (Waycross, GA) 1.40
Petersilia & Turner, 1992 1.31
Petersilia & Turner, 1993 (Des Moines, IO) 1.31
Latessa et al., 1998 (midwestern) 1.27
Erwin, 1986 1.25
Fallen et al., 1981 1.24
Smith & Akers, 1993 1.06
Latessa et al., 1998 (northeastern) 1.04
Brownlee, 1995 .96
Latessa, 1993 (IDU) .95
Petersilia & Turner, 1993 (Los Angeles, CA) .94
Petersilia & Turner, 1993 (Contra Costa, CA) .89
Petersilia & Turner, 1993 (Houston, TX) .85
Petersilia & Turner, 1993 (Macon, GA) .85
Latessa, 1991 (MDO) .81
Latessa, 1991 (IDU) .80
Wagner & Baird, 1993 .76
Latessa, 1991 (ISP) .75
Latessa, 1993 (High-Risk) .68
Petersilia & Turner, 1993 (Dallas, TX) .67
Petersilia & Turner, 1993 (Seattle, WA) .65
Criminal Justice, 1994 .53
Byrne et al., 1989 .45
Petersilia & Turner, 1993 (Santa Fe, NM) .41
Petersilia & Turner, 1993 (Winchester, VA) .35
Petersilia & Turner, 1993 (Atlanta, GA) .31
Petersilia & Turner, 1993 (Milwaukee, WI) .02
Mean Odds-Ratio (31) .89
Favors Control
Favors Treatment

Figure 14.1. Forest plot showing odds ratio and 95 percent confidence interval for studies of intensive supervision parole and intensive supervision probation programs.

TABLE 14.1. *Intensive supervision parole and intensive supervision probation programs showing recidivism rates and length of follow-up*

Study (methods score)	Measure of recidivism	Recidivism				Follow-up period (in months)
		Experimental (%)	N	Control (%) #1/#2/#3	N	
Latessa et al., 1998 (5)	New Arrest					
	Northeastern	58.7	109	59.6	94	5–15
	Midwestern	31.7	101	37.1	97	
	Technical Violation					
	Northeastern	75.2		68.1		
	Midwestern	90.1		90.7		
Petersilia & Turner, 1992 (5)	New Arrest		N/A[1]		N/A[5]	
	Contra Costa, CA	30.0		29.0		12
	Ventura, CA	31.0		52.0*		
	Los Angeles, CA	31.0		30.0		
	Technical Violation					
	Contra Costa, CA	63.0		41.0*		
	Ventura, CA	70.0		71.0		
	Los Angeles, CA	60.0		59.0		
Petersilia & Turner, 1993 (5)	Rearrest					
	Contra Costa, CA	29.0	85	27.0	85	12
	Los Angeles, CA	32.0	76	30.0	76	
	Seattle, WA	46.0	86	36.0	86	
	Ventura, CA	32.0	83	53.0*	83	
	Atlanta, GA	12.0	25	4.0	25	

Macon, GA	42.0	25	38.0	25	
Waycross, GA	12.0	25	15.0	25	
Santa Fe, NM	48.0	29	28.0	29	
Des Moines, IA	24.0	57	29.0	57	
Winchester, VA	25.0	26	12.0	26	
Dallas, TX	39.0	110	30.0	110	
Houston, TX	44.0	219	40.0	219	
Marion, OR	33.0	12	50.0	12	
Milwaukee, WI	58.0	72	3.0*	72	
Reincarceration					
Contra Costa, CA	2.0	85	4.0	85	12
Los Angeles, CA	26.0	76	22.0	76	
Seattle, WA	6.0	86	5.0	86	
Ventura, CA	23.0	83	28.0	83	
Atlanta, GA	23.0	25	4.0	25	
Macon, GA	8.0	25	21.0	25	
Waycross, GA	4.0	25	0.00	25	
Santa Fe, NM	14.0	29	17.0	29	
Des Moines, IA	39.0	57	23.0	57	
Winchester, VA	14.0	26	8.0	26	
Dallas, TX	28.0	110	17.0	110	
Houston, TX	35.0	219	20.0*	219	
Marion, OR	50.0	12	25.0	12	
Milwaukee, WI	35.0	72	3.0*	72	

(continued)

TABLE 14.1 *(continued)*

Study (methods score)	Measure of recidivism	Recidivism: Experimental (%)	N	Control (%) #1/#2/#3	N	Follow-up period (in months)
	Technical Violation					
	Contra Costa, CA	64.0	85	41.0*[4]	85	12
	Los Angeles, CA	61.0	76	57.0	76	
	Seattle, WA	73.0	86	48.0*	86	
	Ventura, CA	70.0	83	73.0	83	
	Atlanta, GA	65.0	25	46.0	25	
	Macon, GA	1.0	25	96.0	25	
	Waycross, GA	38.0	25	31.0	25	
	Santa Fe, NM	69.0	29	62.0	29	
	Des Moines, IA	59.0	57	55.0	57	
	Winchester, VA	64.0	26	36.0*	26	
	Dallas, TX	20.0	110	13.0	110	
	Houston, TX	81.0	219	33.0*	219	
	Marion, OR	92.0	12	58.0	12	
	Milwaukee, WI	92.0	72	17.0*	72	
Criminal Justice Research Center, 1994 (4)	Rearrest					
	6 months	14.0	118	6.0	97	6
	12 months	18.0		10.0		12

Erwin, 1986 (4)	Rearrest					
	Low Risk	41.6	12	27.0/46.2	11/13	18
	Medium Risk	33.9	62	34.5/58.3	58/12	
	High Risk	34.5	69	30.1/57.4	73/47	
	Maximum Risk	43.6	57	44.8/64.0	58/25	
	Reconviction					
	Low Risk	25.0	12	0.0/38.5	11/13	18
	Medium Risk	16.1	62	24.1/50.0	58/12	
	High Risk	27.5	69	24.7/44.7	73/47	
	Maximum Risk	26.3	57	27.6/36.0	58/25	
Fallen, Apperson, Hall-Milligan, & Aos, 1981 (4)	Technical Violation					
	6 months	33.2	289	28.4	102	6
	12 months	25.8	186	30.2	96	12
Latessa, 1993a (4)	Rearrest[2]					
	IDU	35.0	317	34.0	424	6
	High Risk	43.0	502			
	Reconviction[2]					
	IDU	25.0	317	19.0	424	6
	High Risk	27.0	502			
	Technical Violation					
	IDU	43.0	317	37.0	424	6
	High Risk	41.0	502			
Pearson, 1987 (4)	New Arrest[3]	24.7	204	34.6	79	24
	New Arrest That Led to a Conviction[3]	12.3	208	23.1	85	

(continued)

TABLE 14.1 *(continued)*

Study (methods score)	Measure of recidivism	Recidivism				Follow-up period (in months)
		Experimental (%)	N	Control (%) #1/#2/#3	N	
Smith & Akers, 1993 (4)	Rearrest	77.6	219	78.6	266	36
	Reconviction	61.0		56.0		
	Reincarceration	53.4		44.0		
Agopian, 1990 (3)	Reincarceration	40.0	90	27.0	68	6
Brownlee, 1995 (3)	Reconviction					
	12 months	42.2	45	53.8/42.6	26/47	12
	24 months	73.3		81.0/59.9		24
Byrne & Kelly, 1989 (3)	Reconviction	39.4	221	22.4	196	12
	Reconviction/Felony Offenses	17.6		22.4		
	Reincarceration	32.6		28.1		
	Reincarceration/ Technical Violation	5.9		1.5		
Latessa, 1991 (3)	Rearrest[4]					
	ISP	14.0	250	11.0	404	6
	IDU	13.0	151			
	MDO	13.0	61			
	Reconviction[4]					
	ISP	9.0		8.0		
	IDU	3.0				
	MDO	7.0				

	Technical Violation[4]					
	ISP	45.0		33.0		
	IDU	52.0				
	MDO	41.0				
Wagner & Baird, 1993 (3)	Reconviction/New Offense	19.7	630	24.3	630	18
Latessa, 1993b (2)	Rearrest					18–48
	STOP-A	30.0	140	34.0	424	
	STOP-D	43.0	121			
	Sex Offender	32.0	64			
	Mental Health	39.0	76			
	Reconviction					
	STOP-A	17.0	140	19.0	424	
	STOP-D	36.0	121			
	Sex Offender	23.0	64			
	Mental Health	21.0	76			
	Technical Violation					
	STOP-A	30.0	140	37.0	424	
	STOP-D	45.0	121			
	Sex Offender	23.0	64			
	Mental Health	33.0	76			
Mitchell et al., 1987 (2)	Felony Revocation	3.1	57	6.5	382	4
	Technical Violation	12.5		5.2		

[1] Sample size by group not reported for Petersilia and Turner (1992).
[2] Differences were statistically significant at 0.05 level or greater.
[3] Outcomes were obtained from survival analysis.
[4] N may not equal 250 ISP, 151 IDU, 61 MDO, and 404 comparison because of missing data.
* Significantly different from experimental group, $p < 0.05$.

Latessa, Travis, and Fulton (1998), and Petersilia and Turner (1993) include multiple distinct samples]. The study by Petersilia and Turner (1992) was not included in the plot because the study did not report sample size by groups. The recidivism measures used to calculate the effect sizes were rearrests (n = 20), new arrests (n = 6), reconvictions (n = 3), technical violations (n = 1), and reincarceration (n = 1). The effect size listed for the Erwin (1986) study was calculated by combining all four experimental groups used and taking the weighted mean of the groups' recidivism measures, producing a singular comparison measure. The most recent recidivism measures for each study were also used, representing the longest follow-up period. Two studies from Table 14.1 were excluded because of low methods scores (Latessa, 1993b; Mitchell, Zehr, & Butler, 1987). As shown, some of the effect sizes favor the treatment group, whereas others favor the control group. Few studies were significant, and those that were favored the control group. Overall, the effect size favored the control group, but the difference was not significant.

Although research has not revealed a significant relationship between the amount of surveillance and recidivism, there is some evidence that increased treatment of offenders in ISP programs may be related to significant reductions in rearrests. Follow-up analyses by the RAND researchers (Petersilia & Turner, 1993) and researchers evaluating ISP programs in Massachusetts (Byrne & Kelly, 1989), Oregon (Jolin & Stipack, 1991), and Ohio (Latessa, 1993a) have found evidence that rearrests are reduced when offenders receive treatment services in addition to the increased surveillance and control of the ISP programs. For example, Petersilia and Turner (1993) reported a 10–20 percent reduction in recidivism for those who were most active in programs while they were in the community. However, the research designs used in these evaluations do not reach the experimental rigor of the random assignment study by RAND, which examined the effect of increasing the surveillance and control of ISP participants.

ELECTRONIC MONITORING AND HOME CONFINEMENT

Home confinement is designed to regulate and restrict the freedom of the offender within the community (Renzema, 1992; Baumer &

Mendelsohn, 1992). The terms *house arrest, home confinement,* and *electronic monitoring* (EM) are often used interchangeably. However, it is important to note that house arrest, home confinement, and more recently *community control* are terms describing the programs, whereas EM is a tool used to monitor the compliance with the requirements of the sentence.

During the 1980s, technological advances made it possible to monitor offenders electronically to ensure offenders were complying with the requirements of the program. Electronic monitoring (EM) involves the use of electronic devices (usually anklets or bracelets) to monitor offenders' whereabouts. The electronic device, an electronic monitor, emits an electronic signal that is used to track the movement of offenders. EM is often combined with house confinement or arrest as a means to enforce movement restrictions imposed on offenders.

EM was first proposed in 1964 by a Harvard University researcher, Ralph Schwitzgebel. The concept was initially implemented in 1983 by a New Mexico judge, who, inspired by the "Spiderman" comic strip, ordered a probation violator to be subjected to EM for one month. Other states soon adopted the idea, and by 1993, EM was employed in all fifty states (Clear & Dammer, 2000; Renzema, 1992). By this time, approximately seventy thousand offenders were being monitored electronically.

In general, home confinement programs had targeted low risk offenders such as those convicted of driving while intoxicated (DWI). However, more recently, home confinement has been used for parolees (Beck & Klein-Saffran, 1990) or other more serious offenders (Baumer, Maxfield, & Mendelsohn, 1993; Baumer & Mendelsohn, 1991; Austin & Hardyman, 1991). Early research examining the effectiveness of the home confinement programs suffered from poor research designs, lack of program integrity, and the low risk offenders placed in the programs.

Effectiveness of Electronic Monitoring

Table 14.2 lists the nine EM studies along with the methods score, corresponding recidivism rates, and follow-up time. The accompanying Appendix 14.2 provides a description of each study. We identified eight studies with a three or greater on the method scores. Only

TABLE 14.2. *Electronic monitoring studies showing recidivism rates and length of follow-up*

Study (methods score)	Measure of recidivism	Recidivism				Follow-up period (in months)
		Experimental (%)	N	Control (%) #1/#2/#3	N	
Austin & Hardyman, 1991 (5)	Rearrest	13.9	175	11.2	575	3.6
	Technical Violation	14.7		10.1		
Baumer & Mendelsohn, 1991 (5)	New Rearrest	0.01	78	0.08	76	6
Roy & Brown, 1995 (5)	Rearrest	16.9	72	25.9	72	12
Bonta et al., 2000a (4)	Reconviction	26.7	262	37.9*/33.3*	30/240	12
Bonta et al. 2000b (4)	Reconviction	31.5	54	35.3/31.0	17/100	12
Courtright, Berg, & Mutchnick, 1997 (4)	Rearrest[1]	19.3	57	33.3	57	14.8
	New Arrest/M(SD)	0.197(0.553)		0.333 (0.988)		
Jolin & Stipack, 1991 (4)	Rearrest	32.0	98	47.0/33.0	64/96	24
	Reconviction	15.0		30.0/18.0		
	# of Arrests/M[2]	0.58		0.92/0.59		
	# of Convictions/M	0.20		0.66		
Brown & Roy, 1995 (3)	Program Failure	22.0	392	18.0	139	30
Glaser & Watts, 1992 (2)	New Arrest	0.05	124	0.06	200	6

[1] Percentages reflect the total number of rearrests in groups, including multiple arrests for an individual offender.
[2] No standard deviation was reported.
* Significantly different from experimental group, $p < 0.05$.

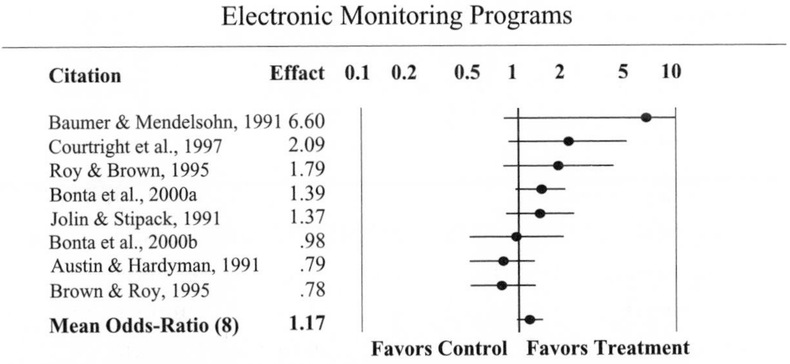

Electronic Monitoring Programs

Citation	Effect
Baumer & Mendelsohn, 1991	6.60
Courtright et al., 1997	2.09
Roy & Brown, 1995	1.79
Bonta et al., 2000a	1.39
Jolin & Stipack, 1991	1.37
Bonta et al., 2000b	.98
Austin & Hardyman, 1991	.79
Brown & Roy, 1995	.78
Mean Odds-Ratio (8)	**1.17**

0.1 0.2 0.5 1 2 5 10

Favors Control Favors Treatment

Figure 14.2. Forest plot showing odds ratio and 95 percent confidence interval for studies of electronic monitoring programs.

one study found significant differences (Bonta, Wallace-Capretta, & Rooney, 2000a). The three studies using experimental designs found no significant difference in recidivism when the behavior of offenders who are electronically monitored on home confinement was compared with those being manually supervised (Baumer & Mendelsohn, 1991; Austin & Hardyman 1991; Roy & Brown, 1995). Initially, recidivism rates of the low risk offenders placed in home confinement programs were very low (e.g., Baumer & Mendelsohn, 1991; Austin & Hardyman, 1991). These studies may not have the power to detect small differences that might be expected between the participants and control groups.

Figure 14.2 represents the results of eight EM studies on offenders' recidivism. Although the principal recidivism measure used in calculating effect sizes is rearrest (n = 5), for those studies that do not include this measure, reconviction (n = 2) and program failure (n = 1) were used. The effect sizes listed for Bonta et al. (2000a; 2000b) and Jolin and Stipack (1991) are calculated by combining both control groups and taking the weighted mean of the groups' recidivism measures, producing a singular comparison measure. The most recent recidivism measures for each study are also used. The Glaser and Watts (1992) study included in Table 14.2 was excluded from the plot because of the low methods score of two. The effect sizes of five of the studies favor the treated group, and three favor the control group. However, as is obvious from the plot, there are no significant differences in the effect sizes nor is the combined effect size significant.

SUMMARY

A large body of research, including random assignment studies, consistently shows the failure of ISP and EM programs to lower recidivism. Restraining offenders in the community by increasing surveillance and control over their activities does not reduce their criminal activities. In general, program participants recidivate as often as their counterparts who receive less surveillance. The increased surveillance may actually increase the probability of detection and, thus, result in more technical violations. Most research has focused on the restraining aspects of these community programs and not the treatment services delivered to the offenders. That is, the research fails to clearly identify and rigorously examine (from a research perspective) the impact of the therapeutic aspects of the programs. When the researchers have mentioned the therapeutic integrity of the programs, it is often to note that the anticipated services or staffing did not occur. In conclusion, ISP and EM programs are not effective in reducing recidivism.

APPENDIX 14.1. STUDY REFERENCE, DESCRIPTION, AND METHODS SCORES (IN PARENTHESES) OF INTENSIVE SUPERVISION PAROLE AND INTENSIVE SUPERVISION PROBATION STUDIES

Agopian, 1990 **(3)**

ISP program in Los Angeles County, California. Adult drug offenders with gang affiliations who were sentenced to ISP were compared to a group of adult drug offenders placed on regular probation supervision matched on sex, education, marital status, and drug offenses.

Brownlee, 1995 **(3)**

ISP program (the Edge) in northern England. Male and female offenders between the ages of seventeen and twenty-one sentenced to ISP between January 1989 and December 1993 were compared to (1) a sample of offenders from the same age group who were recommended for the program but received a custodial sentence and (2) a sample of young adults sent to custody (without having been referred to the program).

Byrne and Kelly, 1989 **(3)**

Massachusetts ISP designed to provide better community protection over offenders placed on probation. The program was implemented on an experiment basis in ten district and three superior court jurisdictions. High risk probationers placed on intensive supervision were compared to a sample of ISP-eligible offenders in thirteen control courts.

Criminal Justice Research Center, 1994 **(4)**

ISP implemented in four districts in Virginia: Richmond, Norfolk, Lynchburg, and Fairfax. A stratified sample of FY 1992 ISP terminated cases were compared to an equivalent matched control group of similar offenders drawn from the Department of Correction's automated Pre/Post Sentence Investigation database.

Erwin, 1986 **(4)**

ISP in Georgia. A sample of offenders diverted to ISP from twenty-six districts during the calendar year of 1984 were compared to (1) a group of regular probationers and (2) a cohort of offenders incarcerated and subsequently released. Recidivism outcomes were broken down to four risk categories: low, medium, high, and maximum.

Fallen et al., 1981 **(4)**

ISP program in Washington State. Low-risk felony offenders released after an average incarceration of three months to the supervision of a specially trained intensive parole supervision officer were compared to a matched group of offenders paroled at the same time as the ISP offenders but incarcerated for an average of sixteen months and released to regular parole supervision. The comparison group would have been eligible for ISP had it existed at the start of their incarceration.

Latessa, 1991 **(3)**

ISP program in Cuyahoga County, Ohio. The program included an ISP unit, an Intensive Diversion Unit, and a Mentally Disordered Offender unit. Offenders sentenced to one of these three units were compared to a group of regular probationers whose cases were randomly selected over a similar time frame as the cases in the ISP group.

Latessa, 1993b **(2)**

Four ISP units were implemented in Lucas County, Ohio, to provide increased supervision and treatment to special-need populations. The units included Sobriety Through Other People Alcohol (STOP-A), Sobriety Through Other People Drug (STOP-D), Sex Offender, and Mental Health. Offenders sentenced to these four units were compared to a group of regular probationers whose cases were randomly selected over a similar time frame as the cases in the ISP units.

Latessa, 1993a **(4)**

Two ISP implemented in Lucas County, Ohio. The purpose of the Incarceration Diversion Unit was to reduce the county commitment rate without seriously increasing the risk to the community, and the High Risk Unit was designed to provide supervision to the county's highest risk offenders. Offenders sentenced to these two ISP units were compared to a group of regular probationers whose cases were randomly selected over a similar time frame as the cases in the ISP units.

Latessa, et al., 1998 **(5)**

Prototypical model (with random assignment) of ISP developed by the American Probation and Parole Association. The program was implemented in a northeastern and a midwestern agency. High risk offenders were randomly selected and assigned between February 1996 and December 1997 to either the ISP or regular probation (control group).

Mitchell et al., 1987 **(2)**

Utah's Intensive Supervision/High Risk Parole (IS/HRP) program aims at reducing the risk to the community posed by high risk offenders. IS/HRP participants were compared to a sample of high risk parolees who received regular supervision between December 1984 and November 1985.

Pearson, 1987 **(4)**

New Jersey ISP. The ISP group, composed of individuals convicted of third- and fourth-degree felonies, were compared to a random sample of third- and fourth-degree felony convictions receiving ordinary term of imprisonment for ISP-eligible crimes prior to ISP implementation.

Petersilia and Turner, 1992 **(5)**

Intensive Supervised Probations (ISPs) implemented in three counties in California. In (1) Contra Costa, adults convicted of drug offenses with no sex-offense history were randomly assigned to either ISP or routine probation. In (2) Ventura and (3) Los Angeles, felons with a high risk score on the NIC scale, serious offense override, or probation revocation for felony plus a high risk score were randomly assigned to either ISP or regular probation.

Petersilia and Turner, 1993 **(5)**

Randomized experiment of ISPs between 1986 and 1991 involving fourteen jurisdictions in nine states. The ISP programs consisted of prison diversion, enhanced probation, and enhanced parole.

1) Contra Costa County, California: ISP probationers (individuals convicted of felony or misdemeanor drug offenses) compared to a matched group of regular probationers.
2) Los Angeles, California: ISP probationers (high risk offenders) compared to a matched group of regular probationers.
3) Seattle, Washington: ISP probationers (offenders convicted of drug-related offenses and drug dependent) compared to a matched group of regular probationers.
4) Ventura County, California: ISP probationers (high risk offenders) compared to a matched group of regular probationers.
5) Atlanta, Georgia: ISP probationers (high-need/low risk felons with a history of drugs) compared to a matched group of felons placed on routine probation.
6) Macon, Georgia: ISP probationers (high-need/low risk felons with a history of drugs) compared to a matched group of felons placed on routine probation.
7) Waycross, Georgia: ISP probationers (high-need/low risk felons with history of drugs) compared to a matched group of felons placed on routine probation.
8) Santa Fe, New Mexico: ISP probationers and parolees (high risk/needs offenders, drug dependent) compared to a matched group of offenders in regular probation and parole caseloads.

9) Des Moines, Iowa: ISP probationers and parolees (individuals convicted of drug offenses or drug-involved burglars) compared to a matched group of probationers and parolees in regular probation and parole caseloads.
10) Winchester, Virginia: ISP probationers and parolees (offenders convicted of drug offenses or who had a drug-abuse history) compared to a matched group of regular probationers and parolees.
11) Dallas, Texas: ISP parolees (high risk offenders with poor performance) compared to a matched group of parolees in regular parole caseloads.
12) Houston, Texas: ISP parolees (high risk offenders with poor performance) compared to a matched group of regular parolees.
13) Marion, Oregon: ISP participants (felons sentenced to prison but who were diverted) compared to a matched group of regular probationers.
14) Milwaukee, Wisconsin: ISP participants (felons recommended to prison on presentence investigation report) compared to a matched group of regular probationers.

Smith and Akers, 1993 **(4)**

Florida's Community Control Program implemented to reduce prison overcrowding. The program's restrictions were more severe than those imposed in regular ISP programs. Program participants between October 1983 and December 1983 were compared to a partially matched sample of prisoners sentenced to prison during the same time period. The subjects were matched on criminal background and current offense.

Wagner and Baird, 1993 **(3)**

Florida Community Control Program (FCCP) aims at reducing prison and jail crowding while ensuring public safety with a punishment-oriented community-based alternative. This is an intensive supervision house arrest program. Offenders sentenced to FCCP were compared to a group of offenders sentenced to prison in 1985 matched on sex, age, offense type and severity, and prior felony convictions.

APPENDIX 14.2. STUDY REFERENCE, DESCRIPTION, AND METHODS SCORES (IN PARENTHESES) OF ELECTRONIC MONITORING STUDIES

Austin and Hardyman, 1991 **(5)**

Pre-Parole Conditional Supervision program in Oklahoma; eligible participants were randomly assigned to the experimental (with EM) or the control group (without EM).

Baumer and Mendelsohn, 1991 **(5)**

Diversion program for offenders charged with suspendible nonviolent offenses; assignment to the program served as a condition of probation; participants were randomly placed in the manually monitored group or the electronic monitored group.

Bonta et al., 2000a **(4)**

EM participants between 1995 and 1997 in three provinces in Canada (British Columbia, Newfoundland, and Saskatchewan) were compared to (1) a sample of probationers and (2) a group of inmates. The groups were matched on risk level by the use of self-report questionnaires.

Bonta et al., 2000b **(4)**

EM participants in Newfoundland, Canada, who received the Learning Resources Program, an intensive cognitive-behavioral treatment, were compared to (1) a sample of probationers receiving the same treatment and (2) a group of released inmates who fit the selection criteria for EM (it was not available in their region).

Brown and Roy, 1995 **(3)**

Electronic supervision program for probationers in Utica, New York; all people sentenced to the electronic supervision program from December 1987 through December 1990 were compared to all people sentenced to the manual supervision program from December 1985 through December 1987.

Courtright et al., 1997 **(4)**

DUI offenders who participated in the EM program beginning in fall 1992 in western Pennsylvania were compared to a group of DUI offenders in the same county receiving a jail sentence.

Glaser and Watts, 1992 **(2)**

EM house arrest program in Los Angeles, California, that requires the offender to wear an anklet or bracelet equipped with an electronic transmitter. Drug offenders sentenced in 1990–91 to probation by house arrest with EM were compared to drug offenders sentenced to ordinary probation during the same period.

Jolin and Stipack, 1991 **(4)**

Clackamas County Community Corrections Division's Electronic Surveillance Program (ESP) in the state of Oregon; ESP participants were compared to (1) a group of clients in the Intensive Drug Program (IDP) and (2) the Work Release (WR) Program. Individuals in the IDP and WR groups were selected using a stratified random sampling procedure that implemented matching on risk assessment categories. All subjects began and terminated their programs between July 26, 1989, and July 31, 1990.

Roy and Brown, 1995 **(5)**

EM home detention program for juvenile offenders in Lake County Superior Court Juvenile Division in Indiana; juvenile offenders in the EM group were compared to a matched sample of juvenile offenders in the manual supervision group between February 1990 and December 1991.

PART SIX

CONCLUSIONS

CHAPTER FIFTEEN

Drawing Conclusions

IMPACT ON RECIDIVISM

In this book I examined correctional interventions, management strategies, and treatment and rehabilitation programs to identify which were effective in reducing the recidivism of offenders and delinquents. Hereafter, in this chapter, I refer to all of these as programs or interventions. Two hundred eighty-four evaluations of the programs were located and scored for the quality of the research methods. The significance and effectiveness were examined for each study. Table 15.1 shows the correctional programs examined, the chapter for each, the number of evaluations located, the number of the evaluations scored five (successful random assignment), the number scored two (too poorly done to include in decision making), and the conclusion drawn about the effectiveness of the program.

What Works

As shown in Table 15.1, at this point in time, the research evidence demonstrates the following programs were effective in reducing recidivism:

- academic education,
- vocation education,
- MRT,
- R&R,
- cognitive restructuring,
- cognitive behavior treatment for sex offenders,
- behavioral treatment for sex offenders,

TABLE 15.1. *Programs, interventions, and strategies examined in this book showing the chapters, intervention, number of evaluations, number of evaluations scored five, number scored two, and conclusions regarding the effectiveness of the programs*

Chapter in book	Program/ intervention strategy	Studies reviewed N =	Studies scored 5 N =	Studies scored 2 N =	Effective?
Education	Academic Ed	25	1	12	Yes
Education	Life Skills	5	0	1	No
Work	Vocation Ed	18	2	2	Yes
Work	Correctional Industries	4	0	2	No
Work	Work/ Multicomponent	8	2	2	No
Cognitive Behavior	MRT	8	0	4	Yes
Cognitive Behavior	R&R	8	0	0	Yes
Cognitive Behavior	Cognitive Restructuring	9	0	0	Yes
Sex Offender	Cognitive Behavior	15	1	8	Yes
Sex Offender	Behavioral	4	0	1	Yes
Sex Offender	Hormonal/Surgical	6	1	2	Yes
Sex Offender	Psychosocial	3	0	3	No
Juvenile	MST	8	7	1	Yes
Juvenile	Residential Treatment	7	1	2	No
Juvenile	Community Supervision	11	3	2	No
Domestic Violence	Feminist	6	1	1	No
Domestic Violence	Cognitive Behavior	6	1	2	No
Domestic Violence	Arrests	9	9	0	No
Drug Courts	Drug Courts	32	2	5	Yes
Drug Treatment	Community	7	1	2	Yes
Drug Treatment	Incarceration Based	29	1	10	Yes
Boot Camps	Adult Boot Camps	14	0	1	No
Boot Camps	Juvenile Boot Camps	17	3	0	No
Intermediate Sanctions	Intensive Supervision	16	3	2	No
Intermediate Sanctions	EM	9	3	1	No
TOTAL		284	42 (14.8%)	66 (23.2%)	

- hormonal/surgical treatment of sex offenders,
- MST for juveniles,
- drug courts,
- drug treatment in the community, and
- incarceration-based drug treatment.

All of the effective programs have what I refer to as human service components except the hormonal/surgical treatment for sex offenders. The effective programs are not based on a control or deterrent philosophy. Furthermore, the results are consistent with the results of the theoretical meta-analyses (see Chapter 4). As found in theoretical meta-analyses such as those conducted by Andrews et al. (1990) and Lipsey (1992; 1995), many of the programs target dynamic criminogenic factors. Furthermore, the effective programs are skill oriented, based on cognitive-behavior/behavior models, and treat deficits simultaneously (i.e., are multimodal).

What Does Not Work

After reviewing research on the following programs and interventions, I concluded they were not effective in reducing recidivism:

- life skills education,
- correctional industries,
- multicomponent work programs,
- psychosocial sex offender treatment,
- residential treatment for juveniles,
- community supervision for juveniles,
- domestic violence treatment using a feminist perspective,
- domestic violence programs using cognitive-behaviorial treatment,
- domestic violence programs using arrest interventions,
- boot camps for adults and juveniles,
- intensive supervision, and
- EM.

My review of Scared Straight research also revealed the ineffectiveness of this program.

No single explanation seems adequate to explain why these programs were not found to be effective in reducing recidivism. Some possible reasons for these findings may be that the programs (1) have poor or no theoretical basis; (2) are poorly implemented; (3) focus on punishment, deterrence, or control instead of providing human service or rehabilitation; and (4) emphasize the formation of ties or bonds without first changing the individual's thought process.

Some programs appear to have little theoretical basis. For example, psychosocial sex offender treatment and community supervision and residential facilities for juveniles appear to fit this description. Most likely this is the reason for their lack of effectiveness. When I reviewed the juvenile programs, I found little consistent theoretical basis for these programs. The psychosocial sex offender treatment is based on a psychodynamic theoretical perspective, not the behavioral or cognitive behavior models that have been found to be effective in correctional treatment.

None of the interventions focusing on punishment, deterrence, or control were found to reduce recidivism. These were major goals of corrections during the 1980s and early 1990s. There is now a sufficient body of research to draw conclusions that programs such as boot camps, Scared Straight, arrests for domestic violence, intensive supervision, and EM are not effective in reducing recidivism. These programs may fulfill other goals of corrections but they are not effective in reducing recidivism.

There is some evidence that punishment, deterrence, or control-type programs could be effective if they included human service, rehabilitation, or treatment components; however, as yet, there is little research examining such combined programs. One hopeful sign comes from the meta-analysis by Wilson and Lipsey (2003) on wilderness and challenge programs (see Chapter 9). Only programs including therapeutic components in the schedule of daily activities were included in the analysis; thus, the programs combined rigorous physical activity with human service components. The researchers found the programs were effective in reducing antisocial or delinquent behavior. Although the sample (at-risk youth) and the target outcomes (antisocial and delinquent behavior) were different from those examined in this book, the findings do suggest the possibility that programs like boot camps, when combined with treatment, may be effective in reducing recidivism. Additionally, exploratory research by myself and colleagues on boot camps as well as research by Petersilia and her colleagues on intensive supervision suggest that adding human service components to such programs may make them effective in reducing recidivism.

When I compared the effective programs to the ineffective programs I noted an interesting difference. Almost all of the effective programs focused on individual-level change. In contrast, the ineffective programs frequently focused on developing opportunities. For example, the cognitive skills programs emphasize individual-level changes in thinking, reasoning, empathy, and problem solving. In contrast, life skills and work programs, examples of ineffective programs, focus on giving the offenders opportunities in the community. Based on these observations, I propose that effective programs must focus on changing the individual. This change is required before the person will be able to take advantage of opportunities in the environment.

Historically, sociology has had a major influence on the theoretical perspective of criminology and criminal justice researchers. Recently, there has been an emphasis on the importance of ties and bonds to social institutions and the relationships between these ties and bonds and desistence from criminal activity. Obviously, from this perspective, programs such as life skills and work programs would be expected to be effective because they would increase an important tie to the community. However, given the results from my analysis of effective programs, I propose the need for individual-level changes before these ties can be formed.

INDIVIDUAL DIFFERENCES AND COGNITIVE TRANSFORMATION

Traditionally most criminologists have come from sociological backgrounds (Andrews & Bonta, 2003). Not surprisingly, their theories emphasize the importance of social conditions in determining criminal behavior. Two major criminological traditions, the Chicago School and Merton's strain theory, continue to be of interest to criminologists and to shape criminal justice policies (Lilly, Cullen, & Ball, 2002). The Chicago School of criminology has focused on the potent criminogenic forces in American cities. Strain theory contends that the pathology lays in the cultural and structural arrangements of America's social fabric. These criminologists rejected individualist explanations for criminal behavior in favor of theories emphasizing crime's social roots.

Recently, some criminologists have emphasized the importance of attachment to a variety of social institutions such as marriage, work, or school. The emphasis is still on social conditions. For example, Sampson and Laub (1995) have proposed a theory of age-graded informal social control to explain crime over the life course. They use social bond theory to describe continuity and change in offending. Individuals form bonds with social institutions. As bonds strengthen, social capital rises. This capital supplies resources to solve problems. Dependence on capital means that much is jeopardized if it is lost. As bonds form and social capital increases, criminal activity becomes more costly.

According to Sampson and Laub, the life course is potentially dynamic and even high-rate delinquents or offenders can reestablish bonds. Offending is marked by both continuity and change across time. Meaningful social bonds established during adulthood can function as critical life events or turning points when offenders begin to conform and turn away from criminal activity. Crime becomes too costly in terms of loss of bonds to such institutions as family, work, or school. The formation of bonds in adulthood is often fortuitous. Once the bonds form, social capital is produced and these constraints begin to control the offender's life.

Research has supported Sampson and Laub's life course theory. Ties or bonds to social institutions influence behavior both during long periods of the life course (Sampson & Laub, 1995) and in relatively local life circumstances (Horney et al., 1995; MacKenzie et al., 1998; 1999; MacKenzie & Li, 2002). However, little is said by these theorists about the mechanisms that lead to the changes in ties or bonds. Although Sampson and Laub do not discount the possibility of early individual differences in such factors as temperament or childhood conduct disorders, they do not discuss how changes within the individual during adulthood may lead to formation of social bonds. The question is what happens within the individual to bring about changes in ties and bonds?

Cognitive Transformation Theory

I propose that individual-level change must precede changes in ties or bonds to social institutions. The individual-level change occurs first and is required before ties can be formed with social institutions. The social environment may be conducive to the formation of ties, but the individual must change if the bond is to form. The original connection (the job) may be fortuitous, but for the bond to form the individual must change. To get along with family, keep a job, support children, or form strong, positive ties with other institutions, the person must change in cognitive reasoning, attitude toward drug use, antisocial attitudes, reading level, or vocation skills. A focus on individual change is critical to our understanding of what works in corrections. Giordano and her colleagues call this change a cognitive transformation (Giordano, Cernkovich, & Rudolph, 2002). Such transformations are necessary before a person makes initial moves toward a different way of life. Only if a transformation occurs is the person able to sustain a new life.

One of the reasons programs such as correctional industries or other work programs may not be effective for correctional populations is that the programs focus on giving opportunities for employment but do not emphasize individual change. The person may not have the individual abilities and/or attitudes to take advantage of the environmental opportunities, and thus a bond with the world of work is not formed.

From this perspective two things are needed. First, a cognitive transformation must occur within the individual. Second, the individual environment must provide the opportunity for the bond or tie to form. An interaction between the individual and the environment is required. In the words of David Farrington, "It is plausible to assume that offending, like all other types of behavior, arises from the interaction between the individual and the environment (Farrington, 1998:241).

Many of the programs and interventions I found to be effective in reducing recidivism focus on individual-level change. For example, vocation and academic education focus on improving the education of the individual. Certainly, such programs may increase an exoffender's ability to find and keep employment. The individual becomes more educated, this makes employment more likely, which in turn permits the person to form a tie or bond to the work world. Similarly, the cognitive skills programs (e.g., R&R, cognitive restructuring, MRT) lead to changes within the individual. These changes would be expected to have an impact on relationships with others, which in turn permits ties or bonds to form within the family, work world, and/or other social institutions. Similarly, drug treatment changes an individual, and these changes result in improved social functioning, which in turn enable the individual to take advantage of environmental opportunities permitting the formation of bonds and ties.

Implications for Re-entry Programs

Recently there has been an explosion of interest in the phenomenon of prisoner re-entry. More than 600,000 individuals a year or 1,600 per day leave state prisons and return home. These ex-prisoners face major difficulties in the process of reintegrating into the community. The interest in re-entry arises from the recognition of the number of exprisoners who return home, the difficulties they confront, and the high recidivism rates.

Well-meaning people want to implement programs to assist the exprisoners in readjusting to the world outside prison. Re-entry programs include all "activities and programming conducted to prepare ex-convicts to return safely to the community and to live as law abiding citizens" (Petersilia, 2004:7).

One of the major goals of re-entry programs is to have an impact on the high recidivism rates of returning offenders. Therefore, the assessments I have conducted on what works in correctional treatment are directly relevant to the issue of re-entry.

The finding that a focus on individual-level change is an important target of effective programs has direct implications for the development of effective re-entry programs. That is, programs would be expected to be effective if they focus on individual-level change. As re-entry programs are developed and implemented, there will be a temptation to focus on programs that increase opportunities for work, reunite families, and provide housing. Obviously, these are important needs of the re-entering exprisoners. Such programs provide opportunities for the formation of ties or bonds to the community. However, my "what works" review suggests that an emphasis on these opportunities for ties with the community will not be effective if there is not also a focus on individual-level transformation. The results from my review suggest that such opportunities should be preceded by programs focusing on changing the individual through cognitive change, education, or drug treatment.

INCAPACITATION

At the beginning of the book I reviewed the literature on the impact of incapacitation on crime. This was important because there has been a strong emphasis on incapacitation since the early 1980s when a control or law and order perspective strongly influenced criminal justice policies in the United States. After reviewing the literature, I concluded that incapacitation prevents crime in the community. The problem is we do not know how much crime is prevented by increasing incarceration rates. Debates continue about the amount of crime reduction that has occurred with the large increase in the incarceration rates. As more offenders are caught and incarcerated there may be diminishing returns because less active criminals who are at the end of their criminal careers may be included in the increased net of control. Furthermore, the increased use of incapacitation may have a negative impact on some locations (inner cities) and with some people (neglected, unsupervised youth) so that increases in crime result from the increased use of incarceration.

Many longitudinal studies have shown that a small number of offenders commit a disproportionate share of crime. Therefore, theoretically, if these career criminals could be identified and incapacitated the crime rate would be substantially reduced. The problem is we have not been successful in identifying who will be career criminals. Habitual offender laws and three-strikes laws have attempted to identify and incapacitate the career criminals but the effectiveness of these laws is questionable for the same reason that incapacitation has failed. That is, increasing punishments for repeat offenders based on official records may identify those who are low-rate offenders, those who commit minor crimes, or those at the end of their careers.

In summary, there is evidence that incapacitation has the potential for reducing crime in the community. The difficulty lies in determining the amount of crime prevented and how much should be considered a large reduction in crime. Questions also revolve around the costs of such policies in terms of money and impact on future generations in inner cities.

FOCUS ON RECIDIVISM

My review of programs focused on the impact of the programs on recidivism. When I present this material in seminars and at professional meetings, I am frequently asked why I did not examine other outcomes and if I believe that other factors are important. *Yes*, I emphatically answer, I believe recidivism is only one of many outcomes and changes that are important to examine. In many of the evaluations I have conducted I examine changes in positive social activities, attitude change, and so forth. These are important, first, because they may help to explain the intermediate, individual-level changes that occur that are related to recidivism. Knowledge of such mediating factors will help us develop a theoretical understanding of the important individual differences associated with criminal activity.

Second, many treatment programs, interventions, and management strategies are designed to assist offenders in other areas of their lives, not only reducing their criminal activities. Although I believe these are important (e.g., intermediate changes, other areas of offender's lives), I also see that the public and many policy makers view recidivism as the bottom line of the outcomes. In their view, successful programs are considered to be programs that are associated with a reduction in recidivism. A program may have many other impacts but if it does not have an impact on recidivism it will not be viewed as effective. If I attempted to look at other outcomes under the assumption that they are related to recidivism, I believe it would muddy the water. These are my reasons for focusing on recidivism.

Here, I am disagreeing with a recent paper by Petersilia (2004) where she argues that research resulting from the "what works" literature does not have face validity. I agree that reintegration is important and measures such as employment, reuniting with family, and healthy children are of critical importance. However, too often we permit practitioners to develop programs on the basis of their intuition and past experiences. To them the programs have face validity. Intuitions, gut feelings, and face validity may be good reasons for developing a pilot program. They are not evidence-based strategies for determining what is effective.

Another important question is, Do I believe that recidivism reduction is the major reason for implementing a program? No, there are many reasons policy makers and corrections professionals might want to implement a program. Costs, safety, public support, and offender needs are just some examples of other important considerations. Reducing recidivism is one of many considerations. The importance of the current work is that it provides understandable information about the results of evaluations and whether the different program areas have an impact on recidivism. This information can be used in conjunction with other information to assist decision makers in the difficult policy decisions. Policy makers can then make clear decisions. For example, in regard to boot camps, they may decide that shortening time in prison is beneficial whether for cost reasons or because it reunites people with their families. They can then make a decision knowing that the program may not reduce recidivism. Too frequently the separate goals are not clearly identified and studied.

Petersilia gives another example. She notes that drug courts may result in healthy children born to sober mothers. She says, "When we use recidivism as the sole criterion for judging whether reentry programs 'work' or 'don't work,' we often miss the more powerful impacts of program participation" (Petersilia, 2004:7). My argument is that we should examine various potential impacts of programs and explicitly examine which goals are achieved and which are not. We can then make informed decisions. If we are willing to ignore recidivism and opt for a program that achieves other goals, then we should do so with evidence about recidivism and the other goals (e.g., healthy children, drug free, etc.).

In summary, reducing recidivism is one of many potential correctional goals. Face validity, gut feelings, and intuitions are not effective ways to determine whether a program has achieved a specific goal. Goals should be clearly identified and research should be conducted to evaluate whether programs reach the desired goals. Recidivism is one of many different goals of correctional programs; however, it is considered by many people including policy makers, the public, and correctional staff to be one of the major goals. The impact of programs on recidivism is, therefore, information to assist decision makers in making evidence-based correctional decisions.

QUALITY OF THE RESEARCH

Two changes would greatly assist us in making better decisions about program implementation. First, I would like to see an increase in the number and quality of outcome evaluations. A great deal of time and money has been wasted on poorly designed outcome studies. Second, a large percentage of the total evaluations conducted have been descriptive studies. We would learn more if we increase the percent of the studies that were outcome studies.

Only forty-two (14.8 percent) of the evaluations shown in Table 15.1 were scored five in research methods, the gold standard of research designs. In contrast, sixty-six (23.2 percent) were scored two. The latter were considered to have used designs that were so poor the research should not be used to draw conclusion about what works. Some of the evaluations reviewed for this book did not rate a score of even two. Many others were descriptive or process evaluations. Although the goal of such work is not to examine outcomes, I do wonder about the number of descriptive studies compared to the number of outcome studies. A large percentage of the total number of evaluations are descriptive and not outcome studies.

Descriptive studies are critically important in setting the context for outcome evaluations. The problem is that a descriptive study alone provides little evidence about effectiveness. However, lest someone begin to complain that I undervalue descriptive studies, let me assure the reader that I have a great respect for quality descriptive studies. A major problem we have found in meta-analysis is that too little information is given about the context of the treatment. Frequently there is no information on program intensity, nor is there detailed information about the exact details of treatment provided. Similarly, little information is given about the characteristics of the participants. We often have difficulty coding such basic information as age, race, sex, or criminal history. Such descriptive information is critical for determining why one treatment program is effective and another is not.

Outcome evaluations need descriptive information to set the context for understanding the outcomes. The problem is separate descriptive and outcome reports make it difficult to know whether the context of the treatment in the outcome study is described in the descriptive report and vice versa. If the descriptive study is published separately from the outcome study, the description of the program may be completed years before the outcome study. The program may have changed dramatically by the time the outcomes are examined. Thus, the descriptive study provides little information to understand the context of the program at the time of the outcome study.

Another finding from my reviews of these studies is the large differences in the numbers of studies completed for different program areas. For example, there were thirty-two studies of drug courts. However, there were only four studies of correctional industries. Given the recent emphasis on the control philosophy of corrections, it is not surprising to see the proportionately large number of studies completed on boot camps and intermediate sanctions. Furthermore, many of the latter studies included multiple sites. Similarly, given the concern about the number of drug offenders entering the correction system, it is not surprising to see the large number of evaluations of programs for drug-involved offenders (e.g., drug courts and drug treatment).

My assessment of studies revealed a large difference in research methods scores in the different research areas. In some topic areas, a large percent of the studies used random assignment and were scored five in research methods. Particularly notable are the MST for juveniles where seven of the eight studies scored five, and arrests for domestic violence offenders where all the studies scored five. Overall, however, it is disappointing that only 14.8 percent of the studies scored five (see Table 15.1).

Conversely, in some topic areas the studies had a higher percentage that were scored two on research methods. A score of two means the study was so poorly designed that many alternative explanations for the results could not be ruled out. My colleagues and I believe evaluations with scores of two should not be used to make policy decisions about the effectiveness of programs and whether such programs should be implemented (Sherman et al., 1997; 2002). Three topic areas that are particularly problematic because a large percentage of the studies were scored two are academic education, cognitive behavior for sex offenders, and drug treatment in facilities. Approximately 50 percent of the academic education and cognitive behavior for sex offenders evaluations were scored two, and about one-third of the incarceration-based drug treatment evaluations were scored two. This is a serious deficit in the research, particularly when you consider the number of such programs and the costs of implementing such programs in correctional facilities. Given the number of drug-involved offenders requiring treatment, the large percentage of poorly designed studies in this area is disappointing. Another consideration is the cost of the research in terms of both time and money. Such poorly designed studies do not provide data necessary to adequately inform policy. In fact, one of the reasons my colleagues and I designed the research methods scoring system was to assist policy makers is determining the quality of the research so they would not be misled by results from poorly designed studies.

One research problem that continually occurs particularly in the area of drug treatment is the comparison of program completers to dropouts. Frequently the researchers refer to this as a comparison of the motivated (e.g., completers) to the nonmotivated (dropouts). The problem is that such a comparison does not tell us much about the program effects. Certainly, the completers seem more motivated. The problem is that the groups probably differed prior to entering the program: the motivated group wanted to change, the nonmotivated group did not. A comparison of how these groups do later in drug use and criminal behavior does not tell us much about the effect of the program because we cannot rule out the obvious fact that the two groups most likely differed prior to starting the program. From another perspective, it is as if we separated the groups into the "good" prospects and "bad" prospects at the start of the study. We expect the "good guys" to do better than the "bad guys" regardless of whether they enter a program. Thus, research comparing the two groups only says that there were "good guys" and "bad guys." It does not tell us the effect of the program.

EVIDENCE-BASED POLICY

Several recent developments in the field of criminology may help to increase evidence-based policy and improve the quality of the research (Sherman et al., 2002; MacKenzie, 2000; 2001; Cullen & Gendreau, 2000). One such development is the international Campbell Collaboration (Petrosino, Boruch, Soydan, Duggan, & Sanchez-Meca, 2001). The Campbell Collaboration is modeled after the Cochrane Collaboration in health care. It was created to "prepare, update, and disseminate systematic reviews of evidence on what works relevant to social and education intervention" (Petrosino et al., 2001:15). Decision makers, practitioners, citizens, media, and researchers are the target audience. The reviews will continually be updated. In addition, to maximize the use of the information for decision making, the reviews will be presented in a form that is reader-friendly for policy makers and practitioners. The systematic reviews will describe the details of the research design and methods of each study reviewed. Most of the criminal justice reviews have not been able to limit the research to randomized trials because there are too few completed. However, one of the goals of the Collaboration is to increase the rigor of the evaluations completed.

A second recent development that acknowledges and supports rigorous scientific research in criminology and criminal justice is the Academy of Experimental Criminology. The Academy was founded in 1999 to recognize criminologists who have successfully led randomized, controlled field experiments in criminology. The Academy recognizes such scholars by electing them as Fellows in the Academy. The Academy sponsors a commercially published *Journal of Experimental Criminology*, which publishes major advances in field experiments as well as quasi-experiments.

CONCLUSIONS

A large body of scientific evidence has been completed to evaluate the effectiveness of correctional programs and interventions. Although only a small percentage of these studies used strong research designs and methods, it is possible to draw some conclusions from the results of the evaluations. There is sufficient evidence to reject the "nothing works" mantra. Correctional programs do reduce recidivism. Specifically, effective programs provide human service treatment and focus on changing the individual. We have learned much from correctional evaluations. This information should be used to guide policy makers in decisions about which programs to implement and support (MacKenzie, 2005).

References

Abadinsky, H. (2001). *Drugs: An introduction.* Belmont, CA: Wadsworth.

Adams, K. (1968). *College-level instruction in U.S. prisons.* Unpublished manuscript.

Adams, K., Bennett, K. J., Flanagan, T. J., Marquart, J. W., Cuvelier, S. J., Fritsch, E., et al. (1994). A large-scale multidimensional test of the effect of prison education programs on offenders' behavior. *The Prison Journal, 74,* 433–449.

Agopian, M. W. (1990). The impact of intensive supervision probation on gang-drug offenders. *Criminal Justice Policy Review, 4*(3), 214–222.

Alaska Department of Corrections. (1996). *Sex offender treatment program: Initial recidivism study.* Anchorage, AK: Alaska Justice Statistical Analysis Unit Justice Center, University of Alaska.

Allen, L. C., Mackenzie, D. L., & Hickman, L. J. (2001). The effectiveness of cognitive behavioral treatment for adult offenders: A methodological, quality-based review. *International Journal of Offender Therapy and Comparative Criminology, 45,* 498–514.

Aloisi, M., & LeBaron, J. (2001). *The Juvenile Justice Commission's stabilization and reintegration program: An updated recidivism analysis.* Trenton, NJ: Juvenile Justice Commission Research & Evaluation Unit, New Jersey Department of Law and Public Safety.

American Friends Service Committee. (1971). *Struggle for justice: A report on crime and punishment in America.* New York: Hill & Wang.

American Psychiatric Association. (1994). *Diagnostic and statistical manual of mental disorders.* Washington, DC: American Psychiatric Association.

American University. (2001). *Drug court activity update: Composite summary information.* Washington, DC: U.S. Department of Justice, Office of Justice Programs, Drug Court Clearinghouse and Technical Assistance Project.

Anderson, D. (1981). The relationship between correctional education and parole success. *Journal of Offender Counseling, Services, and Rehabilitation, 5*, 13–25.

Anderson, S. V. (1995a). *Evaluation of the impact of correctional education programs on recidivism.* Columbus, OH: Office of Management Information Systems Bureau of Planning and Evaluation, Ohio Department of Rehabilitation and Correction.

Anderson, S. V. (1995b). *Evaluation of the impact of participation in Ohio penal industries on recidivism.* Columbus, OH: Office of Management Information Systems Bureau of Planning and Evaluation, Ohio Department of Rehabilitation and Correction.

Andrews, D. A., & Bonta, J. (2003). *The psychology of criminal conduct.* Cincinatti, OH: Anderson Publishing.

Andrews, D. A., Bonta, J., & Hoge, R. D. (1990). Classification for effective rehabilitation: Rediscovering psychology. *Criminal Justice and Behavior, 17*, 19–52.

Andrews, D. A., Dowden, C., & Gendreau, P. (1999). *Clinically relevant and psychologically informed approaches to reduced re-offending: A meta-analytic study of human service, risk, need, responsibility, and other concerns in justice contexts.* Unpublished manuscript.

Andrews, D. A., Zinger, I., Hoge, R. D., Bonta, J., Gendreau, P., & Cullen, F. T. (1990). Does correctional treatment work? A clinically relevant and psychologically informed meta-analysis. *Criminology, 28*, 369–397.

Anglin, D. M., & Hser, Y.-I. (1992). Drug abuse treatment. In Ronald R. Watson (Ed.), *Drug abuse treatment* (pp. 1–36). Totowa, NJ: Humana Press.

Anglin, D. M., & Hser, Y.-I. (1990). Treatment of drug abuse. In Michael Tonry & James Q. Wilson (Eds.), *Drugs and crime* (Vol. 13, pp. 393–460). Chicago, IL: University of Chicago Press.

Anglin, D. M., & McGlothlin, W. (1988). Outcome of narcotic addict treatment in California. In Frank M. Tims & Jacqueline P. Ludford (Eds.), *Drug abuse treatment evaluation: Strategies, progress, and prospects* (pp. 106–128). Washington, DC: Department of Health and Human Services.

Anspach, D. F., & Ferguson, A. S. (1999). *Cumberland County's drug court program: An evaluation report of Project Exodus.* Portland, ME: University of Southern Maine, Department of Sociology.

Antonowicz, D., & Ross, R. (1994). Essential components of successful rehabilitation programs for offenders. *International Journal of Offender Therapy and Comparative Criminology, 38*, 97–104.

Applegate, B. K., Cullen, F. T., & Fisher, B. S. (1997). Public support for correctional treatment: The continuing appeal of the rehabilitative ideal. *Prison Journal, 77*, 237–258.

Arbuthnot, J., & Gordon, D. A. (1988). Crime and cognition: Community applications of sociomoral reasoning development. *Criminal Justice and Behavior, 15*, 498–514.

Austin, J., & Hardyman, P. (1991). *The use of early parole with electronic monitoring to control prison crowding: Evaluation of the Oklahoma Department of Corrections pre-parole supervised release with electronic monitoring.* Madison, WI: National Council on Crime and Delinquency.

Austin, J., Jones, M., & Bolyard, M. (1993). *Assessing the impact of a county operated boot camp: Evaluation of the Los Angeles County regimented inmate diversion program.* San Francisco, CA: National Council on Crime and Delinquency.

Austin, T. (1997). *Life skills for inmates: An evaluation of Dauphin County Prison's LASER program.* Unpublished manuscript.

Babcock, J. C., & La Taillade, J. J. (2000). Evaluating interventions for men who batter. In J. P. Vincent & E. N. Jouriles (Eds.), *Domestic violence: Guidelines for research-informed practice* (pp. 37–77). Philadelphia: Jessica Kingsley Publishers.

Babcock, J. C., & Steiner, R. (1999). The relationship between treatment, incarceration, and recidivism of battering: A program of evaluation of Seattle's coordinated community response to domestic violence. *Journal of Family Psychology, 13*, 46–59.

Baer, D. J., Jacobs, P., & Carr, F. E. (1975). Instructors' ratings of delinquents after Outward Bound survival training and their subsequent recidivism. *Psychological Reports, 36*, 547–553.

Baird, S. C., & Wagner, D. (1990). Measuring diversion: The Florida community control program. *Crime and Delinquency, 36*, 112–125.

Ball, J. C., & Ross, A. (1991). *The effectiveness of methadone maintenance treatment: Patients, programs, services, and outcomes.* New York: Springer-Verlag.

Ball, J., Shaffer, J., & Nurco, D. (1983). Day to day criminality of heroin addicts in Baltimore: A study of offense rates. *Drug and Alcohol Dependence, 12*, 119–142.

Bandura, A. (1977). *Social learning theory.* Englewood Cliffs, NJ: Prentice-Hall.

Baro, A. L. (1999). Effects of a cognitive restructuring program on inmate institutional behavior. *Criminal Justice and Behavior*, 26, 466–484.

Barton, W. H., & Butts, J. A. (1990). Accommodating innovation in a juvenile court. *Criminal Justice Policy Review, 4*(2), 144–158.

Batiuk, M. E., Moke, P., & Rountree, P. W. (1997). Crime and rehabilitation: Correctional education as an agent of change. *Justice Quarterly, 14*, 167–180.

Baumer, T. L., Maxfield, M. G., & Mendelsohn, R. I. (1993). A comparative analysis of three electronically monitored home detention programs. *Justice Quarterly, 10*(1), 121–141.

Baumer, T., & Mendelsohn, R. (1992). Electronically monitored home confinement: Does it work? In J. Byrne, A. Lurigio, & J. Petersilia (Eds.), *Smart sentencing: The emergence of intermediate sanctions* (pp. 54–67). Newbury Park, CA: Sage.

Bavon, A. (2001). The effect of the Tarrant County drug court project on recidivism. *Evaluation and Program Planning, 24*(1), 13–22.

Beck, J. L., & Klein-Saffran, J. (1990). Home confinement and the use of electronic monitoring with federal parolees. *Federal Probation, 54*(4), 22–34.

Belenko, S. R. (1999). Research on drug courts: A critical review 1999 update. *National Drug Court Institute Review*, 2(2), 1–58.

Belenko, S. (1998a). *Behind bars: Substance abuse and America's prison population.* Retrieved January 5, 2005, from http://www.casacolumbia.org/pdshopprov.

Belenko, S. R. (1998b). Research on drug courts: A critical review. *National Drug Court Institute Review, 1*(1), 1–42.

Benekos, P. J., & Merlo, A. V. (1995). Three strikes and you're out! The political sentencing game. *Federal Probation, 59*, 3–9.

Bench, L. L., Kramer, S. P., & Erickson, S. (1997). A discriminant analysis of predictive factors in sex offender recidivism. In B. K. Schwartz & H. R. Cellini (Eds.), *The sex offender: New insights, treatment innovations and legal developments* (pp. 15.1–15.15). Kingston, NJ: Civic Research Institute.

Berk, R. A., Campbell, A., Klap, R., & Western, B. (1992). A Bayesian analysis of the Colorado Springs spouse abuse experiment. *Journal of Criminal Law and Criminology, 83*, 170–200.

Berlin, F. S. (2000). The etiology and treatment of sexual offending. In D. H. Fishbein (Ed.), *The science, treatment, and prevention of antisocial behaviors: Application to the criminal justice system.* Kingston, NJ: Civic Research Institute.

Blackburn, F. S. (1981). The relationship between recidivism and participation in a community college associate of arts degree program for incarcerated offenders. Paper presented at the meeting of the Thirty-Sixth Annual Conference of the Correctional Education Association, Costa Mesa, CA.

Blanchette, K. (1996). *Sex offender assessment, treatment and recidivism: A literature review.* Correctional Services of Canada, Ottawa, Ontario.

Bloom, H., Orr, L. L., Cave, G., Bell, S. H., Doolittle, F., & Lin, W. (1994). *The national JTPA study: Overview of impacts, benefits, and costs of Title IIA.* Cambridge, MA: ABT Associates.

Blumstein, A. (1995). Prisons. In J. Q. Wilson, & J. Petersilia (Eds.), *Crime* (pp. 387–419). San Francisco: Institute for Contemporary Studies.

Blumstein, A., & Beck, A. J. (1999). Population growth in U.S. prisons, 1980–1996. In M. Tonry & J. Petersilia (Eds.), *Prisons* (pp. 17–62). Chicago: University of Chicago Press.

Blumstein, A., & Cohen, J. (1979). Estimation of individual crimes rates from arrest records. *Journal of Criminal Law and Criminology, 70,* 561–585.

Blumstein, A., & Cohen, J. (1973). A theory of the stability of punishment. *Journal of Criminal Law and Criminology, 64,* 198–207.

Blumstein, A., Cohen, J., & Miller, H. (1980). Demographically disaggregated projections of prison populations. *Journal of Criminal Justice, 8,* 1–26.

Blumstein, A., Cohen, J., Roth, J., & Visher, C. A. (1986). *Criminal careers and career criminals,* Vol. 1. Washington, DC: National Academy Press.

Bonta, J., Wallace-Capretta, S., & Rooney, J. (2000a). Can electronic monitoring make a difference? An evaluation of three Canadian programs. *Crime and Delinquency, 46*(1), 61–75.

Bonta, J., Wallace-Capretta, S., & Rooney, J. (2000b). A quasi-experimental evaluation of an intensive rehabilitation supervision program. *Criminal Justice and Behavior,* 27(3), 312–329.

Bottcher, J. (1997). *A boot camp and intensive parole program: The final impact evaluation (report to the California legislature).* Sacramento, CA: California Department of Youth Authority.

Bourdin, C. M., Henggeler, S. W., Blaske, D. M., & Stein, R. J. (1994). Multisystemic treatment of adolescent sexual offenders. In D. West (Ed.), *Sex crimes* (pp. 271–279). Brookfield, VT: Dartmouth.

Bourdin, C. M., Henggeler, S. W., Blaske, D. M., & Stein, R. J. (1990). Multisystemic treatment of adolescent sexual offenders. *International Journal of Offender Therapy and Comparative Criminology, 34,* 105–113.

Bourdin, C. M., Mann, B. J., Cone, L. T., Henggeler, S. W., Fucci, B. R., Blaske, D. M., & Williams, R. A. (1995). Multisystemic therapy of serious juvenile offenders: Long-term prevention of criminality and violence. *Journal of Consulting and Clinical Psychology, 63,* 569–578.

Boudouris, J. (1985). *Recidivism and rehabilitation.* Des Moines, IA: Iowa Department of Corrections.

Bouffard, J. A., MacKenzie, D. L., & Hickman, L. (2000). Effectiveness of vocational education and employment programs for adult offenders: A methodology-based analysis of the literature. *Journal of Offender Rehabilitation, 31,* 1–41.

Boyles, C. E., Bokenkamp, E., & Madura, W. (1996). *Evaluation of the Colorado juvenile regimented training program.* Golden, CO: Colorado Department of Human Services, Division of Youth Corrections.

Brewster, M. P. (2001). An evaluation of the Chester County (PA) drug court program. *Journal of Drug Issues, 31*(1), 177–206.

Brownlee, I. D. (1995). Intensive probation with young adult offenders: A short reconviction study. *British Journal of Criminology, 35*(4), 599–612.

Buhrich, N., Bailey, J. M., & Martin, N. G. (1991). Sexual orientation, sexual identity, and sex-dimorphic behaviors in male twins. *Behavioral Genetics, 21*, 75–96.

Bureau of Justice Statistics. (2001). *Key facts at a glance – Correctional populations, 1980–2000.* Washington, DC: U.S. Department of Justice.

Bureau of Justice Statistics. (2000). *Drug use, testing, and treatment in jails.* Washington, DC: U.S. Department of Justice.

Bureau of Justice Statistics. (1999). *Substance abuse and treatment, state and federal prisoners, 1997.* Washington, DC: U.S. Department of Justice.

Bureau of Justice Statistics. (1997). *Characteristics of adults on probation, 1995.* Washington, DC: U.S. Department of Justice.

Burke, L. O., & Vivian, J. E. (2001). The effect of college programming on recidivism rates at the Hampden County House of Correction: A 5-year study. *Journal of Correctional Education, 52*, 160–162.

Burnett, W. L. (1996). Treating post-incarcerated offenders with moral reconation therapy: A one-year recidivism study. Unpublished master's thesis: University of Phoenix, Phoenix, AZ.

Burns, J. C., & Vito, G. F. (1995). An impact analysis of the Alabama boot camp program. *Federal Probation, 59*, 63–67.

Bush, J., & Bilodeau, B. (1993). *Options: A cognitive change program.* Longmont, CO: National Institute of Corrections.

Bushway, S. D. (1998). Impact of an arrest on the job stability of young white American men. *Journal of Research in Crime and Delinquency, 35*, 454–479.

Bushway, S., & Reuter, P. (1997). Labor markets and crime risk factors. In L. W. Sherman, D. Gottfredson, D. MacKenzie, J. Eck, P. Reuter, & S. Bushway (Eds.), *Preventing crime: What works, what doesn't, what's promising* (pp. 6-1–6-49). Washington, DC: Office of Justice Programs, U.S. Department of Justice.

Buzawa, E. S., & Buzawa, C. G. (1996a). *Domestic violence: The criminal justice response.* Thousand Oaks, CA: Sage.

Buzawa, E. S., & Buzawa, C. G. (1996b). The role of arrest in domestic versus stranger assault: Is there a difference? In E. S. Buzawa & C. G. Buzawa (Eds.), *Do arrests and restraining orders work?* (pp. 150–175). Thousand Oaks, CA: Sage.

Byrne, J., & Kelly, L. (1989). *Final report to the National Institute of Justice, research program of the punishment and control of offenders.* Washington, DC: U.S. Department of Justice.

Byrne, J. M., Lurigio, A. J., & Petersilia, J. (1992). *Smart sentencing: The emergence of intermediate sanctions.* Newbury Park, CA: Sage.

Camp, G., & Camp, C. (1990). *Preventing and solving problems involved in operating therapeutic communities in a prison setting.* South Salem, NY: Criminal Justice Institute.

Camp, D. A., & Sandhu, H. S. (1995). Evaluation of female offender regimented treatment program (FORT). *Journal of the Oklahoma Criminal Justice Research Consortium, 2*, 50–57.

Castellano, T. C., & Soderstrom, I. R. (1992). Therapeutic wilderness programs and juvenile recidivism: A program evaluation. *Journal of Offender Rehabilitation, 17*(3/4), 19–46.

Cecil, D. K., Drapkin, D. A., MacKenzie, D. L., & Hickman, L. J. (2000). The effectiveness of adult basic education and life-skills programs in reducing recidivism: A review and assessment of the research. *Journal of Correctional Education, 51*, 207–226.

Chaiken, J. M., & Chaiken, M. R. (1982). *Varieties of criminal behavior* (Rand Report R-2814-NIJ). Santa Monica, CA: Rand Corporation.

Chen, H., Bersani, C., Myers, S. C., & Denton, R. (1989). Evaluating the effectiveness of a court sponsored abuser treatment program. *Journal of Family Violence, 4*, 309–322.

Chown, B., & Davis, S. (1986). *Recidivism among offenders incarcerated by the Oklahoma Department of Corrections who received vocational-techinical training: A survival data analysis of offenders released January 1982 through July 1986.* Oklahoma City, OK: Oklahoma State Department of Corrections.

Clark, D. D. (1991). *Analysis of return rates of the inmate college program participants.* Albany, NY: New York State Department of Correctional Services.

Clark, C. L., & Aziz, D. W. (1996). Shock incarceration in New York State: Philosophy, results, and limitations. In D. L. MacKenzie & E. E. Hebert (Eds.), *Correctional boot camps: A tough intermediate sanction* (pp. 39–68). Washington, DC: National Institute of Justice, U.S. Department of Justice.

Clark, P. M., Hartter, S., & Ford, E. (1992). *An experiment in employment of offenders.* Paper presented at the meeting of the American Society of Criminology, New Orleans, LA.

Clarke, S. H. (1974). Getting 'em out of circulation: Does incarceration of juvenile offenders reduce crime? *Journal of Criminal Law and Criminology, 65*, 528–535.

Clear, T., & Dammer, H. R. (2000). *The offender in the community.* Blemont, CA: Wadsworth.

Clear, T. R., Flynn, S., & Shapiro, C. (1987). Intensive supervision in probation: A comparison of three projects. In B. R. McCarthy (Ed.),

Intermediate punishments: Intensive supervision, home confinement, and electronic surveillance (Vol. 31–51). Monsey, NY: Criminal Justice Press.

Coffey, B. B. (1983). The effectiveness of vocational education in Kentucky's correctional institutions as measured by employment status and recidivism (Doctoral dissertation, University of Kentucky, 1983). *Dissertation Abstracts International, 44-09A*, 2745–2877.

Coffey, O. D., & Gemignani, M. G. (1994). *Effective practices in juvenile correctional education: A study of the literature and research 1980–1992*. Washington, DC: Office of Juvenile Justice and Delinquency Prevention.

Cohen, J. (1988). *Statistical power analysis for the behavioral sciences*. Hillsdale, NJ: Erlbaum.

Cohen, J. (1983). Incapacitation as a strategy for crime control: Possibilities and pitfalls. In N. Morris & M. Tonry (Eds.), *Crime and justice: An annual review of research* (Vol. 5, pp. 1–84). Chicago: University of Chicago Press.

Cohen, J., & Canela-Cacho, J. A. (1994). Incapacitation and violent crime. In A. J. Reiss & J. Roth (Eds.), *Understanding and preventing violence*, (Vol. 4, pp. 296–388). Washington, DC: National Academy of Sciences.

Collaer, M. L., & Hines, M. (1995). Human behavioral sex differences: A role for gonadal hormones during early development? *Psychological Bulletin, 118*, 55–107.

Cosden, M., Crothers, L., & Peerson, S. (1999). *Ventura County drug court: Summary findings*. Santa Barbara, CA: University of California, Graduate School of Education.

Courtright, K. E., Berg, B. L., & Mutchnick, R. J. (1997). Effects of house arrest with electronic monitoring on DUI offenders. *Journal of Offender Rehabilitation, 24*(3/4), 35–51.

Craven, D. (1997). *Sex differences in violent victimization, 1994*. Washington, DC: Bureau of Justice Statistics.

Criminal Justice Research Center. (1994). *Evaluation of the Virginia Department of Corrections' intensive supervision program*. Richmond, VA: Virginia Department of Criminal Justice Services.

Cullen, F. T., & Gendreau, P. (2000). Assessing correctional rehabilitation: Policy, practice, and prospects. In J. Horney (Ed.), *Criminal justice 2000: Vol. 3. Policies, processes, and decisions of the criminal justice system*. Washington, DC: U.S. Department of Justice, National Institute of Justice.

Cullen, F. T., & Gendreau, P. (1989). *The effectiveness of correctional rehabilitation: Reconsidering the "nothing works" debate*. In L. Goodstein & D. L. MacKenzie (Eds.), *The American Prison: Issues in Research Policy*: Plenum Press, New York.

Cullen, F. T., Skovron, S. E., & Scott, J. E. (1990). Public support for correctional treatment: The tenacity of rehabilitative ideology. Survey of Cincinnati and Columbus residents. *Criminal Justice and Behavior, 17,* 6–18.

Cullen, F. T., Wright, J. P., & Applegate, B. K. (1996). Control in the community: The limits of reform? In A. T. Harland (Ed.), *Choosing correctional options that work: Defining the demand and evaluating the supply.* Thousand Oaks, CA: Sage.

Curulla, V. L. (1991). Aggression replacement training in the community for adult learning-disabled offenders (Doctoral dissertation, University of Washington, 1991). *Dissertation Abstracts International, 53,* 627).

Davidson, P. (1984, March). Outcome data for a penitentiary-based treatment program for sex offenders. Paper presented at the meeting of the Conference on the Assessment and Treatment of the Sex Offender, Kingston, Ontario.

Davis, R. C., & Lurigio, A. J. (1996). *Fighting back: Neighborhood antidrug strategies.* Thousand Oaks, CA: Sage.

Davis, R. C., & Taylor, B. G. (1999). Does batterer treatment reduce violence? A synthesis of the literature. *Women and Criminal Justice, 10,* 69–93.

DeLeon, G. (1986). Program-based evaluation research in therapeutic communities. In F. M. Tims & J. P. Ludford (Eds.), *Drug abuse treatment evaluation: Strategies, progress, and prospect* (pp. 69–87). Rockville, MD: National Institute on Drug Abuse.

Deschenes, E. P., Greenwood, P. W., & Marshall, G. (1996). *The Nokomis Challenge program evaluation* (DRU-1147-1-MDoSS). Michigan Department of Social Services, Lansing.

Deschenes, E. P., Iman, I., Foster, T. L., Diaz, L., Moreno, V., Patascil, L., & Ward, D. (1999). *Evaluation of Orange County drug courts.* Richmond, CA: Center for Applied Local Research.

Deschenes, E. P., Turner, S., & Greenwood, P. W. (1995). Drug court or probation? An experimental evaluation of Maricopa County's drug court. *Justice System Journal, 18*(1), 55–73.

Devine, J. A., Sheley, J. F., & Smith, M. D. (1988). Macroeconomic and social-control policy influences on crime rate changes, 1948–1985. *American Sociological Review, 53,* 407–420.

Ditton, P. M., & Wilson, D. J. (1999). *Truth in sentencing in state prisons.* Washington, DC: Bureau of Justice Statistics.

Di Vito, R. J. (1991). Survey of mandatory education policies in state penal institutions. *Journal of Correctional Education, 42,* 126–130.

Dobash, R. E., & Dobash, R. P. (2000). Evaluating criminal justice interventions for domestic violence. *Crime and Delinquency, 46,* 252–271.

Dobson, K. S., & Craig, K. D. (1996). *Advances in cognitive behavioral therapy.* Newbury Park, CA: Sage.

Dobson, K. S., & Khatri, N. (2000). Cognitive therapy: Looking backward, looking forward. *Journal of Clinical Psychology, 56*, 907–923.

Dole, V. P., & Nyswander, M. E. (1965). A medical treatment of diacetylmorphine (heroin) addiction. *Journal of the American Medical Association, 193*, 646–650.

Donohue, J. J. (1998). Understanding the time path of crime. *Journal of Criminal Law and Criminology, 88*, 1423–1451.

Downes, E. A., Monaco, K. R., & Schreiber, S. O. (1989). Evaluating the effects of vocational education on inmates: A research model and preliminary results. In S. Duguid (Ed.), *The yearbook of correctional education* (pp. 249–262). Burnaby, BC, Canada: Simon Fraser University.

Dugan, J. R., & Everett, R. S. (1998). An experimental test of chemical dependency therapy for jail inmates. *International Journal of Offender Therapy and Comparative Criminology, 42*, 360–368.

Duguid, S. (1981). Rehabilitation through education: A Canadian model. *Journal of Offender Counseling, Services and Rehabilitation, 6*, 53–67.

Duguid, S., Hawkey, C., & Pawson, R. (1996). Using recidivism to evaluate effectiveness in prison education programs. *Journal of Correctional Education, 47*, 74–85.

Dunford, F. W. (2000). Determining program success: The importance of employing experimental research designs. *Crime and Delinquency, 46*, 425–434.

Dunford, F. W. (1992). The measurement of recidivism in cases of spouse assault. *Journal of Criminal Law and Criminology, 83*, 120–136.

Dunford, F. W. (1990). System-initiated warrants for suspects of misdemeanor domestic assault: A pilot study. *Justice Quarterly, 7*, 621–653.

Dunford, F. W., Huizinga, D., & Elliott, D. S. (1990). The role of arrest in domestic assault: The Omaha police experiment. *Criminology, 28*, 183–206.

Dutton, D. G. (1998). *The abusive personality: Violence and control in intimate relationships.* New York: Guilford Press.

Dutton, D. G., Bodnarchuk, M., Kropp, R., Hart, S. D., & Ogloff, J. R. P. (1997). Wife assault treatment and criminal recidivism: An 11-year follow-up. *International Journal of Offender Therapy and Comparative Criminology, 41*, 9–23.

Edleson, J. L., & Grusznski, R. J. (1988). Treating men who batter: Four years of outcome data from the domestic abuse project. *Journal of Social Service Research, 12*, 3–22.

Edleson, J. L., & Syers, M. (1991). The effects of group treatment for men who batter: An 18-month follow-up study. *Research on Social Work Practice, 1*, 227–244.

Eisenberg, M. (2001). *The substance abuse felony punishment program: Evaluation and recommendations.* Austin, TX: Criminal Justice Policy Council.

Eisenberg, M., & Fabelo, T. (1996). Evaluation of the Texas correctional substance abuse treatment initiative: The impact of policy research. *Crime and Delinquency, 42*, 296–308.

Elrod, H. P., & Minor, K. I. (1992). Second wave evaluation of a multi-faceted intervention for juvenile court probationers. *International Journal of Offender Therapy and Comparative Criminology, 36*, 247–262.

English, K. (1993). Self-reported crime rates of women prisoners. *Journal of Quantitative Criminology, 9*(4), 357–382.

English, K., & Mande, M. (1992). *Measuring crime rates of prisoners.* Unpublished report to the National Institute of Justice. Denver, CO: Colorado Division of Criminal Justice.

Ericson, R., Welter, S., & Johnson, T. L. (1999). *Evaluation of the Hennepin County drug court.* Minneapolis, MN: Minnesota Citizens Council on Crime and Justice.

Erwin, B. S. (1986, June). Turning up the heat on probationers in Georgia. *Federal Probation, 50*, 17–24.

Fagan, J. (1996). *The criminalization of domestic violence: Promises and limits.* Washington, DC: National Institute of Justice.

Fagan, J. (1995). Legal work and illegal work: Crime, work and unemployment. In B. Weisbrod and J. Worthy (Eds.), *Dealing with urban crisis: Linking research to action.* Evanston, IL: Northwestern University Press.

Falkin, G. P., Strauss, S., & Bohen, T. (1999). Matching drug-involved probationers to appropriate drug interventions. *Federal Probation, 63*(1), 3–8.

Fallen, D. L., Apperson, C. D., Hall-Milligan, J., & Aos, S. (1981). *Intensive parole supervision.* Olympia, WA: Department of Social and Health Services, Analysis and Information Services Division.

Farrington, D. P. (1998). Individual differences and offending. In M. Tonry (Ed.), *The handbook of crime and punishment* (pp. 241–268). Oxford: Oxford University Press.

Farrington, D. (1986). Age and crime. In M. Tonry and N. Morris (Eds.), *Crime and justice* (Vol. 7, pp. 189–250). Chicago: University of Chicago Press.

Farrington, D. P., Ditchfield, J., Hancock, G., Howard, P., Jolliffee, D., Livingston, M. S., & Painter, K. A. (2002). *Evaluation of two intensive regimes for young offenders*, British Home Office, London.

Farrington, D. P., Gallagher, B., Morley, L., Ledger, R. J. St. (1986). Unemployment, school leaving and crime. *British Journal of Criminology. 26*:335–356.

Farrington, D. P., Hancock, G., Livingston, M., Painter, K., & Towl, G. (2001). *Evaluation of intensive regimes for young offenders.* London, England: Home Office Research, Development and Statistics Directorate.

Farrington, D. P., & Petrosino, A. (2001). The Campbell Collaboration crime and justice group. *Annals of the American Academy of Political and Social Science, 578*, 35–49.

Feder, L., & Dugan, L. (2002). A test of the efficacy of court-mandated counseling for domestic violence offenders: The Broward experiment. *Justice Quarterly, 19*, 343–375.

Federal Bureau of Investigation. (2004). *Crime in the United States 2004*, Washington, DC: U.S. Department of Justice.

Federoff, J. P., Wisner-Carlson, R., Dean, S., & Berlin, F. S. (1992). Medroxy-progesterone acetate in the treatment of paraphilic sexual disorders. *Journal of Offender Rehabilitation, 18*, 109–123.

Feeley, M. M., & Simon, J. (1992). The new penology: Notes on the emerging strategy of corrections and its implications. *Criminology, 30*(4), 449–470.

Feldman, C. M., & Ridley, C. A. (1995). The etiology and treatment of domestic violence between partners. *Clinical Psychology: Science and Practice*, 2, 317–348.

Field, G. (1989). A study of the effects of intensive treatment on reducing the criminal recidivism of addicted offenders.

Field, G. (1985). The Cornerstone Program: A client outcome study. *Federal Probation, 49*, 50–55.

Finckenauer, J. O. (1982). *Scared Straight and the panacea phenomenon.* Englewood Cliffs, NJ: Prentice-Hall.

Finigan, M. W. (1998). *An outcome program evaluation of the Multnomah County S. T. O. P. drug diversion program.* Portland, OR: NPC Research.

Finn, P. (1998). *The Delaware Department of Corrections life skills program.* Washington, DC: National Institute of Justice.

Flanagan, T. (1989). Prison labor and industry. In L. I. Goodstein & D. L. MacKenzie (Eds.), *The American Prison.* New York: Plenum Press.

Florida Department of Juvenile Justice. (1997a). *Bay County sheriff's office boot camp: A follow-up of the first seven platoons.* Bay County, FL: Bureau of Data and Research.

Florida Department of Juvenile Justice. (1997b). *Martin County sheriff's office boot camp: A follow-up study of the first four platoons.* Martin County, FL: Bureau of Data and Research.

Florida Department of Juvenile Justice. (1997c). *Polk County juvenile boot camp: A follow-up of the first four platoons.* Tallahassee, FL: Bureau of Data and Research.

Florida Department of Juvenile Justice. (1997d). *Polk County juvenile boot camp female program: A follow-up study of the first seven platoons.* Polk County, FL: Bureau of Data and Research.

Florida Department of Juvenile Justice. (1996a). *Leon County sheriff's department boot camp: A follow-up study of the first five platoons.* Tallahassee, FL: Bureau of Data and Research.

Florida Department of Juvenile Justice. (1996b). *Manatee County sheriff's boot camp: A follow-up study of the first four platoons.* Tallahassee, FL: Bureau of Research and Data.

Florida Department of Juvenile Justice. (1996c). *Pinellas County boot camp: A follow-up study of the first five platoons.* Tallahassee, FL: Bureau of Data and Research.

Flowers, G. T., Carr, T. S., & Ruback, B. R. (1991). *Special alternative incarceration evaluation.* Atlanta, GA: Georgia Department of Corrections.

Foglia, W. D. (2000). Adding an explicit focus on cognition to criminological theory. In D. H. Fishbein (Ed.), *The science, treatment, and prevention of antisocial behaviors: Application to the criminal justice system.* Kingston, NJ: Civic Research Institute.

Furby, L., Weinrott, M. R., & Blackshaw, L. (1989). Sex offender recidivism: A review. *Psychological Bulletin, 105,* 3–30.

Gaither, C. (1976). *An evaluation of the Texas Department of Corrections' Junior College program.* Huntsville, TX: Department of Correction Treatment Directorate, Research and Development Division.

Gallagher, C. A., Wilson, D. B., Hirschfield, P., Coggeshall, M. B., & MacKenzie, D. L. (1999). The effects of sex offender treatment on sexual reoffending. *Corrections Management Quarterly, 3,* 19–29.

Gallagher, C. A., Wilson, D. B., & MacKenzie, D. L. (1999). A meta-analysis of the effectiveness of sex offender treatment programs. College Park, MD: University of Maryland.

Garner, J., Fagan, J., & Maxwell, C. (1995). Published findings from the spousal assault replication program: A critical review. *Journal of Quantitative Criminology, 11,* 3–28.

Gendreau, P., Andrews, D. A., Goggin, C., & Chanteloupe, F. (1992). The development of clinical and policy guidelines for the prediction of criminal behavior in criminal justice settings. Unpublished manuscript.

Gendreau, P., Little, T., & Goggin, C. E. (1996). A meta-analysis of the predictors of adult recidivism: What works! *Criminology, 34,* 575–607.

Gendreau, P., & Ross, R. R. (1987). Revivification or rehabilitation: Evidence from the 1980s. *Justice Quarterly,* 4, 349–407.

Gendreau, P., & Ross, R. R. (1981). Offender rehabilitation: The appeal of success. *Federal Probation, 45,* 45–48.

Gendreau, P., & Ross, R. R. (1979). Effective correctional treatment. Bibliotherapy for cynics. *Crime and Delinquency,* 25, 463–489.

General Accounting Office (GAO). (1997). *Drug courts: Overview of growth, characteristics, and results.* Washington, DC: Author.

General Accounting Office (GAO). (1996). *Sex offender treatment: Research result inconclusive about what works to reduce recidivism.* Washington, DC: Author.

Gerber, J., & Fritsch, E. J. (1995). Adult academic and vocational correctional education programs: A review of recent research. *Journal of Offender Rehabilitation,* 22, 119–142.

Giancola, P. R. (2000). Neuropsychological functioning and antisocial behavior: Implications for etiology and prevention. In D. H. Fishbein (Ed.), *The science, treatment, and prevention of antisocial behaviors: Application to the criminal justice system.* Kingston, NJ: Civic Research Institute.

Giordano, P. C., Cernkovich, S. A., & Rudolph, J. L. (2002). Gender, crime, and desistance: Toward a theory of cognitive transformation. American Journal of Sociology, 107(4), 990–1064.

Glaser, D. (1969). *The effectiveness of a prison and parole system.* Indianapolis, IN: Bobbs-Merrill.

Glaser, D., & Watts, R. (1992). Electronic monitoring of drug offenders on probation. *Judicature, 76*(3), 112–117.

Glueck, S., & Glueck, E. (1930). *500 criminal careers.* New York: A. A. Knopf.

Godley, M. D., Dennis, M. L., Funk, R., Siekmann, M., & Weisheit, R. (1998). *Madison County alternative treatment and court final evaluation report.* Bloomington, IL: Chestnut Health Systems.

Godwin, G., Stone, S., & Hambrock, K. (1995). Recidivism study: Lake County, Florida Detention Center. *Cognitive-Behavioral Treatment Review,* 4, 6.

Goldkamp, J. S. (October 3, 2000). What we know about the impact of drug courts: Moving research from "do they work?" to "when and how they work." Testimony before the Senate Judiciary Subcommittee on Youth Violence.

Goldkamp, J. S. (1999). When is a drug court not a drug court? In C. Terry (Ed.), *The early drug courts: Case studies in judicial innovation.* Beverly Hills, CA: Sage.

Goldkamp, J. S., & Weiland, D. (1993). *Assessing the impact of Dade County's felony drug court: Final report.* Philadelphia: Crime and Justice Research Institute.

Goldkamp, J. S., White, M. D., & Robinson, J. B. (2000). *Retrospective evaluation of two pioneering drug courts: Phase I findings from Clark County, Nevada, and Multnomah, Oregon: An interim report of the national evaluation of drug courts.* Philadelphia: Crime and Justice Research Institute.

Gondolf, E. W. (1999). A comparison of four batterer intervention systems: Do court referral, program length, and services matter? *Journal of Interpersonal Violence, 14,* 41–61.

Gordon, D. A., & Arbuthnot, J. (1987). Individual, group, and family interventions. In H. C. Quay (Ed.), *Handbook of juvenile delinquency* (pp. 290–324). New York: Wiley.

Gordon, A., & Nicholaichuk, T. (1996). *Applying the risk principle to sex offender treatment, Correctional Service of Canada, Ottawa, Ontario.*

Gottfredson, D. C., & Barton, W. H. (1993). Deinstitutionalization of juvenile offenders. *Criminology, 31*(4), 591–611.

Gottfredson, D. C., Coblentz, K., & Harmon, M. A. (1996). *A short-term outcome evaluation of the Baltimore City drug treatment court program.* College Park, MD: University of Maryland, Department of Criminology and Criminal Justice.

Gottfredson, S. D., & Gottfredson, D. M. (1986). Behavioral prediction and the problem of incapacitation. *Criminology, 32*(3), 441–474.

Gottfredson, M., & Hirschi, T. (1990). *A general theory of crime.* Stanford, CA: Stanford University Press.

Gottfredson, D. C., Najaka, S. S., & Kearley, B. (2003). Effectiveness of drug treatment courts: Evidence from a randomized trial. *Criminology and Public Policy,* 2(2), 171–196.

Gowdy, V. B. (1996). Historical perspective. In *Correctional boot camps: A tough intermediate sanction* (pp. 1–16). Washington, DC: National Institute of Justice, U.S. Department of Justice.

Granfield, R., Eby, C., & Brewster, T. (1998). An examination of the Denver drug court: The impact of a treatment-oriented drug-offender system. *Law and Policy,* 20(2), 183–202.

Gransky, L. A., & Jones, R. J. (1995). *Evaluation of the post-release status of substance abuse program participants.* Chicago: Illinois Criminal Justice Information Authority.

Greenberg, D. F. (1975). The incapacitative effects of imprisonment: Some estimates. *Law and Society, 9*(4), 541–586.

Greenfeld, L. A. (1997). *Sex offenses and offenders: An analysis of data on rape and sexual assault.* Washington, DC: Bureau of Justice Statistics.

Greenwood, P. W., & Abrahamse, A. (1982). *Selective incapacitation: Report prepared for the National Institute of Justice.* Santa Monica, CA: Rand Corporation.

Greenwood, P. W., Deschenes, E. P., & Adams, J. (1993). *Chronic juvenile offenders: Final results from the Skillman Aftercare Experiment.* RAND, Santa Monica, CA.

Greenwood, P. W., Rydell, C. P. Abrahamse, A. F., Caulkins, J. P., Chiesa, J., Model, K. E., & Klein, S. P. (1996). Estimated benefits and costs of California's new mandatory-sentencing law. In D. Shichor & D. K. Sechrest (Eds.), *Three strikes and you're out: Vengeance as public policy* (pp. 53–89). Thousand Oaks, CA: Sage.

Greenwood, P. W., & Turner, S. (1993). Evaluation of the Paint Creek Youth Center: A residential program for serious delinquents. *Criminology, 31*(2), 263–279.

Greenwood, P. W., & Turner, S. (1987a). *Selective incapacitation revisited: Why the high-rate offenders are hard to predict.* Santa Monica: Rand.

Greenwood, P. W., & Turner, S. (1987b). The VisionQuest program: An evaluation (R-3445-OJJDP). Office of Juvenile Justice and Delinquency Prevention, U.S. Department of Justice, Washington, DC.

Groth, A. N. (1979). Sexual trauma in the life histories of rapists and child molesters. *Victimology: An International Journal, 4*, 10–16.

Groth, A. N. (1978). Patterns of sexual assault against children and adolescents. In A. W. Burgess, A. N. Groth, L. L. Holmstrom, & S. M. Sgroi (Eds.), *Sexual assault of children and adolescents.* Lexington, MA: Lexington Books.

Guarino, G. S., & Kimball, L. M. (1998). Juvenile sex offenders in treatment. *Corrections Management Quarterly*, 2, 45–54.

Hagan, J., & Dinovitzer, R. (1999). Collateral consequences of imprisonment. In M. Tonry & J. Petersilia (Eds.), *Crime and justice: A review of research* (Vol. 26, pp. 121–162). Chicago: University of Chicago Press.

Hall, N. G. (1995). Sexual offender recidivism revisited: A meta-analysis of recent treatment studies. *Journal of Consulting and Clinical Psychology, 63*, 802–809.

Hamberger, L. K., & Hastings, J. E. (1988). Skills training for treatment of spouse abusers: An outcome study. *Journal of Family Violence, 3*(2), 121–130.

Hanson, R. K., & Bussiere, M. T. (1998). Predicting relapse: A meta-analysis of recent treatment studies. *Journal of Consulting and Clinical Psychology, 66*, 348–362.

Hanson, R. K., Steffy, R. A., & Gauthier, R. (1993). Long-term recidivism of child molesters. *Journal of Consulting and Clinical Psychology, 61*(4), 646–652.

Harer, M. D. (1995a). *Prison education program participation and recidivism: A test of the normalization hypothesis.* Washington, DC: Federal Bureau of Prisons, Office of Research and Evaluation.

Harer, M. D. (1995b). Recidivism among federal prisoners released in 1987. *Journal of Correctional Education, 46*, 98–127.

Harer, M. D., & Klein-Saffran, J. (1996). *An evaluation of the Federal Bureau of Prisons Lewisburg Intensive Confinement Center.* Washington, DC: Federal Bureau of Prisons, Research and Evaluation.

Harland, A. T. (1996). *Choosing correctional options that work: Defining the demand and evaluating the supply.* Thousand Oaks, CA: Sage.

Harrell, A., Hirst, A., Mitchell, O., Marlowe, D., & Merrill, J. (2001). *Evaluation of the breaking the cycle demonstration in Birmingham, Alabama: Final report.* Washington, DC: Urban Institute.

Harrell, A., Roman, J., & Sack, E. (2001). *Evaluation of the Brooklyn Treatment Court: 1996–1999.* Washington, DC: Urban Institute.

Harrison, R. S., Parsons, B. V., Byrnes, E. I., & Sahami, S. (n.d.). *Salt Lake County drug court evaluation report July, 1996 through September, 1998.* Salt Lake City, UT: University of Utah, Social Research Institute.

Hartmann, D. J., Wolk, J. L., Johnston, L. S., & Colyer, C. J. (1997). Recidivism and substance abuse outcomes in a prison-based therapeutic community. *Federal Probation, 61,* 18–25.

Healey, K., Smith, C., & O'Sullivan, C. (1998). *Batterer intervention: Program approaches and criminal justice strategies.* Washington, DC: National Institute of Justice.

Henggeler, S. W., & Bourdin, C. M. (1990). *Family therapy and beyond: A multisystemic approach to treating the behaviour problems of children and adolescents.* Pacific Grove, CA: Brooks/Cole.

Henggeler, S. W., Bourdin, C. M., Melton, G. B., Mann, B. J., Smith, L. A., Hall, J. A., Cone, L., & Fucci, B. R. (1991). Effects of multisystemic therapy on drug use and abuse in serious juvenile offenders: A progress report from two outcome studies. *Family Dynamics of Addiction Quarterly, 1*(3), 40–51.

Henggeler, S. W., Cligempeel, W. G., Brondino, M. J., & Pickrel, S. G. (2002). Four year follow-up of multisystemic therapy with substance abusing and dependent juvenile offenders. *Journal of the American Academy of Child and Adolescent Psychiatry, 41,* 868–874.

Henggeler, S. W., Metlon, G. B., Brondino, M. J., Scherer, D. G., & Hanley, J. H. (1997). Multisystemic therapy with violent and chronic juvenile offenders and their families: The role of treatment fidelity in successful dissemination. *Journal of Consulting and Clinical Psychology, 65,* 821–833.

Henggeler, S. W., Melton, G. B., Smith, L. A., Schoenwald, S. K., & Hanley, J. H. (1993). Family preservation using multisystemic therapy: Long-term follow-up to a clinical trial with serious juvenile offenders. *Journal of Child and Family Studies,* 2, 283–293.

Henning, K. R., & Frueh, B. C. (1996). Cognitive-behavioral treatment of incarcerated offenders: An evaluation of the Vermont Department of Corrections cognitive self-change program. *Criminal Justice and Behavior, 23,* 31–42.

Hildebran, D. D., & Pithers, W. D. (1992). Relapse prevention: Application and outcome. In W. O'Donohue & J. H. Geer (Eds.), *The sexual abuse of children* (2nd ed.). Hillsdale, NJ: Erlbaum.

Hirschel, J. D., & Hutchinson, I. W. (1992). Female spouse abuse and the police response: The Charlotte, North Carolina experiment. *Journal of Criminal Law and Criminology, 83*, 73–119.

Holloway, J., & Moke, P. (1986). *Post-secondary correctional education: An evaluation of parolee performance.* Unpublished manuscript.

Home Builders Institute. (1996). *Project TRADE. A program of training, restitution, apprenticeship, development and education.* Washington, DC: Home Builders Institute.

Horney, J., & Marshall, I. H. (1991). Measuring lambda through self-reports. Rand methodology. *Criminology, 29*, 471–495.

Horney, J., Osgood, W. D., & Marshall-Ineke, H. (1995). Criminal careers in the short-term: Intra-individual variability in crime and its relation to local life circumstances. *American Sociological Review, 60*, 655–673.

Hughey, R., & Klemke, L. W. (1996). Evaluation of a jail-based substance abuse treatment program. *Federal Probation, 60*, 40–44.

Hull, K. A. (1995). Analysis of recidivism rates for participants of the academic/vocational/transition education programs offered by the Virginia Department of Correctional Education. Richmond, VA: Commonwealth of Virginia Department of Correctional Education.

Hull, K. A., Forrester, S., Brown, J., Jobe, D., & McCullen, C. (2000). Analysis of recidivism rates for participants of the academic/vocational/transition education programs offered by the Virginia Department of Correctional Education. *Journal of Correctional Education, 51*, 256–261.

Huot, S. (1999). *Sex offender treatment and recidivism.* Minnesota Department of Corrections, St. Paul.

Husband, S. D., & Platt, J. J. (1993). The cognitive skills component in substance abuse treatment in correctional settings: A brief review. *Journal of Drug Issues, 23*, 31–42.

Inciardi, J. A. (1996). The therapeutic community: An effective model for corrections-based drug abuse treatment. In K. E. Early (Ed.), *Drug treatment behind bars: Prison-based strategies for change* (pp. 65–74). Westport, CT: Praeger.

Inciardi, J. A., Martin, S. S., Butzin, C. A., Hooper, R. M., & Harrison, L. D. (1997). An effective model of prison-based treatment for drug-involved offenders. *Journal of Drug Issues, 27*, 261–278.

Izzo, R. L., & Ross, R. R. (1990). Meta-analysis of rehabilitation programs for juvenile delinquents. *Criminal Justice and Behavior, 17*, 134–142.

Jaffe, P. G., Hastings, E., Reitzel, D., & Austin, G. W. (1993). The impact of police laying charges. In N. Z. Hilton (Ed.), *Legal responses to wife assault: Current trends and evaluation* (pp. 62–95). Newbury Park, CA: Sage.

Jeffords, C. R., & McNitt, S. (1993). *The relationship between GED attainment and recidivism.* Texas Youth Commission Department of Research and Planning, Austin.

Johnson, G. D., Formichella, C. M., & Bowers, D. A. Jr. (1998). Do drug courts work? An outcome evaluation of a promising program. *Journal of Applied Sociology, 15*(1), 44–62.

Johnson, G., & Hunter, R. M. (1995). Evaluation of the specialized drug offender program. In R. R. Ross & B. Ross (Eds.), *Thinking straight* (pp. 215–234). Ottawa, Canada: Cognitive Center.

Johnson, S., & Latessa, E. J. (2000). *The Hamilton County drug court: Outcome evaluation findings.* Cincinnati, OH: University of Cincinnati, Center for Criminal Justice Research.

Jolin, A., & Stipak, B. (1991). *Clackamas County community corrections intensive drug program: Program evaluation report.* Portland, OR: Portland State University, Department of Public Administration.

Jones, M. (1996). Do boot camp graduates make better probationers? *Journal of Crime and Justice, 19,* 1–14.

Jones, M., & Ross, D. L. (1997). Is less better? Boot camp, regular probation and rearrest in North Carolina. *American Journal of Criminal Justice, 21,* 147–161.

Jones, R. J. (1998). *Annual report to the governor and the general assembly: Impact incarceration program.* Springfield, IL: Illinois Department of Corrections.

Kelly, F. J., & Baer, D. J. (1971, October). Physical challenge as a treatment for delinquency. *Crime and Delinquency,* 437–445.

Kempinen, C., & Kurlychek, M. (2003). An outcome evaluation of Pennsylvania's boot camp: Does rehabilitative programming within a disciplinary setting reduce recidivism? *Crime and Delinquency, 49,* 581–602.

Kirkpatrick, B. L. H. (1996). Cognitive restructuring: Effects on recidivism (Doctoral dissertation, Ball State University, 1996). *Dissertation Abstracts International, 57,* 2680).

Knight, K., Simpson, D. D., & Hiller, M. (1999). Three-year reincarceration outcomes for in-prison therapeutic community treatment in Texas. *Prison Journal, 79,* 337–351.

Knight, R. A. (1988). A taxonomic analysis of child molesters. In R. A. Prentky & V. L. Quinsey (Eds.), *Human sexual aggression: Current perspectives.* New York: New York Academy of Science.

Knight, R. A., & Prentky, R. A. (1990). The developmental antecedents and adult adaptations of rapist subtypes. *Criminal Justice and Behavior, 14,* 403–426.

Knott, C. (1995). The STOP Programme: Reasoning and rehabilitation in a British setting. In J. McGuire (Ed.), *What works: Reducing reoffending – Guidelines from research and practice* (pp. 115–126). New York: Wiley.

Koch Crime Institute. (2001), http://www.kci.org/forms/kccreach.htm.

Kohlberg, L. (1976). Moral stages and moralization: The cognitive developmental approach. In T. Lockona (Ed.), *Moral development and behavior:*

Theory, research and social issue (pp. 31–53). New York: Holt, Rinehart, & Winston.

Krueger, S. (1997). Five-year recidivism study of MRT-treated offenders in a county jail. *Cognitive-Behavioral Treatment Review, 6*, 3.

Lab, S. P., Shields, G., & Schondel, C. (1993). Research note: An evaluation of juvenile sexual offender treatment. *Crime and Delinquency, 39*, 543–553.

Land, K. C. M. P. L., & Williams, J. R. (1990). Something that works in juvenile justice: An evaluation of the North Carolina court counselors' intensive protective supervision randomized experimental project, 1987–1989. *Evaluation Review, 14*(6), 574–605.

Langenbach, M., North, M. Y., Aagaard, L., & Chown, W. (1990). Televised instruction in Oklahoma prisons: A study of recidivism and disciplinary actions. *Journal of Correctional Education, 41*, 87–94.

Langevin, R., Paitich, D., Hucker, S., Newman, S., Ramsay, G., Pope, S., Geller, G., & Anderson, C. (1979). The effect of assertiveness training, provera and sex of therapist in the treatment of genital exhibitionism. *Journal of Behavior Therapy and Experimental Psychiatry, 10*, 275–282.

Latessa, E. J. (1993a). *An evaluation of the Lucas County adult probation department's IDU & high risk groups.* Cincinnati, OH: University of Cincinnati, Department of Criminal Justice.

Latessa, E. J. (1993b). *Profile of the special units of the Lucas County adult probation department.* Cincinnati, OH: University of Cincinnati, Department of Criminal Justice.

Latessa, E. J. (1991). *A preliminary evaluation of the Cuyahoga County adult probation department's intensive supervision groups.* Cincinnati, OH: University of Cincinnati, Department of Criminal Justice.

Latessa, E. J., Travis, L., Fulton, B., & Stichman, A. (1998). *Evaluating the prototypical ISP: Final report.* Cincinnati, OH: University of Cincinnati, Division of Criminal Justice.

Lattimore, P. K., Witte, A. D., & Baker, J. R. (1990). Experimental assessment of the effect of vocational training on youthful property offenders. *Evaluation Review, 14*, 115–133.

Laws, D. R. (1995). Central elements in relapse prevention procedures with sex offenders. *Crime and Law*, 2, 41–53.

Lee, K. M. (1983). *The Wichita work release center: An evaluative study (Kansas).* Unpublished doctoral dissertation, Kansas State University.

Leschied, A. W., Bernfeld, G. A., & Farrington, D. P. (2001). Implementation issues. In G. A. Bernfeld, D. P. Farrington, & A. W. Leschied (Eds.), *Offender rehabilitation in practice* (pp. 3–19). Chichester, England: Wiley.

Levitt, S. (1996). The effect of prison population size on crime rates: Evidence from prison overcrowding litigation. *Quarterly Journal of Economics, 111*(2), 319–351.

Lilly, J. R., Cullen, F. T., & Ball, R. A. (2002). *Criminological theory: Context and consequences.* Thousand Oaks, CA: Sage.

Linden, R., & Perry, L. (1983). The effectiveness of prison education programs. *Journal of Offender Counseling, Services and Rehabilitation, 6,* 43–57.

Linden, R., Perry, L., Ayers, D., & Parlett, T. A. (1984). An evaluation of a prison education program. *Canadian Journal of Criminology, 26,* 65–73.

Lindsey, M., McBride, R. W., & Platt, C. M. (1993). *Amend: Philosophy and curriculum for treating batterers.* Littleton, CO: Gylantic.

Lipsey, M. W. (1995). What do we learn from 400 research studies on the effectiveness of treatment with juvenile delinquents? In J. McGuire (Ed.), *What works? Reducing offending* (pp. 63–78). New York: Wiley.

Lipsey, M. W. (1992). Juvenile delinquency treatment: A meta-analytic inquiry into the variability of effects. In T. D. Cook, H. Cooper, D. S. Cordray, H. Hartmann, L. V. Hedges, R. J. Light, T. A. Louis, & F. Mosteller (Ed.), *Meta-analysis for explanation: A casebook.* New York: Russell Sage Foundation.

Lipsey, M. W., & Wilson, D. B. (2001). *Practical meta-analysis.* Thousand Oaks, CA: Sage.

Lipsey, M. W., & Wilson, D. B. (1998). Effective intervention for serious juvenile offenders: A synthesis of research. In R. Loeber & D. Farrington (Eds.), *Serious and violent juvenile offenders: Risk factors and successful interventions* (pp. 313–345). Thousand Oaks, CA: Sage.

Lipsey, M. W., & Wilson, D. B. (1993). The efficacy of psychological, educational, and behavioral treatment: Confirmation from meta-analysis. *American Psychologist,* 48, 1181–1209.

Lipton, D., Martinson, R., & Wilkes, L. (1975). *The effectiveness of correctional treatment and what works: A survey of treatment evaluation studies.* New York: Praeger.

Littell, J. H. (2005 August). A systematic review of effects of multisystemic therapy. Paper presented at the 14th World Congress of Criminology, University of Pennsylvania.

Little, G. L., & Robinson, K. D. (1989). Treating drunk drivers with moral reconation therapy: A one-year recidivism report. *Psychological Reports, 64,* 960–962.

Little, G. L., & Robinson, K. D. (1988). Moral reconation therapy: A systematic step-by-step. *Psychological Reports, 62,* 135–151.

Little, G. L., Robinson, K. D., & Burnette, K. D. (1994). Treating offenders with cognitive-behavioral therapy: 5-year recidivism report. *Cognitive-Behavioral Treatment Review, 3,* 1–3.

Little, G. L., Robinson, K. D., & Burnette, K. D. (1993a). 42 month alcohol treatment data: Multiple DWI offenders treated with MRT show lower recidivism rates. *Cognitive-Behavioral Treatment Review,* 2, 5.

Little, G. L., Robinson, K. D., & Burnette, K. D. (1993b). Cognitive behavioral treatment of felony drug offenders: A five-year recidivism report. *Psychological Reports, 73*, 1089–1090.

Little, G. L., Robinson, K. D., & Burnette, K. D. (1991a). Treating drug offenders with moral reconation therapy: A three-year recidivism report. *Psychological Reports, 69*, 953–954.

Little, G. L., Robinson, K. D., & Burnette, K. D. (1991b). Treating drunk drivers with moral reconation therapy: A three-year report. *Psychological Reports, 69*, 953–954.

Little, G. L., Robinson, K. D., & Burnette, K. D. (1990). Treating drunk drivers with moral reconation therapy: A two-year recidivism study. *Psychological Reports, 66*, 1379–1387.

Little, G. L., Robinson, K. D., Burnette, K. D., & Swan, S. (1996). Review of outcome data with MRT: Seven year recidivism results. *Cognitive-Behavioral Treatment Review, 5*, 1–7.

Little, G. L., Robinson, K. D., Burnette, K. D., & Swan, S. (1995a). Seven-year recidivism of felony offenders treated with MRT. *Cognitive-Behavioral Treatment Review, 4*, 6.

Little, G. L., Robinson, K. D., Burnette, K. D., & Swan, S. (1995b). Six-year MRT recidivism data on felons and DWI offenders: Treated offenders show significantly lower reincarceration. *Cognitive-Behavioral Treatment Review, 4*(1), 4–5.

Lo, C. C., & Stephens, R. C. (2000). Drugs and prisoners: Treatment needs on entering prison. *American Journal of Drug and Alcohol Abuse, 26*, 229–245.

Lockwood, D. (1991). Prison higher education and recidivism: A program evaluation. In *Yearbook of Correctional Education* (pp. 187–201). Burnaby, BC, Canada: Simon Fraser University, Institute for the Humanities.

Losel, F. (1995a). The efficacy of correctional treatment: A review and synthesis of meta-evaluations. In J. McGuire (Ed.), *What works: Reducing reoffending – Guidelines from research and practice* (pp. 79–111). New York: Wiley.

Losel, F. (1995b). Increasing consensus in the evaluation of offender rehabilitation? Lessons from recent research synthesis. *Psychology, Crime, and Law*, 2, 19–39.

Losel, F., & Koferl, P. (1989). Evaluation research on correctional treatment in West Germany: A meta-analysis. In H. Wegener, F. Losel, & J. Haisch (Eds.), *Criminal behavior and the justice system: Psychological perspectives* (pp. 334–355). New York: Springer Verlag.

Luftig, J. T. (1978). Vocational education in prison: An alternative to recidivism. *Journal of Studies in Technical Careers, 1*, 31–42.

Lurigio, A. J., & Petersilia, J. (1992). The emergence of intensive probation supervision programs in the United States. In J. M. Byrne, A. J. Lurigio, &

J. Petersilia (Eds.), *Smart sentencing: The emergence of intermediate sanctions* (pp. 3–17). Newbury Park, CA: Sage.

Lynch, J. P., & Sabol, W. J. 2000. Prison use and social control. In J. Horney (Ed.), *Policies, processes, and decisions of the criminal justice system: Criminal justice 2000* (Vol. 3, pp. 7–44). Washington, DC: National Institute of Justice.

Maciekowich, Z. D. (1976). Academic education/vocational training and recidivism of adult prisoners (Doctoral dissertation, Arizona State University, 1976). *Dissertation Abstracts International, 37-08A,* 5080–5195.

MacKenzie, D. L. 2005. The importance of using scientific evidence to make decisions about correctional programming. *Criminology and Public Policy, 4*(2), 1001–1010.

MacKenzie, D. L. (2001). Corrections and sentencing in the 21st century: evidence-based corrections and sentencing. *Prison Journal, 81,* 299–312.

MacKenzie, D. L. (2000). Evidence-based corrections: Identifying what works. *Crime and Delinquency, 46*(4), 457–471.

MacKenzie, D. L. (2002). Reducing the criminal activities of known offenders and delinquents: Crime prevention in the courts and corrections. In W. L. Sherman, B. C. Welsch, D. P. Farrington & D. L. MacKenzie (Eds.), *Evidence-Based Crime Prevention,* London, UK: Harwood Academic Publishers.

MacKenzie, D. L. (1997). Criminal justice and crime prevention. In L. W. Sherman, D. Gottfredson, D. L. MacKenzie, J. Eck, P. Reuter, & S. Bushway (Eds.), *Preventing crime: What works, what doesn't, what's promising* (Report to the U.S. Congress). Washington, DC: National Institute of Justice.

MacKenzie, D. L. (1989). Prison classification: The management and psychological perspectives. In L. Goodstein & D. MacKenzie (Eds.), *The American prison: Issues in research and policy.* New York: Plenum Press.

MacKenzie, D. L., Brame, R., McDowall, D., & Souryal, C. (1995). Boot camp prisons and recidivism in eight states. *Criminology, 33,* 327–357.

MacKenzie, D. L., Browning, K., Priu, H., Skroban, S., & Smith, D. (1998). Probationer compliance with conditions of supervision. Unpublished report. Washington, DC: National Institute of Justice, U.S. Department of Justice.

MacKenzie, D. L., Browning, K., Skroban, S., & Smith, D. (1999). The impact of probation on the criminal activities of offenders. *Journal of Research in Crime and Delinquency, 36*(4), 423–453.

MacKenzie, D. L., & S. D. Li. (2002). The impact of formal and informal social controls on the criminal activities of probationers. *Journal of Research in Crime and Delinquency, 39*(3), 243–276.

Mackenzie, D. L., & Hebert, E. E. (1996). *Correctional boot camps: A tough intermediate sanction.* Washington, DC: National Institute of Justice, U.S. Department of Justice.

MacKenzie, D. L., & L. J. Hickman. (1998). *What works in corrections? An examination of the effectiveness of the type of rehabilitation programs offered by Washington State Department of Corrections* (Report to the State of Washington Legislature Joint Audit and Review Committee). College Park, MD: University of Maryland.

MacKenzie, D. L., & Parent, D. (1992). Boot camp prisons for young offenders. In *Smart sentencing: The emergence of intermediate sanctions.* Newbury Park, CA: Sage.

MacKenzie, D. L., & Parent. D. (1991). Shock incarceration and prison overcrowding in Louisiana. *Journal of Criminal Justice, 19,* 225–237.

MacKenzie, D. L., & Piquero, A. (1994). The impact of shock incarceration programs on prison overcrowding. *Crime and Delinquency, 40,* 222–249.

MacKenzie, D. L., & Shaw, J. W. (1990). Inmate adjustment and change during shock incarceration. *Justice Quarterly,* 7, 125–150.

MacKenzie, D. L., & Souryal, C. (1995). Inmate attitude change during incarceration: A comparison of boot camp with traditional prison. *Justice Quarterly, 12,* 325–354.

MacKenzie, D. L., Souryal, C., Sealock, M., & Bin Kashem, M. (1997). *Outcome study of the Sergeant Henry Johnson Youth Leadership Academy (YLA).* Washington, DC: University of Maryland, National Institute of Justice, U.S. Department of Justice.

MacKenzie, D. L., Tracy, G. S., & Williams, G. (1988). Incarceration rates and demographic changes: A test of the demographic change hypothesis. *Journal of Criminal Justice, 16,* 241–253.

MacKenzie, D. L., Wilson, D. B., Armstrong, G. S., & Gover, A. (2001). The impact of boot camps and traditional institutions on juvenile residents: Adjustment, perception of the environment and changes in social bonds, impulsivity, and antisocial attitudes. *Journal of Research in Crime and Delinquency, 38*(3), 279–313.

MacKenzie, D. L., Wilson, D. B., & Kider, S. B. (2001). Effects of correctional boot camps on offending. *Annals of the American Academy of Political and Social Sciences, 578 (Nov),* 126–143.

Maguire, K. E., Flanagan, T. J., & Thornberry, T. P. (1988). Prison labor and recidivism. *Journal of Quantitative Criminology, 4,* 3–18.

Magura, S., Nwakeze, P. C., Kang, S. Y., & Demsky, S. (1999). Program quality effects on patient outcomes during methadone maintenance: A study of 17 clinics. *Substance Use Misuse, 34*(9), 1299–1327.

Magura, S., Rosenblum, A. L. C., & Joseph, H. (1993). The effectiveness of in-jail methadone maintenance. *Journal of Drug Issues, 23,* 75–99.

Mahoney, M. J., & Arnkoff, D. B. (1978). Cognitive and self-control therapies. In S. L. Garfield & A. E. Bergin (Eds.), *Handbook of psychotherapy and behavior change: An empirical analysis* (pp. 689–722). New York: Wiley.

Maletzky, B. M. (1991). The use of medoxyprogesterone acetate to assist in the treatment of sexual offenders. *Annals of Sex Research, 4,* 117–129.

Marcus-Mendoza, S. T. (1995). Preliminary investigation of Oklahoma's shock incarceration program. *Journal of the Oklahoma Criminal Justice Research Consortium,* 2, 44–49.

Marques, J. K., Day, D. M., Nelson, C., & West, M. A. (1994). Effects of cognitive-behavioral treatment on sex offender recidivism. *Criminal Justice and Behavior, 21,* 28–34.

Marquis, H. A., Bourgon, G. A., Armstrong, B., & Pfaff, J. (1996). Reducing recidivism through institutional treatment programs. *Forum on Corrections Research, 8,* 3–5.

Marquis, J. K. (1981). *Quality of prisoner self-reports, arrest and conviction response errors.* Santa Monica, CA: Rand.

Marshall, W. L., & Barbaree, H. E. (1988). The long-term evaluation of a behavioral treatment program for child molesters. *Behavior Research & Therapy, 26,* 499–511.

Marshall, W. L., Eccles, A., & Barbaree, H. E. (1991). The treatment of exhibitionists: A focus on sexual deviance versus cognitive and relationship features. *Behavior Research and Therapy, 29,* 129–135.

Marshall, W. L., Jones, R., Ward, T., Johnston, P., & Barbaree, H. E. (1991). Treatment outcome with sex offenders. *Clinical Psychology Review, 11,* 465–485.

Martinson, R. (1979). What works: Questions and answers about prison reform. *Public Interest, 35,* 22–54.

Martinson, R. (1976). California research at the crossroads. *Crime and Delinquency,* 22, 178–191.

Martinson, R. (1974). What works? Questions and answers about prison reform. *Public Interest, 10,* 22–54.

Marvell, T. B., & Moody, C. E. (1998). The impact of out-of-state prison population on state homicide rates: Displacement and free-rider effects. *Criminology, 36*(3), 513–531.

Marvell, T. B., & Moody, C. E. (1994). Prison population and crime reduction. *Journal of Quantitative Criminology, 10,* 109–139.

McConaghy, N., Blasczynski, A., & Kidson, W. (1988). Treatment of sex offenders with imaginal desensitization and /or medroxyprogesterone. *Acta Psychiatrica Scandinavica,* 77, 199–206.

McFall, R. M. (1990). The enhancement of social skills: An information-processing analysis. In W. L. Marshall, D. R. Laws, & H. E. Barbaree (Eds.), Handbook of sexual assault: Issues, theories, and treatment of the offender (pp. 311–330). New York: Plenum.

McGee, C. J. (1997). *The positive impact of corrections education on recidivism and employment.* Springfield, IL: Illinois Department of Corrections and Illinois Council on Vocational Education.

McGrath, R. J., Hoke, S. E., & Vojtisek, J. E. (1998). Cognitive-behavioral treatment of sex offenders: A treatment comparison and long-term follow-up study. *Criminal Justice and Behavior, 25*, 203–225.

McKelvey, B. (1972). *American prisons: A study in American social history prior to 1915.* Montclair, NJ: Patterson Smith Publishing.

McNeece, C. A., & Byers, J. B. (1995). *Hillsborough County drug court two year follow-up study.* Tallahassee, FL: Florida State University, Institute for Health and Human Services Research.

Melton, R., & Pennell, S. (1998). *Staying out successfully: An evaluation of an in-custody life skills training program.* San Diego, CA: San Diego Association of Governments.

Menon, R., Blakely, C., Carmichael, D., & Silver, L. (1992). *An evaluation of Project RIO outcomes: An evaluative report.* College Station, TX: Texas A&M University, Public Policy Resources Laboratory.

Menton, P. C. (1999). The effect of a domestic violence program on incarcerated batterers (Doctoral dissertation, Boston University, 1999). *Dissertation Abstracts International, 59*, 3217.

Meyer, W. J., Cole, C., & Emory, E. (1992). Depo provera treatment for sex offending behavior: An evaluation of outcome. *Bulletin of the American Academy of Psychiatry and Law, 20*, 249–259.

Miethe, T. D., Lu, H., & Reese, E. (2000). Reintegrative shaming and recidivism risks in drug court: Explanations for some unexpected findings. *Crime and Delinquency, 46*(4), 522–541.

Milhalic, S. W., & Elliott, D. (1997). A social learning theory model of marital violence. *Journal of Family Violence, 12*, 21–47.

Milkman, R. H., Timrots, A. D., Peyser, A. V., Toborg, M. A., Gottlieb, B. E., Yezer, A. M. J., et al. (1985). *Employment services for ex-offenders field test: Summary report* (Report to the National Institute of Justice). McLean, VA: Lazar Institute.

Miller, M. (1997). *Evaluation of the life skills program.* Division of Correctional Education, Delaware State Department of Corrections, Dover.

Miller, M. (1995). The Delaware life skills program: Evaluation report. *Cognitive-Behavioral-Treatment Review, 4*, 1–4.

Miller, M. L., Scocas, E. A., & O'Connell, J. P. (1998). *Evaluation of the juvenile drug court diversion program.* Dover, DE: Statistical Analysis Center.

Minnesota Department of Corrections. (1987). *Transistional sex offender program.* St. Paul, MN: Minnesota Department of Corrections.

Minor, K. I., & Elrod, H. P. (1990). The effects of a multi-faceted intervention on the offense activities of juvenile probationers. *Journal of Offender Counseling, Services and Rehabilitation, 15*(2), 87–108.

Miranne, A. C., & Geerken, M. R. (1991). The New Orleans inmate survey: A test of Greenwood's predictive scale. *Criminology, 29*(3), 497–518.

Mitchell, O., & MacKenzie, D. L. (2003). Crime prevention via prison-based drug treatment: A systematic review and assessment of the research. In H. Kury & J. Obergfell-Fuchs (Eds.), *Crime prevention: New approaches.* Weberstrabe, Mainz: Weisser Ring, Germany.

Mitchell, O., MacKenzie, D. L., & Wilson, D. B. (2005). The effectiveness of incarceration-based drug treatment: An empirical synthesis of the research. In D. P. Farrington & B. C. Welsh (Eds.), *In preventing crime: What works for children, offenders, victims, and places.* Belmont, CA: Wadsworth.

Mitchell, C., Zehr, J., & Butler, C. (1987). *Intensive supervision/high risk parole: Utah Department of Corrections. Crime and juvenile delinquency: 1987 update.* Ann Arbor, MI: University Microfilms International.

M M Bell, Inc. (1998). *King County drug court evaluation: Final report.* Seattle, WA: M M Bell, Inc.

Moody, E. E., Jr. (1997). Lessons of pair counseling with incarcerated juvenile delinquents. *Journal of Addictions and Offender Counseling, 18,* 10–25.

Moon, M. M., & Latessa, E. J. (1994). Drug treatment in adult probation: An evaluation of an outpatient and acupunture program. *Evaluation and Program Planning, 17*(2), 217–226.

Money, J. (1980). *Love and love sickness.* Baltimore, MD: Johns Hopkins University Press.

Money, J. A., Wideling, P. S., Walker, & Gain, D. (1976). Combined antiandrogenic and counseling program for treatment of 46 XY and 47 XYY sex offenders. In E. J. Sachar (Ed.), *Hormones, behavior and psychopathology.* New York: Raven Press.

Morash, M., & Rucker, L. (1990). A critical look at the idea of boot camp as correctional reform. *Crime and Delinquency, 36,* 204–222.

Morris, N., & Tonry, M. (1990). *Between prison and probation: Intermediate punishments in a rational sentencing system.* New York: Oxford University Press.

Mumola, C. J. (1999). *Substance abuse and treatment, state and federal prisoners, 1997.* Washington, DC: Bureau of Justice Statistics.

Murphy, C. M., Musser, P. H., & Maton, K. I. (1998). Coordinated community intervention for domestic abusers: Intervention system involvement and criminal recidivism. *Journal of Family Violence, 13,* 263–284.

National Institute of Justice. (2003) *2000: Arrestee drug abuse monitoring: Annual report.* Retrieved January 13, 2005, from http://www.ojp.usdoj.gov/nij/.

Needels, K. (1996). Go directly to jail and do not collect? A long-term study of recidivism, employment and earnings patterns among prison releasees. *Journal of Research on Crime and Delinquency, 33*, 471–496.

Nicholaichuk, T. (1996). Sex offender treatment priority: An illustration of the risk/need principle. *Forum, 8*, 30–32.

Nicholaichuk, T., Gordon, A., Andre, G., & Gu, D. (1995, Nov). Long-term outcome of the Clearwater sex offender treatment. Paper presented to the 14th Annual Conference of the Association for the Treatment of Sexual Abusers, New Orleans, LA.

Nielson, A. L., & Scarpitti, F. R. (1997, Spring). Changing the behavior of substance abusers: Factors influencing the effectiveness of therapeutic communities. *Journal of Drug Issues, 27*, 279–298.

O'Neil, M. (1990). Correctional higher education: Reduced recidivism? *Journal of Correctional Education, 41*, 28–31.

Oregon Department of Corrections. (1994). *Comparison of outcomes and costs residential and outpatient treatment programs for inmates alcohol and drug, mental health, sex offender, and social skills treatment.* Corrections Treatment Program and Corrections Treatment Services Executive Summary. Salem, OR: Oregon Department of Corrections.

Palmer, T. (1996). Programmatic and nonprogrammatic aspects of successful implementation. In A. T. Harland (Ed.), *Choosing correctional options that work: Defining the demand and evaluating the supply* (pp. 131–182). Thousand Oaks, CA: Sage.

Palmer, T. (1992). *The re-emergence of correctional intervention.* Newbury Park, CA: Sage.

Palmer, T. (1983). The "effectiveness" issue today: An overview. *Federal Probation, 47*, 3–10.

Palmer, T. (1975). Martinson revisited. *Journal of Research in Crime and Delinquency, 12*, 133–152.

Palmer, S. E., Brown, R. A., & Barrera, M. E. (1992). Group treatment for abusive husbands: Long term evaluation. *American Journal of Orthopsychiatry, 62*, 276–283.

Pate, A. M., & Hamilton, E. E. (1992). Formal and informal deterrents to domestic violence: The Dade County spouse assault experiment. *American Sociological Review, 57*, 691–697.

Pearson, F. S. (1987). *Final report of research on New Jerseys's intensive supervision program.* New Brunswick, NJ: Rutgers – the State University of New Jersey, Department of Sociology.

Pearson, F. S., & Lipton, D. S. (1999). A meta-analytic review of the effectiveness of corrections-based treatment for drug abuse. *Prison Journal, 79*, 384–410.

Pelissier, B. M., Gaes, G., Rhodes, W., Camp, S., O'Neil, J., Wallace, S., & Saylor, W. (1998). *TRIAD drug treatment evaluation project, six-month interim report.* Federal Bureau of Prisons, Office of Research and Evaluation, Washington, DC.

Pence, E. (1989). Batterer programs: Shifting from community collusion to community confrontation. In P. L. Caesar & L. K. Hamberger (Eds.), *Treating men who batter: Theory, practice, and programs* (pp. 24–50). New York: Springer.

Peters, M. (1996a). *Evaluation of the impact of boot camps for juvenile offenders: Denver interim report.* Fairfax, VA: Office of Juvenile Justice and Delinquency Prevention, U.S. Department of Justice.

Peters, M. (1996b). *Evaluation of the impact of boot camps for juvenile offenders: Mobile interim report.* Fairfax, VA: Office of Juvenile Justice and Delinquency Prevention, U.S. Department of Justice.

Peters, R. H., Greenbaum, P. E., Edens, J. F., Carter, C. R., & Ortiz, M. M. (1998). Prevalence of DSM-IV substance abuse and dependence disorders among prison inmates. *American Journal of Drug and Alcohol Abuse, 24*, 573–587.

Peters, R. H., Kearns, W. D., Murrin, M. R., Dolente, A. S., & May, R. L. II. (1993). Examining the effectiveness of in-jail substance abuse treatment. *Journal of Offender Rehabilitation, 19*, 1–39.

Peters, R. H., & Murrin, M. R. (2000). Effectiveness of treatment-based drug courts in reducing criminal recidivism. *Criminal Justice and Behavior, 27*(1), 72–96.

Petersilia, J. (2004). What works in prisoner reentry? Reviewing and questioning the evidence. *Federal Probation, 68*(2), 4–8.

Petersilia, J., & Greenwood, P. (1978). Mandatory prison sentences: Their projected effects on crime and prison populations. *Journal of Criminal Law and Criminology, 69*, 604–615.

Petersilia, J., & Turner, S. (1993). Intensive probation and parole. *Crime and Justice, 17*, 281–335.

Petersilia, J., & Turner, S. (1992). An evaluation of intensive probation in California. *Journal of Criminal Law and Criminology, 82*(3), 610–658.

Peterson, M. A., & Braiker, H. B. (1980). *Doing crime: A survey of California prison inmates* (Report R-2200-DOJ). Santa Monica, CA: Rand Corporation.

Peterson, M. A., Braiker, H. B., & Polich, S. M. (1981). *Who commits crimes: A survey of prison inmates.* Cambridge, MA: Oelgeschlager, Gunn, and Hain.

Peterson, M. A., Chaiken, J., Ebener, P., & Honig, P. (1982). *Survey of prison and jail inmates: Background and methods.* Santa Monica, CA: Rand Corporation.

Petrosino, A., Boruch, R. F., Farrington, D., Sherman, L., & Weisburd, D. (2003). Towards evidence-based criminology and criminal justice: Systematic reviews and the Campbell Collaboration crime and justice group. *International Journal of Comparative Criminology, 3*, 18–41.

Petrosino, A., Boruch, R. F., Soydan, H., Duggan, L., & Sanchez-Meca, J. (2001). Meeting the challenges of evidence-based policy: The Campbell Collaboration, *The Annals of the American Academy of Political and Social Science, 578*, 14–34.

Petrosino, A., Turpin-Petrosino, C., & Buehler, J. (2003, September). Scared Straight and other juvenile awareness programs for preventing juvenile delinquency: A systematic review of the randomize experimental evidence. *Annals of the American Academy of Political and Social Sciences, 589*, 41–62.

Piaget, J. (1965). *The moral judgement of the child.* New York: Free Press.

Piehl, A. M. (1995). *Learning while doing time.* Unpublished manuscript, John F. Kennedy School of Government, Harvard University, Cambridge, MA.

Platt, J. J., & Labate, C. (1976). *Heroin addiction: Theory, research, and treatment.* New York: Wiley.

Polizzi, D. L., MacKenzie, D. L., & Hickman, L. (1999). What works in adult sex offender treatment? A review of prison and non-prison-based treatment programs. *International Journal of Offender Therapy and Comparative Criminology, 43*, 357–374.

Porporino, F. J., Fabiano, E. A., & Robinson, D. (1991). *Focusing on successful reintegration: Cognitive skills training for offenders, R-19.* Canada: Research and Statistics Branch, Correctional Service of Canada, Ottawa, Ontario.

Porporino, F. J., & Robinson, D. (1995). An evaluation of the reasoning and rehabilitation program with Canadian federal offenders. In R. R. Ross & B. Ross (Eds.), *Thinking straight* (pp. 155–191). Ottawa, Canada: Cognitive Centre.

Porporino, F. J., & Robinson, D. (1992). The correctional benefits of education: A follow-up of Canadian federal offenders participating in ABE. *Journal of Correctional Education, 43*, 92–98.

Postmus, J. L. (2000). Analysis of the family violence option: A strengths perspective. *Journal of Women and Social Work, 15*, 244–259.

Prendergast, M. L., Podus, D., Chang, E., & Urada, D. (2002, June). The effectiveness of drug abuse treatment: A meta-analysis of comparison group studies. *Drug and Alcohol Dependence, 67*(1), 53–73.

President's Commission on Law Enforcement and Administration of Justice. (1967). *Task force report: Corrections.* Washington, DC: U.S. Government Printing Office.

Quinsey, V. L. (1986). Men who have sex with children. In D. N. Weisstub (Ed.), *Law and mental health: International perspectives* (Vol. 2, pp. 140–172). New York: Pergamon.

Quinsey, V. L., & Chaplin, T. C. (1988). Preventing faking in phallometric assessments of sexual preference. In R. Prentky & V. L. Quinsey (Eds.), *Human sexual aggression: Contemporary perspectives: Vol. 528.* New York: New York Academy of Sciences.

Quinsey, V. L., & Earls, C. M. (1990). The modification of sexual preferences. In D. R. L. & H. E. B. W. L. Marshall (Eds.), *Handbook of sexual assault: Issues, theories, and treatment of the offender* (pp. 279–296). New York: Plenum.

Quinsey, V. L., Harris, G., Rice, M., & Lalumiere, M. (1993). Assessing treatment efficacy in outcome studies of sex offenders. *Sex Offender Treatment, 8,* 512–523.

Ramsey, C. (1988). *The value of receiving a General Education Development certificate while incarcerated in the South Carolina Department of Corrections on the rate of recidivism.* Columbia, SC: South Carolina Department of Corrections.

Raynor, P., & Vanstone, M. (1996). Reasoning and rehabilitation in Britain: The results of the Straight Thinking on Probation (STOP) programme. *International Journal of Offender Therapy and Comparative Criminology,* 40, 272–284.

Reagan, M. V., & Stoughton, D. M. (1976). *A descriptive overview of correctional education in the American prison system.* Metuchen, NJ: Scarecrow.

Redondo, S., Sanchez-Meca, J., & Garrido, V. (1999). The influence of treatment programmes on the recidivism of juvenile and adult offenders: An European meta-analytic review. *Psychology, Crime, and Law, 5,* 251–278.

Reichel, P. L., & Sudbrack, B. D. (1994). Differences among eligibles: Who gets an ISP sentence? *Federal Probation, 58*(4), 51–59.

Reitz, K. R. (1998). Sentencing. In M. Tonry (Ed.), *The handbook of crime and punishment* (pp. 542–562). New York: Oxford University Press.

Rennison, C. M. (2001). *Criminal victimization 2000.* Washington, DC: Bureau of Justice Statistics.

Renzema, M. (1992). Home confinement programs: Development, implementation, and impact. In J. M. Byrne, A. J. Lurigio, & J. Petersilia (Eds.), *Smart sentencing: The emergence of intermediate sanctions* (Vol. 41–53). Newbury Park, CA: Sage.

Rhodes, W., & Gross, M. (1997). Case management reduces drug use and criminality among drug-involved arrestees: An experimental study of an HIV prevention intervention. Washington, DC: U.S. National Institute of Justice.

Rice, M. E., Quinsey, V. L., & Harris, G. T. (1991). Sexual recidivism among child molesters released from a maximum security psychiatric institution. *Journal of Counseling and Clinical Psychology, 29,* 381–386.

Rickards, W. (1987). Evaluation report for the pilot project in electronic monitoring with juvenile offenders. Kenosha County Department of Social Services.

Robinson, D. (1995). *The impact of cognitive skills training on post-release recidivism among Canadian federal offenders.* Canada: Correctional Research and Development, Correctional Service of Canada, Ottawa, Ontario.

Robinson, D., Grossman, M., & Porporino, F. (1991). *Effectiveness of the cognitive skills training program: From pilot to national implementation, B-07.* Canada: Research and Statistics Branch, Correctional Service of Canada, Ottawa, Ontario.

Roehl, J. (1998). *Monterey County drug court: Evaluation report #1.* Pacific Grove, CA: Justice Research Center.

Rose, D. R., & Clear, T. R. (1998). Incarceration, social capital, and crime: Implications for social disorganization theory. *Criminology, 36*(3), 441–479.

Rosenfeld, R. (2000). Patterns in adult homicide: 1980–1995. In A. Blumstein & J. Wallman (Eds.), *The crime drop in America* (pp. 130–163). New York: Cambridge University Press.

Rosner, A. (1988). Evaluation of a drinking-driver rehabilitation program for first offenders. In G. Kaiser & I. Geissler (Eds.), *Crime and criminal justice: Criminological research in the 2nd decade at the Max Planck Institute in Freiburg* (pp. 319–336). Frieburg, West Germany: Max-Planck-Institute.

Ross, R. R. (1995). The reasoning and rehabilitation program for high-risk probationers and prisoners. In D. H. A. & G. K. D. R. R. Ross (Eds.), *Going straight: Effective delinquency prevention and offender rehabilitation* (pp. 195–222). Ottawa, Canada: AIR Training and Publications.

Ross, R., Fabiano, E. A., & Ewles, C. D. (1988). Reasoning and rehabilitation. *International Journal of Offender Therapy and Comparative Criminology, 32*, 29–35.

Ross, R., & Fabiano, E. A. (1985). Time to think: A cognitive model of delinquency prevention and offender rehabilitation. Johnson City, TN: Institute of Social Science and Arts.

Ross, R. R., & Gendreau, P. (1980). *Effective correctional treatment.* Toronto, Canada: Butterworths.

Rothman, D. J. (1980). *Conscience and convenience: The asylum and its alternatives in progressive America.* Boston: Little, Brown.

Roy, S., & Brown, M. P. (1995). The juvenile electronic monitoring program in Lake County, Indiana: An evaluation. In J. O. Smykla & W. L. Selke (Eds.), *Intermediate sanctions: Sentencing in the 1990s.* Cincinnati, OH: Anderson Publishing.

Russell, L. C., Sharp, B., & Gilbertson, B. (2000). Acupuncture for addicted patients with chronic histories of arrest. A pilot study of the Consortium Treatment Center. *Journal of Substance Abuse Treatment, 19*(2), 199–205.

Ryan, T. P. (1997). A comparison of recidivism rates for Operation Outward Reach (OOR) participants and control groups of non-participants for the years 1900 through 1994 (Program evaluation report). Youngwood, PA: Operation Outward Reach.

Ryan, T. P. (1990, Nov). *Effects of literacy training on reintegration of offenders.* Paper presented at Freedom to Read, International Conference on Literacy in Corrections, Ottawa, Ontario, Canada.

Sampson, R. J. (1987). Urban black violence: The effect of male joblessness and family disruption. *American Journal of Sociology, 93*(2), 348–382.

Sampson, R. J., & Laub, J. H. (1995). *Crime in the making: Pathways and turning points through life.* Cambirdge, MA: Harvard University Press.

Sampson, R. J., & Laub, J. H. (1990). Crime and deviance over the life course: The salience of adult social bonds. *American Sociological Review, 55*, 609–627.

Sampson, R. J., Raudenbush, S. W., & Earls, F. (1997). Neighborhoods and violent crime: A multilevel study of collective efficacy. *Science,* 277(5328), 918–924.

Sampson, R. J., & Wilson, W. J. (1995). Toward a theory of race, crime, and urban inequality. In J. Hagan & R. D. Peterson (Eds.), *Crime and inequality* (pp. 37–54). Stanford, CA: Stanford University Press.

Sandhu, T. S. (1981). The effectiveness of community-based correctional programs. In H. Sandhu (Ed.), *Community corrections: New horizons* (pp. 296–351). Springfield, IL: BannerStone House.

Santa Clara County Courts. (1997). *Santa Clara County courts drug treatment court: Third progress report one year period (March 1, 1996–March 31, 1997).* Santa Clara, CA: Santa Clara County Courts.

Sapp, A., & Vaughn, M. (1990). Juvenile sex offender treatment at state-operated correctional institutions. *International Journal of Offender Therapy and Comparative Criminology, 34*, 131–146.

Saunders, K. W. (1996). *Violence as obscenity: Limiting the media's first amendment protection.* Durham, NC: Duke University Press.

Saylor, W. G., & Gaes, G. G. (1992). PREP study links UNICOR work experience with successful post-release outcome. Washington, DC: U.S. Federal Bureau of Prisons.

Scherer, D. G., & Brondino, M. J. (1994). Multisystemic family preservation therapy: Preliminary findings from a study of rural and minority serious adolescent offenders. *Journal of Emotional and Behavioral Disorders,* 2(4), 198–206.

Schumacker, R. E., Anderson, D. B., & Anderson, S. L. (1990). Vocational and academic indicators of parole success. *Journal of Correctional Education, 41*, 8–12.

Sealock, M. D., Gottfredson, D. C., & Gallagher, C. A. (1997). Drug treatment for juvenile offenders: Some good and bad news. *Journal of Research in Crime and Delinquency, 34*, 210–236.

Sechrest, D. D. (1989). Prison "boot camps" do not measure up. *Federal Probation, 53*, 15–20.

Sechrest, D. K., Shichor, D., Artist, K., & Briceno, G. (1998). *The Riverside County drug court: Final research report for the Riverside County Probation Department.* San Bernardino, CA: California State University San Bernardino, Criminal Justice Department.

Sechrest, L., White, S., & Brown E. (1979). *The rehabilitation of criminal offenders: Problems and prospects.* Washington, DC: National Academy of Science.

Selman, R. L., & Schultz, L. H. (1990). *Making a friend in youth: Developmental theory and pair therapy.* Chicago: University of Chicago Press.

Shaw, J. W., & MacKenzie, D. L. (1992). The one-year community supervision performance of drug offenders and Louisiana DOC-identified substance abusers graduating from shock incarceration. *Journal of Criminal Justice, 20*, 501–516.

Sherman, L. W. (1992). *Policing domestic violence.* New York: Free Press.

Sherman, L. W., & Berk, R. A. (1984). The specific deterrent effects of arrest for domestic assault. *American Sociological Review, 49*, 261–272.

Sherman, L. W., Farrington, D. P., Welsh, B. C., & MacKenzie, D. L. (2002). *Evidence-based crime prevention.* New York: Routledge.

Sherman, L. W., Gottfredson, D., MacKenzie, D. L., Eck, J., Reuter, P., & Bushway, S. (1997). *Preventing crime: What works, what doesn't, what's promising. 1997.* Washington, DC, National Institute of Justice.

Sherman, L. W., Schmidt, J. D., Rogan, D. P., Gartin, P. R., Cohn, E. G., Collins, D. J., & Bacich, A. R. (1992). The variable effects of arrest on criminal careers: The Milwaukee domestic violence experiment. *Journal of Criminal Law and Criminology, 83*, 137–169.

Sherman, L. W., Schmidt, J. D., Rogan, D. P., Gartin, P. R., Cohn, E. G., Collins, D. J., & Bacich, A. R. (1991). From initial deterrence to long-term escalation: Short-custody arrest for poverty ghetto domestic violence. *Criminology, 29*, 821–850.

Sherman, L. W., & Smith, D. A. (1992) Crime, punishment and stake in conformity, *American Sociological Review* 57(5), 680–691.

Siegel, G. R., & Basta, J. (1997). *The effect of literacy and General Education Development programs on adult probationers.* Tucson, AZ: Adult Probation Department of the Superior Court in Pima County.

Siegal, H. A., & Cole, P. A. (1993). Enhancing criminal justice based treatment through the application of the intervention approach. *Journal of Drug Issues,* 23, 131–142.

Siegal, H. A., Wang, J., Falck, R. S., Rahman, A. M., & Carlson, R. G. (1997). *An evaluation of Ohio's prison-based therapeutic community treatment programs for substance abusers.* Dayton, OH: Wright State University, School of Medicine.

Simpson, D. (1988). National Treatment system evaluation based on the Drug Abuse Reporting Programs (DARP) follow-up research. In F. M. Tims & J. P. Ludford (Eds.), *Drug abuse treatment evaluations: Strategies, progress, and prospects.* Rockville, MD: National Institute on Drug Abuse.

Smith, C. J. (1996). *The California Civil Addict program: An evaluation of implementation and effectiveness.* Unpublished doctoral dissertation, University of California, Irvine.

Smith, L. G., & Akers, R. L. (1993). A comparison of recidivism of Florida's community control and prison: A five-year survival analysis. *Journal of Research in Crime and Delinquency, 30*(3), 267–292.

Smykla, J. O., & Selke, W. L. (1995). *Intermediate sanctions: Sentencing in the 1990s.* Cincinatti, OH: Anderson Publishing and Academy of Criminal Justice Sciences.

Song, L., & Lieb, R. (1995). The Twin Rivers sex offender treatment program: Recidivism rates. In *Washington state sex offenders: Overview of recidivism studies.* Olympia, WA: Washington State Institute for Public Policy.

Sonkin, D. J. (1995). *The counselor's guide to learning to live without violence.* Volcano, CA: Volcano Press.

Sontheimer, H., & Goodstein, G. L. (1993). An evaluation of juvenile intensive aftercare probation: Aftercare versus system response effects. *Justice Quarterly, 10*(2), 197–227.

Sourcebook of criminal justice statistics. (2000). Washington, DC: U.S. Department of Justice, Bureau of Justice Statistics.

Spelman, W. (2000). The limited importance of prison expansion. In A. Blumstein & J. Wallman (Eds.), *The crime drop in America* (pp. 97–129). New York: Cambridge University Press.

Spelman, W. (1994). *Criminal incapacitation.* New York: Plenum Press.

Spohn, C., Piper, R. K., Martin, T., & Frenzel, E. D. (2001). Drug courts and recidivism: The results of an evaluation using two comparison groups and multiple indicators of recidivism. *Journal of Drug Issues, 31*(1), 149–176.

Stageberg, P., Wilson, B., & Moore, R. G. (2001). *Final Report on the Polk County adult drug court.* IA: Iowa Department of Human Rights, Division of Criminal and Juvenile Justice Planning, Des Moine, IA.

State of New York Department of Correctional Services Division of Parole, (1996). *The Eight Annual Shock Legislative Report,* Albany, NY: State of New York Department of Correctional Services Division of Parole.

Stephan, J. J. (1997). *Census of state and federal correctional facilities, 1995*. Washington, DC: Bureau of Justice Statistics.

Steurer, S., Smith, L., & Tracy, A. (2001). *Three state recidivism study* (Report to the U.S. Department of Education Office of Correctional Education). Lanham, MD: Correctional Education Association.

Straus, M., Gelles, R. J., & Steinmetz, S. K. (1980). *Behind closed doors: Violence in the American family*. New York: Doubleday.

Studer, L. H., Reddon, J. R., Roper, V., & Estrada, L. (1996). Phoenix: An in-hospital treatment program for sex offenders. *Journal of Offender Rehabilitation, 23*, 91–97.

T3 Associates Training and Consulting. (2000). *Project Turnaround outcome evaluation.* (Final report). Ottawa, ON, Canada: T3 Associates Training and Consulting.

Taxman, F. S., & Spinner, D. L. (1996). The Jail Addiction Services (JAS) project in Montgomery County, Maryland. College Park, MD: University of Maryland.

Taylor, J. M. (1994). Should prisoners have access to collegiate education? A policy issue. *Educational Policy, 8*, 315–338.

Teeters, N. K. (1955). *The cradle of the penitentiary*. Philadelphia: Pennsylvania Prison Society.

Terry, W. C., III (1999). Broward County's dedicated drug treatment court: From postadjudication to diversion. In W. C. Terry III (Ed.), *The early drug courts: Case studies in judicial innovation* (pp. 77–107). Thousand Oaks, CA: Sage.

Terry, W. C., III. (1995). *Repeat offenses of the first year cohort of Broward County, Florida's drug court.* Miami, FL: International University, College of Public Affairs, School of Policy and Management.

Tewksbury, R. A., & Vito, G. F. (1996). Improving the educational skills of jail inmates: Preliminary program findings. *Federal Probation, 58*, 55–59.

Thomas, D., & Peters, M. (1996). *Evaluation of the impact of boot camps for juvenile offenders: Cleveland interim report.* Fairfax, VA: Office of Juvenile Justice and Delinquency Prevention, U.S. Department of Justice.

Tjaden, P., & Thoennes, N. (2000). Extent, nature, and consequences of intimate partner violence: Findings from the National Violence Against Women Survey. Washington, DC: National Institute of Justice.

Tonry, M. (1996a). Intermediate sanctions. In M. Tonry (Ed.), *The handbook of crime and punishment.* New York: Oxford University Press.

Tonry, M. (1996b). *Sentencing matters.* New York: Oxford University Press.

Tonry, M. (1995). *Malign neglect: Race, crime and punishment in America.* New York: Oxford University Press.

Tonry, M., & Lynch, M. (1996). Intermediate sanctions. In M. Tonry (Ed.), *Crime and justice: A review of research* (Vol. 20). Chicago: University of Chicago Press.

Tonry, M., & Wilson, J. E. (1990). *Drugs and crime.* Chicago: University of Chicago Press.

Tracy, C., & Johnson, C. (1994). Review of various outcome studies relating prison education to reduced recidivism. Austin, TX: Windham School System.

Troia, N. (1994). *An evaluation of the intensive aftercare pilot program* (Final report). Madison, WI: Office of Policy and Budget, Wisconsin Department of Health and Social Services.

Tunis, S., Austin, J., Morris, M., Hardyman, P., & Bolyard, M. (1995). *Evaluation of drug treatment in local corrections* (Final report). San Francisco: National Council on Crime and Delinquency.

Turner, S., & Petersilia, J. (1996). *Work release: Recidivism and corrections costs in Washington state* (Research in Brief). Washington, DC: National Institute of Justice.

Uggen, C. (2000). Work as a turning point in the life course of criminals: A duration model of age, employment, and recidivism. *American Sociological Review, 65*, 529–546.

Uggen, C. (1997, Nov). *Age, employment and the duration structure of recidivism: Estimating the "true effect" of work on crime.* Paper presented at the meeting of the American Society of Criminology, San Diego, CA.

Van Dine, S., Conrad, J. P., & Dinitz, S. (1977). The incapacitation of the dangerous offender: A statistical experiment. *Journal of Research in Crime and Delinquency, 14*, 22–35.

Van Stelle, K. R., Lidbury, J. R., & Moberg, D. P. (1995). *Final evaluation report: Specialized Training and Employment Project (STEP).* Madison, WI: University of Wisconsin-Madison Medical School, Department of Preventive Medicine, Center for Health Policy and Program Evaluation.

Van Stelle, K. R., Mauser, E., & Moberg, D. P. (1994). Recidivism to the criminal justice system of substance-abusing offenders diverted into treatment. *Crime and Delinquency, 40*(2), 175–196.

Van Voorhis, P. (1997). An overview of offender classification systems. In P. Van Voorhis, M. Braswell, & D. Lester (Eds.), *Correctional counseling and rehabilitation* (pp. 81–108). Cincinatti, OH: Anderson.

Van Voorhis, P. (1993). Psychological determinants of the prison experience. *Prison Journal, 73*, 72–102.

Visher, C. A. (1987). Incapacitation and crime control: Does a "lock 'em up" strategy reduce crime? *Justice Quarterly, 4*(4), 513–543.

Vito, G. F., & Tewksbury, R. A. (1998). The impact of treatment: The Jefferson County (Kentucky) drug court program. *Federal Probation, 62*(2), 46–51.

von Hirsch, A., & Gottfredson, D. M. (1984). Selective incapacitation: Some queries about research design and equity. *New York University Review of Law and Social Change, 12*, 11–51.

Wagner, D., & Baird, C. (1993). Evaluation of the Florida community control program. Washington, DC: U.S. Department of Justice, National Institute of Justice.

Walsh, A. (1985). An evaluation of the effects of adult basic education on rearrest rates among probationers. *Journal of Offender Counseling, Services, and Rehabilitation, 9*, 69–76.

Washington State Department of Corrections. (1998). *Substance abuse treatment program evaluation of outcomes and management report.* Olympia, WA: Washington State Department of Corrections.

Washington State Department of Corrections. (1997). *Work ethic camp: One year after (1993–1994)* (Program report). Seattle, WA: Washington State Department of Corrections.

Weinrott, M. R., & Saylor, M. (1991). Self report of crimes committed by sex offenders. *Journal of Interpersonal Violence, 6*, 286–300.

Welle, R., & Beier, K. M. (1989). Castration in Germany. *Annals of Sex Research,* 2, 103–133.

Welsh, B. C., & Farrington, D. P. (2000a). Correctional intervention programs and cost-benefit analysis. *Criminal Justice and Behavior,* 27(1):115–113.

Welsh, B. C., & Farrington, D. P. (2000b). Monetary Costs and Benefits of Crime Prevention Programs. In M. Tonry (Ed.), *Crime and Justice: A Review of Research* (pp. 305–61). Chicago: The University of Chicago Press.

Wexler, H. K., DeLeon, G., Thomas, G., Kressel, D., & Peters, J. (1999, June). The Amity Prison TC evaluation: Reincarceration outcomes. *Criminal Justice and Behavior,* 26, 147–167.

Wexler, H. K., Falkin, G. P., & Lipton, D. S. (1990). Outcome evaluation of a prison therapeutic community for substance abuse treatment. *Criminal Justice and Behavior, 17,* 71–92.

Wexler, H. K., Graham, W. F., Koronkowski, R., & Lowe, L. (1995). *Amity therapeutic community substance abuse program: Preliminary return to custody data.* Laguna Beach, CA: National Development and Research Institutes.

Wexler, H. K., Williams, R., Early, K., & Trotman, C. (1996). Prison treatment for substance abusers: Stay 'N Out revisited. In K. E. Early (Ed.), *Drug treatment behind bars: Prison-based strategies for change* (pp. 101–108). Westport, CT: Praeger.

Whitehead, J. T., Miller, L. S., & Myers, L. B. (1995). The diversionary effectiveness of intensive supervision and community corrections programs. In J. O. Smykla & W. L. Selke (Eds.), *Intermediate sanctions: Sentencing in the 1990s* (pp. 135–151). Cincinatti, OH: Anderson Publishing and Academy of Criminal Justice Sciences.

Wiebush, R. G. (1993). Juvenile intensive supervision: The impact on felony offenders diverted from institutional placement. *Crime and Delinquency, 39*(1), 68–89.

Wiehe, V. R. (1998). *Understanding family violence: Treating and preventing partner, child, sibling, and elder abuse.* Thousand Oaks, CA: Sage.

Willman, H., & Chun, R. (1973). An alternative to the institutionalization of adjudicated juvenile offenders. *Federal Probation, 37,* 52–58.

Wilson, D. B., Allen, L. C., & MacKenzie, D. L. (2001). A quantitative review of structured, group-oriented, cognitive-behavioral programs for offenders. *Criminal Justice and Behavior: 32*(2,) 174–204.

Wilson, D. B., Gallagher, C. A., Coggeshall, M. B., & MacKenzie, D. L. (1999). A quantitative review and description of corrections based education, vocation and work programs. *Corrections Management Quarterly, 3,* 8–18.

Wilson, D. B., Gallagher, C. A., & MacKenzie, D. L. (2000). A meta-analysis of corrections-based education, vocation, and work programs for adult offenders. *Journal of Research on Crime and Delinquency, 37,* 347–368.

Wilson, S. J., & Lipsey, M. W. (2003). Wilderness challenge programs for delinquent youth: A meta-analysis of outcome evaluations. *Evaluation and Program Planning, 23,* 1–12.

Wilson, W. J. (1996). *When work disappears.* New York: Knopf.

Winterton, J. L. (1995). *Transformations: Technology boot camp. Summative evaluation.* Unpublished manuscript.

Wish, E. P., & Johnson, B. D. (1986). The impact of substance abuse on criminal careers. In A. Blumstein, J. Cohen, J. A. Roth, & C. A. Visher (Eds.), *Criminal Careers and Career Criminals* (Vol. 2, pp. 54–59). Washington, DC: National Academy Press.

Wolfgang, M. E., Figlio, R. M., & Sellin, T. (1972). *Delinquency in a birth cohort.* Chicago: University of Chicago Press.

Wright, D. T., & Mays, G. L. (1998). Correctional boot camps, attitudes, and recidivism: The Oklahoma experience. *Journal of Offender Rehabilitation, 28,* 71–87.

G. E., Axelrod, J., Chin, D., Vargas-Carmona, J. V., & Burns-Loeb, T. B. (2000). Examining patterns of vulnerability to domestic violence among African American women. *Violence Against Women, 6,* 495–514.

Yochelson, S., & Samenow, S. (1976). *The criminal personality: A profile for change.* Northvale, NJ: Jason Aronson.

Zedlewski, E. W. (1987). *Making confinement decisions.* Washington, DC: National Institute of Justice.

Zhang, S. X. (2000). *An evaluation of the Los Angeles County juvenile drug treatment boot camp.* Washington, DC: National Institute of Justice, U.S. Department of Justice.

Zimring, F. E., & Hawkins, G. (1995). *Incapacitation: Penal confinement and the restraint of crime.* New York: Oxford University Press.

Index

Other Books in the Series (*continued from page iii*)

Companions in Crime: The Social Aspects of Criminal Conduct, by Mark Warr

The Criminal Career: The Danish Longitudinal Study, by Britta Kyvsgaard

Gangs and Delinquency in Developmental Perspective, by Terence P. Thornberry, Marvin D. Krohn, Alan J. Lizotte, Carolyn A. Smith, and Kimberly Tobin

Early Prevention of Adult Antisocial Behaviour, by David P. Farrington and Jeremy W. Coid

Violent Crime, by Darnell F. Hawkins

Errors of Justice, by Brian Forst

Rethinking Homicide: Exploring the Structure and Process in Homicide Situations, by Terance D. Miethe and Wendy C. Regoeczi

Understanding Police Use of Force: Officers, Suspects, and Reciprocity, by Geoffrey P. Alpert and Roger G. Dunham

Marking Time in the Golden State: Women's Imprisonment in California, by Candace Kruttschnitt and Rosemary Gartner

Economic Espionage and Industrial Spying, by Hedieh Nasheri

The Virtual Prison: Community Custody and the Evolution of Imprisonment, by Julian Roberts

Prisoner Reentry and Crime in America, by Jeremy Travis and Christy Visher

Choosing White-Collar Crime, by Neal Shover and Andrew Hochstetler

The Crime Drop in America, Revised Edition, edited by Alfred Blumstein and Joel Wallman

Police Innovation: Contrasting Approaches and Perspectives, edited by David Weisburd and Anthony A. Braga

Policing Gangs in America, by Charles M. Katz and Vincent J. Webb

Third Party Policing, by Lorraine Mazerolle and Janet Ransley

Street Justice: Retaliation in the Criminal Underworld, by Bruce Jacobs and Richard Wright